MW01235369

Elements of Mineralogy

You are holding a reproduction of an original work that is in the public domain in the United States of America, and possibly other countries.You may freely copy and distribute this work as no entity (individual or corporate) has a copyright on the body of the work.This book may contain prior copyright references, and library stamps (as most of these works were scanned from library copies).These have been scanned and retained as part of the historical artifact.

This book may have occasional imperfections such as missing or blurred pages, poor pictures, errant marks, etc. that were either part of the original artifact, or were introduced by the scanning process. We believe this work is culturally important, and despite the imperfections, have elected to bring it back into print as part of our continuing commitment to the preservation of printed works worldwide. We appreciate your understanding of the imperfections in the preservation process, and hope you enjoy this valuable book.

ELEMENTS

OF

MINERALOGY

CONTAINING

A GENERAL INTRODUCTION TO THE SCIENCE,
WITH DESCRIPTIONS OF THE SPECIES

BY

JAMES NICOL, F.R.S.E., F.G.S.,

PROFESSOR OF NATURAL HISTORY IN THE UNIVERSITY OF ABERDEEN

SECOND EDITION

Illustrated by Numerous Woodcuts

EDINBURGH
ADAM AND CHARLES BLACK
1873

188. f. 50.

PREFACE.

THIS Treatise was originally intended to furnish a summary of the leading principles and more important facts of Mineralogy, specially for the use of persons wishing to acquire a knowledge of the science,—some it might be as a branch of general education, others with a view to its practical applications to geology, mining, agriculture, or other connected pursuits. Hence the facts and principles were stated in the simplest language consistent with scientific accuracy, and the more important results ascertained in regard to the physical properties and chemical composition of minerals were given without those details which often prove more embarrassing than useful to the student.

The call for a new edition shows that it has so far served the purpose for which it was prepared. But in the last few years most important additions have been made to this science. The forms and composition of many, even of the older known minerals, have been determined with more accuracy, and several highly interesting new species have been discovered. In the present edition this new matter has been introduced so far as consistent with the plan of the work. Every portion of it has been carefully revised and corrected, so

as to render the definitions and descriptions of the leading minerals fuller, more precise, and more easily intelligible to the student. Supposed species, which have
not stood the test of investigation, have been omitted,
or are noticed only as varieties, while the more interesting of those recently discovered have taken their
place. No change has been made on the classification,
the mixed system being preferred, both as admitting of a
more natural grouping of minerals, and as better adapted
to promote the progress of the student than either a
rigid chemical or crystallographic arrangement. The
Author has been glad to find his views on this point
confirmed by the adoption of like or identical groups
and families of minerals in several recent publications
on the subject.

The Author regrets that the plan and limits of this
treatise do not admit of full references to the many
authors whose works and memoirs he has consulted,
and to which he is indebted for much valuable
material. In revising this volume he has found much
assistance from the last edition of the admirable manual
of Professor Naumann, whose system and symbols of
the forms of crystals he retains, regarding them as
simpler, more philosophical, more generally used, and
thus also more useful, than any other. In the chemical
department the works of Rammelsberg are still our best
guides. The changes in that science are, however, one
of the chief difficulties the teacher of mineralogy has to
encounter. Though, for reasons stated in the text, and
on the advice of some esteemed scientific friends and

teachers of the science, he has chiefly retained the old formulæ, he has also given others of the more important species, conformable to the new views. It need hardly be stated that the chemical composition, as given in per cents, is the same on either theory.

Those families and species which, from their frequent occurrence, their geological importance as constituents of rock formations, or from their economic properties or products, are most worthy of notice, have now been indicated throughout,—the most important by two (**), the less by one (*) asterisk. For a first course in the science, or for reading our best works on geology, the former selection (**) contains almost all the species to which the student's attention need be specially directed.

In conclusion, the Author would anew express his trust that, notwithstanding any errors or omissions, which in a work so full of minute facts and figures he can hardly hope to have avoided, this volume may still continue to promote—what was his chief object in first preparing it—an increased knowledge of this most important and beautiful portion of the works of the Creator.

ABERDEEN, 12th July 1873.

CONTENTS.

PART II.

DESCRIPTION OF MINERAL SPECIES.

MINERALOGY.

MINERALOGY is sometimes understood as comprising the natural history of every portion of inorganic nature. Here we consider it as limited to the natural history of simple minerals or mineral species. In the strictest sense, a mineral species is a natural inorganic body, possessing a definite chemical composition, and assuming a regular determinate form or series of forms. This definition excludes many bodies often regarded as minerals : as, all the artificial salts of the chemist, all the inorganic secretions of plants and animals, all the remains of former living beings now imbedded in rocks. Some substances originally organic products have indeed, by common consent, found a place in mineral systems, as coal, amber, and mineral resins; but this is a departure from the strictness of the definition, and in most cases had better have been avoided. So also some amorphous substances, with no precise form or chemical composition, as some kinds of clay, have been introduced into works on mineralogy, but we believe often improperly, and with no beneficial result. Aggregates of simple minerals or rocks are likewise excluded from this science, though the various associations of minerals, their modes of occurrence, and their geological position, are important points in the history of the different species.

One most important object of a treatise on mineralogy is to give such descriptions of minerals, their essential properties and distinctive characters, as will enable the student to distinguish the various species, and to recognise them when he meets with them in nature. But to accomplish this he must first become acquainted with the terminology or nomenclature of the science; that is, with the meaning of the terms used in describing these properties, and the various modifications they may undergo. With this is necessarily conjoined an account of the properties themselves, and of the more general laws by which their various changes are regulated. Closely related to this is an account of the system or classification, explaining the order in which the species are arranged, and the reasons for which it has been adopted. The second and most important part of mineralogy, to which the former is properly preparatory, is the physiography or description of the various species, pointing out the characters by which they may be recognised, and giving an account of their appearance or external aspect and forms; their principal physical and chemical properties; their mode of occurrence, with their geological and geographical distribution; and their various uses, whether in nature or in the arts. Each of these departments will be considered in the following treatise in the order just mentioned.

PART I.—TERMINOLOGY.

———◆———

THE more important properties of a mineral regarded as a body existing in space, and consisting of matter aggregated in a peculiar way, are—its form as shown in crystallisation ; its structure as determining its mode of cleavage and fracture ; its hardness and tenacity ; its weight or specific gravity ; and its relations to light, heat, electricity, and magnetism.

CHAPTER I.

FORM OF MINERALS.

Crystalline and Amorphous.—Mineral substances occur in two distinct modes of aggregation. Some consist of minute particles simply collected together, with no regularity of structure or constancy of external form, and are named amorphous. All fluid minerals are in this condition, together with some solid bodies, which appear to have condensed either from a gelatinous condition like opal, when they are named *porodine*, or from a state of igneous fluidity like obsidian and glass, when they are named *hyaline*. The other class have their ultimate atoms evidently arranged according to definite law, and are named *crystalline*, when the regularity of structure appears only in the internal disposition of the parts ; and *crystallised*, when it also produces a determinate external form, or a *crystal*.

Faces, Edges, Angles, Axes of Crystals.—The word *crystal* in mineralogy designates a solid body exhibiting an

original (not artificial) more or less regular polyhedric form.
It is bounded by plane surfaces, named *faces*, which intersect
in straight lines or *edges*, and these again meet in points and
form *solid angles*, bounded by three or more faces.   The
space occupied by a crystal is often named a *form of crystallisation*, which is thus the mathematical figure regarded as independent of the matter that fills it.   Crystals bounded by
equal and similar faces are named *simple forms*. The cube or
hexahedron (Fig. 1), bounded by six equal and similar
squares ; the octahedron (Fig. 2), by eight equilateral triangles ; and the rhombohedron, by six rhombs,—are thus
simple forms.   Crystals of which all the faces are not equal
and similar are named *compound forms*, or *combinations*, being
regarded as produced by the union or combination of two
or more simple forms.   An *axis* of a crystal is a line passing
through its centre and terminating either in the middle of
two faces, or of two edges, or in two angles ; and axes terminating in similar parts of a crystal are named similar axes.
In describing a crystal, one of its axes is supposed to be
vertical or upright, and is then named the *principal axis*, and
that axis is chosen which is the only one of its kind in the
figure.   Round this axis the faces belonging to a certain
form of crystal often group themselves in regular zones.
A few other technical terms used in describing crystals
will be explained as they occur.

Systems of Crystallisation.—The forms of crystals that
occur in nature seem almost innumerable.   On examining
them, however, more attentively, it is discovered that these
forms can be arranged in certain groups, of which each
member is intimately related to all the others—specially
they all agree in the proportion of their axes and in the
angles at which these intersect each other.   Then they can
all be deduced or derived from one simple form, or *Primary
form* as it is named, by changes produced on it according
to definite laws.   When viewed in this manner, the vast
variety of crystals occurring in nature may all be reduced
to six distinct groups, or, as they are named, Systems of Crystallisation.   The following are the names given to these
systems of crystallisation in some of the best authors :—

Naumann.	Mohs.	Weiss and G. Rose.
I. Tesseral System.	Tessular.	Regular.
II. Tetragonal System.	Pyramidal.	2 and 1 axial.
III. Hexagonal System.	Rhombohedral.	3 and 1 axial.
IV. Rhombic System.	Orthotype.	1 and 1 axial.
V. Monoclinic System.	Hemiorthotype.	2 and 1 membered.
VI. Triclinic System.	Anorthotype.	1 and 1 membered.

Miller names them—I. Cubic, II. Pyramidal, III. Rhombohedral, IV. Prismatic, V. Oblique, and VI. Anorthic.

In the following treatise the terminology of Naumann is adopted, his method of classifying and describing crystals appearing the simplest and best adapted to promote the progress of the student. Formerly he named systems V. and VI. Monoclinohedric and Triclinohedric, but the shorter names are preferable.

The first, or *Tesseral System*, named from *tessera*, a cube, which is one of the most frequent varieties, is characterised by three equal axes intersecting each other at right angles. Properly speaking, this system has no chief axis, as they are all similar, and with similar faces formed round them, so that any one axis may be placed upright in drawing and describing the crystals. Of these there are thirteen varieties, named from the number of their faces :—

1. One Tetrahedron, or form with four faces.
2. One Hexahedron, with six faces.
3. One Octahedron, with eight faces.
4. Four Dodecahedrons, with twelve faces.
5. Five Icositetrahedrons, with twenty-four faces.
6. One Tetracontaoctahedron, with forty-eight faces.

The dodecahedrons are further distinguished, according to the form of their faces, into rhombic, trigonal, deltoid, and pentagonal dodecahedrons ; and some of the icositetrahedrons have also received peculiar names.

The following is a description, with figures, of the different forms above mentioned :—

1. The hexahedron or cube (Fig. 1) is bounded by six equal squares, has twelve edges, formed by faces meeting at 90°, and eight solid trigonal angles. The principal axes join the centre points of each two opposite faces.—Examples are fluor spar, galena, boracite.

2. The octahedron (Fig. 2), bounded by eight equilateral triangles, has twelve equal edges, with planes meeting at

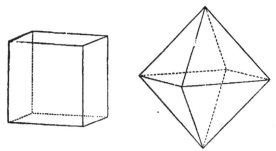

Fig. 1. The Hexahedron.   Fig. 2. The Octahedron.

109° 28', and six tetragonal angles. The principal axes join the opposite angles, two and two.—Examples, alum, spinel, magnetite.

3. The rhombic-dodecahedron (Fig. 3) is bounded by twelve equal and similar rhombs (diagonals as 1 and $\sqrt{2}$), has twenty-four equal edges of 120°, and six tetragonal and eight trigonal angles. The principal axes join two opposite tetragonal angles.—Ex., garnet, boracite, cuprite.

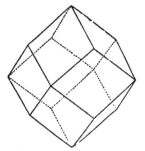
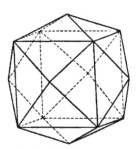

Fig. 3. Rhombic-dodecahedron.   Fig. 4. Tetrakishexahedron.

4. The tetrakishexahedrons (variety of icositetrahedron, Fig. 4) are bounded by twenty-four isosceles triangles,

arranged in six groups of four each. They have twelve longer edges, which correspond to those of the primitive or inscribed cube, and twenty-four shorter edges placed over each of its faces. The angles are eight hexagonal and six tetragonal; the latter joined two and two by the three principal axes. This form varies in general aspect, approaching, on the one hand, to the cube; on the other, to the rhombic-dodecahedron.—Ex., fluor spar, gold.

5. The triakisoctahedrons (variety of icositetrahedron, Fig. 5) are bounded by twenty-four isosceles triangles, in eight groups of three, and, like the previous form, vary in general aspect from the octahedron on one side, to the rhombic-dodecahedron on the other. The edges are twelve longer, corresponding with those of the inscribed octahedron, and twenty-four shorter, three and three over each of the faces. The angles are eight trigonal and six ditetragonal (formed by eight faces); the latter angles joined two and two by the principal axes.—Ex., galena, diamond.

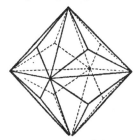 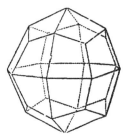

Fig. 5. Triakisoctahedron.   Fig. 6. Icositetrahedron.

6. The icositetrahedrons (most common variety, Fig. 6) are bounded by twenty-four deltoids or figures with four sides, of which two and two adjacent ones are equal. This form varies from the octahedron to the cube, sometimes approaching the former and sometimes the latter in general aspect. The edges are twenty-four longer and twenty-four shorter. The angles are six tetragonal joined by the principal axes, eight trigonal, and twelve rhombic, or tetragonal with unequal angles.

7. The hexakisoctahedrons (Fig. 7), bounded by forty-eight scalene triangles, vary much in general aspect, approaching more or less to all the preceding forms; but most frequently they have the faces arranged either in six groups of eight, or eight of six, or twelve of four faces. There are

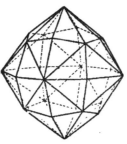

twenty-four long edges, often corresponding to those of the rhombic-dodecahedron; twenty-four intermediate edges lying in pairs over each edge of the inscribed octahedron; and twenty-four short edges in pairs over the edges of the inscribed cube. There are six ditetragonal angles joined by the principal axes, eight hexagonal and twelve rhombic angles.—Ex., fluor spar, garnet, diamond.

Fig. 7. Hexakisoctahedron.

The seven forms of crystals now described are related to each other in the most intimate manner. This will appear more distinctly from the following account of the derivation of the forms, with which is conjoined an explanation of the crystallographic signs or symbols by which they are designated. We have adopted these symbols throughout this work, in the belief that they not only mark the forms in a greatly abbreviated manner, but also exhibit the relations of the forms and combinations in a way which words could hardly accomplish.

The *derivation of forms* is that process by which, from one form chosen for the purpose, and considered as the *type* —the *fundamental* or *primary form*—all the other forms of a system may be produced, according to fixed principles or general laws. In order to understand this process or method of derivation, the student should keep in mind that the position of any plane is fixed when the positions of any three points in it, not all in one straight line, are known. To determine the position, therefore, of the face of a crystal, it is only necessary to know the distance of three points in it from the centre of the crystal, or the point in which the axes intersect each other. Usually the points in which the face or its supposed extension meets the three axes of the crystal are chosen, and the portion of the axes between these points and the centre are named parameters, and the position of the face is sufficiently known when the relative length or proportion of these parameters is ascertained. When the position of one face of a simple form is thus fixed or described, all the other faces are in like manner fixed, since they are all equal and similar, and have equal parameters—that is, intersect the axes in a uniform manner. Hence the expression which marks or describes one face, marks and describes the whole figure, with all its faces.

The octahedron is adopted as the primary or fundamental form of the tesseral system, and distinguished by the first letter of the name, O. Its faces cut the half-axes at equal distances from the centre; so that these semi-axes, or the parameters of the faces, have to each other the proportion $1 : 1 : 1$. In order to derive the other forms from the octahedron, the following construction is employed. The numbers in brackets refer to the descriptions above.

Suppose a plane so placed in each angle of the octahedron as to be vertical to the axis passing through that angle, and consequently parallel to the two other axes (or to cut them at an infinite distance $= \infty$); then the hexahedron or cube (1) is produced, designated by the crystallographic sign $\infty O \infty$; expressing the proportion of the parameters of its faces, or $\infty : \infty : 1$. If a plane is supposed placed on each edge parallel to one axis, and cutting the two other axes at equal distances, the resulting figure is the rhombic-dodecahedron (3), designated by the sign ∞O, the proportion of the parameters of its faces being $\infty : 1 : 1$. The triakisoctahedron (5) arises when on each edge of the octahedron planes are placed cutting the axis not belonging to that edge at a distance from the centre m which is a rational number greater than 1. The proportion of its parameters is therefore $m : 1 : 1$, and its sign mO; the most common varieties being $\frac{3}{2}O$, $2O$, and $3O$. When, on the other hand, from a similar distance m in each two semiaxes pro-

longed, a plane is drawn to the other semiaxis, or to each
angle, an ikositetrahedron (6) is formed; the parameters of
its faces have consequently the proportion $m : m : 1$, and its
sign is mOm; the most common varieties being 2O2 and
3O3, the former very frequent in leucite, analcime, and
garnet. When, again, planes are drawn from each angle,
or the end of one semiaxis of the octahedron, parallel to a
second axis, and cutting the third at a distance n, greater
than 1, then the tetrakishexahedron (4) is formed, the
parameter of its faces $\infty : n : 1$; its sign ∞On; and the
most common varieties in nature $\infty O\frac{3}{2}$, $\infty O2$, and $\infty O3$.
Finally, if in each semiaxis of the octahedron two distances,
m and n, be taken, each greater than 1, and m also greater
than n, and planes be drawn from each angle to these
points, so that the two planes lying over each edge cut the
second semiaxis belonging to that edge, at the smaller distance n, and the third axis at the greater distance m, then
the hexakisoctahedron (7) is produced, the parameters, which
are $m : n : 1$, its sign mOn, and the most common varieties
3O$\frac{3}{2}$, 4O2, and 5O$\frac{4}{3}$.

It must be observed that the numbers in these signs
refer to the parameters of the faces, not to the axes of the
crystal, which are always equal. One parameter also is
always assumed $= 1$, and then that either one only of the
two other parameters marked by the number before O, or
both of them marked by the numbers before and after O
may be changed, and in the proportion of these numbers.

The forms of crystals now described are named *Holohedral*, the whole faces of each form being seen on them.
But there are other crystals which appear as if formed by
one half the faces of these forms, which have increased so
as to suppress the other half of the faces alternating with
them. These are named *Hemihedral*, and occur both in this
system and in all the others.

These *Hemihedral*, or, as they are sometimes named in
this system, *Semitesseral*, forms are :—

(1.) The tetrahedron (Fig. 8), bounded by four equilateral
triangles. It has six equal edges with faces meeting at 70°
32′, and four trigonal angles. The principal axes join the

middle points of each two opposite edges.—Ex., fahlore, boracite, and helvine.

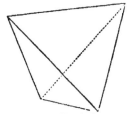

Fig. 8. Tetrahedron.

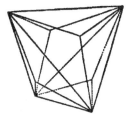

Fig. 9. Trigonal-dodecahedron.

(2.) The trigonal-dodecahedrons (Fig. 9) are bounded by twelve isosceles triangles, and vary in general form from the tetrahedron to the hexahedron. There are six longer edges corresponding to those of the inscribed tetrahedron, and twelve shorter, placed three and three over each of its faces ; and four hexagonal and four trigonal angles.—Ex., fahlore.

(3.) The deltoid-dodecahedrons (Fig. 10) are bounded by twelve deltoids, and vary in general form from the tetrahedron on the one hand, to the rhombic-dodecahedron on the other. They have twelve longer edges lying in pairs

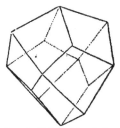

Fig. 10. Deltoid-dodecahedrons.

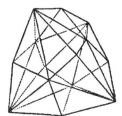

Fig. 11. Hexakistetrahedron.

over the edges of the inscribed tetrahedron ; and twelve shorter edges, three and three over each of its faces. The angles are six tetragonal (rhombic), four acute trigonal, and four obtuse trigonal angles. The principal axes join two and two opposite rhombic angles.—Ex., fahlore.

(4.) The hexakistetrahedrons (Fig. 11) are bounded by twenty-four scalene triangles, and most commonly have their faces grouped in four systems of six each. The edges are twelve shorter and twelve longer, lying in groups of three over each face of the inscribed tetrahedron, and twelve intermediate in pairs over its edges. The angles are six rhombic, joined in pairs by the principal axes, and four acuter and four obtuser hexagonal angles.—Ex., diamond.

In these forms, often named tetrahedral, the faces are oblique to each other. Their derivation and signs are as follows :—The tetrahedron arises when four alternate faces of the octahedron, two opposite above, and two intermediate below, are enlarged, so as to obliterate the other four, and its sign is hence $\frac{O}{2}$. But, as either four faces may be thus enlarged or obliterated, two tetrahedrons can be formed similar in all respects except in position, and together making up the octahedron. These are distinguished by the signs + and −, added to the above symbol, but only the latter in general expressed thus $-\frac{O}{2}$. In all hemihedric systems two forms similarly related occur, which may thus be named complementary forms. The trigonal dodecahedron is derived from the icositetrahedron by the expansion of the alternate trigonal groups of faces. Its sign is $\frac{mOm}{2}$, the most common variety being $\frac{2O2}{2}$. The deltoid-dodecahedron is in like manner the result of the increase of the alternate trigonal groups of faces of the triakisoctahedron, and its sign is $\frac{mO}{2}$. Lastly, the hexakistetrahedron arises in the development of alternate hexagonal groups of faces in the hexakisoctahedron, and its sign is $\frac{mOn}{2}$.

Two semitesseral forms with parallel faces occur. (1.) The pentagonal dodecahedrons (Fig. 12) bounded by twelve symmetrical pentagons, and varying in general aspect

between the hexahedron and rhombic-dodecahedron. They
have six regular (and in general longer) edges, lying over
the faces of the inscribed hexahedron, and twenty-four
generally shorter (seldom longer) edges, usually lying in
pairs over its edges. The angles are eight of three equal

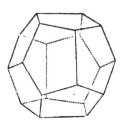
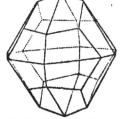

Fig. 12. Pentagonal-dodecahedrons.   Fig. 13. Dyakisdodecahedron.

angles, and twelve of three unequal angles. Each principal
axis unites two opposite regular edges. This form is de-
rived from the tetrakishexahedron, and its sign is $\frac{\infty O n}{2}$, one
of the most common varieties being $\frac{\infty O 2}{2}$, found frequently
in iron pyrites and cobaltine. (2.) The dyakisdodecahedron
(Fig. 13), bounded by twenty-four trapezoids with two sides
equal, has twelve short, twelve long, and twenty-four inter-

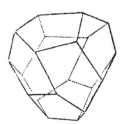
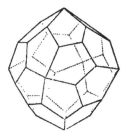

Fig. 14. Pentagonal-dodecahedron.   Fig. 15. Pentagonal-icositetrahedron.

mediate edges. The angles are six equiangular rhombic,
united in pairs by the principal axes, eight trigonal, and

twenty-four irregular tetragonal angles. It is derived from the hexakisoctahedron, and its sign is $\left[\dfrac{mOn}{2}\right]$, the brackets being used to distinguish it from the hexakistetrahedron, also derived from the same primary form. It occurs in iron pyrites and cobaltine. There are two other tetrahedral forms, the pentagonal dodecahedron (Fig. 14), and the pentagonal icositetrahedron (Fig. 15), both bounded by irregular pentagons, but not yet observed in nature.

Combinations.—These forms of the tesseral system (and this is true also of the five other systems of crystallisation) not only occur singly, but often two, three, or more united in the same crystal, forming what are named combinations. In this case it is evident that no one of the individual forms can be complete, because the faces of one form must partially interfere with the faces of other forms. A combination therefore implies that the faces of one form shall appear symmetrically disposed between the faces of other forms, and consequently in the room of certain of their edges and angles. These edges and angles are thus, as it were, cut off, and new ones produced in their place, which properly belong neither to the one form nor the other, but are edges or angles of combination. Usually, one form predominates more than the others, or has more influence on the general aspect of the crystal, and hence is distinguished as the predominant form, the others being named subordinate. The following terms used on this subject require explanation. A combination is *developed* when all the forms contributing to its formation are pointed out; and its sign consists of the signs of these forms, written in the order of their influence on the combination, with a point between. An angle or edge is said to be *replaced* when it is cut off by one or more secondary planes; it is *truncated* when cut by one plane, forming equal angles with the adjacent faces; and an edge is *bevelled* when replaced by two planes, which are equally inclined to the adjacent faces.

It will be readily seen that such combinations may be exceedingly numerous, or rather infinite; and only a few of the more common can be noticed, simply as specimens of the class. Many others more complicated will occur in the descriptive part of this treatise. Among holohedral combinations, the cube, octahedron, and also the rhombic-dodecahedron, are the predominant forms. In Fig. 16 the

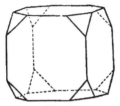

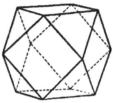

Fig. 16.

Fig. 17.

Combination : Hexahedron and Octahedron.

Octahedron and Hexahedron.

cube has its angles replaced by the faces of the octahedron, and the sign of this combination is $\infty O\infty . O$. In Fig. 17 this process may be regarded as having proceeded still farther, so that the faces of the octahedron now predominate, and the sign, of the same two elements but in reverse order, is $O . \infty O\infty$. In Fig. 18 the cube has its edges replaced

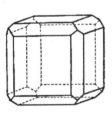

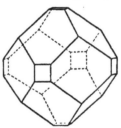

Fig. 18.

Fig. 19.

by the faces of the rhombic-dodecahedron, the sign being $\infty O\infty . \infty O$; whilst in Fig. 19 there is the same combination, but with the faces of the cube subordinate, and hence the sign is $\infty O . \infty O\infty$. The former figure, it will be seen, has more the general aspect of the cube; the latter of the dodecahedron.

In combinations of semitesseral forms with oblique faces,

the tetrahedron, the rhombic-dodecahedron, or even the hexahedron, seldomer a trigonal-dodecahedron, are the more

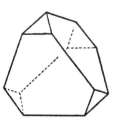

Fig. 20.

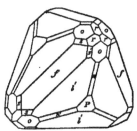

Fig. 21.

common predominant forms. In Fig. 20 two tetrahedrons in opposite positions, $\frac{O}{2} . - \frac{O}{2}$, are combined. In Fig. 21 a very complex combination of seven forms is represented in a crystal of fahlore, its full sign being—

$$\frac{2O2}{2}(l') . \infty O \infty (f) . \infty O(o) . \frac{O}{2}(P) . - \frac{2O2}{2}(r) . \frac{\frac{3}{2}O}{2}(n') . \infty O 3(s) ;$$

the letters in brackets connecting them with the respective faces of the figure. As examples of combinations of semi-

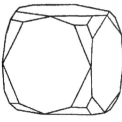

Fig. 22.

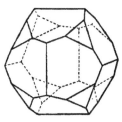

Fig. 23.

tesseral forms with parallel faces, we may take Fig. 22, in which each of the angles of the cube is unsymmetrically replaced by three faces of the dyakisdodecahedron, and hence $\infty O \infty . \left[\frac{4O2}{2} \right]$; or Fig. 23, in which the pentagonal-dodecahedron has its trigonal angles replaced by the faces of the octahedron, consequently with the sign $\dfrac{\infty O2}{2}.O.$

Figure 24 represents the same combination but with greater predominance of the faces of the octahedron, the crystal being bounded by eight equilateral and twelve isosceles triangles.

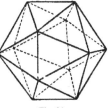

Fig. 24.

In interpreting a combination it should be observed that the faces of each form are all similar. When in a combination, therefore, there are only 4 faces similar to each other, they belong to the tetrahedron; if only 6, to the hexahedron; if only 8, to the octahedron; if only 12 parallel, to the rhombic or pentagonal dodeca-hedron; and if 12 not parallel, to the trigonal or deltoid dodecahedron.

In the following systems there is always one axis un-equal to (longer or shorter than) the others. This is placed vertical and named the *chief axis;* its ends are *poles,* and the edges connected with them *polar edges.* The other axes are named subordinate or lateral axes, and the plane that passes through them is the *base.* A plane through the chief and a lateral axis is a normal chief section. In these systems also the three following forms occur:—1st, *Pyra-mids,* of which the faces are triangles, and each composed of two geometric pyramids placed base to base, and named *closed forms,* as the crystals are shut in by definite faces on every side. 2d, *Prisms* bounded by plain faces parallel to one axis. They are thus of unlimited extent in the direction of that axis, and therefore named *open forms,* but in crystals are shut in by faces of other forms. 3d, *Pina-coids* or *Tables*—two faces intersecting one axis and parallel to the others, and thus also open forms, or unlimited in the direction of these axes.

II. *Tetragonal System.*—This system has three axes at right angles, two of them equal, and one, the chief axis, unequal. The name tetragonal is derived from the form of

C

the basis, which is usually quadratic. There are eight
tetragonal forms, of which five are *closed*.

(1.) Tetragonal pyramids (Figs. 25, 26) are inclosed by
eight isosceles triangles, with four middle edges all in one

Tetragonal Pyramids.

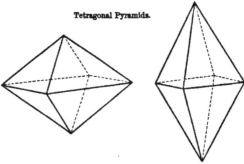

Fig. 25. Obtuse.   Fig. 26. Acute.

plane, and eight polar edges. There are three kinds of this
form, distinguished by the position of the lateral axes. In
the first these axes unite the opposite angles; in the second
they intersect the middle edges equally; and in the third

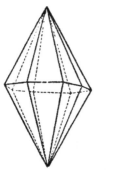

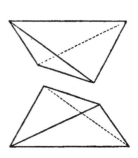

Fig. 27. Ditetragonal Pyramid.   Fig. 28. Tetragonal Sphenoids.

they lie in an intermediate position, or divide these edges
unequally; the latter being hemihedral forms. These pyramids are also distinguished as obtuse (Fig. 25) or acute (Fig.

26), according as the vertical angle is greater or less than in the octahedron, which, though intermediate, is never a tetragonal form. (2.) Ditetragonal pyramids (Fig. 27) are bounded by sixteen scalene triangles, whose base-lines are all in one plane. This form rarely occurs except in combinations. (3.) Tetragonal sphenoids (Fig. 28), bounded by four isosceles triangles, are the hemihedral forms of the first variety of tetragonal pyramids. (4.) The tetragonal scalenohedron (Fig. 29), bounded by eight scalene triangles, whose bases rise and fall in a zigzag line, is the hemihedral form

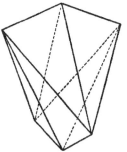

Fig. 29. Tetragonal Scalenohedron.   Fig. 30. Tetragonal Prism.

of the ditetragonal pyramid. The latter two forms are rare. *Open forms.*—(1.) Tetragonal prisms (Fig. 30), bounded by four planes parallel to the principal axis ; (2.) ditetragonal prisms by eight similar planes ; and (3.) the basal pinacoid, consisting merely of two parallel faces bounding the prisms at the ends above and below.

The various series of tetragonal crystals are distinguished from each other only by their relative dimensions. To determine these, one of the series must be chosen as the primary form, and for this purpose a tetragonal pyramid of the first variety, designated by P as its sign, is selected. The angle of one of its edges, especially the middle edge, found by measurement, determines its angular dimensions ; whilst the proportion of the principal axis (a) to the lateral axes supposed equal to 1, gives its linear dimensions. The parameters, therefore, of each face of the fundamental form are $1 : 1 : a$.

Now if m be any (rational) number, either less or greater than one, and if from any distance ma in the principal axis planes be drawn to the middle edge of P, then new tetragonal pyramids of the first kind, but more or less acute or obtuse than P, are formed. The general sign of these pyramids is mP, and the most common varieties $\frac{1}{2}$P, 2P, 3P ; with the chief axis equal to $\frac{1}{2}$, twice or thrice that of P. If m becomes infinite, or $= \infty$, then the pyramid passes into a prism, indefinitely extended along the principal axis, and with the sign ∞P ; if $m = 0$, which is the case when the lateral axes are supposed infinite, then it becomes a pinacoid, consisting properly of two basal faces open towards the lateral axes, and designated by the sign 0P. The ditetragonal pyramids are produced by taking in each lateral axis distances n greater than 1, and drawing two planes to these points from each of the intermediate polar edges. The parameters of these planes are therefore $m : 1 : n$, and the general sign of the form mPn, the most common values of n being $\frac{3}{2}$, 2, 3, and ∞. When $n = \infty$, a tetragonal pyramid of the second kind arises, designated generally by mP∞, the most common in the mineral kingdom being P∞ and 2P∞. The relation of these to pyramids of the first kind is shown in Fig. 31, where ABBBX is the first, and ACCCX the second kind of pyramid. In like manner from the prism ∞P,

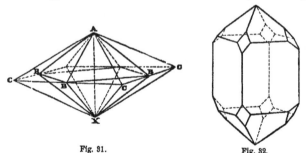

Fig. 31.   Fig. 32.

the ditetragonal prisms ∞Pn are derived, and finally when $n = \infty$, the tetragonal prism of the second kind, whose sign is ∞P∞.

The combinations of the tetragonal system are either holohedral or hemihedral; but the latter are rare. Prisms and pinacoids must always be terminated on the open sides by other forms. Thus in Fig. 32 a square prism of the first kind is terminated by the primary pyramid, and has its lateral angles again replaced by another more acute pyramid of the second kind, so that its sign is $\infty P . P . 2P\infty$.

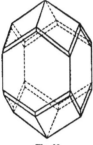

Fig. 33.

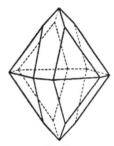

Fig. 34.

In Fig. 33 a prism of the second kind is first bounded by the fundamental pyramid, and then has its edges of combination replaced by a ditetragonal pyramid, and its sign is here $\infty P\infty . P . 3P3$. In Fig. 34 the polar edges of the pyramid are replaced by another pyramid, its sign being $P . P\infty$. In Fig. 35 a hemihedric form very characteristic of chalcopyrite is represented, P and P′ being the two sphenoids, a the basal pinacoid, and b, c, two ditetragonal pyramids.

Fig. 35.

III. *The Hexagonal System.*—The essential character of this system is, that it has four axes—three equal lateral axes intersecting each other in one plane at 60°, and one principal axis at right angles to them. The plane through the lateral axes or the basis, from its hexagonal form gives the name to the system. As in the last system, its forms are either closed or open ; and are divided into holohedral, hemihedral, and tetartohedral—the last forms with only a fourth part of their faces developed. Many of the latter forms are rare, and only a few of the more common require to be here described.

The hexagonal pyramids (Figs. 36, 37) are bounded by twelve isosceles triangles, and are of three kinds, according as the lateral axes fall in the angles, in the middle of the lateral edges, or in another point of these edges, the latter being hemihedral forms. They are also classed as acute or obtuse, but without any very precise limits. The trigonal

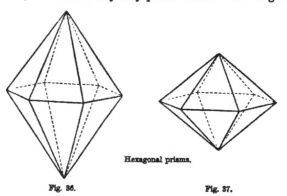

Hexagonal prisms.

Fig. 36.   Fig. 37.

pyramid is bounded by six triangles, and may be viewed as the hemihedral form of the hexagonal. The dihexagonal pyramid is bounded by twenty-four scalene triangles, but has never been observed alone, and rarely even in combinations. The more common prisms are the hexagonal of six sides, and the dihexagonal of twelve sides.

As the fundamental form of this system a particular pyramid P is chosen, and its dimensions determined either from the proportion of the lateral to the principal axis $(1 : a)$, or from the measurement of its angles. From this form (mP) others are derived exactly as in the tetragonal system. Thus dihexagonal pyramids are produced with the general sign mPn, the chief peculiarity being that, whereas in the tetragonal system n might have any rational value from 1 to ∞, in the hexagonal system it can only vary from 1 to 2, in consequence of the geometric character of the figure. When $n = 2$ the dihexagonal changes into a hexagonal pyramid of the second kind, whose sign is mP2. When m is $= \infty$ various prisms arise from similar changes in the value of n; and when $m = 0$ the basal pinacoid.

Few hexagonal mineral species form perfect holohedral combinations. Though quartz and apatite appear as such, yet properly the former is a tetartohedral, the latter a hemihedral species. In holohedral species the predominant faces are usually those of the two hexagonal prisms ∞P and ∞P2, or of the pinacoid 0P; whilst the pyramids P and 2P2, are the most common subordinate forms. Figure 38 represents the prism, bounded on the extremities by two pyramids; one, P, forming the point, the other 2P2 the rhombic faces on the angles, or ∞P . P . 2P2. In some crystals the lateral edges of the prism are replaced by the

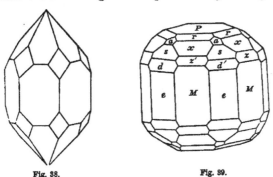

Fig. 38.   Fig. 39.

second prism ∞P2, producing an equiangular twelve-sided prism, which always represents the combination ∞P . ∞P2, and cannot occur as a simple form. An example of a more complicated combination is seen in Fig. 39, of a crystal of apatite, whose sign with the corresponding letters is ∞P(M) . ∞P2(e) . 0P(P) . $\frac{1}{2}$P(r) . P(x) . 2P(z) . P2(a) . 2P2(s) . 4P2(d).

Hexagonal minerals more frequently crystallise in those series of hemihedral forms that are named rhombohedral, from the prevalence in them of rhombohedrons. These are (Fig. 40) bounded by six rhombs, whose lateral edges

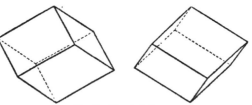

Fig. 40. Rhombohedrons.

do *not* lie in one plane, but rise and fall in a zig-zag manner. The principal axis unites the two trigonal angles, formed by three equal plane angles, and in the most common variety the secondary axes join the middle points of two opposite edges. When the polar edges form an angle of more than 90° the rhombohedrons are named obtuse ; when of less, acute. Hexagonal scalenohedrons (Fig. 41) are bounded by twelve scalene triangles, whose lateral edges do not lie in one plane. The principal axis joins the two hexagonal angles, and the secondary axis the middle points of two opposite lateral edges.

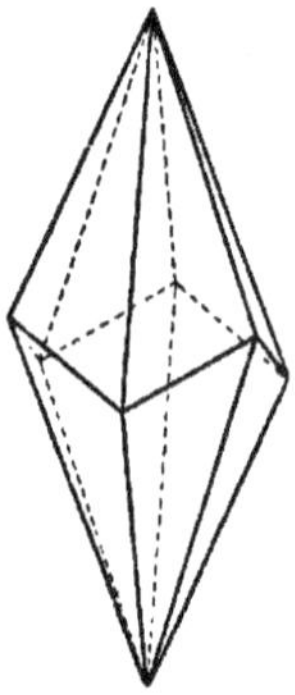

The rhombohedron is derived from the first kind of hexagonal pyramid by the hemihedral development of its alternate faces. Its general sign should therefore be $\frac{m\mathrm{P}}{2}$; but on several grounds it is found

Fig. 41.
Scalenohedron.

better to designate it by R or mR, and its complimentary figure by $-m$R. When the prism or pinacoid arise as its limiting forms, they are designated by ∞R and 0R, though in no respect changed from the limiting forms ∞P and 0P of the pyramid. The scalenohedron is properly the hemihedral form of the dihexagonal

pyramid, but is better derived from the inscribed rhombohedron mR. If the halves of the principal axis of this are
multiplied by a definite number
n, and then planes drawn from
the extremities of this enlarged
axis to the lateral edges of the
rhombohedron, as in Figure 42,
the scalenohedron is constructed.
It is now designated by mRn (the
n on the right though referring
to the chief axis) and the dihexagonal prism in this series by
∞Rn (formerly mR^n and ∞R^n).

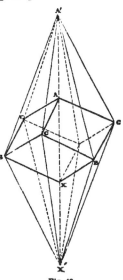

Fig. 42.

The combinations of rhombohedral forms are very numerous,
some hundreds being described
in calc-spar alone. Among the
more common is the prism in
combination with a rhombohedron, as in the twin crystal of
calc-spar (Fig. 43), with the sign
$\infty R . -\frac{1}{2}R$, the lower half being
the same form with the upper,
but turned round 180°. In Fig.
44, the rhombohedron mR has its polar edges replaced by

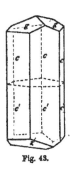

Fig. 43.

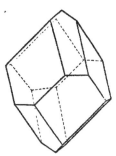

Fig. 44.

another rhombohedron $-\frac{1}{2}mR$; and in Fig. 45 its lateral edges bevelled by the scalenohedron mRn. A more complex combination of five forms is represented in the crystal of calc-spar, Fig. 46, its sign with the letters on the faces being $R5(y)$. $R3(r)$. $R(P)$. $4R(m)$. $\infty R(c)$. Tetartohedral combinations are seen most distinctly in pure quartz or rock-crystal.

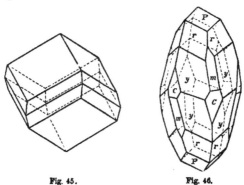

Fig. 45.   Fig. 46.

IV. *Rhombic System.*—The rhombic system is characterised by three axes, all unequal, but at right angles to each

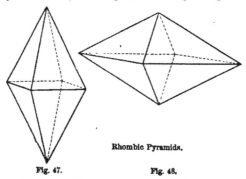

Rhombic Pyramids.

Fig. 47.   Fig. 48.

other. Any one of these may be assumed as the chief axis, when the others are named subordinate. The plane passing through the secondary axes or the basis forms a rhomb, and from this the name is derived. This system comprises only a few varieties of forms that are essentially distinct, and its relations are consequently very simple.

The closed forms are—(1*st.*) The rhombic pyramids (Figs. 47, 48), bounded by eight scalene triangles, whose lateral edges lie in one plane, and form a rhomb. They have eight polar edges—four acute and four more obtuse —and four lateral edges, and six rhombic angles, the most acute at the extremities of the longest axis. (2*d.*) The rhombic sphenoids (Fig. 49) are bounded by four scalene triangles with their lateral edges not in one plane; and are a hemihedral form of the rhombic pyramid of unfrequent occurrence. The open forms again are, (3*d.*) Rhombic prisms bounded by four planes parallel to one of the axes

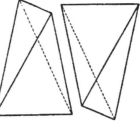

Fig. 49.   Rhombic sphenoids.

which is indefinitely extended. They are divided into upright and horizontal prisms, according as either the principal or one of the lateral axes is supposed to become infinite. For the latter form the name doma or dome has been used ; and two kinds, the macrodome and the brachydome, have been distinguished. Rhombic pinacoids also arise when one axis becomes $= 0$, and the two others are indefinitely extended.

In deriving these forms from a primary, a particular rhombic pyramid P is chosen, and its dimensions determined either from the angular measurement of two of its edges, or by the linear proportion of its axes $a : b : c$; the greater lateral axis b being assumed equal to 1. To the greater lateral axis the name macrodiagonal is frequently given ; to the shorter, that of brachydiagonal ; and the two principal sections are in like manner named macrodiagonal and brachydiagonal, according to the axis they intersect. The same terms are applied throughout all the derived forms, where they consequently mark only the position of the faces in respect to the axes of the fundamental crystal, without reference to the relative magnitude of the derived axes.

By multiplying the principal axis by any rational number m, greater or less than 1, a series of pyramids arise, whose general sign is mP, and their limits the prism and pinacoid, the whole series being contained in this formula, $0P \text{-----} mP \text{----} P \text{----} mP \text{----} \infty P$; which is the fundamental series, the lateral axes always remaining unchanged.

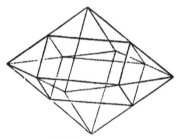

Fig. 50.   Macrodome.

From each member a new series may, however, be developed in two directions by increasing one or other of the lateral axes. When the macrodiagonal is thus multiplied by any number n greater than 1, and planes drawn from the distance n to the polar edges, a new pyramid is produced, named a macropyramid, with the sign $m\bar{P}n$, the mark over the P pointing out the axis enlarged. When $n = \infty$ a macrodome results, with the sign $m\bar{P}\infty$. If the shorter axis is multiplied, then brachypyramids and brachydomes are produced with the signs $m\bar{P}n$ and $m\bar{P}\infty$. So also from the prism ∞P, on the one side, numerous macroprisms $\infty \bar{P}n$, with the limiting macropinacoid $\infty \bar{P}\infty$; on the other, numerous brachyprisms $\infty \bar{P}n$, with the limit form $\infty \bar{P}\infty$, or the brachypinacoid. In Figs. 50, 51, the two domes are shown in their relation to the primitive pyramid.

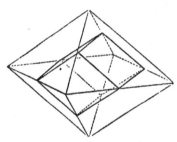

Fig. 51.   Brachydome.

The pyramids seldom occur independent, or even as the

predominant forms in a combination—sulphur, however,
being an exception. Prisms or pinacoids usually give the

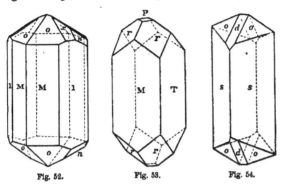

Fig. 52.   Fig. 53.   Fig. 54.

general character to the crystal, which then appears either
in a columnar or tabular, or even in a rectangular pyramidal
form. The determination of the position of these crystals,
as vertical or horizontal,
depends on the choice of
the chief axis of the fundamental form. In the topaz
crystal (Fig. 52) the
brachyprism and the
pyramid are the predomi-
nant elements, associated
with the prism, its sign
and letters being $\infty\breve{P}2(l)$.
$P(o)$. $\infty P(m)$. Fig. 53 of
stilbite is another example,
the macropinacoid $\infty\bar{P}\infty$

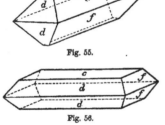

Fig. 55.

Fig. 56.

or M, being combined with the pyramid $P(r)$, the brachypinacoid $\infty\breve{P}\infty$ (T), and the basal pinacoid $0P$ (P). Another instance is Fig. 54 of a lievrite crystal, where the
brachyprism and pyramid combine with the macrodome,
or $\infty\breve{P}2.P.\bar{P}\infty$. The above figures are very common
forms of barytes; Figs. 55 and 56 being both composed

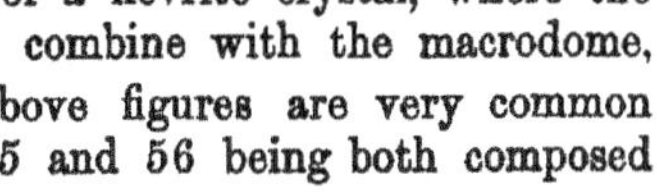

of the pinacoid, a brachydome and macrodome, with sign
OP (c) . $\bar{P}\infty$ (f) $\frac{1}{2}\bar{P}\infty$(d), the variation in aspect arising
from the predominance of
different faces ; and Fig.
57 consisting of the mac-
rodome $\frac{1}{2}P\infty$, the prism
∞P (g), and the pinacoid
OP.

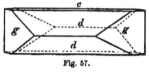

Fig. 57.

V. *The Monoclinic System.*—This system is characterised
by three unequal axes, two of which intersect each other at
an oblique angle, and are cut by the third at right angles.
One of the oblique axes is chosen as the chief axis, and the
other axes are then distinguished as the orthodiagonal (right-
angled), and clinodiagonal (oblique-angled). The same terms
are applied to the chief sections, and the name of the system
refers to the fact that these two planes and the base, together with two right angles, form also one oblique angle C.

The forms of this system approach very near to those of
the rhombic series, but the inclination of the axes, even
when almost a right angle, gives them a peculiar character,
by which they are always readily distinguished. Each pyramid thus separates into two altogether independent forms
or hemipyramids. Three varieties of prism also occur—vertical, inclined, and horizontal
—with faces parallel to the
chief axis, the clinodiagonal or
the orthodiagonal. The horizontal prisms, like the pyramids, separate into two independent partial forms, named
hemiprisms or hemidomes.
The inclined prisms are often
designated clinodomes, the
term prism being restricted to
the vertical forms. Orthopina-
coids and clinopinacoids are
also distinguished from their
position in relation to the axes.

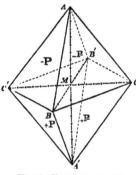

Fig. 58. Monoclinic pyramid.

The monoclinic pyramids (Fig. 58) are bounded by eight

scalene triangles of two kinds, four and four only being
similar. Their lateral edges lie all in one plane, and the
similar triangles are placed in pairs on the clinodiagonal
polar edges. The two pairs in the acute angle between the
orthodiagonal and basal section are designated the positive
hemipyramid ; whilst the two pairs in the obtuse angles of
the same sections form together the negative hemipyramid.
But as these hemipyramids are wholly independent of each
other, they are rarely observed combined. More frequently
each occurs alone, and then forms a prism-like figure, with
faces parallel to the polar edges, and open at the extremities.
Hence, like all prisms, they can only appear in combination
with other forms. The vertical prisms are bounded by four
equal faces parallel to the principal axis, and the cross
section is a rhomb ; the clinodomes have a similar form and
section ; whilst the horizontal prisms or domes have unequal
faces, and their section is a rhomboid.

The mode of derivation of these forms closely resembles
that of the rhombic series. A complete pyramid is assumed
as the fundamental form, and designated $\pm$ P, in order to
express the two portions of which it consists. Its dimensions are given when the proportion of its axes $a : b : c$, and
the angular inclination of the oblique axes C, which is also
that of the orthodiagonal section to the basis, are known.
The fundamental series of forms is, $0\mathrm{P} \ldots \ldots \pm m\mathrm{P} \ldots \ldots$
$\pm \mathrm{P} \ldots \ldots \pm m\mathrm{P} \ldots \ldots \infty\mathrm{P}$; from each of whose members,
by changing the dimensions of the other axes, new forms
may be again derived. Thus from $\pm m\mathrm{P}$, by multiplying the
orthodiagonal by any number n, a series of orthopyramids
$\pm m\mathrm{P}^{\circ}n$ is produced, with the orthodomes $m\mathrm{P}^{\circ}\infty$ as limiting
forms. . The clinodiagonal produces a similar series of clino-
pyramids $\pm m\mathrm{P}^{\circ}n$, with the limiting clinodome $m\mathrm{P}^{\circ}\infty$
always completely formed, and therefore without the signs
$\pm$ attached. From $\infty\mathrm{P}$ arise orthoprisms $\infty\mathrm{P}^{\circ}n$, and the
orthopinacoid $\infty\mathrm{P}^{\circ}\infty$, and clinoprisms $\infty\mathrm{P}^{\circ}n$, and the clinopinacoid $\infty \mathrm{P}^{\circ}\infty$. In these signs the o or c attached to the
P indicates that the orthodiagonal or clinodiagonal axis has
been multiplied. Formerly the latter forms were enclosed
in brackets, thus $(m\mathrm{P}\infty) = m\mathrm{P}^{c}\infty$.

The combinations of this system may be easily understood from their resemblance to those of the rhombic; the chief difficulty being in the occurrence of partial forms, which, however, closely resemble the hemihedral forms of the previous systems. We shall therefore only select a few examples frequently observed in the mineral kingdom.

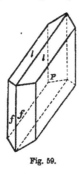 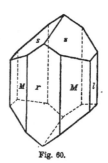

Fig. 59.   Fig. 60.

Fig. 59 represents a very common form of gypsum crystals $\infty P^s \infty$. (P). $\infty P(f)$. $P(b)$. The most common form of augite is represented in Fig. 60, with the sign $\infty P(m)$. $\infty P^s \infty$ (r). $\infty P^s \infty$ (l). $P(s)$. Fig. 61 is a crystal of common felspar or orthoclase, composed of the clinopinacoid

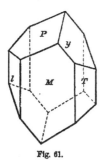 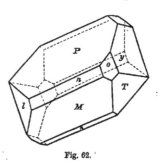

Fig. 61.   Fig. 62.

$\infty P^s \infty$ (M), the prism ∞P (T), the basal pinacoid $0P\,(P)$, and the hemidomes $2P^s \infty$ (y): to which, in Fig. 62 of the same mineral, the hemipyramid $P(o)$, and the clinodome $2P^s \infty$ (n) are added.

VI. *Triclinic System.*—This is the least regular system,
and departs the most widely from symmetry of form. The
axes are all unequal, and inclined at angles none of which
are right angles, so that to determine any crystal, or series of
forms, the proportion of the axes $a : b : c$, and also their
angles, or those of the inclination of the chief sections, must
be known. As in the previous system, one axis is chosen
as the principal axis, and the two others distinguished as
the macrodiagonal and brachydiagonal axes. In consequence
of the oblique position of the principal sections, this system
consists entirely of partial forms wholly independent on
each other, and each composed only of two parallel faces.
The complete pyramid is thus broken up into four distinct
quarter pyramids and the prism into two hemiprisms.
Each of these partial forms is thus nothing more than a pair
of parallel planes, and the various forms consequently mere
individual faces. This circumstance renders many triclinic
crystals very unsymmetrical in appearance.

Triclinic pyramids (Fig. 63) are bounded by eight
triangles whose lateral edges lie in
one plane. They are equal and
parallel two and two to each other;
each pair forming, as just stated, a
tetartopyramid or open form, only
limited by combination with other
forms, or, as we may suppose, by
the chief sections. The prisms are
again either vertical or inclined;
the latter named domes, and their
section is always rhomboidal. In
deriving the forms, the fundamental
pyramid is placed upright with its
brachydiagonal axis to the spectator, and the partial forms
designated, the two upper by 'P and P', the two lower by
,P and P,, as in the figure. The further derivation now
follows as in the rhombic system, with the modifications
already mentioned, so that we need not delay on it longer,
especially as the minerals crystallising in these forms are
not numerous.

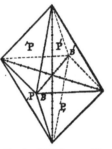

Fig. 63. Triclinic pyramid.

D

Some combinations of this system, as the series exhibited by most of the felspars, approach very near to the monoclinic system; whilst others, as cyanose or blue vitriol and axinite, show great incompleteness and want of symmetry. In the latter case the determination of the forms is often difficult and requires great attention. As specimens, we may notice the albite crystal (Fig. 64), in which P is the basal

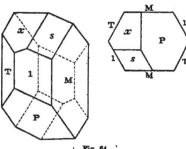

Fig. 64.

pinacoid 0P; M the brachydiagonal pinacoid $\infty \breve{P} \infty$; s the upper right pyramid P'; l the right hemiprism ∞ P'; T the left hemiprism ∞'P, and x the hemidome $\overline{'P} \infty$. Figures 65 and 66 are crystals of axinite, the former from Dauphiné, the

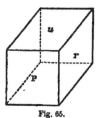

Fig. 65.

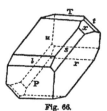

Fig. 66.

latter common in Cornwall, of whose faces the following is the development :—r the macropinacoid $\infty \overline{P} \infty$; P the left hemiprism ∞'P; u the left upper quarter pyramid 'P; l the left upper quarter pyramid 2'P; s the left upper partial form of the macropyramid 3$\overline{P}$3, and x the hemidome 2'P' ∞.

Imperfections of Crystals.

In the foregoing description of the forms of crystals the planes have been supposed smooth and even, the faces equal and uniform, or at the same distance from the centre or point of intersection of the axes, and each crystal also perfect or fully formed and complete on every side. In nature, however, these conditions are rarely if ever realised, and the edges of crystals are seldom straight lines, or the faces mathematical plane surfaces. A very interesting variety of these irregularities, which pervades all the systems except the tesseral, is named *hemimorphism*. In this the crystals are bounded at the opposite ends of their chief axis by faces belonging to distinct forms, and hence only the upper or under half of each form is produced, or the crystal, as the name implies, is half-formed. Figure 67 represents

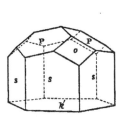

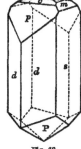

Fig. 67.   Fig. 68.

a common variety of tourmaline, bounded on the upper end by the planes of the rhombohedrons R and − 2R, and on the lower end by the basal pinacoid. In Fig. 68 of galmei the upper extremity shows the basis k, two brachydomes o and p; and two macrodomes m and l; whilst on the lower end it is bounded by the faces P of the primary form. This appearance becomes more interesting from the fact that many hemimorphic crystals acquire polar electricity from heat—that is, exhibit opposite kinds of electricity at opposite ends of the crystal.

The faces of crystals are very frequently rendered imperfect by *striæ* or minute linear and parallel elevations and depressions. These arise in the oscillatory combination of two crystal forms, alternately prevailing through small spaces. The striæ, therefore, are in reality the edges of combined forms. They are very common on quartz, shorl, and some other minerals; and frequently indicate combinations where only a simple form would otherwise appear to exist. The cubes and pentagonal dodecahedrons of iron pyrites are frequently striated, and in three directions at right angles to each other. In calc-spar the faces of the rhombohedron, $-\frac{1}{2}R$ (*g* in Fig. 43 above), are almost never without striæ parallel to the oblique diagonal. The striation is said to be simple when only one series of parallel lines appears on each face, or feathered when two systems diverge from a common line. In other crystals the faces, then said to be *drusy*, are covered by numerous projecting angles of smaller crystals; an imperfection often seen in fluor spar. The faces of crystals occasionally appear curved either as in tourmaline and beryl from the peculiar oscillatory combination mentioned, or by the union of several crystals at obtuse angles, like stones in a vault, as in stilbite and prehnite. A true curvature of the faces probably occurs in the saddle-shaped rhombohedrons of dolomite and siderite, in the lens-like crystals of gypsum, and in the curved faces so common on diamond crystals. In chabasite similar curved faces occur, but concave. In galena and augite the crystals are often rounded on the corners, as if by an incipient state of fusion. On other crystals the faces are rendered uneven from inequalities following no certain rule. These imperfections furnish valuable assistance in developing very complex combinations, all the faces of each individual form being distinguished by the same peculiarity of surface.

Irregularities in the forms of crystals are produced when the corresponding faces are placed at unequal distances from the centre, and consequently differ in form and size. Thus the cubes and octahedrons of iron pyrites, galena, and fluor spar, are often lengthened along one axis. Quartz is subject

to many such irregularities, which are seen in a very remarkable manner on the beautiful transparent and sharply
angular crystals from Dauphiné. In such irregular forms,
instead of one line, the axes are then represented by an infinite number of lines, parallel to the ideal axis of the figure.
The same irregularity carried to a greater extent frequently
causes certain faces, required for the symmetry of the form,
altogether to disappear. Again, some crystals do not fill
the space marked out by their outline, holes and vacancies
being left in the faces, occasionally to such an extent that
they seem little more than mere skeletons. This appearance is very common on crystals produced artificially, as in
common salt, alum, bismuth, silver, etc. A perfect crystal
can only be produced when during its formation it is completely isolated, so as to have full room to expand on every
side. Hence the most perfect crystals have been originally
imbedded singly in some uniform rock mass. Next to them
in perfection are forms that grow singly on the surface of
some mass of similar or distinct composition, especially when
the point of adherence is small. An incompleteness of form,
or at least a difficulty in determining it, arises from the
minuteness of some crystals, or from their contracted dimensions in certain directions. Thus some appear mere tabular
or lamellar planes, whilst others run out into acicular, needle-
shaped, or capillary crystals. Amid all these modifications
of the general form of the crystal, of the condition and
aspect of its individual faces, or of its linear dimensions, one
important element, the angular measurement, remains constant. In some crystals, indeed, increase of temperature
produces an unequal expansion in different directions, slightly
changing the relative inclination of the faces, but so small
as to be scarcely perceptible in common measurements, and
hence producing no ambiguity. More important are the
angular changes which in many species accompany slight
changes in chemical composition, particularly in the relative
proportions of certain isomorphous elements. But notwithstanding these limitations, the great truth of the permanence
of the angular dimensions of crystals, announced by Romé
de l'Isle, remains unaffected ; only, as Mohs well states, it

must not be interpreted with a rigid immutability, incon-
sistent with the whole analogy of other parts of nature.

The Goniometer and Measurement of Crystals.

The fact just stated of the permanence of the angular
dimensions of crystals shows the importance of some accurate method of measuring their angles; that is the inclination of two faces to each other. Two instruments have
been specially used for this purpose,—the common or contact goniometer, invented by Caringeau, and the reflecting
goniometer of Wollaston.

The former is simply two
brass rulers turning on a
common centre, between
which the crystal is so placed
that its faces coincide with
the edges of the rulers, and
the angle is then measured
on a graduated arc. This
instrument is sufficiently
accurate for many purposes
and for large crystals; but
for precise determination is
far inferior to the reflecting
goniometer. This requires
smooth and even faces, but
these may be very small,
even the hundredth of an
inch, in skilful hands; and
as small crystals are generally most perfect, far greater
accuracy can be attained,
and the measurement de-
pended on to one minute (1′).

Fig. 69. Goniometer.

The reflecting goniometer
is represented in the annexed
figure. It consists essentially of a graduated circle mm,
divided on its edge into twice 180°, or more often into half-

degrees, the minutes being read off by the vernier *hh.* This circle turns on an axis connected with *tt,* so that by turning this the circle is moved round, but is stopped at 180°, when moving in one direction, by a spring at *k.* The other part of the instrument is intended to attach and adjust the crystal to be measured. The first axis of *mn* is hollow, and a second axis, *aa,* passes through it from *ss,* so that this and all the connected parts from *b* to *f* can be turned without moving the circle *mm.* The axis *d* passes through a hole in *bc,* so that it can turn the arm *de* into any required position ; *f* is a similar axis turning the arm *og* ; and *pq* a fourth axis, in like manner movable in *g,* and with a small knob at *q,* to which the crystal to be measured is attached.

When about to use the instrument it should be placed on a table, with its base horizontal, which is readily done by the screws in it, and opposite to a window at about 12 or 15 feet distance, so that its axis shall be parallel to the horizontal bars of the window. One of the upper bars of the window, and also the lower bar, or, instead of the latter, a white line on the floor or table parallel to the window, should then be chosen in order to adjust the crystal. The observer places himself behind the instrument with the side *a* at his right hand. The crystal is then attached to *q* by a piece of wax with the two faces to be measured upwards. The axis *fo* is made parallel to *aa,* and the eye being brought near to the first face of the crystal, the axes *aa* and *p* are turned till the image of the window is seen reflected in the face with the horizontal and vertical bars in their position. The axis *d* is then turned through a considerable angle (say 60°), and the image of the window again sought and brought into its proper place by turning the axis *f,* without moving *p.* When this is done that face is brought into its true position, normal to *d,* so that no motion of *d* can disarrange it. Hence the image of the window may now be sought in the second face and brought into its true position, with the horizontal bars seen horizontal, by moving the axes *d* and *a.* When this is done the crystal is properly adjusted, and the angle is thus measured. First bring the zero of the circle and vernier to coincide, and then turn the inner axis *a* or *ss*, and move the eye till the image of the upper bar of the window reflected from the more distant face of the crystal coincides with the lower bar or horizontal line seen directly. Keeping the eye in its place, turn the outer axis *tt* till the reflected image of the upper bar in the other face in like manner coincides with the lower line, and the angle of the two faces is then read off on the divided circle. As the angle measured is not directly that of the faces, but of the rays of light reflected from them, or the difference of the angle wanted from 180°, the circle has the degrees numbered in the reverse direction, so as to give the angle without the trouble of subtracting the one from the other.

The above apparatus for adjusting the crystal is an improvement suggested by Naumann. In the original instrument the axis *fo* was made to push in or out in a sheath, and had a small brass plate, bent at right angles, inserted in a cleft at *o*, to which the crystal was attached. The crystal was adjusted, as formerly, by moving the plate, or the axis *fo*, and by slight motion of the arm *de*, which should be at right angles nearly to *bc* when used. A considerable improvement is, to have a small mirror fixed on the stand below the crystal, with its face parallel to the axis *aa*, and inclined at 45° to the window, when the lower line can be dispensed with, and the instrument used for various other purposes of angular measurement. Many alterations have been suggested for the purpose of insuring greater accuracy; but the simple instrument is sufficient for all purposes of determinative mineralogy, and the error from the instrument will in most cases be less than the actual variations in the dimensions of the crystals. Greater simplicity is indeed rather desirable, and the student will often find it sufficient to attach the crystal by a piece of wax to the axis *a* directly, and give it the furthur adjustment by the hand. The only use of the parts from *b* to *q* is to enable the observer to place the crystal properly; that is, with the edge to be measured parallel to the axis of the instrument, and as nearly as possible coinciding with its centre. This is effected when the reflection of the horizontal bar in the two faces appears parallel to that edge.

Macles or Twin Crystals.

When two similar crystals are united with all their similar faces and axes parallel, the one is merely a continuation or enlargement of the other, and every crystal may be regarded as thus built up of a number of smaller crystals. Where, however, crystals are united with only some, not all, their similar faces and axes parallel, they are named macles or twin crystals. There are two kinds of macles, the first with the axes of the separate crystals parallel; the second with these axes inclined or oblique. The first only occur in hemihedral forms, and the two crystals are then combined in the exact position in which they would be derived from or reproduce the primary holohedral form. The second class, with oblique axes, occur both in holohedral and hemihedral forms, and the two individuals are placed in perfect symmetry to each other, in reference to a particular face of the crystal which forms the plane of union or the equator of the macle. We may also suppose the two crystals originally parallel, and the one turned round the normal of the united faces by 180°, whilst the other is stationary. Or we may suppose a crystal cut into halves in a particular direction, and one-half turned 180° on the other; and hence the name of hemitrope given to them by Hauy. The position of the two individuals in this case corresponds with that of an object and its image in a mirror, whose surface then represents the plane of union.

The manner in which the crystals unite also differs. Some are merely opposed, or the faces of union in simple contact; others are, as it were, grown together, and mutually interpenetrate, occasionally so completely as to appear like one individual. The twin edges and angles in which the two unite are often re-entering; or the faces may coincide in one plane, when the line of union is either imperceptible, or is only marked by the meeting of two systems of striæ, or other diversity in the physical characters of the two faces.

The formation of twin crystals may be again repeated, forming groups of three, four, or more. When the planes

of union are parallel to each other, the crystals form rows
of indeterminate extent; where they are not parallel, they
may return into each other in circles, or form bouquet-like
or other groups. Where crystals are merely in juxtaposition,
they are sometimes much shortened in the direction of the
twin axis; and where many occur in a series with parallel
position, are often compressed into very thin plates, frequently not thicker than paper, giving to the surface of the
aggregate a peculiar striated aspect.

Only a few twin crystals in the different systems can

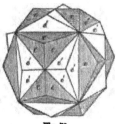

Fig. 70.

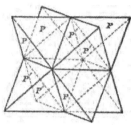

Fig. 71.

be noticed, chiefly as examples of this mode of formation.
In the tesseral system forms that unite with parallel axes
produce intersecting macles like the pentagonal dodeca-

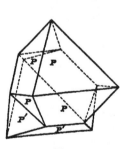

Fig. 72.

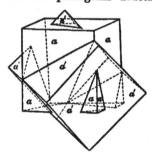

Fig. 73.

hedrons of iron pyrites in Fig. 70, and the tetrahedrons of
fahlore in Fig. 71, a similar formation also occurring in the

diamond. In macles with inclined axes the two forms almost always unite by a face of the octahedron, and the two individuals are then generally apposed and shortened in the direction of the twin axis by one-half, so that they appear like a crystal that has been divided by a plane parallel to one of its faces, and the two halves turned round on each other by an angle of 180°. In this manner two octahedrons of the spinel, magnetite automolite (Fig. 72), are frequently united. The same law prevails in the intersecting cubes of fluor spar, iron pyrites, and galena, represented in Fig. 73. In Fig. 74 of blende two rhombic dodecahedrons are united by a face of the octahedron.

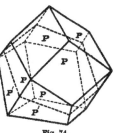

Fig. 74.

In the tetragonal system twin crystals with parallel axes rarely occur, but are seen in chalcopyrite, and one or two other minerals. Where the axes are inclined the plane of union is very often one of the faces of the pyramid P∞, or one of those faces that would regularly replace the polar edges of the fundamental form P. The crystals of tin ore

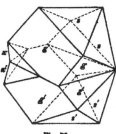

Fig. 75.

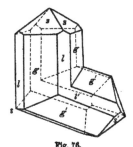

Fig. 76.

obey this law, as seen in Fig. 75, where the individuals are pyramidal, and in the knee-shaped crystal (Fig. 76), where they are more prismatic. Hausmanite appears like Fig. 77, in which the fundamental pyramid P prevails, on whose

polar edges other crystals are often very symmetrically repeated, a central individual appearing like the support of
all the others. Almost identical
forms occur in chalcopyrite.

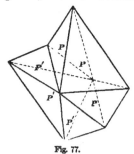

In the hexagonal system twin
crystals with parallel axes are
common, as in calc-spar, chabasite,
hæmatite, and other rhombohedral
minerals. In calc-spar they often
form very regular crystals, the two
individuals uniting by a plane
parallel to the base, so as to
appear like a single crystal, as
in Fig. 78, where each end

Fig. 77.

shows the forms ∞R − ¼R, but in a complementary
position ; or in Fig. 79 of two scalenohedrons R3 from
Derbyshire. The rhombohedric crystals of chabasite often
appear intersecting each other, like those of fluor spar
in Fig. 73 above. The purer varieties of quartz or rock-

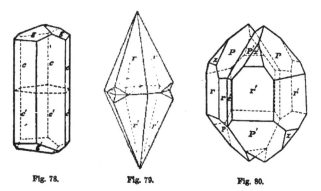

Fig. 78.   Fig. 79.   Fig. 80.

crystal, in consequence of the tetartohedral character of
its crystallisation, often exhibit twins. In these the
pyramid P separates into two rhombohedrons P and r,
which, though geometrically similar, are yet physically distinct. In Fig. 80 the two individuals are only grown to-

gether, but more commonly they penetrate each other in an irregular manner, forming apparently a single crystal. Twins with oblique axes are also common, the plane of union being usually one face of the rhombohedron. Thus in calc-spar two rhombohedrons are often joined by a face of $-\frac{1}{2}$R, the

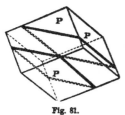

Fig. 81.

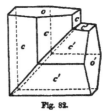

Fig. 82.

two axes forming an angle of 127° 34′; occasionally a third individual is interposed in a lamellar form, as in Fig. 81, when the two outer crystals become parallel. This latter arrangement is very common in the highly cleavable varieties or Iceland spar. When the crystals unite in a face of the rhombohedron R, Fig. 82, they form an angle of 89° 8′, differing little from a right angle, by which the occurrence of this law is very easily recognised, especially in prismatic varieties.

Fig. 83.

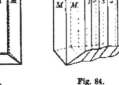

Fig. 84.

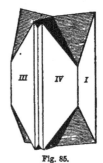

Fig. 85.

In the rhombic system twin crystals with parallel axes are very rare, but those with oblique axes common, the plane

of union being one of the faces of the prism ∞P. Twins
of this kind are very distinctly seen in arragonite, cerussite,
marcasite, stephanite, mispickel, and other minerals. In
arragonite the crystals partly interpenetrate, partly are in
mere juxtaposition, as in Fig. 83, where the individuals are
formed by the combination ∞P(m) . ∞P̆∞ (h), P̆∞ (k), and
in Fig. 84 where several crystals of the same combination
form a series with parallel planes of union ; the inner members being so shortened that they appear like mere lamellar
plates producing striæ on the faces P̆∞ and ∞P̆∞ of the
macle. In Fig. 85 four crystals, each of the combination
∞P . 2P̆∞ , having united in inclined planes, form a circular
group, returning into itself. Cerussite often occurs in macles

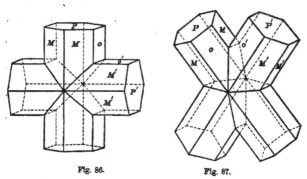

Fig. 86.   Fig. 87.

in all respects similar. In staurolite, individuals of the prismatic combination ∞P . ∞P̆∞ . 0P, combine either, as in
Fig. 86, by a face of the brachydome $\frac{3}{2}$P̆∞ , with their chief
axes almost at right angles ; or, as in Fig. 87, by a face of
the brachypyramid $\frac{3}{2}$P̆$\frac{3}{2}$, the chief axes and the brachypinacoids (o) of the two single crystals meeting at an angle of
about 60°. Harmotome (Fig. 88) is often regarded as forming macles of two crystals intersecting so nearly at right
angles that their principal axes seem to coincide.

In the monoclinic system the most common macles are
those in which the principal axes and the chief sections of

the two crystals are parallel to each other, and consequently the principal axis is also the twin axis. Usually the two individuals are united by a face parallel to the orthodiagonal chief section, as in Figure 89 of gypsum, where two crystals of the combination $\infty P^\circ \infty . \infty P. - P$, shown in Fig. 59, unite

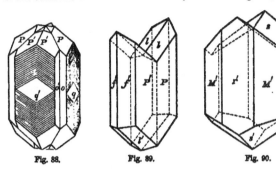

Fig. 88.   Fig. 89.   Fig. 90.

so regularly that the faces of the pinacoids (P and P) form only one plane. In a similar manner the augite crystals of the combination $\infty P . \infty P^\circ \infty . \infty P^\circ \infty . P$, represented singly in Fig. 60, are in Fig. 90 united in a macle so very symmetrical and regular that the line of junction cannot be observed on the face of the clinopinacoid. The two hemipyramids P (s) (like $-$ P (l) in the gypsum crystal above) form on one side a re-entering, on the other a salient angle. Hornblende, wolfram, and other minerals, exhibit a similar appearance. In other cases the individuals partially penetrate each other, being, as it were, crushed together in the direction of the orthodiagonal. This mode of union is not uncommon

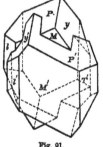

Fig. 91.

in gypsum, and very frequent in orthoclase felspar. Two crystals of the latter, of the combination $\infty P^\circ \infty . \infty P. 0P. 2P^\circ \infty$, as in Fig. 61 above, are often pushed sidewise into each other as shown in Fig. 91.

In the triclinic system some twin formations are of great importance as a means of distinguishing the triclinic from the monoclinic species of felspar. In one variety the twin axis is the normal to the brachydiagonal chief section. But in the triclinic felspars this section is not perpendicular to the bases, and consequently the two bases form on one side a re-entering, on the other a salient angle ; whereas in the monoclinic felspars (where the brachydiagonal chief section corresponds to the clinodiagonal) no twin crystals can be produced in conformity to this law, and the two bases fall in one plane. The albite and oligoclase very often exhibit such twins as in Figure 92, where the very obtuse angles

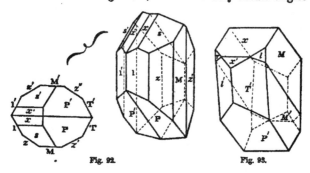

Fig. 92.   Fig. 93.

formed by the faces of OP, or P and P' (as well as those of $\overline{P}\infty$, or z and z') are a very characteristic appearance, marking out this mineral at once as a triclinic species. Usually the twin formation is repeated, three or more crystals being combined, when those in the centre are reduced to mere plates. When very numerous, the surfaces P and z are covered with fine striæ, often only perceptible with a microscope. A second law observed in triclinic felspars, particularly the albite and labradorite, is that the twin axis corresponds with that normal of the brachydiagonal which is situated in the plane of the base. In pericline, a variety of albite, these twins appear as in Fig. 93, where the two crystals are united by a face of the basil pinacoid P, whilst the faces of the two brachypinacoids (M and M') form edges with very obtuse angles (173° 22'), re-entering on the one side and salient on the other. These edges, or the line of junction between M and M', are also parallel to the edges formed by these faces and the base, or those between M and P. In this case also the macles are occasionally several times repeated, when the faces appear covered with fine striæ.

Irregular Aggregation of Crystals.

Besides the regular unions now described, crystals are often aggregated in peculiar ways, to which no fixed law can be assigned. Thus some crystals, apparently simple, are composed of concentric crusts or shells, which may be removed one after the other, always leaving a smaller crystal like a kernel, with smooth distinct faces. Some specimens of quartz from Beeralston in Devonshire consist apparently of hollow hexagonal pyramids placed one within another. Other minerals, as fluor spar, apatite, heavy spar, and calc-spar, exhibited a similar structure by bands of different colours.

Many large crystals, again, appear like an aggregate of numerous small crystals, partly of the same, partly of different forms. Thus some octahedrons of fluor spar from Schlaggenwald are made up of small dark violet-blue cubes, whose projecting angles give a drusy character to the faces of the larger form. Such polysynthetic crystals, as they may be called, are very common in calc-spar.

A similar, but still more remarkable formation, is where two crystals of distinct species are conjoined. Such unions of cyanite and staurolite have been long well known, and the graphic granite exhibits a similar union between large felspar crystals and many smaller ones of mica and quartz.

Forms of Crystalline Aggregates.—Crystals have often been produced under conditions preventing the free development of their forms. They then compose crystalline aggregates, of which the following may be distinguished :— *Granular,* formed of grains, generally angular, but rarely rounded or flattened. *Lamellar* consist of broad plates, which are *tabular* when of uniform thickness, *lenticular*

E

when becoming thinner on the edges, *wedge-shaped* when
sharpened towards one edge, and *scaly* when the plates are
very small. *Columnar*, in which the individuals are drawn
out in one direction more than in the others ; *bacillary* or
rod-like, in which the columns are of uniform thickness ;
acicular or needle-shaped, in which they are pointed ; and
fibrous, in which they are very fine. In the broad-colum-
nar the columns are, as it were, compressed, or broader in
one direction than the other. The distinctions of large,
coarse, small, or fine-granular ; thick or thin scaly ; straight,
curved, or twisted-columnar ; parallel, diverging, or con-
fused-fibrous ; and such like, are easily understood.

Aggregates which have been able to crystallise, at least
with a certain degree of freedom, have been distinguished
by Mohs into crystal groups and druses ; the former including all unions of several imbedded crystals with no distinct
basis ; the latter those of crystals that have grown together
on a common support. In the groups crystals with their
faces otherwise perfect are conjoined in various ways.
Sometimes they radiate, as it were, from a common centre,
and produce spheroidal, ellipsoidal, or other forms, frequent
in gypsum, iron pyrites, and other minerals imbedded in
clay. Where many such masses are united, they are named
botryoidal when like bunches of grapes, *mammellated* where
the spheres are larger and less distinct, and *reniform* or kid-
ney-shaped where the masses are still larger. Some groups
are partially attached by a small point ; but the mass is
generally free.

Crystals are often grouped in rows or in one direction,
forming, when they are very small, capillary or hair-like,
and filiform, thread, or wire-like forms, which are common
among native metals, as gold, silver, copper, and bismuth,
in argentite and a few other minerals. Sometimes the
masses are dentiform, consisting of portions resembling
teeth ; as is very common in silver. Often these groups
expand in several directions, and produce arborescent, dendritic, foliated, feathered, or other forms, very common in
copper. In these groups, however, a certain dependence
on the crystallographic character of the species may be ob-

served. The lamellar minerals often form fan-shaped, wheel-like, almond-shaped, comb-like, or other groups. The fibrous types, again, are disposed in parallel or diverging bundles, or in radiating, stellar, and other masses. Coralloidal (like coral), fruticose (like cauliflower), and other forms, have also been observed.

In druses, many crystals rise side by side from a common support; in some only the granular mass composed of their united bases, in others a distinct body. The form of a druse is determined by that of the surface on which it grows, and consequently is often very irregular or wholly accidental. Where completely inclosed they have been named drusy cavities, and when of a spheroidal form, geodes. A drusy crust, again, consists of a thin layer of small crystals investing the surface of a large crystal or of some other body.

The minute or cryptocrystalline minerals form similar aggregates. When globular or oolitic the minute crystals often appear to radiate from a centre, or form concentric crusts. Somewhat similar are the stalactites and stalagmites, in which the mineral, especially rock-salt, calc-spar, chalcedony, opal, limonite, has been deposited from a fluid dropping slowly from some overhanging body. In this case the principal axis of the figure, generally a hollow tube, is vertical, whilst the individual parts are arranged at right angles to it. In other cases the mineral has apparently been deposited from a fluid mass moving slowly in a particular direction, which may be regarded as the chief axis of the figure, whilst the axes of the individual crystals may assume a different position.

By far the largest masses of the mineral kingdom have, however, been produced under conditions in which a free development of their forms was excluded. This has been the case with the greater portion of the minerals composing rocks or filling veins and dykes. The structure of these masses on the large scale belongs to geology, but some varieties of the texture, visible even in hand specimens, may be noticed. The individual grains or masses have seldom any regular form, but appear round, long, or flat, according to circumstances, and as each has been more or less checked in the process of formation. Even then, however, a certain regularity in the position of the parts is often observable, as in granite, in which the cleavage planes, and consequently the axes of the felspar crystals, are parallel. Where these grains are all pretty similar in size and shape, the rock is named massive when they are small, or granular when they are larger and more distinct. Sometimes the rock becomes slaty, dividing into thin plates; or concretionary, forming roundish masses; at other times the interposition of some foreign substance (gas or vapour) has rendered it porous, cellular, or vesicular, giving rise to drusy cavities. These cavities are often empty, but have occasionally been filled by other minerals, when the rock is named amygdaloidal, from the almond-like shape of the inclosed masses.

Many of the above external forms appear also in the amorphous solid minerals, in which no trace of individual parts, and consequently of internal structure, is observable. They are not unfrequently disposed in parallel or concentric layers, of uniform or distinct colours; and may assume spherical, cylindrical, stalactitic, and other appearances.

Pseudomorphism.

When the substance of one mineral assumes the external form of some other mineral it is named a pseudomorph. In some named incrusting pseudomorphs the original crystal is covered by a rough or drusy surface of the second mineral, frequently not thicker than paper. Occasionally the first crystal has been removed, and the shell alone remains; or the cavity has been filled by a distinct mineral species, or a crystalloid, as it may be named, forming an exact representation of the original, but of a different substance.

More commonly the new mineral substance has gradually expelled the old, and replacing it, as it were, atom by atom, has assumed its exact form. In other cases not the whole substance of the original crystal, but only one or more of its elements, has been changed, or the whole matter has remained, but in a new condition. Thus arragonite crystals have been converted into calc-spar, the chemical composition of both being identical ; or gaylussite has been changed into calc-spar, andalusite into cyanite, by the loss of certain elements. On the other hand, anhydrite becomes gypsum, cuprite malachite, by addition of new matter. Or the elements are partially changed, as felspar into kaolin, iron pyrites into hæmatite or limonite, azurite into malachite, augite into green earth. The true nature of such bodies is shown by the internal structure having no relation to the external form or apparent system of crystallisation.

The process of petrification of organic bodies is in reality a species of pseudomorphic formation, and has been produced in all the above modes. External and internal casts of organic bodies are not uncommon. In other cases the original substance has been replaced by some mineral which has preserved not merely the external form, but even the minutest detail of internal structure ; so that the different kinds of wood have been distinguished in their silicified trunks. The most common petrifying substances are silica and carbonate of lime. In encrinites, echinites, belemnites, and other fossils, the crystals of calc-spar often occur in very regular positions. In some varieties of petrified wood both the ligneous structure and the cleavage of the calc-spar are observable.

Different from the above are mineralised bodies, in which the original structure is still retained, but their chemical nature partially changed. In these a complete series may be often traced, as from wood or peat, through the varieties of brown coal, common coal, anthracite, and graphite, perhaps even to the diamond.

CHAPTER II.

PHYSICAL PROPERTIES OF MINERALS.

THE physical character of minerals comprehend — 1*st*, Those properties derived from the nature of the substance itself, as coherence, mode of fracture, elasticity, and density or specific gravity. 2*d*, Those phenomena called forth in minerals by the influence of some external power or agent, as their optical, electric, or thermal relations ; and, 3*d*, Other characters depending on the personal sensation of the observer, on his taste, smell, and touch. All these properties furnish useful characters in distinguishing and describing mineral species.

Cleavage and Fracture.

In many species there are certain planes, at right angles to which cohesion seems to be at a minimum, so that the mineral separates along, or parallel to, these planes far more readily than in any other direction. This property is named cleavage, and these planes cleavage-planes. They have a strictly definite position, and do not show any transition or gradual passage into the greater coherence in other directions. The number of these parallel cleavage-planes is altogether indefinite ; so that the only limit that can be assigned to the divisibility of some minerals, as gypsum and mica, arises from the coarseness of our instruments.

These minima of coherence or cleavage-planes are always parallel to some face of the crystal, and similar equal minima occur parallel to every other face of the same form. Hence they are always equal in number to the faces of the form, and the figures produced by cleavage agree in every point with true crystals, except that they are artificial. They are thus most simply and conveniently described by

the same terms and signs as the faces of crystals. Some
minerals cleave in several directions parallel to the faces of
different forms, but the cleavage is generally more easily
obtained and more perfect in one direction than in the
others. This complex cleavage is well seen in calc-spar
and fluor spar, and very remarkably in zinc-blende, where
it takes place in no less than six directions. As in each of
these the division may be indefinitely continued, it is clear
that no lamellar structure in any proper sense can be assigned to the mineral. All that can be affirmed is, that
contiguous atoms have less coherence in the normal of these
planes than in other directions. When the cleavage takes
place in three directions, it, of course, produces a perfect
crystal form, from which the system of crystallisation and
angular dimensions of the species may be discovered, and
is thus often of very great importance.

The common cleavage in the different systems is as follows, those of most frequent occurrence being put in italics:
—(1.) In the tesseral, *Octahedral,* O, along the faces of the
octahedron; *Hexahedral,* $\infty O \infty$, along those of the cube;
and Dodecahedral, ∞O. (2.) In the tetragonal system,
Pyramidal, P or $2P\infty$; *Prismatic,* ∞P or $\infty P\infty$; or *Basal,*
0P. (3.) In the hexagonal system with holohedral forms,
Pyramidal, P or P2; *Prismatic,* ∞P or $\infty P2$; or *Basal*
0P; with rhombohedral forms, *Rhombohedral,* R; Prismatic, ∞R; or *Basal,* 0R. (4.) In the rhombic system,
Pyramidal, P; *Prismatic,* ∞P; Makro or Brachydomatic,
$\bar{P}\infty$ or $\breve{P}\infty$; *Basal,* 0P; Macrodiagonal, $\infty \bar{P}\infty$; or
Brachydiagonal, $\infty \breve{P}\infty$. (5.) In the monoclinic system,
Hemipyramidal, P or $-P$; *Prismatic,* ∞P; Clinodomatic,
$P^{\circ}\infty$; Hemidomatic, $P^{\circ}\infty$ or $-P^{\circ}\infty$; *Basal,* 0P; *Ortho-*
diagonal, $\infty P^{\circ}\infty$; or *Clinodiagonal,* $\infty P^{\circ}\infty$. (6.) In the
triclinic system, Hemiprismatic, $\infty P'$ or ∞P; Hemido-
matic either along the macrodome or brachydome; *Basal,*
0P; Macrodiagonal, $\infty \bar{P}\infty$; or *Brachydiagonal,* $\infty \breve{P}\infty$.

In some minerals, as mica and gypsum, the cleavage is
readily procured; these may be held in the hand and
divided by a knife. Others only cleave with more or less

difficulty; these must be placed on a firm support resting on lead, folded paper, or cloth, and a sharp blow struck on a chisel applied in a proper direction. This may often be ascertained by examining the specimen in a strong light. The planes produced also vary much in their degree of perfection, being *highly* perfect in some, as mica and calc-spar; imperfect in others, as garnet and quartz. In a very few crystalline minerals cleavage-planes can hardly be said to exist. Cleavage must be carefully distinguished from the planes of union in twin crystals, and the division-planes in the laminar minerals.

Fracture Surfaces are formed when a mineral breaks in a direction different from the cleavage-planes. They are consequently most readily observed when the cleavage is least perfect. The form of the fracture is named *conchoidal* when composed of concave and convex surfaces like shells, *even* when nearly free from inequalities. The character of the surface is *smooth;* or *splintery* when covered by small wedge-shaped splinters adhering by the thicker end; or *hackly* when covered by small slightly-bent inequalities, as in iron and other malleable bodies; or *earthy* when it shows only fine dust.

Hardness and Tenacity.

The hardness of minerals, or their power of resisting any attempt to separate their parts, is also an important character. As it differs considerably in the same species, according to the direction and the surface on which the trial is made, its accurate determination is difficult, and the utmost that can usually be obtained is a mere approximation found by comparing different minerals one with another. For this purpose Mohs has given the following scale :—

1. *Talc*, of a white or greenish colour.
2. *Rock-salt*, a pure cleavable variety, or semi-transparent uncrystal-lised gypsum, the transparent and crystallised varieties being generally too soft.
3. *Calc-spar*, a cleavable variety.
4. *Fluor spar*, in which the cleavage is distinct.
5. *Apatite*, the as aragus-stone, or phosphate of lime.

  6. *Adularia felspar*, any cleavable variety.
  7. *Rock-crystal*, a transparent variety.
  8. *Prismatic topaz*, any simple variety.
  9. *Corundum* from India, which affords smooth cleavage surfaces.
 10. The *Diamond*.

Two other degrees are obtained by interposing foliated mica between 2 and 3, and scapolite, a crystalline variety, between 5 and 6. The former is numbered 2·5, the latter, 5·5.

To ascertain the hardness of a mineral, first try which of the members of the scale is scratched by it, and in order to save the specimens, begin with the highest numbers, and proceed downwards, until reaching one which is scratched. Then take a fine hard file, and draw along its surface, with the least possible force, the specimen to be examined, and also that mineral in the scale whose hardness is immediately above the one which has been scratched. From the resistance they offer to the file, from the noise occasioned by their passing along it, and from the quantity of powder left on its surface, their relative hardness is deduced. When, after repeated trials, we are satisfied to which member of the scale of hardness the mineral is most nearly allied, we say its hardness (suppose it to be felspar) is equal to 6, and write after it H. = 6·0. If the mineral do not exactly correspond with any degree of the scale, out is found to be between two of them, it is marked by the lower with a decimal figure added. Thus, if more than 6 but less than 7, it is expressed H. = 6·5. In these experiments we must be careful to employ specimens which nearly agree in form and size, and also as much as possible in the shape of their angles.

Where the scale of hardness is wanting, or for a first rough determination, the following experiments may serve:—

Every mineral that is scratched by the finger-nail has H. = 2·5 or less.
Minerals that scratch copper have H. = 3 or more.
Polished white iron has H. = 4·5.
Window-glass has H. = 5 to 5·5.
Steel point or file has H. = 6 to 7.
Hence every mineral that will cut or scratch with a good penknife has H. less than 6.
Flint has H. = 7, and only about a dozen minerals, including the precious stones or gems, are harder.

Closely allied to hardness is the TENACITY of minerals, of which the following varieties have been distinguished: —A mineral is said to be *brittle* when, as in quartz, on attempting to cut it with a knife, it emits a grating noise, and the particles fly away in the form of dust. It is *sectile* or *mild* when, as in galena and some varieties of mica, on cutting, the particles lose their cohnection in a considerable degree; but this takes place without noise, and they do not fly off, but remain on the knife. And a mineral is said to be *soft* or *ductile* when, like native gold or lead, it can be cut into slices with a knife, extended under the hammer, and drawn into wire. From tenacity it is usual to distinguish *frangibility*, or the resistance which minerals oppose when we attempt to break them into pieces or fragments. This property must not be confounded with hardness. Quartz is hard, and hornblende comparatively soft; yet the latter is more difficultly frangible than the former. *Flexibility*, again, expresses the property possessed by some minerals of bending without breaking. They are *elastic*, like mica, if, when bent, they spring back again into their former direction; or merely flexible, when they can be bent in different directions without breaking, but remain in their new position, as gypsum, talc, asbestus, and all malleable minerals.

Specific Gravity.

The density or the relative weight of a mineral, compared with an equal volume of pure distilled water, is named its specific gravity. This is a most important character for distinguishing minerals, as it varies considerably in different species, and can be readily ascertained with much accuracy, and, in many cases, without at all injuring the specimen. The whole process consists in weighing the body, first in air, and then immersed in water, the difference in the weight being that of an equal bulk of the latter fluid. Hence assuming, as is commonly done, the specific gravity of pure distilled water to be equal to 1 or unity, the specific gravity (G) of the other body is equal to its weight in air (w), divided by the loss or difference (d) of

weight in water (or $G = \frac{w}{d}$). A simple and portable instrument for finding the specific gravity is the areometer of Nicholson, Fig. 94. A delicate hydrostatic balance gives the gravity with most accuracy;
but a good common balance is often sufficient. The mineral may be suspended from one arm or scale by a fine silk thread or hair, and its weight ascertained, first in the air, and then in water.

There are some precautions necessary to insure accuracy. Thus, a pure specimen must be selected which is not intermixed with other substances, and when weighed in air it should be quite dry. It must also be free from cavities, and care must be taken that when weighed in water no globules of air adhere to its surface, which render it lighter. If the body imbibes moisture, it

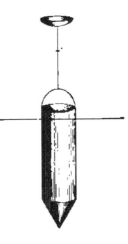

Fig. 94. Areometer.

should be allowed to remain till fully saturated before determining its weight when immersed, and it is sometimes even necessary to boil the specimen in order to expel the air from its pores. Small crystals or fragments, whose freedom from mixture can be seen, are best adapted for the purpose. The specimen experimented on should not be too heavy; thirty grains being enough where the gravity is low, and even less where it is high. It is also of importance to repeat the trial, if possible with different specimens, which will show whether any cause of error exists, and to take the mean of the whole. A correction should be made for the variation of the temperature of the water from 60° Fahr., which is that usually chosen as the standard in mineralogical works. Where the difference, however, does not exceed ten or fifteen degrees this correction may be neglected, as it only affects the third or second decimal figure of the result.

Optical Properties of Minerals.

There are few more interesting departments of science than the relations of mineral bodies to light, and the modifications which it undergoes either, 1st, when passing through them, or 2d, when reflected from their surface. In this place, however, we only notice these phenomena so far as they point out distinctions in the internal constitution of minerals, or furnish characters for distinguishing one species from another.

Minerals, and even different specimens of the same species, vary much in pellucidity, or in the quantity of light which can pass through them. Some transmit so much light, that small objects can be clearly seen, or letters read when placed behind them, and are named *transparent.* They are *semitransparent* when the object is only seen dimly, as through a cloud; and *translucent* when the light that passes through is so obscured that the objects can be no longer discerned. Some minerals are only thus *translucent on the* thinnest *edges,* others transmit no light, and are named *opaque.* These degrees pass gradually into each other, and cannot be separated by any precise line; and this is also the case in nature, where some minerals pass through the whole scale, as quartz, from the fine transparent rock-crystal to opaque dark-black varieties. Such minerals may be described generally as *pellucid.* This change often arises from some mixture in their composition, especially of metallic substances. Perfect opacity is chiefly found in the metals or their compounds with sulphur, though even these seem to transmit light when reduced to laminæ of sufficient thinness.

Double Refraction.—When a ray of light passes obliquely from one medium into another of different density, it is bent or refracted from its former course. The line which it then follows forms an angle with the perpendicular, which in each body bears a certain proportion to that at which the ray fell upon it, or, as definitely stated, the sine of the angle of refraction has a fixed ratio to the sine of the angle of incidence, this ratio being named the index of réfraction. Simple refraction occurs in all transparent bodies, whether crystalline, amorphous, or fluid; but some crystals produce a still more remarkable result. The ray of light which entered them as one is divided into two rays, each following a different angle, or is doubly refracted. In minerals of the tesseral system this property does not exist, but it has been observed in all minerals belonging to the other systems, though in some only after they have been cut in a particular manner, or have been otherwise properly prepared. It is most distinctly seen in crystals of calc-spar, especially in the beautiful transparent variety from Iceland, in which it was first observed and described by Erasmus Bartholin in a work published at Copenhagen in 1669.

The subjoined figure will illustrate this singular property. It represents a rhomb of Iceland spar, on the surface of which a ray of light *Rr* falls. As seen in the figure, this ray divides into two, one of which *roo'* follows the ordinary law of refraction, or the sines of the angles of incidence and refraction maintain a constant ratio. This is named the ordinary ray O.

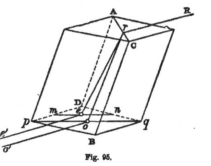

Fig. 95.

The other, *ree'*, named the extraordinary ray E, does not obey the usual law of the sines, and has no general index of refraction. In the plane perpendicular to the axis of the crystal, it is most widely separated from the ordinary ray, but in others oblique to it approaches nearer to O, and in one at right angles to the first coincides, or then shows no double refraction. This plane, or rather direction, in which there is no double refraction, is named the optical axis of the crystal, or the axis of double refraction. Now, in certain minerals it is found that there is only one plane with this property, whereas in others there are two such planes, and they have in consequence been divided into monoaxial and binaxial. To the former (monoaxial) belong all crystals of the tetragonal and hexagonal systems ; to the latter (binaxial) all those of the three other systems. In the former the optic axis coincides with, or is parallel to, the crystallographic chief axis. In some crystals the index of refraction for the extraordinary ray E is greater than for the ordinary ray O ; and in others it is smaller. When greater, they are said to have positive (or attractive), when less, negative (or repulsive) double refraction. Quartz is an example of the former, the index of refraction, according to Malus, being for $O = 1\cdot5484$, for $E = 1\cdot5582$; and calc-spar of the latter, the index of O being $= 1\cdot6543$, of $E = 1\cdot4833$. The index of E is in both cases taken at its maximum.

It should be observed that the optic axes are not single lines, but directions parallel to a line, or innumerable parallel lines, passing through every atom of the crystal. It is also important to remark that this property divides crystals into three precise groups—the tesseral, with single refraction ; the tetragonal and hexagonal, with double refraction and monoaxial ; those of the three other systems also, double, but binaxial. It is therefore of use to determine the system to which a mineral belongs, but is not of great value as a character for distinguishing species.

Polarisation of Light.—Intimately connected with this property is that of the polarisation of light, which being more easily and precisely observable than double refraction, is in many cases of higher value as a mineralogical character. By this term is meant a peculiar modification which a ray of light undergoes, in consequence of which its capability of being transmitted or reflected towards particular sides is either wholly or partially destroyed. Thus, if from a transparent prism of tourmaline two thin plates are cut parallel to its axis, they will transmit light, as well as the prism itself, when they are placed above each other with the chief axis of both in the same direction. But when the one slip of tourmaline is turned at right angles to the

other, either no light at all or very little is transmitted, and
the plates consequently appear black. Hence, in passing
through the first slip the rays of light have acquired a
peculiar property, which renders them incapable of being
transmitted through the second, except in a parallel position, and they are then said to be polarised. The same
property is acquired by a ray of light when reflected, at an
angle of $35\frac{1}{2}°$ (or angle of incidence $54\frac{1}{2}°$), from a plate of
glass, one side of which is blackened, or from some other
non-metallic body. When such a ray falls on a second
similar mirror at an equal angle, but so that the plane of
reflection in the second is at right angles to that in the
first, it is no longer reflected, but wholly absorbed. When,
on the other hand, the planes of reflection are parallel, the
ray is wholly and at any intermediate angle partially
reflected. A ray of light polarised by reflection is also
incapable of transmission through a tourmaline slip in one
position, which, however, is at right angles to that in which
a ray polarised by passing through another slip is not
transmitted.

In order to observe the polarisation of light, either two
tourmaline plates, properly prepared, or this simple instru-

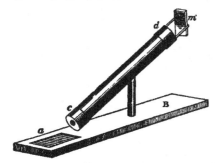

Fig. 96. Polarising instrument.

ment will be found useful (Fig. 96). At one end of a horizontal board B a black mirror a is fixed. In the middle is
a pillar to which a tube cd is fastened, with its axis directed

to the mirror at an angle of $35\frac{1}{2}°$. On the lower end is a cover c, with a small hole in the centre, and at the upper end another cover with a small black mirror m attached to it by two arms, as in the figure, and also at an angle of $35\frac{1}{2}°$. With this instrument the mirror m can be so placed in relation to a that the planes of reflection shall have any desirable inclination to exhibit the simple polarisation of light.

This instrument furnishes a simple test whether minerals that cleave readily into thin lamellæ are optically monoaxial or binaxial. Place the two mirrors with their polarisation-planes at right angles, and fix a plate of the mineral with a little wax over the hole c, and then observe what takes place in the second mirror during the time that the cover c is turned round. If the mineral belongs to the binaxial system, the light from the first mirror a, in passing through it, is doubly refracted and has its polarisation changed, and consequently can be again reflected from the second mirror m, and in each revolution of c will show four maxima and four minima of intensity. If, on the contrary, the mineral

is monoaxial, the ray will pass through the lamina unaltered, and will not be entirely reflected from the second mirror in any position of c.

Another beautiful phenomenon of polarised light, in like manner connected with the crystalline structure of minerals, is the coloured rings which la-

Fig. 97.

minæ of the doubly refract-ing species, when of a proper thickness, exhibit in certain positions. These rings are easily seen in the above apparatus, by interposing a thin plate of gypsum or mica between the two mirrors. When the interposed plate belongs to a monoaxial mineral, there is seen in the second mirror a system (Fig. 97) of circular concentric coloured rings intersected by a black cross. If the mineral is binaxial, one or two systems of elliptical coloured rings appear, each intersected by a black stripe (Fig. 98). In certain

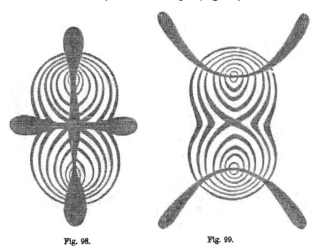

Fig. 98.   Fig. 99.

cases this stripe is curved, or the two systems of rings unite in a lemniscoidal form (Fig. 99). When the planes of polarisation are parallel, the black cross and stripe appear white (Fig. 100), showing that in this direction the crystals act like singly-refracting minerals. Quartz, again, in close relation to its system of crystallisation, exhibits a circular polarisation of splendid prismatic colours, which on turning the plate change in each point in the order of the spectrum, from red to yellow, green, and blue. In order to pro-

Fig. 100.

duce these changes, however, in some specimens the plate must be turned to the right, in others to the left, showing a difference in the crystalline structure.

Pleochroism.—Closely connected with double refraction

F

is that property of transparent minerals named pleochroism (many-coloured), in consequence of which they exhibit distinct colours when viewed by transmitted light in different directions. Crystals of the tesseral system do not show this property; whilst in those of the other systems it appears in more or less perfection; and in the tetragonal and hexagonal minerals as dichroism (two colours), in the rhombic and clinic systems as trichroism (three colours). In most cases these changes of colour are not very decided, and appear rather as different tints or shades than as distinct colours. The most remarkable of dichromatic minerals are the magnesian mica from Vesuvius, the tourmaline and ripidolite; of trichromatic, the iolite, the andalusite from Brazil, the diaspore from Schemnitz, and the axinite.

Some crystalline minerals exhibit a very lively play or change of colours from reflected light in certain directions. It is well seen in many various hues on the cleavage-planes of labradorite, and seems produced by a multitude of very thin quadrangular pores, interposed in the mineral like minute parallel laminæ. On the cleavage-planes of the hypersthene it appears copper-red, and is occasioned by numerous small brown or black laminæ of some foreign substance interposed in a parallel position between the planes of the hypersthene. The chatoyant, or changing colours of the sun-stone, arise from scales of hæmatite similarly interposed. The play of colour in the noble opal seems to be produced very nearly in the same manner with that in the labradorite. A similar opalescence is seen in certain minerals when cut in particular forms. In the sapphire, cut hemispherically over the chief axis, it appears like a star with six rays; in certain varieties of chrysoberl and adularia it has a bluish tint; and is also very remarkable in the cat's-eye variety of quartz. Iridescence often arises from very fine fissures, producing semicircular arches of prismatic tints, which, like the colours of thin plates in general, are referred to the interference of light.

Lustre and Colour.

Though these properties admit of no precise or mathematical determination, they are of considerable value in mineralogy. One highly important distinction founded on them is that of minerals of metallic and non-metallic aspect or character. This distinction can hardly be described in words, and the student will best learn to distinguish metallic colours and lustre from non-metallic, by observing them in nature. Transparency and opacity nearly coincide with this division, the metallic minerals being almost constantly opaque; the non-metallic more or less transparent. Minerals which are perfectly opaque, and show metallic colour and lustre, are named metallic; those with only two of these three properties, semi-metallic or metalloid; and those with the opposite properties, non-metallic.

Lustre has reference to either the intensity or the quality of the reflected light, considered as distinct from colour. Several degrees in intensity have been named. (1.) *Splendent*, when a mineral reflects light so perfectly as to be visible at a great distance, and lively, well-defined images are formed in its faces, as galena, rock-crystal, or calcspar. (2.) *Shining*, when the reflected light is weak, and only forms indistinct and cloudy images, as heavy-spar. (3.) *Glistening*, when the reflected light is so feeble as not to be observable at a greater distance than arm's length, and no longer forms an image. (4.) *Glimmering*, when the mineral held near the eye in full clear daylight presents only a number of small shining points, as red hæmatite and granular limestone. When, as in· chalk, the lustre is so feeble as to be indiscernible, it is said to be *dull*.

In regard to the kind or quality of the lustre, the following varieties are distinguished :—(1.) The *metallic*, seen in much perfection in native metals and their compounds with sulphur, and imperfectly in glance coal. (2.) *Adamantine*, found in beautiful perfection in the diamond, and in some varieties of blende and cerussite. (3.) *Vitreous* or glassy, seen in rock-crystal or common glass, or inclining to adamantine in flint-glass. (4.) *Resinous*, when the body appears as if smeared with oil, as in pitch-stone and garnet. (5.) *Pearly*, like mother-of-pearl, seen in stilbite, gypsum, mica. (6.) *Silky*, the glimmering lustre seen on fine fibrous aggregates like amianthus.

Colour.—This property is not in all cases of equal value as a character. Thus some minerals are naturally coloured, showing in all modes of their occurrence one determinate colour, which is therefore essential, and forms a characteristic of the species. This class includes the metals, pyrites, blendes, with many metallic oxides and salts. A second class of minerals are colourless, their purest forms being white, or clear like water, as ice, calc-spar, quartz, felspar, and many silicates. But these minerals are occasionally coloured,—that is, accidentally tinged, in some from the chemical or mechanical admixture of some colouring substance, as a metallic oxide, carbon, or particles of coloured minerals ; in others, from the substitution of a coloured for an uncoloured element. The colours of these minerals, therefore, vary indefinitely, and never characterise the species, but only its varieties. Thus, quartz, calc-spar, fluor spar, gypsum, and felspar, are often coloured accidentally by pigments mechanically mixed ; and hornblende, augite, garnet, and other colourless silicates, acquire green, brown, red, or black tints from the introduction of metallic elements.

Werner, who bestowed much attention on this portion of mineralogy, distinguished eight principal colours,—white, grey, black, blue, green, yellow, red, and brown,—each with several varieties or shades arising from intermixture with the other colours. He also divided them into metallic and non-metallic as follows :—

METALLIC COLOURS.

1. *White.*—(1.) Silver-white, as in leucopyrite and native silver. (2.) Tin-white ; native antimony.

2. *Grey.*—(1.) Lead-grey ; galena or lead glance. (2.) Steel-grey ; native platina.

3. *Black.*—(1.) Iron-black ; magnetite.

4. *Yellow.*—(1.) Brass-yellow ; chalcopyrite. (2.) Bronze-yellow ; iron pyrites. (3.) Gold yellow ; native gold.

5. *Red.*—(1.) Copper-red ; native copper and nickeline.

NON-METALLIC COLOURS.

1. *White.*—(1.) Snow-white ; new fallen snow, Carrara marble, and

common quartz. (2.) Reddish-white; heavy spar. (3.) Yellowish-white; chalk. (4.) Greyish-white; quartz. (5.) Greenish-white; amianthus. (6.) Milk-white; skimmed milk, chalcedony.

2. *Grey.*—(1.) Bluish-grey; limestone. (2.) Pearl-grey; porcelain jasper. (3.) Smoke-grey or brownish-grey; dense smoke, dark varieties of flint. (4.) Greenish-grey; clay slate. (5.) Yellowish-grey; chalcedony. (6.) Ash-grey; wood-ashes, zoisite, zircon, and slate-clay.

3. *Black.*—(1.) Greyish-black; basalt. (2.) Velvet-black; obsidian and schorl. (3.) Pitch-black or brownish-black; cobalt ochre, bituminous coal. (4.) Greenish-black or raven-black; hornblende. (5.) Bluish-black; fluor spar.

4. *Blue.*—(1.) Blackish-blue; dark varieties of azurite. (2.) Azure-blue; bright varieties of azurite and Lapis lazuli. (3.) Violet-blue; amethyst and fluor spar. (4.) Lavender-blue; lithomarge and porcelain jasper. (5.) Plum-blue; spinel and fluor spar. (6.) Berlin-blue; sapphire, cyanite. (7.) Smalt-blue; pale-coloured smalt, gypsum. (8.) Duck-blue; talc and corundum. (9.) Indigo-blue; vivianite. (10.) Sky-blue; liroconite.

5. *Green.*—(1.) Verdigris-green; amazon stone. (2.) Celandine-green; green earth, beryl. (3.) Mountain-green; beryl, aqua-marine, topaz. (4.) Leek-green; common actynolite and prase. (5.) Emerald-green; emerald. (6.) Apple-green; chrysoprase. (7.) Grass-green; uranite, smaragdite. (8.) Blackish-green; augite and precious serpentine. (9.) Pistachio-green; chrysolite and epidote. (10.) Asparagus-green; the apatite or asparagus-stone. (11.) Olive-green; garnet and olivine. (12.) Oil-green; olive-oil, blende, beryl. (13.) Siskin green; uranite and pyromorphite.

6. *Yellow.*—(1.) Sulphur-yellow; native sulphur. (2.) Straw-yellow; pycnite. (3.) Wax-yellow; opal and wulfenite. (4.) Honey-yellow; dark honey, fluor spar, and beryl. (5.) Lemon-yellow; rind of ripe lemons, orpiment. (6.) Ochre-yellow; yellow-earth and jasper. (7.) Wine-yellow; topaz and fluor spar. (8.) Cream-yellow or Isabella-yellow; bole and compact limestone. (9.) Orange-yellow, rind of the ripe orange, uran-ochre, and some varieties of wulfenite.

7. *Red.*—(1.) Aurora, or morning-red; zealgar. (2.) Hyacinth-red; hyacinth or zircon, and garnet. (3.) Tile-red; fresh-burned bricks and heulandite. (4.) Scarlet-red; light red cinnabar. (5.) Blood-red; blood, pyrope. (6.) Flesh-red; felspar and barytes. (7.) Carmine-red; carmine, spinel, particularly in thin splinters. (8.) Cochineal-red; cinnabar. (9.) Crimson-red; oriental ruby and erythrine. (10.) Columbine-red; precious garnet. (11.) Rose-red; diallogite and rose-quartz. (12.) Peach-blossom red; blossoms of the peach, red cobalt ochre. (13.) Cherry-red; spinel and precious garnet. (14.) Brownish-red; reddle and columnar-clay ironstone.

8. *Brown.*—(1.) Reddish-brown; brown blende and zircon. (2.) Clove-brown; the clove, rock-crystal, and axinite. (3.) Hair-brown; wood-opal and limonite. (4.) Broccoli-brown; zircon. (5.) Chestnut-brown; Egyptian jasper. (6.) Yellowish-brown; iron-flint and jasper. (7.) Pinchbeck-brown; tarnished pinchbeck, mica. (8.) Wood-brown; mountain wood and old rotten wood. (9.) Liver-brown; boiled liver, common jasper. (10.) Blackish-brown; mineral pitch and brown coal.

The accidentally coloured minerals sometimes present

two or more colours or tints, even on a single crystal ; very remarkable examples occurring in fluor spar, apatite, sapphire, amethyst, tourmaline, and cyanite. This is still more common in compound minerals, on which the colours are variously arranged in points, streaks, clouds, veins, stripes, bands, or in brecciated and ruin-like forms. Some minerals again change their colour from exposure to the light, the air, or damp. Then either the surface alone is affected or *tarnished*, and appears covered as with a thin film, producing in some minerals, as silver, arsenic, bismuth, only one colour ; in others, as chalopyrite, hæmatite, stibine, and common coal, various or iridescent hues. Or occasionally the change pervades the whole mineral, the colour either becoming paler, or disappearing as in chrysoprase and rose-quartz ; or darker, as in brown spar, siderite, and rhodo-nite. In a few minerals a complete change of colour takes place, as in the chlorophæite of the Western Isles, which, on exposure for a few hours, passes from a transparent yellow-green to black. These mutations are generally connected with some chemical change. The tarnished colours sometimes only appear on certain faces of a crystal belonging to a peculiar form. Thus a crystal of copper pyrites (like Fig. 35) has one face P' free from tarnish ; the faces b and c, close to P', dark-blue ; the remainder of c, first violet, and then, close to P, gold-yellow. *Streak* is the colour of the powder formed when a mineral is scratched by a hard body. This is often different from that of the solid mass, and is very characteristic of many minerals. It also often shows a peculiar lustre where the mineral is soft, as in talc and steatite.

Phosphorescence, Electricity, Magnetism.

Phosphorescence is the property possessed by particular minerals of producing light in certain circumstances without combustion or ignition. Thus some minerals appear luminous when taken into the dark after being for a time exposed to the sun's rays, or even to the ordinary daylight. Many diamonds and calcined barytes exhibit this property in a remarkable degree ; less so, arragonite, calc-spar, and chalk. Many minerals, including the greater part of those thus rendered phosphorescent by the influence of the sun, also become so through heat. Thus some topazes, diamonds, and varieties of fluor spar become luminous by the heat of the hand; other varieties of fluor spar and the phosphorite require a temperature near that of boiling water; whilst calc-spar and many silicates are only phosphorescent at from 400° to 700° Fahr. Electricity produces it in some minerals, as in green fluor spar and calcined barytes. In others it is excited when they are struck, rubbed, split, or broken; as many varieties of zinc-blende and dolomite when scratched with a quill, pieces of quartz when rubbed on each other, and plates of mica when suddenly separated.

Friction, pressure, and heat also excite *electricity* in minerals. To observe this property delicate electroscopes are required, formed of a light needle, terminating at both ends in small balls, and suspended horizontally on a steel pivot by an agate cup. Such an instrument can be electrified negatively by touching it with a stick of sealing-wax, excited by rubbing, or positively, by only bringing the wax so near as to attract the needle. When the instrument is in this state, the mineral, if also rendered electric by heat or friction, will attract or repel the needle according as it has acquired electricity of an opposite or similar kind; but if the mineral is not electric, it will attract the needle in both conditions alike. Most precious stones become electric from friction, and are either positive or negative according as their surface is smooth or rough. Pressure even between the fingers will excite distinct positive electricity in pieces of transparent double-refracting calc-spar. Topaz, arragonite, fluor spar, carbonate of lead, quartz, and other minerals, show this property, but in a much smaller degree.

Heat or change of temperature excites electricity in many crystals, as in tourmaline, calamine, topaz, calc-spar, beryl, barytes, fluor spar, diamond, garnet, and others, which are hence said to be thermo- or pyro-electric. Some acquire polar pyro-electricity, or the two electricities appear in opposite parts of the crystal, which are named its electric poles. Each pole is alternately positive and negative— the one when the mineral is heating, the other when it is cooling. As already noticed, many polar electric minerals are also remarkable for their hemimorphic crystal forms.

Magnetism, or the power to act on the magnetic needle, is very characteristic of the few minerals in which it occurs, chiefly ores of iron or nickel. It is either simple, attracting both poles of the needle; or polar, when one part attracts, and another repels the same pole. Some magnetic iron ores possess polar magnetism, or are natural magnets; whilst the common varieties, meteoric iron, magnetic pyrites, precious garnet, and other minerals, are simply magnetic. Most minerals are only attracted by the magnet, but do not themselves attract iron.

Smell, taste, and *touch* furnish a few characters of minerals. Most have no smell, but some give out a peculiar odour when rubbed: as quartz an empyreumatic odour, or smell of burning; fluor spar of chlorine; clay of clay; some lime-stones and marls of bitumen, or a fœtid odour. Aluminous minerals acquire a smell when breathed on. Other odours caused by heat, and often highly characteristic, are noticed under tests by the blow-pipe.

Taste is produced by all the salts soluble in water. Some are saline like common salt; sweetish astringent, like alum; astringent, like blue vitriol; bitter, like epsom salt; cooling, like saltpetre; pungent, like sal-ammoniac; alkaline, like soda; acid or sour, like sassoline, etc.

Touch.—Some minerals are distinguished by a greasy feeling like talc; others feel meagre, like clay; others cold. The last character readily distinguishes true gems from their imitations in glass.

CHAPTER III.

CHEMICAL PROPERTIES OF MINERALS.

THE consideration of the chemical nature of minerals—that is, of the elements that enter into their composition—of the manner in which these elements are combined, and the variations in proportion which they may undergo without destroying the identity of the species—forms an important branch of mineralogical science. The methods of detecting the different elements, and particularly the characters thus obtained for the discrimination of minerals, are also of much value. This is especially true of the metallic ores and other substances sought for their economic qualities.

N.B.—It is well known that views and theories regarding the chemical constitution of mineral bodies different from those of Berzelius, have recently been adopted by many distinguished mineral chemists. These views, however, affect only the theoretical constitution of minerals as expressed in formula, leaving the actual composition of the body, as stated in analyses by percentages, unchanged. It has therefore seemed to me better, in what must be regarded as a transition state of the science, to retain the old language and formula as probably most acceptable to the greater number of those using this work. No new rational formulæ, also, have as yet definitely taken the place of the old Berzelian formulæ, which, from their short condensed form, are more readily caught by the eye, and more easily remembered, than any that have been substituted for them. In the following Tables, however, both the old and new atomic weights are given; and in the more important species, the new formulæ are added, distinguished by being put in [ ]; thus $\dot{H} = [H^2O]$.*

Composition of Minerals.

At present above sixty elements, or substances which have not been decomposed, are known. These are divided into *metallic* and *non-metallic*, a distinction of importance in mineralogy, though not always to be carried out with precision. The *non-metallic* elements are rarely of semimetallic aspect, and are bad conductors of heat and electricity. Some of them are commonly gaseous—oxygen, hydrogen, nitrogen, chlorine, and fluorine ; one fluid—bromine ; the others solid—carbon, phosphorus, sulphur, boron, selenium, silicium or silicon, and iodine. The *metallic* elements are, except mercury, solid at usual temperatures, have generally a metallic aspect, and are good conductors of heat and electricity. They are divided into light and heavy metals, the former with a specific gravity under 5, and a great affinity for oxygen, and again distinguished as either alkali-metals, potassium (or kalium), sodium (or natrium), lithium, barium, strontium, and calcium ; — or earth metals, magnesium, lanthanium, yttrium, glucinum, aluminium, zirconium. The heavy metals, with a specific gravity above 5, are divided into noble, which can be reduced, or separated from oxygen, by heat alone ; and ignoble, whose affinity for oxygen renders them irreducible without other agents. Some of the latter are brittle and difficultly fusible— thorium, titanium, tantalium, tungsten (wolframium), molyb-

---

* Naummann, in the last edition of his valuable Manual, follows the same course, for reasons more fully stated.—See *Elemente der Mineralogie*, 8te Auf. 1871, pp. 150-153. We quote one sentence only :—

" Es bedarf wohl dieses Verfahren um so weniger einer Entschuldigung, als doch noch manche recht bedeutende Chemiker sich der älteren, nach Berzelius' Methode geschriebenen Formeln bedienen, und als gar nicht geläugnet werden kann, dass diese Formeln eine sehr klare und compendiöse Uebersicht der qualitativen und quantitativen Zusammensetzung der Mineralien gewähren, dem practischen Bedürfnisse des Hüttenmannes und Technikers vollkommen Genüge leisten, und sich sehr leicht in die modernen empirischen Formeln übersetzen lassen."

denum, vanadium, chromium, uranium, manganese, and cerium; others are brittle and easily fusible or volatile—arsenic, antimony, tellurium, and bismuth; and others malleable—zinc, cadmium, tin, lead, iron, cobalt, nickel, and copper. The noble metals are—quicksilver, silver, gold, platinum, palladium, rhodium, iridium, and osmium.

All the chemical combinations observed in the mineral kingdom follow the law of definite proportions; that is, two elements always combine either in a fixed proportion, or so that the quantity of the one is multiplied by two, three, four, or some other definite number seldom very large. As this law prevails throughout the whole range of elements, by assuming any one, usually hydrogen, as unity or 1, and determining from experiment the simple proportion in which the others combine with it, a series of numbers is obtained which also expresses the proportions in which all these elements combine with each other. These numbers, therefore, mark the combining proportions or equivalents, as they are named, of the elements. They are also named atomic weights, on the supposition that matter consists of definite atoms, and that its combinations consist of one atom (or sometimes two atoms) of one substance, with one, two, three, or more atoms of another. This theory is not free from difficulties, but the language is convenient. To designate the elements, chemists generally employ the first letter or letters of their Latin names. These signs also indicate one atom or equivalent of the element. Thus, O means oxygen in the proportion of one atom; H, hydrogen in the same proportion; N, an atom of nitrogen; Na, an equivalent proportion of natrium or sodium. These signs and the equivalent weights are given in the following Table, in which hydrogen is taken as unity :—

TABLE I.—Elements, etc.

Name.	Sign.	Atomic Weight. Old.	Atomic Weight. New.
Aluminium - - -	Al	13·7	27·5
†Antimony - - -	Sb	122	122
†Arsenic - - -	As	75	75
Barium - - -	Ba	68·5	137
† Bismuth - - -	Bi	208	208
† Boron - - -	B	11	11
† Bromine - - -	Br	80	80
Cadmium - - -	Cd	56	112
Cæsium - - -	Cs		133
Calcium - - -	Ca	20	40
Carbon - - -	C	6	12
Cerium - - -	Ce	46	92
†Chlorine - - -	Cl	35·5	35·5
Chromium - - -	Cr	26·1	52·2
Cobalt - - -	Co	30	60
Copper - - -	Cu	31·7	63·4
Didymium - - -	D		95
†Fluorine - - -	Fl	19 ·	19
Glucinum - · -	Gl	4·6	9·2
†Gold - - -	Au	197	197
†Hydrogen - - -	H	1	1
Indium - - -	In		72
†Iodine - - -	I	127	127
Iridium ＼ - -	Ir	99	198
Iron - - -	Fe	28	56
Lanthanium - - -	La	46	92
Lead - - -	Pb	103·5	207
†Lithium - - -	Li	7	7
Magnesium - - -	Mg	12	24
Manganese - - -	Mn	27·5	55
Mercury - - -	Hg	100	200
Molybdenum - - -	Mo	48	96
Nickel - - -	Ni	29	58

TABLE I.—ELEMENTS, ETC.—*continued.*

NAME				Sign.	Atomic Weight.	
					Old.	New.
Niobium	-	-	-	Nb	47	94
† Nitrogen	-	-	-	N	14	14
Osmium	-	-	-	Os	100	200
Oxygen	-	-	-	O	8	16
Palladium	-	-	-	Pd	53	106
† Phosphorus	-	-	-	P	31	31
Platinum	-	-	-	Pt	99	198
†Potassium	-	-	-	K	39	39
Rhodium	-	.	.	Rh	52	104
Rubidium	.		-	Rb		85·5
Ruthenium	-	-		Ru	52	104
Selenium	-	-	-	Se	39·5	79
Silicium	-	-	-	Si	14	28
†Silver	-	-	-	Ag	108	108
†Sodium	-	-	-	Na	23	23
Strontium	-	.	-	Sr	44	88
Sulphur	-	-	-	S	16	32
Tantalium	-	-	-	Ta	91	182
Tellurium	-	-	-	Te	64	128
Thallium	-	-	-	Tl		204
Thorium	-	-	-	Th	115·7	231·4
Tin	-	-	-	Sn	59	118
Titanium	-	-	-	Ti	25	50
Tungsten	-	-	-	W	92	184
Uranium	-	-	-	U	60	120
Vanadium	-	-	-	V	68·6	137·2
Yttrium	-	-	-	Y	30·8	61·6
Zinc	-	-	-	Zn	32·8	65·6
Zirconium	-	-	-	Zr	44·8	89·6

It will be seen that the elements marked † have the same atomic weights on both theories, whilst the others are doubled on the new theory.

All these elements occur in minerals, but not more than twenty are common, and only about twelve abundant. They are also very rare in their simple or uncombined state ; carbon (in the diamond and graphite), sulphur, and about a dozen of the native metals only, being thus known. More frequently minerals consist of two or more elements combined in accordance with those laws which prevail in inorganic compounds. The most important of these laws is that the combinations are binary ; that is, that the elements unite in pairs, which may again unite either with another compound of two, or with a single element. Inorganic compounds, also, are generally distinguished from organic by their greater simplicity.

The following principles are observed in designating the combinations of these elementary substances :—For those of the first order the signs of the two components are conjoined, and the number of atoms or equivalents of each expressed by a number following the sign, like an algebraic exponent. Thus, SO, SO^2, SO^3, are the combinations of one atom of sulphur with one, two, or three atoms of oxygen ; FeS, FeS^2, of one atom of iron with one or two of sulphur. But as combinations with oxygen and sulphur are very numerous in the mineral kingdom, Berzelius marks the atoms of oxygen by dots over the sign of the other element, and those of sulphur by an accent ; the above compounds being then designated thus—$\dot{S}$, $\ddot{S}$, $\dddot{S}$, and Fe', Fe''. In some cases two atoms of a base combine with three or five of oxygen or sulphur, as Al^2O^3, Fe^2S^3. In such cases Berzelius marks the double atom by a line drawn through the sign of the single atom ; thus $\bar{Al}$ is two atoms aluminium with three of oxygen or alumina ; $\bar{Cu}$, two of copper with one of oxygen or oxide of copper. Where a number is prefixed to the sign, like a coefficient in algebra, it includes both elements of the combination ; thus $\dot{H}$ is one atom water, $2\dot{H}$ two atoms ; $Ca\ddot{C}$ is one atom carbonate of lime, $2Ca\ddot{C}$ two atoms, including, of course, two of calcium, two of carbon, and six of oxygen.

The most common and important binary compounds

are those with oxygen, contained in the following Table, with their signs, atomic numbers, and amount of oxygen in 100 parts. The more electro-negative are named acids, which are often soluble in water, and then render blue vegetable colours red. The more electro-positive are named oxides or bases, and show great affinity or attractive power for the former. The most powerful are the alkaline bases, which are colourless and soluble in water; less powerful are the earths, also colourless, but insoluble in water :—

TABLE II.—BINARY COMPOUNDS WITH OXYGEN.

Name.	Old Atoms.		New Atoms.	
Alumina - - -	$\ddot{A}l$	51·4	Al^2O^3	102·8
Antimony oxide -	$\dot{S}b$	146	Sb^2O^3	292
Antimonic acid -	$\ddot{S}b$	162	Sb^2O^5	324
Arsenious acid -	$\dot{A}s$	99	As^2O^3	198
Arsenic acid - -	$\ddot{A}s$	115	As^2O^5	230
Baryta - - -	$\dot{B}a$	76·5	BaO	153
Bismuth peroxide -	$\dot{B}i$	232	Bi^2O^3	464
Boracic acid - -	$\dot{B}$	35	B^2O^3	70
Carbonic acid - -	$\dot{C}$	22	CO^2	44
Cerium protoxide -	$\dot{C}e$	54	CeO	108
Chromium oxide -	$\ddot{C}r$	76·5	Cr^2O^3	153
Chromic acid - -	$\ddot{C}r$	50·25	CrO^3	100·5
Cobalt protoxide -	$\dot{C}o$	38	CoO	76
Copper suboxide -	$\dot{C}u$	71·4	Cu^2O	142·8
„ protoxide -	$\dot{C}u$	39·7	CuO	79·4
Glucina - - -	$\dot{G}l$	12·8	GlO	25·4
Iron protoxide - -	$\dot{F}e$	36	FeO	72
„ peroxide - -	$\ddot{F}e$	80	Fe^2O^3	160
Lead protoxide -	$\dot{P}b$	111·5	PbO	223
Lime or Calcia -	$\dot{C}a$	28	CaO	56

TABLE II.—BINARY COMPOUNDS WITH OXYGEN—*continued.*

Name.		Old Atoms.		New Atoms.	
Lithia - - -	L̇i	15	Li²O	30
Magnesia - -	Ṁg	20	MgO	40
Manganese protoxide	Ṁn	35·5	MnO	71
,, peroxide	M̈n	78	Mn²O³	156
Molybdic acid - -	M̈o	72	MoO³	144
Nickel protoxide -	Ṅi	37	NiO	74
Nitric acid - -	N̈	54	N²O⁵	108
Phosphoric acid -	P̈	71	P²O⁵	142
Potassa - - -	K̇	47	KO	94
Silica - - -	S̈i	30	SiO²	60
Soda - - -	Ṅa	31	NaO	62
Strontia - - -	Ṡr	52	SrO	104
Sulphuric acid -	S̈	40	SO³	80
Tantalic acid - -	T̈a	222	Ta²O⁵	444
Thorina - - -	T̈h	131·7	ThO²	263·4
Tin peroxide - -	Ṡn	74	SnO²	148
Titanic acid - -	T̈i	41	TiO²	82
Tungstic acid - -	Ẅ	116	WO³	232
Uranium protoxide -	U̇	68	UO	136
,, peroxide -	Ü	144	U²O³	288
Vanadic acid -	V̈	92·5	VO³	185
Water - - -	Ḣ	9	H²O	18
Yttria - - -	Ẏ	38·8	VO	77·7
Zinc oxide - -	Żn	40·8	ZnO	81·6
Zirconia - - -	Z̈r	60·8	ZrO²	121·6

Similar to the compounds of oxygen are those with
sulphur, usually named sulphurets, and considered analo-
gous to the oxidised bases. A few of more electro-negative

character, resembling acids, have been distinguished as sulphides.

Many of these combinations occur as independent species in the mineral kingdom, especially those with oxygen and sulphur. Thus the most abundant of all minerals, quartz, is an oxide, and corundum is of similar nature. Many oxides of the heavy metals, as of iron, tin, copper, and antimony, are very common. Compounds with sulphur also abound, and either as sulphides, like realgar, orpiment, and stibine; or as sulphurets, like galena, argentite, and pyrite. Less frequent are haloid salts, with chlorine and fluorine, as common salt and fluor spar; and still rarer those with iodine and bromine. On the other hand, metallic alloys, or combinations of two metals, are far from uncommon, especially those with arsenic, tellurium, or antimony.

Combinations of these binary compounds with each other are still more common, the greater number of minerals being composed of an acid and base. By far the greater number are oxygen-salts, distinguished by giving to the acid the termination *ate*; thus sulphate of lead, silicate of lime, and in like manner numerous carbonates, phosphates, arseniates, aluminates. The sulphur-salts (two metals combined with sulphur, and again combined with each other) are next in number, and perform a most important part in the mineral kingdom. The hydrates, or combinations of an oxide with water, are also common, and much resemble the oxygen salts, the water sometimes acting as an electro-positive, at other times as an electro-negative element. Combinations of a higher order are likewise common, especially the double salts, or the union of two salts into a new body; and even these again with water, as alum and many hydrous silicates. The chemical formulæ for these compound salts are formed by writing the signs of the simple salts with the sign of addition between them: thus dolomite is $Ca\ddot{C} + Mg\ddot{C}$, or, in the new form, $[CaO . CO^2 + MgO . CO]$—*i.e.* carbonate of lime and carbonate of magnesia; orthoclase, $\ddot{A}l \overset{...}{Si}^3 + \dot{K} \overset{...}{Si}^3 = [Al^2O^3 . 3 SiO^2 +$

G

K^{2}O . 3 SiO^2] ; and cryolite, 3 NaF + Al^{2}F^3, consisting of
three compound atoms of fluorine and sodium united to
one compound atom, consisting of three of fluorine and
two of aluminium.   Mere empiric formulæ are also used,
written thus in the above instances : — [Ca . Mg . C^2 . O^6],
[Al . K . Si^3 . O^8], and [Na^3 . Al . F^6].

Influence of the Chemical Composition on the External Characters of Minerals.

That the characters of the compound must in some way
or other depend on those of its component elements seems,
as a general proposition, to admit of no doubt.   Hence it
might be supposed possible, from a knowledge of the composition of a mineral, to draw conclusions in reference to
its form and other properties ; but practically this has not
yet been effected.   The distinction between the mineralis-
ing and mineralisable, or the forming and formed, elements,
lies at the foundation of all such inquiries.   Certain elements in a compound apparently exert more than an equal
share of influence in determining its physical properties.
Thus the more important non-metallic elements, as oxygen,
sulphur, chlorine, fluorine, are remarkable for the influence
they exert on the character of the compound.   The sulphurets, for example, have more similarity among themselves than the various compounds of one and the same
metal with the non-metallic bodies.   Still more generally
it would appear that the electro-negative element in the
compound is the most influential, or exerts the greatest
degree of active forming power.   After the non-metallic
elements the brittle, easily fusible metals rank next in
power ; then the ductile ignoble metals ; then the noble
metals ; then the brittle, difficultly fusible ; and last of all,
the metals of the earths and alkalies.

Generally each chemical substance crystallises only in
one form or series of forms.   Some substances, however,
show *dimorphism*, or crystallise in two forms, and thus may
compose two or more minerals.   Thus sulphur, which usually crystallises in the rhombic system, when melted may

form monoclinic crystals.   Carbon in one form is the diamond, in another graphite; carbonate of lime appears as
calc-spar or arragonite; the bisulphuret of iron as pyrite
and marcasite.   An example of *trimorphism* occurs in the
titanic acid, forming the three distinct species, anatase,
rutile, and brookite.   It is curious that of dimorphic minerals one form is almost always rhombic; thus—

				Rhombic form.
Cyanite, Triclinic	-	-	-	{ Sillimanite. Andalusite.
Calc-spar, Hex.	-	-	-	Arragonite.
Susannite, Hex. R.	-	-	-	Leadhillite.
Rutile } Tetr. Anatase }	-	-	-	Brookite.
Pyrolusite, Rhom.	-	-	-	Polianite.
Cuprite, Tess.	-	-	-	Chalcotrichite.
Senarmontite, Tess.	-	-	-	Valentinite.
Pyrite, Tess.	-	-	-	Marcasite.
Rammelsbergite, Tess.	-	-	-	Chloanthite.
Argentite, Tess.	-	-	-	Acanthite.
Freieslebenite, Monocl.	-	.	-	Diaphorite.
Sulphur, Monocl.	-	-	-	Sulphur.

Even the temperature at which a substance crystallises
influences its forms, and so far its composition, as seen in
arragonite, Glauber salt, natron, and borax.

Still more important is the doctrine of *isomorphism*,
designating the fact that two or more simple or compound
substances crystallise in one and the same form; or often
in forms which, though not identical, yet approximate very
closely.   This similarity of form is generally combined
with a similarity in other physical and in chemical properties.   Among minerals that crystallise in the tesseral system,
isomorphism is of course common and perfect, there being
no diversity in the dimensions of the primary form; but
for this very reason it is often of less interest.   It is of
more importance among crystals of the other systems, the
various series of which are separated from each other by
differences in the proportion of the primary form.   In

these perfect identity is seldom observed, but only very great similarity.

The more important isomorphic substances are either simple substances, as (1) fluorine and chlorine; (2) sulphur and selenium; (3) arsenic, antimony, tellurium; (4) cobalt, iron, nickel; (5) copper, silver, quicksilver, gold (?); or combinations with oxygen, as (6) lime, magnesia, potassa, soda, and the protoxides of iron, manganese, zinc, nickel, cobalt; (7) lime, baryta, strontia, lead-oxide; (8) alumina, and the peroxides of iron, manganese, chromium; (9) phosphoric acid, arsenic acid; (10) sulphuric, selenic, chromic acids; or combinations with sulphur, as (11) sulphuret of iron and of zinc; (12) sulphuret of antimony and of arsenic; (13) sulphuret of copper and of silver.

These substances are named vicarious, from the singular property that in chemical compounds they can mutually replace each other in indefinite proportions, and very often without producing any important change in the form or other physical properties. But there are numerous instances among the silicates, where the mutual replacement of the isomorphic bodies, especially when the oxides of the heavy metals come in the room of the earths and alkalies, exerts a most essential influence on the external aspect of the species, particularly in regard to colour, specific gravity, and transparency. The varieties of hornblende, augite, garnet, epidote, and many other minerals, are remarkable proofs of this influence. This intermixture of isomorphic elements confers many valuable properties on minerals, and to it this department of nature owes much of its variety and beauty. Without the occasional presence of the colouring substances, especially the oxides of iron and manganese, the non-metallic combinations would have exhibited a very monotonous aspect. It is also remarkable that in some silicates the substitution of a certain portion of the metallic oxides for the earthy bases seems to be almost a regular occurrence; whilst in others, as the felspars and zeolites, this rarely happens. This fact is also of great economic interest, as drawing attention to important elements often combined with others of less value. Thus iron oxide and chrome oxide, sulphuret of copper and sulphuret of silver, nickel and cobalt, may be looked for in connection. The general chemical formula for such compounds is formed by writing R (= radicle or basis) for the whole isomorphic elements ; and in special instances to place their signs either one below the other, connected by a bracket, or, as is more convenient, to inclose them in brackets one after the other, separated by a comma. Thus the general sign for the garnet is $\dot{R}^3\,\ddot{S}i^2 + \ddot{R}\,\ddot{S}i$, which, when fully expressed, becomes $(\dot{C}a^3, \dot{F}e^3, \dot{M}n^3)\,\ddot{S}i^2 + (\ddot{A}l, \ddot{F}e)\,\ddot{S}i$, and the mineral forms many varieties as the one or other element preponderates.

Chemical Reaction of Minerals.

The object of the chemical examination of minerals is the discovery of those elementary substances of which they consist. This examination is named *qualitative* when the nature of the elements alone, *quantitative* when also their relative amount, is sought to be determined. Mineralogists are, in general, content with such an examination as will discover the more important elements, and which can be carried on with simple apparatus, and small quantities of the substance investigated. The indications thus furnished of the true character of the mineral are, however, frequently of high importance. Two methods of testing minerals are employed, the one by heat chiefly applied through the blowpipe, the second by acids and other reagents in solution.

Use of the Blowpipe.

The blowpipe in its simplest form is merely a conical tube of brass or other metal, curved round at the smaller extremity, and terminating in a minute circular aperture not larger than a fine needle. Other forms have been proposed, one of the most useful being a cone of tin open for the application of the mouth at the smaller end, and with a brass or platina beak projecting from the side near the other or broad end. With this instrument a stream of air is conveyed from the mouth to the flame of a lamp or candle, so that this can be turned aside, concentrated, and directed upon any small object. The flame thus acted on consists of two parts—the one nearest the beak of the blowpipe forming a blue obscure cone, the other external to this being of a shining yellow or reddish-yellow colour. The blue cone consists of the inflammable gases not yet fully incandescent, and the greatest heat is just beyond its point, where this is fully effected. The blue flame still needs oxygen for its support, and consequently tends to withdraw it from any body placed within its influence, and is named the reducing flame. At the extremity of the yellow cone, on the other hand, the whole gases being consumed, and the external air having free access, bodies are combined with oxygen, and this part is named the oxidating flame. Their action being so distinct, it is of great importance to learn to distinguish accurately these two portions of the flame. . This is best done by experimenting on a piece of metallic tin, which can only be kept pure in a good reducing flame, and acquires a white crust when acted on by the oxidating flame.

The portion of the mineral to be examined should not be larger than a peppercorn, or a fine splinter a line or two long. It is supported in the flame either by a pair of fine pincers pointed with platinum, or on slips of platinum-foil, or on charcoal. Platinum is best for the siliceous minerals, whereas for metallic substances charcoal must be employed. For this purpose solid uniform pieces are chosen, and a small cavity formed in the surface, in which the mineral to be tested can be deposited.

In examining a mineral by heat, it should be first tested alone, and then with various reagents. When placed alone in a matrass or tube of glass closed at one end, and heated over a spirit lamp, water or other volatile ingredients, as mercury, arsenic, tellurium, often sulphur, may readily be detected, being deposited in the cooler part of the tube, or, like fluorine, acting on the glass. It may next be tried in an open tube of glass, through which a current of air passes, more or less strong, according to the inclination at which the tube is held, so that volatile oxides or acids may be formed; and in this way the chief combinations of sulphur, selenium, tellurium, and arsenic, are detected. On charcoal, in the reducing flame, arsenic, and in the oxidating flame, selenium or sulphur, are shown by their peculiar odour; antimony, zinc, lead, and bismuth leave a mark or coloured ring on the charcoal; and other oxides and sulphurets are reduced to the pure metal. On charcoal or in the platinum pincers the fusibility of minerals is tested, and some other phenomena should be observed—as whether they intumesce (bubble up), effervesce, give out fumes, become shining, or impart a colour to the flame. The colour is seen when the assay is heated at the point of the inner flame, and is—

Reddish-yellow, from soda and its salts;
Violet, from potash and most of its salts;
Red, from lithia, strontia, and lime;
Green, from baryta, phosphoric acid, boracic acid, molybdic acid, copper oxide, and tellurium oxide;
Blue, from chloride of copper, bromide of copper, selenium, arsenic, antimony and lead.

The fusibility, or ease with which a mineral is melted, should also be observed; and is expressed by stating whether it is easy or difficult, and takes place in large or small grains, in fine splinters, or only on sharp angles. The result or product of fusion also yields important characters, being in some cases a glass, clear, opaque, or coloured; in others an enamel, or a mere slag.

The most important reagents for testing minerals with the blowpipe are the following:—(1.) Soda (the carbonate), acting as a flux for quartz and many silicates, and especially for reducing the metallic oxides. For the latter purpose, the assay (or mineral to be tried) is reduced to powder, kneaded up with moist soda into a small ball, and placed in a cavity of the charcoal. Very often both the soda and assay sink into the charcoal, but by continuing the operation they either again appear on the surface, or, when it is completed, the charcoal containing the mass is finely pounded and washed away with water, when the reduced metal is found in the bottom of the vessel. (2.) Borax (biborate of soda) serves as a flux for many minerals, which are best fused in small splinters on platina wire. The borax when first exposed to the flame swells up or intumesces greatly, and it should therefore be first melted into a small bead, in which the assay is placed. During the process the student should observe whether the assay melts easily or difficultly, with or without effervescence, what colour it imparts to the product both when warm and when cold, and also the effect both of the oxidating and reducing flames. (3.) Microcosmic salt, or salt of phosphorus (phosphate of soda and ammonia) is specially important as a test for metallic oxides, which exhibit far more decided colours with it than with borax. It is also a useful reagent for many silicates, whose silica is separated from the base and remains undissolved in the melted salt. (4.) Solution of cobalt (nitrate of cobalt dissolved in water), or dry oxalate of cobalt, serve as tests of alumina, magnesia, and zinc oxide.

In examining minerals in the moist way, the first point to be considered is their solubility, of which three degrees may be noted : (1) minerals soluble in water ; (2) minerals soluble in hydrochloric or nitric acid ; and (3) those unaffected by any of these fluids. The minerals soluble in water are either acids (almost only the boracic acid or sassolin and the arsenious acid), or oxygen and haloid salts. These are easily tested, one part of the solution being employed to find the electro-positive element or basis, the other the electro-negative or acid.

Minerals insoluble in water may next be tested with the above acids ; the nitric acid being preferable when it is probable, from the aspect of the mineral or its conduct before the blowpipe, that it contains an alloy, a sulphuret, or arseniate of some metal. In this manner the carbonic, phosphoric, arsenic, and chromic acid salts, many hydrous and anhydrous silicates, many sulphurets, arseniates, and other metallic compounds, are dissolved, so that further tests may be employed.

The minerals insoluble either in water or these acids are sulphur, graphite, cinnabar, some metallic oxides, some sulphates, and compounds with chlorine and fluorine, and especially quartz, and various silicates. For many of these no test is required, or those furnished by the blowpipe are sufficient. The silicates and others may be fused with four times their weight of anhydrous carbonate of soda when they are rendered soluble, so that further tests may be applied.

Chemical Reaction of the more Important Elements.

It is not intended in this place to describe the whole of those marks by which the chemist can detect the various elements. Our object is limited principally to the conduct of minerals before the blowpipe, and to a few simple tests by which their more important constituents may be discovered.

I.—NON-METALLIC ELEMENTS, AND THEIR COMBINATIONS WITH OXYGEN.

Nitric Acid is not abundant in minerals. Most of its salts detonate when heated on charcoal. In the closed tube they form nitrous acid, easily known by its orange colour and smell; clearly exhibited when the salt is mixed with copper filings and treated with concentrated sulphuric acid.

Sulphur and its compounds, in the glass tube or on charcoal, form sulphurous acid, easily known by its smell. The minutest amount of sulphur or sulphuric acid may be detected by melting the pulverised assay with two parts soda and one part borax, and placing the bead moistened with water on a plate of clean silver (or a coin), which is then stained brown or black.

Phosphoric Acid.—Most combinations with this acid tinge the blowpipe flame green, especially if previously moistened with sulphuric acid. When the experiment is performed in the dark, even three per cent of the acid may be detected.

Selenium and *Selenic Acid* are readily detected by the strong smell of decayed horse-radish, and leave a grey deposit with a metallic lustre on the charcoal. In the glass tube selenium sublimes with a red colour.

Chlorine and its salts.   When oxide of copper is melted with salt of phosphorus into a very dark-green bead, and an assay containing chlorine fused with this, the flame is tinged of a beautiful reddish-blue colour.

Iodine and its salts, treated like chlorine, impart a very beautiful bright-green colour to the flame ; and heated in the closed tube with sulphate of potassa, yield violet-coloured vapours.

Bromime and its salts, treated in the same manner with salt of phosphorus and oxide of copper, colour the blow-pipe flame greenish-blue.   Both it and iodine are rare in minerals.

Fluorine is shown by heating the assay with sulphate of potassa in a closed tube with a strip of logwood paper in the open end.   The paper becomes straw-yellow, and the glass is corroded.

Boracic Acid.—The mineral alone, or moistened with sulphuric acid when fusing, colours the flame momentarily green.   If the assay be heated with sulphuric acid, and alcohol added, and set on fire, the flame is coloured green from the vapours of the boracic acid.

Carbon, pulverised and heated with saltpetre, detonates, leaving carbonate of potassa.   *Carbonic acid* is not easily discovered with the blowpipe, but the minerals containing it effervesce in hydrochloric acid, and the colourless gas that escapes renders litmus paper red.   In solution it forms a precipitate with lime-water, which is again dissolved with effervescence in acids.

Silica, before the blowpipe, alone is unchanged ; is very slowly acted on by borax, very little by salt of phosphorus, but with soda melts entirely with a brisk effervescence into a clear glass.   The silicates are decomposed by salt of phosphorus, the silica being left in the bead as a powder or a skeleton.   Most of them melt with soda to a transparent glass.   Some silicates are dissolved in hydrochloric acid, and this the more readily the more powerful the basis, the less proportion of silica, and the greater the amount of water they contain.

II.—THE ALKALIES AND EARTHS.

Ammonia, heated with soda in a closed tube, is readily known by its smell. Its salts, heated with solution of potassa, also yield the vapour, known from its smell, its action on turmeric paper, and the white fumes that rise from a glass tube dipped in hydrochloric acid and held over it.

Soda imparts a reddish-yellow colour to the external flame when the assay is fused or kept at a strong red heat.

Lithia is best recognised by the beautiful carmine red colour it imparts to the flame during the fusion of a mineral containing it in considerable amount. Where the proportion is small, the colour appears if the assay be mixed with 1 part fluor spar and 1½ part sulphate of potassa.

Potassa gives a violet colour to the external cone when the assay is heated at the extremity of the oxidating flame. The presence of lithia or soda, however, disturbs this reaction. It may still be discovered by melting the assay in borax glass coloured brown by nickel oxide, which is changed to blue by the potassa.

Baryta, strongly heated at the point of the blue flame, imparts a green tinge to the outer flame.

Strontia and its salts colour the flame carmine red.

Lime and its salts colour the flame yellowish-red; the colour weakest in its compounds with sulphuric acid and silica.

The colour is most distinct in the sulphates of lime, baryta, and strontia, when the assay is first heated on charcoal and moistened with hydrochloric acid. The solutions of strontia and lime in hydrochloric acid impart their colours to the flames of alcohol.

Magnesia, ignited with solution of cobalt, or the oxalate of cobalt, forms a light-red mass; but the alkalies, earths, and metallic oxides more or less interfere with this test.

Alumina alone is infusible. In many combinations, when ignited with solution of cobalt, it assumes a fine blue colour, but iron peroxide or the alkalies interfere with the reaction.

Glucina, Yttria, Zirconia, and *Thorina* are not properly distinguished by blowpipe tests, though the minerals in which they occur are well marked in this way.

III.—THE METALS.

Arsenic on charcoal yields fumes with a smell like garlic, and sublimes in the closed tube. Most of its alloys in the reducing flame leave a white deposit on the charcoal, and some also yield metallic arsenic in the closed tube.

Antimony melts easily on charcoal, emitting dense white fumes, and leaving a ring of white crystalline oxide on the support. Antimony oxide on charcoal melts easily, fumes, and is reduced, colouring the flame pale greenish-blue.

Bismuth melts easily, fumes, and leaves a yellow oxide on the charcoal. Its oxides are easily reduced, and the bead left is known by its brittleness.

Tellurium fumes on charcoal, and becomes surrounded by a white mark with a reddish border, which, when the reducing flame is turned on it, disappears with a bluish-green light. Its combinations, heated in concentrated sulphuric acid, colour it red.

Mercury in all its combinations is volatile, and yields a metallic sublimate when heated alone, or with tin or soda in the closed tube.

Zinc, when heated with soda on charcoal, forms a deposit, which, when warm, is yellow; when cold, white; is tinged of a fine green by solution of cobalt, and is not further volatile in the oxidating flame.

Tin forms a white deposit on the charcoal behind the assay, which takes a bluish-green colour with the solution of cobalt. The oxide is easily reduced by soda.

Lead colours the flame pale blue, and forms a yellow deposit with a white border on the charcoal when heated in the oxidating flame, and with soda is easily reduced.

Cadmium produces, with soda, a reddish-brown or orange-yellow ring, with iridescent border on the charcoal, and also on platinum-foil.

Manganese alone, melted with borax or salt of phosphorus on the platinum wire in the oxidating flame, forms a fine amethystine glass, which becomes colourless in the reducing flame. In combination with other metals, the pulverised assay mixed with two or three times as much soda, and melted in the oxidating flame on platinum-foil, forms a bluish-green glass.

Cobalt, melted with borax in the oxidating flame, gives a beautiful blue glass. Minerals of metallic aspect must be first roasted on charcoal. The salts of protoxide of cobalt form bright-red solutions, from which potassa throws down a blue flaky hydrate, which becomes olive-green in the air.

Nickel, the assay, first roasted in the open tube and on charcoal, produces in the oxidating flame, with borax, a glass, which, hot, is reddish or violet-brown; when cold, yellowish or dark red; and by the addition of saltpetre changes to blue. In the reducing flame the glass appears grey. The salts in solution have a bright-green colour, and with potassa form a green precipitate, which is unchanged in the air.

Copper (the assay, if apparently metallic, first roasted) forms with borax or salt of phosphorus in the oxidating flame, an opaque reddish-brown glass, a small addition of tin aiding in the result. In the reducing flame the glass, when warm, is green; when cold, blue. With soda metallic copper is produced. A small proportion of copper may often be detected by heating the assay, moistened with hydrochloric acid, in the oxidating flame, which is then tinged of a beautiful green colour.

Silver from many combinations is readily extracted on charcoal with soda as a white malleable bead. From its solution in nitric acid silver is thrown down by hydrochloric acid as a white chloride, which in the light soon becomes black.

Gold is easily separated from its combinations with

tellurium on charcoal. The bead, if pure, is insoluble in
nitric or hydrochloric acids. If the grain is white, it contains more silver than gold, and must then be heated in a
porcelain capsule with nitric acid, which gives it a black
colour, and gradually removes the silver, if the gold is only
a fourth part or less. If the proportion of gold is greater,
the nitro-chloric acid must be used, which then removes
the gold. From its solution in this acid the protochloride
of tin throws down a purple precipitate (*purple of Cassius*),
and the sulphate of iron, metallic gold.

Platinum, and the metals usually found with it, cannot
.be separated from each other by heat. Only the *Osmium-
iridium* strongly heated in the closed tube with saltpetre is
decomposed, forming osmium acid, known from its peculiar
pungent odour. The usual mixture of platinum grains is
soluble in nitro-chloric acid, leaving osmium-iridium. From
this solution the *platinum* is thrown down by sal-ammonia
as a double chloride of platinum and ammonium. From
the solution evaporated, and again diluted, with cyanide of
mercury, the *palladium* separates as cyanide of palladium.
The *rhodium* may be separated by its property of combining with fused bisulphate of potassa, which is not the case
with platinum or iridium.

Cerium, when no iron-oxide is present, produces, with
borax and salt of phosphorus, in the oxidating flame, a red
or dark-yellow glass, which becomes very pale when cold,
and colourless in the reducing flame. *Lanthanium* oxide
forms a white colourless glass; *didymium* a dark amethystine glass.

Iron, the peroxide and hydrated peroxide, become black
and magnetic before the blowpipe, and form, with borax or
salt of phosphorus, in the oxidating flame, a dark-red glass,
becoming bright-yellow when cold; and in the reducing
flame, especially on adding tin, an olive-green or mountain-
green glass. The peroxide colours a bead of borax containing copper oxide bluish-green; the protoxide produces
red spots. Salts of protoxide of iron form a green solution, from which potassa or ammonia throws down the protoxide as a hydrate, which is first white, then dirty-green,

and finally yellowish-brown. Carbonate of lime produces
no precipitate. The salts of the peroxide, on the other
hand, form yellow solutions from which the peroxide is
thrown down by potassa or ammonia as a flaky-brown
hydrate. Carbonate of lime also causes a precipitate.

Chromium forms, with borax or salt of phosphorus, a
glass, fine emerald-green when cold, though when hot often
yellowish or reddish. Its solutions are usually green, and
the metal is thrown down by potassa as a bluish-green
hydrate, again dissolved in excess of the alkali. The
chrome in many minerals is very certainly discovered by
melting the assay with three times its bulk of saltpetre,
which, dissolved in water, gives with acetate of lead a
yellow precipitate.

Vanadium, melted on platinum wire with borax or salt
of phosphorus, gives a fine green glass in the reducing
flame, which becomes yellow or brown in the oxidating
flame, distinguishing it from chrome.

Uranium, with salt of phosphorus, forms in the oxidating flame a clear yellow, in the reducing flame a fine green,
glass. With borax its reaction is similar to that of iron.

Molybdenum forms in the reducing flame, with salt of
phosphorus, a green, with borax a brown, glass.

Tungsten or *Wolfram* forms, with salt of phosphorus, in
the oxidating flame, a colourless or yellow, in the reducing
flame a very beautiful blue, glass, which appears green
when warm. When accompanied by iron the glass is
blood-red, not blue.

Tantalium, as tantalic acid, is readily dissolved by salt
of phosphorus, and in large quantity into a colourless glass,
which does *not* become opaque in cooling, and does *not*
acquire a blue colour from solution of cobalt. Or fuse the
assay with two times as much saltpetre, and three times as
much soda, in a platinum spoon ; dissolve this, filter and
decompose the fluid by hydrochloric acid ; the tantalic acid
separates as a white powder, which does *not* become yellow
when heated.

Titanium in anatase, rutile, brookite, and titanite, is
shown by the assay forming, with salt of phosphorus, in the

oxidating flame, a glass which is and remains colourless; in the reducing flame, a glass which appears yellow when hot, and whilst cooling, passes through red into a beautiful violet. When iron is present, however, the glass is blood-red, but is changed to violet by adding tin. When titanate of iron is dissolved in hydrochloric acid, and the solution boiled with a little tin, it acquires a violet colour from the oxide of titanium. Heated with concentrated sulphuric acid, the titanate of iron produces a blue colour.

CHAPTER IV.

CLASSIFICATION OF MINERALS.

A MINERAL species was formerly defined as a natural inorganic body, possessing a definite chemical composition and peculiar external form. The account given of these properties shows that the form of a mineral species comprehends not only the primary or fundamental figure, but all those that may be derived from it by the laws of crystallography. Irregularities of form arising from accidental causes, or that absence of form which results from the limited space in which the mineral has been produced, do not destroy the identity of the species. Even amorphous masses, when the chemical composition remains unaltered, are properly classed under the same species as the crystalline.

The definite chemical composition of mineral species must be taken with equal latitude. Pure substances, such as they are described in works on chemistry, are very rare in the mineral kingdom. In the most transparent quartz crystals, traces of alumina and iron oxide can be detected ; the purest spinel contains a small amount of silica, and the most brilliant diamond, consumed by the solar rays, leaves some ash behind. Such non-essential mixtures must be neglected, or each individual crystal would form a distinct mineral species. The isomorphous elements introduce a wider range of varieties, and render the limitation of species more difficult. Carbonate of lime, for instance, becomes mixed with carbonate of magnesia or of iron in almost innumerable proportions ; and the latter substances also with the former. Where these mixtures are small in amount, variable in different specimens, and do not sensibly affect the form or physical characters, they may be neglected, and the mineral reckoned to that species with which it

H

most closely agrees. Where, however, the two substances
are frequently found in definite chemical proportions, these
compounds must be considered as distinct species, especially
when they also show differences in form and other external
characters.

Amorphous minerals with definite composition must
also be considered as true species. But when they show
no definite composition, like many substances classed as
clays and ochres, they cannot be accounted true minerals.
Some of them, however, from their importance in the arts,
others from other circumstances, have received distinct
names and a kind of prescriptive right to a place in mineralogical works, from which they can now scarcely be
banished. Many of them are properly rocks, or indefinite
combinations of two or more minerals; others are the
mere products of the decomposition of such bodies.

In collecting the species into higher groups, and arranging them in a system, several methods have been pursued.
Some, like Mohs, have looked only at the external characters, and asserted that they alone were sufficient for all the
purposes of arranging and classifying minerals.   Others,
led by Berzelius, have, on the contrary, taken chemistry as
the foundation of mineralogy, and classed the species by
their composition, without reference to form or physical
characters.

Neither system can be exclusively adopted, and a natural classification of minerals should take into account all
their characters, and that in proportion to their relative
importance.   Among these the chemical composition un-
doubtedly holds a high rank, as being that on which the
other properties will probably be ultimately found to depend.   Next in order is their crystalline form, especially
as exhibited in cleavage; and then the physical characters,
gravity, hardness, and tenacity.   But the properties of
minerals are as yet far from showing that subordination
and co-relation which has been observed in the organic
world, where the external forms and structures have a
direct reference to the functions of the living being.
Hence, even when all the characters are taken into account,

there is not that facility in classifying the mineral that is presented by the other kingdoms of nature. Many, or rather most, of the species stand so isolated that it is scarcely possible to find any general principle on which to collect them into larger groups, especially such groups as, like the natural families of plants and animals, present important features of general resemblance, and admit of being described by common characteristics. Certain groups of species are indeed united by such evident characters, that they are found together in almost every method; but other species are not thus united, and the general order of arrangement is very uncertain. Hence, though some classifications of very considerable merit have been proposed, no natural system of minerals commanding general assent has yet appeared.

The arrangement followed in this treatise is chiefly founded on that proposed by Professor Weiss of Berlin. We have, however, made considerable changes, which the progress of the science and the more accurate knowledge of many species require. This classification appears to us to come nearer than any other we have seen to a natural system, which in arranging and combining objects takes account of all their characters, and assigns them their place, from a due consideration of their whole nature, and is thus distinguished from artificial systems, which classify objects with reference only to one character.

Besides species, two higher grades in classification seem sufficient at once to exhibit the natural relations, and to facilitate an easy and complete review of the species composing the mineral kingdom. These are families and orders. In forming the families, those minerals are first selected which occupy the more important place in the composition of rocks, and consequently in the crust of the globe. Thus quartz, felspar, mica, hornblende, garnet, among siliceous minerals; calc-spar, gypsum, rock-salt, less so fluor spar and heavy spar, among those of saline composition stand out prominently as the natural centres or representatives of so many distinct families. To these certain metallic minerals, as iron pyrites, lead-glance or galena, blende, magnetite, the sparry iron ore or siderite, and a few more, are readily associated as important families. But the minerals thus geologically distinguished are not sufficient to divide the whole mineral kingdom into convenient sections, and additional groups must be selected from the peculiarity of their natural-historical or chemical properties. Thus the zeolites are easily seen to form such a natural group. The precious stones or gems also, notwithstanding their diverse chemical composition, must ever appear a highly natural family, when regarded as individual objects. Their great hardness, tenacity, high specific gravity without the metallic aspect, their brilliant lustre, transparent purity, and vivid colours,—all mark them out as a peculiar group. Only the diamond, which might naturally seem to take the chief place in this class, differs so much, not only in elementary composition, but in physical properties, that it must be assigned to a diverse place.

Round these species thus selected the other less important minerals are arranged in groups or families. It is evident that no precise definition of these families can be given, as the connection is one of resemblance in many points, not of identity in any single character. In other words, it is a classification rather according to types than from definitions, as every true natural classification must be. The same cause, however, leaves the extent of the families somewhat undefined, and also permits considerable license in the arrangement of species. But both circumstances are rather of advantage in the present state of the science, as allowing more freedom in the grouping of species than could be obtained in a more rigid system of classification.

In collecting the families into orders, the guidance of chemistry is followed rather than of natural history, though the latter is also taken into consideration. Chemical names are assigned to the orders, but still regarded *as names* derived from the prevailing chemical characters, and *not as definitions*. Hence it must not be considered an error should two or three mineral species be found in an order with whose name, viewed as a definition, they may not agree.

Guided by these and similar considerations, minerals may be divided into the following orders and families :—

ORDER I.—THE OXIDISED STONES.

Families :—
1. Quartz.
2. Felspar.
3. Scapolite.
4. Haloid stones.
5. Leucite.
6. Zeolite.
7. Mica.
8. Serpentine.
9. Hornblende.
10. Clays.
11. Garnet.
12. Cyanite.
13. Gems.
14. Metallic stones.

ORDER II.—SALINE STONES.

Families :—
1. Calc spar.
2. Fluor spar.
3. Heavy spar.
4. Gypsum.
5. Rock salt.

ORDER III.—SALINE ORES.

Families :—
1. Sparry iron ores.
2. Iron salts.
3. Copper salts.
4. Lead salts.

ORDER IV.—OXIDISED ORES.

Families :—
1. Iron ores.
2. Tinstone.
3. Manganese ores.
4. Red copper ores.
5. White antimony ores.

ORDER V.—NATIVE METALS.

Form only one family.

ORDER VI.—SULPHURETTED METALS.

Families :—
1. Iron pyrites.
2. Galena.
3. Gray antimony ore.
4. Gray copper ore.
5. Blende.
6. Ruby-blende.

ORDER VII.—THE INFLAMMABLES.

Families :—
1. Sulphur.
2. Diamond.
3. Coal.
4. Mineral resins.
5. Combustible salts.

In describing the species we have followed this general

plan. First, that name which it seems most expedient to adopt is given, with the principal synonyms, followed in the same line by the probable chemical formula. The new formulæ are also, as stated, given for the more important species, and distinguished by being enclosed in brackets [thus]. In the descriptions the system of crystallisation is noted, and the mineral more precisely characterised by enumerating some of its more common forms and combinations with their characteristic angles. The physical characters of the species, its state of aggregation, cleavage, fracture, hardness (H.), and specific gravity (G.), follow; then its lustre, pellucidity, colour, and any other marked peculiarities. Next come its chemical characters, or its conduct before the blowpipe (B.B.), and the effect of acids, specially the hydrochloric (h.), nitric (n.), and sulphuric (s.). The chemical composition, or the amount of the different elements in 100 parts, generally deduced from the formula, but with notices of the more important variations indicated by the best analyses either from the substitution of isomorphous elements or other substances, are then noted. The principal localities where each species occurs, especially in our own country, with certain miscellaneous particulars, conclude the description.

We have also given characters of the orders and families, so far as possible. These, of course, apply chiefly to the more important and better marked or typical species (indicated by one or two asterisks [* or **] prefixed to the name), but in most points are also descriptive of the others. The possibility of forming such general characters is the best proof that the groups are so far natural, and that the object of a scientific classification has been partially at least attained.

PART II.

DESCRIPTION OF MINERAL SPECIES.

—◆—

ORDER I.—THE OXYDISED STONES.

THE minerals contained in this order are either simple oxides or compounds of oxides. The earths and alkalies compose the greater number, whilst oxides of the true metals are not abundant, and occur generally as isomorphous with or replacing them. Silica almost always occurs as the acid element, but in a very few alumina appears to take its place. They are not soluble in water (or in very minute amount). They have all a stony aspect, non-metallic lustre, and most of them are white or colourless, and more or less translucent, except the metallic stones. All translucent stones that do not scratch with the knife (except boracite and diamond) belong to this order.

**FAMILY I.—QUARTZ.

Characters of family chiefly those of the first species. Silica usually occurs either crystalline with G. = 2·6, or amorphous with G. = 2·2 ; but a third form crystalline and with G. = 2·3, is also known. Generally it is insoluble in water or acids, but in certain conditions, as when separating from decomposing silicates, it is soluble, and hence found in springs and rivers, and more abundant in hot springs. It is then of great importance in many organic and inorganic processes. Quartz is the true type or representative of the mineral kingdom.

**1.—QUARTZ.—$\ddot{S}i = [SiO^3]$.

Hexagonal ; the purest varieties tetartohedral. The primary pyramid P has the middle edge = 103° 34′, and the polar edges = 133° 44', and is often perfect. Very frequently it appears as a rhombohedron R (or ¼ P), with

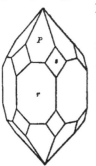

Fig. 101.

polar edges = 94° 15'. Crystals often of ∞P . P; ∞P . P . 4P, the forms ∞P and 4P being combined in an oscillatory manner, producing striæ on the face of the prism ; ∞P . P . ¼(2P2) (*v, p,* 5) (Fig. 101), the last face appearing as a rhomb replacing the angles between the two other forms. They are prismatic, or pyramidal, or rhombohedral, when P is divided into R and − R ; the latter very often wanting.

Twins or macles common, with parallel axes, and either merely in juxtaposition (see Fig. 80), or interpenetrating. The crystals occur either single, attached, or imbedded, or in groups and druses. Most frequently granular, massive, fibrous, or columnar; also in pseudomorphs, petrifactions, and other forms. Cleavage, rhombohedral along R very imperfect ; prismatic along ∞P still more imperfect. Fracture conchoidal, uneven, or splintery. H. = 7; G. = 2·5...2·8, or 2·65 in the purest varieties. Colourless, but more often white, gray, yellow, brown, red, blue, green, or even black. Lustre vitreous, inclining to resinous ; transparent or translucent, when impure almost opaque. B.B. infusible alone ; with soda effervesces and melts into a clear glass. Insoluble in acids, except the fluoric ; when pulverised, slightly soluble in solution of potash. Chem. com. 48·05 silicium and 51·95 oxygen, but frequently a small amount of the oxides of iron or titanium, of lime, alumina, and other substances.

Varieties are—*Rock-crystal,* highly transparent and colourless ; Dauphiné, Switzerland, Tyrol, Hungary, Madagascar, and Ceylon. *Amethyst,* violet-blue (from iron peroxide or manganese), and often marked by zig-zag or undulating lines, and the colour disposed in clouds ; Siberia, Persia, India, Ceylon, Brazil (white or yellow named topaz), Hungary, Siebenburg, Ireland, near Cork, and Aberdeenshire. Wine yellow, or *citrin* and *gold topaz;* the brown or *smoky quartz* (coloured by a substance containing carbon and nitrogen); and the black or *morion;* Siberia, Bohemia, Pennsylvania, and other places. *Cairngorm stone,* brown or yellow; Aberdeenshire mountains. The above are valued as ornamental stones; less so :—

Rose-quartz, red inclining to violet-blue; Ben Macdhui, and Rabenstein in Bavaria. *Milk quartz,* milk-white, and slightly opalescent; Greenland. *Prase,* leek and other shades of green; Saxony and Cedar Mountain in South Africa. *Cat's-eye,* greenish-white or gray, olive-green, red, brown, or yellow; Ceylon and Malabar. *Avanturine,* yellow, red, or brown; India, Spain, and Scotland. *Siderite,* indigo or Berlin blue; Golling in Salzburg.

Common quartz, crystallised or massive, white or gray, also red, brown, etc., is a frequent constituent in many rocks. Some impure varieties are properly rocks, as—

(1.) *Ferruginous quartz,* or iron-flint, red, yellow, or brown, often associated with iron ores.

(2.) *Jasper,* red, yellow, brown, also green, gray, white, and black alone, or in spots, veins, and bands (*Ribbon* or *Egyptian jasper*); the Ural, Tuscan Apennines, the Hartz, and many parts of Scotland.

(3.) *Lydian stone,* or *flinty slate,* black, gray, or white; has a splintery or conchoidal fracture, breaks into irregular fragments, and passes by many transitions into clay-slate, of which it is often merely an altered portion, as in Scotland; used as a touchstone for gold, and at Elfdal manufactured into ornaments.

(4.) *Hornstone* or *chert,* compact, conchoidal splintery fracture; translucent on the edges, and dirty gray, red, yellow, green, or brown; passes into flint, flinty slate, or common quartz; common in the mountain limestone, oolite, and greensand formations; and often contains petrifactions, as shells, corals, and wood.

Other siliceous minerals seem intimate mixtures of quartz and opal, as,—*Flint,* grayish-white, gray, or grayish-black, also yellow, red, or brown; sometimes in clouds, spots, or stripes; semitransparent; lustre dull; fracture flat conchoidal; occurs chiefly in the chalk formation, as in England, Ireland, Aberdeenshire, France, Germany, and other countries; sometimes in beds or vertical veins, oftener in irregular lumps or concretions, inclosing petrifactions, as sponges, echinoids, shells, or siliceous infusoria. The colour is partly derived from carbon or organic matter. It is used for gun-flints, and for the manufacture of glass and pottery, and cut into cameos or other ornaments.

Calcedony, semitransparent or translucent; white, gray, blue, green, yellow, or brown; stalactitic, reniform, or botryoidal, and in pseudomorphs or petrifactions; Trevascus mine in Cornwall, Scotland, Hungary, Tyrol, Bohemia, Oberstein. *Carnelian*, chiefly blood-red, but also yellow, brown, or almost black; India, Arabia, Surinam, and Siberia; also Bohemia, Saxony, and Scotland (Perthshire). *Plasma*, leek or grass green, and waxy lustre; Olympus, Schwarzwald, India, and China. *Chrysoprase*, apple-green; Silesia, and Vermont in North America. *Heliotrope* or *bloodstone*, dark-green, sprinkled with deep-red spots; Siberia, Bohemia, the Fassa Valley, the island of Rum and other parts of Scotland. *Agates*, mixtures chiefly of calcedony in layers, with jasper, amethyst, or common quartz, abound in the amygdaloids of our own and other countries. *Onyx*, alternate layers of white, brown, or black, was much used in ancient times for cameos.

Some crystals are remarkable for their great size, as one in the Museum at Paris, measuring 3 feet in diameter, and weighing nearly 8 cwt. Other specimens contain cavities inclosing various substances, more than 40 known, as silver, iron pyrites, rutile, magnetite, tremolite, amianthus, mica, tourmeline, topaz; also air, water, naphtha, and fluid carbonic acid.

2. TRIDYMITE.—$\ddot{S}i$.

Hexagonal; P middle edge 124° 4', polar edges 127° 35'. Single crystals very minute hexagonal tables of 0P. ∞P, but with the edges replaced by P and ∞P2, are rare. Mostly conjoined in macles of two, or oftener three. Cleavage, basal indistinct; fracture conchoidal. H. = 7; G. =

2·282...2·326. Colourless and transparent. Vitreous, pearly on the basis. B.B. like quartz. Chem. com. 96 silica, with some alumina, magnesia, and iron peroxide, probably from the matrix. Discovered by Von Rath in the trachyte of San Cristobal, near Pachucho, in Mexico. Also in the trachyte of Mont-Dore, Puy Capucine, the Drachenfels, and of Hungary. Many opals, treated with solution of potash, leave tridymite crystals, as those from Zimapan, Caschau, Silesia, and the cacholong from Iceland. Where they are abundant, the opal becomes opaque or snow-white. Said also in meteoric iron, Breitenbach.

*3. OPAL.—$\ddot{S}i$, $\dot{H}$, *or* $\ddot{S}i\ \dot{H}^3$.

Amorphous; fracture conchoidal; very brittle. H = 5·5...6·5; G. = 2...2·2. Transparent to opaque; vitreous, inclining to resinous. Colourless, but often white, yellow, red, brown, green, or gray, with a beautiful play of colours. B.B. decrepitates and becomes opaque, but is infusible; in the closed tube yields water; almost wholly soluble in solution of potash. Chem. com. silica, with 5 to 13 per cent water; or probably a mere hardened natural gelatine of silica with water; but most are mixtures of various minerals.

Varieties are—(1.) *Hyalite, glassy-opal,* or *Muller's glass,* transparent, colourless, very glassy; small botryoidal, or incrusting; Kaiserstuhl in the Breisgau, Schemnitz, Silesia, Moravia, Mexico, and other places. (2.) *Fire-opal* or *girasol,* transparent, brilliant vitreous lustre; bright hyacinth red or yellow; Zimapan in Mexico, and the Faroe Islands. (3.) *Noble opal,* semitransparent or translucent; resinous inclining to vitreous; bluish or yellowish-white, with brilliant prismatic colours; most show double refraction and are binaxial; in irregular masses or veins near Eperies in Hungary. (4.) *Common opal,* semitransparent, vitreous; white, yellow, green, red, or brown; Hungary, also Faroe, Iceland, the Giant's Causeway, and the Western Isles of Scotland. (5.) *Semi-opal,* duller and less pellucid. *Wood-opal* or *lithoxylon,* with the form and texture of wood distinctly seen; Hungary, Bohemia, and other countries.

(6.) *Menilite*, compact, reniform; opaque and brown or bluish-gray; Mont Menil, near Paris. (7.) *Opal jasper*, blood red, brown, or yellow. (8.) *Cacholong*, opaque, dull, glimmering, or pearly, and yellowish or rarely reddish-white; in veins or reniform and incrusting; Faroe, Iceland, the Giant's Causeway. One variety is named *Hydrophane*, from imbibing water and becoming translucent. (9.) *Siliceous sinter*, deposited from the Geyser and other hot springs; and *Pearl sinter*, incrusting volcanic tufa at Santa-Fiora in Tuscany (*Fiorite*), and in Auvergne. That from the Geyser contains 84·4 silica, 3·1 alumina, 1·9 peroxide of iron, 1·1 magnesia, 0·7 lime, 0·9 potash and soda, and 7·9 water.

4. EARTHY SILICA.

(*a.*) *Spongiform quartz*, coarse, earthy, soft, and often friable, and yellow or grayish-white; porous, and swims on water till saturated; St. Ouen, near Paris. (*b.*) *Tripoli*, coarse or fine earthy; white, gray, or yellow; near Tripoli in Africa, Corfu, Bohemia, Saxony, and Bavaria. (*c.*) *Polishing slate* (*Polirschiefer*), white or yellow; slaty texture, opaque, brittle, and swims on water; at Bilin in Bohemia; consists chiefly of the siliceous remains of plants (*Diatomaceæ*). (*d.*) *Adhesive slate*, from Montmartre, near Paris. And (*e.*) *Mountain meal*, snow-white, pearly, gray, or greenish; have a similar origin; Santa Fiora in Tuscany, Oberohe in Hanover, Kymmenegard in Sweden (where used as food), in Bohemia, and the Isle of France.

** FAMILY II.—FELSPAR.

Crystallisation monoclinic or triclinic, both very similar in aspect and angles. Cleavage very distinct, especially the basal *P*; less so the clino- or brachy-diagonal *M*. G. = 2·4...3·2, but mostly 2·5...2·8; H. = 6, or a little more. Slightly or not at all soluble in acids. B.B. fusible, but often with difficulty. Translucent, pure varieties highly transparent. Colourless, white, or shades of red; less common, green or yellow. Chem. com. anhydrous silicates of alumina, and of an alkali or lime.

The felspars are very important constituents of the earth's crust, occurring in nearly all the igneous rocks, and in many of the stratified crystalline schists. In true strata they are found chiefly as fragments or decomposed, and in the latter state form a large part of most soils and clays. In the older mineralogists and popular language many species are conjoined under the common name of felspar which are now considered as distinct, each of them having not only its peculiar physical and chemical characters, but also geognostic position and associated group of minerals. Thus orthoclase, and the other more siliceous felspars with potash, abound in granite and the plutonic rocks; the less siliceous, with soda and lime, characterise the volcanic rocks—as labradorite the basaltic group, glassy felspar the trachytic. Orthoclase is associated with quartz, hornblende, and mica; glassy felspar either with hornblende and mica or with augite; labradorite only with augite, rarely with quartz or hornblende.

The felspars are best known from similar minerals by their hardness (scarce scratch with a good knife), difficult fusibility, and unequal cleavages. The following marks may aid the student in distinguishing the more common species. In orthoclase the basal cleavage plane forms a right angle with the clinodiagonal cleavage planes M on both hands; in the triclinic or plagioclase felspars the angles are unequal. Orthoclase, albite, andesin, and oligoclase are insoluble in acids; ryacolite, labradorite, and anorthite more or less soluble. In granite, when decomposing, orthoclase often becomes reddish or dark-red; oligoclase dull green, and at length white.

S. von Walterhausen stated that the felspars were mixtures of three true species, forming a series with the oxygen of the silica, alumina and $\dot{R} = x : 3 : 1 :$—x ranging from 24 to 4. Tschermak and most mineralogists now take a similar view, regarding orthoclase, albite, and anorthite alone as true species, of which the others are mixtures. Those consisting essentially of potash and soda only, are mechanical mixtures of orthoclase and albite, the distinct lamellæ visible by the microscope; those again that contain essentially lime and soda together, are chemical, isomorphous compounds of albite and anorthite in various proportions, and with corresponding transitions in crystallographic and physical properties.

**5. ORTHOCLASE. $\begin{cases} \ddot{A}l\ \ddot{S}i^3 + \dot{K}\ \ddot{S}i^3, \textit{or} \\ [Al^2O^3 . 3\ SiO^2 + K^2O . 3\ SiO^2]. \end{cases}$

Monoclinic; $C = 63°\ 57'$; ∞P (T and l) $118°\ 47'$, P°∞ $65°\ 46'$, 2 P°∞ $90°\ 71'$, 2P°∞ (y) $35°\ 45'$; crystals often of ∞P . 0P . P°∞; or ∞P°∞ (M) . ∞P . 0P (P). 2P°$_\infty$ (Fig. 102), are short rhombic prisms, when ∞P predominates; or tabular when ∞P°∞; or short hexagonal prismatic when ∞P and ∞P°∞; or rectangular prismatic when 0P and ∞P°∞ predominate; and occur single, at-

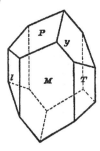
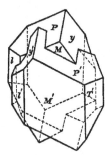

Fig. 102.　　　Fig. 103.

tached, or in druses. Macles are frequent, especially with the twin axis parallel to the chief axis, and often partially interpenetrating, as in Fig. 103. Also massive and coarse or fine granular. Cleavage, basal (P) very perfect; clino-diagonal (M) perfect (P to M = 90°); and hemiprismatic ∞P in traces. Fracture conchoidal or uneven and splintery. H. = 6 ; G. = 2·53...2·58. Transparent to translucent on the edges; vitreous, but often pearly on the more perfect cleavage; and also opalescent, with bluish or changing colours. Colourless, but generally red, yellow, gray, or green. B.B. fuses with difficulty to an opaque vesicular glass; not affected by acids. Chem. com. 64·6 silica, 18·5 alumina, and 16·9 potash, but generally 10 to 14 potash, 1 to 4 soda, 0 to 1·3 lime, 0 to 2 iron peroxide.

Varieties are—(1.) *Adularia* and *Ice-spar*, transparent or translucent, splendent, and almost, or wholly, colourless. Some with a bluish opalescence are named *Moonstone;* St. Gotthardt, Mont Blanc, Dauphiné, Arendal, Southern Norway, Greenland, and Ceylon.

(2.) *Common felspar*, less splendent and transparent, and generally white or red, especially flesh-red, is a very common constituent of many rocks. Crystals at Baveno on Lago Maggiore, Lomnitz in Silesia, Mourne Mountains and Wicklow in Ireland, Aberdeenshire (at Rubislaw, 4 or 5 inches long) in Scotland, and at Carlsbad and Elnbogen in Bohemia. *Amazon stone*, verdigris-green, from Lake Ilmen; and *Murchisonite*, golden or grayish-yellow, from Arran and Dawlish, seem varieties.

(3.) The *Glassy felspar* or *Sanidine* ($C = 64°\ 1'$, ∞P $119°\ 16'$) contains 3 to 12 potash, 3 to 10 soda, 0 to 3 lime, and 0 to 2 magnesia. Crystals imbedded, yellowish-white or gray; vitreous; transparent or translucent, and

Macles of common Felspar

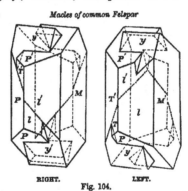

RIGHT.   **Fig. 104.**   LEFT.

often much cracked; Drachenfels, Auvergne, Italy, Iceland, Mexico, and other countries; also in Arran, Rum, and other parts of Scotland. *Rhyacolite*, from Vesuvius and Lake Laach, is only an impure variety. *Loxoclase*, from Hammond, New York, also a variety with much soda. *Baulite* and *Krablite* from Iceland, probably mixtures with quartz.

Orthoclase occurs in granite, gneiss, and porphyry in many countries. It is commonly associated with quartz, sometimes, as in the graphic granite of Portsoy and Aberdeenshire, in regular combinations. It is very liable to decomposition, when it is converted especially into kaolin, used for manufacturing porcelain and stoneware. The adularia or moonstone, and the green amazon stone, are cut as ornamental stones.

Compact felspar, or *feldstein*, a mixture of orthoclase and quartz, often harder than the pure mineral. G. = 2·59...3. White, gray, red, or yellow, sometimes in spots or bands. The softer varieties, or *claystones*, often bluish or purplish. G. = 2·21. B.B. most melt with difficulty to a white enamel (hornstone is infusible). Common in the porphyry rocks of many countries, as in Scotland (Cheviots, Pentland, and Ochil Hills), and Sweden (*Leelite* from Grythyttan).

**6. ALBITE. $\begin{cases} \ddot{A}l\ \dot{S}i^3 + \dot{N}a\ \dot{S}i^3,\ or \\ [Al^2O^3.\ 3SiO^2 + Na^2O.\ 3SiO^2]. \end{cases}$

Triclinic; 0P (*P*) to $\infty\bar{P}\infty$ (*M*) = 86° 24′, ∞P′ (*l*) to ∞P (*T*) = 122° 15′, but angles very variable. Crystals, generally like those of orthoclase, are tabular or prismatic

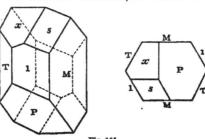

Fig. 105.

(Fig. 105). Macles very common, especially united by a face of ∞ P ∞ (Fig. 106), the re-entering angle between the faces of 0P (*P* and *P′*) = 172° 48′ being very characteristic. Fig. 107 is another macle common in pericline. Also massive and foliated, or radiating. Cleavage, basal and brachydiagonal almost equally perfect, prismatic along ∞P imperfect; fracture conchoidal or uneven. H. = 6... 6·5; G. = 2·6...2·67. Rarely transparent, usually translucent or only on the edges; vitreous, pearly on the cleavage. Colourless, but generally white, gray, green, red, or yellow; streak white. B.B. difficultly fusible, tinging the flame yellow, to a white semi-opaque glass; not affected

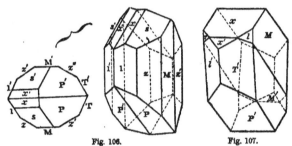

Fig. 106.　　　　　　　　Fig. 107.

by acids. Chem. com. 68·6 silica, 19·6 alumina with 0·1 to 1 iron peroxide and 11·8 soda with 0·3 to 4 lime, 0 to 2·5 potash, and 0 to 0·5 magnesia. Hence albite and orthoclase both contain soda and potash, only in different proportions. Albite is best marked by the frequent reentering angles, its more easy fusibility, and the obliquity (93° 36′) of its cleavage planes, often marked with striæ. *Pericline*, with G. = 2·54...2·6, and slight diversity in angles, is only a variety.

Albite is a constituent of many greenstones (Edinburgh), of granite (Aberdeenshire), syenite, gneiss, porphyry, and trachyte; also in beds and veins; crystals at Barèges in the Pyrenees, Bourg d'Oisans in Dauphiné, St. Gotthardt, the Tyrol, Salzburg, and Arendal. *Adinole* is a compact gray or red mixture of albite and quartz.

7. ANDESINE.—$\ddot{A}l \ddot{S}i^3 + (\dot{N}a, \dot{C}a) \ddot{S}i$.

Triclinic; crystals and physical properties similar to albite; but the cleavage less distinct. B.B. more easily

I

fusible to a milky somewhat porous glass. Chem. com.
59·7 silica, 25·6 alumina, 7·7 soda and 7 lime, and thus
nearly 1 albite and 1 anorthite, but some a little potash
and magnesia ; and others nearer oligoclase, from which
scarce distinct. Andes, Vosges, and Iceland.

Saccharite, compact, or fine granular ; white or apple-
green ; Silesia and Canada ; also a variety.

**8. LABRADORITE.— $\begin{cases} \ddot{A}l \ \ddot{S}i^3 + (\dot{C}a, \dot{N}a) \ \ddot{S}i = \\ [Al^2 \ O^3 . \ 2Si \ O^3 + RO . \ Si \ O^2]. \end{cases}$

Triclinic ; $0P : \infty \bar{P} \infty = 86° 40', 0P : \infty'P = 111°$. Crystals rare ; mostly massive and granular ; macles like those
of albite (Fig. 107). Cleavage, basal very perfect ; brachydiagonal less so ; both usually striated. $H. = 6$; $G. = 2·68$
...2·74. Translucent, or only on the edges ; vitreous, on
the cleavage pearly or resinous. Gray, passing into white,
green, yellow, or red. The faces of $\infty \bar{P} \infty$ often exhibit
very beautiful changing colours—blue, green, yellow, red,
or brown—sometimes in bands intersecting at certain
angles. B.B. fuses more readily than orthoclase to a compact colourless glass ; soluble when pulverised in n. acid.
Chem. com. 52·9 silica, 30·3 alumina with 1 to 2 iron peroxide, 12·3 lime, and 4·5 soda with 0·3 to 2 potash, 0·1 to
2 magnesia, and 1 to 3 water—the latter probably not
essential. It is thus = 1 albite and 3 anorthite.

Common constituent of dolerite, greenstone, the gabbro,
and hypersthene rocks. Labrador, Finland, Harz, Meiss-
ner, Tyrol, Mourne Mountains, Campsie and Milngavie near
Glasgow, and Skye ; also Etna and Vesuvius, and in
meteoric stones.

*9. ANORTHITE, $\begin{cases} \ddot{A}l \ \ddot{S}i + \dot{C}a \ \ddot{S}i, \ or \\ [Al^2 \ O^3 . \ Si \ O^2 + CaO . \ Si \ O^2]. \end{cases}$
  Christianite.

Triclinic ; $0P : \infty \bar{P} \infty = 85° 50'$; $\infty P' : \infty'P = 120° 30'$.
Crystals and macles like albite, with angle between P and
$P' = 188° 24'$. Cleavage, basal and brachydiagonal perfect. $H. = 6$; $G. = 2·7...2·76$. Transparent or translucent ; vitreous. Colourless or white. B.B. fuses to a clear
glass ; soluble without gelatinising in con. h. acid. Chem.

com. 43·0 silica, 36·9 alumina, and 20·1 lime with 1 to 5 magnesia, 0·3 to 8 soda, 0·2 to 1 potash, and 0·1 to 2 iron peroxide. Monte Somma, Iceland, Java.

Amphodelite has the same composition and a close resemblance in crystalline forms, cleavage, and macles; is reddish-gray, or dirty peach-blossom red. Lojo in Finland, and Tunaberg in Sweden.

Latrobite, massive or in indistinct crystals of a red colour from Amitok in Labrador, and Bolton, Massachusetts, is a similar variety with the alumina partly replaced by manganese peroxide. *Lepolite* from Lojo is similar. *Bytownite* from Canada, a mixture of anorthite and hornblende.

*10. OLIGOCLASE.—2 $\ddot{\text{Al}}$ $\ddot{\text{Si}}^{\text{i}}$ + $(\dot{\text{Na}}, \dot{\text{Ca}})^{\text{s}}$ $\ddot{\text{Si}}^{\text{i}}$.

Triclinic; $0P : \infty\breve{P}\infty = 86° 10'$; $\infty P' : \infty'P = 120° 42'$. Crystals, rather rare, and macles resemble albite. Cleavage, basal perfect; brachydiagonal less perfect; $\infty P'$ imperfect. H. = 6; G. = 2·64...2·68. More or less translucent; vitreous, pearly or resinous on the cleavage. White, with a tinge of green, gray, or red. B.B. melts easier than orthoclase or albite to a clear glass; not affected by acids. Chem. com. 63 silica, 23·4 alumina, 8·4 soda, and 4·2 lime; but 20 to 24 alumina, 7 to 12 soda, 1 to 4 potash, 5 to 4 lime, 0 to 1 magnesia, and 0 to 4 iron peroxide. Thus nearly = 3 albite and 1 anorthite. Scandinavia, Ural, Harz, and North America. In granite near Aberdeen, and Rhiconich, Sutherlandshire. Distinguished from orthoclase by the marked striæ on the faces; less readily from albite, but more fusible, and G. higher. The *Sunstone* from Norway, Lake Baikal, and Ceylon, with a fine play of colour, belongs to this species.

11. PETALITE, Castor.—4 $\ddot{\text{Al}}$ $\ddot{\text{Si}}^{\text{i}}$ + 3 $(\dot{\text{Li}}, \dot{\text{Na}})$ $\ddot{\text{Si}}^{\text{i}}$.

Monoclinic, castor with C. = 67° 34′ and ∞P 87°, in irregular rectangular prisms, or petalite massive and coarse granular. Cleavage, basal distinct, in a second direction (meet at $141\frac{1}{2}°$) less so, and mere traces of a third. H. = 6·5; G. = 2·4...2·5. Greenish, grayish, or reddish white,

to pale red. Translucent; vitreous or pearly. B.B. melts
easily into an obscure porous glass, colouring the flame red;
not affected by acids. Chem. com. 78·3 silica, 17·4 alumina,
3·2 lithia, and 1·1 soda. Utoe, Bolton in Massachusetts,
York in Canada, and castor in Elba.

12. Spodumene, $\{$ 4 $\ddot{A}$l $\ddot{S}i^3$ + 3 ($\dot{L}i$, $\dot{N}a$, $\dot{K}$) $\ddot{S}i$, *or*
    Triphane. $\{$ [4 (Al² O³ . 3 Si O³)+3 (Li²O . Si O³)].
Monoclinic; C. = 69° 40′ ∞P = 87°; isomorphous with
augite (diopside). Cleavage, prismatic ∞P, and orthodiagonal perfect; chiefly massive or foliated. H. = 6·5...7;
G. 3·1...3·2. Translucent; vitreous or pearly. Pale
greenish-gray or white to apple-green; streak white. B.B.
intumesces slightly, tinging the flame momentarily purplish-
red, and fuses easily to a colourless glass; not affected by
acids. Chem. com. 65·0 silica, 28·7 alumina, and 6·3 lithia,
with 0·1 to 2·5 soda, 0 to 4·5 potash, and 0 to 1 lime.
Utoe in Sweden, Tyrol, Killiney near Dublin, Peterhead in
Scotland, and crystals at Norwich in Massachusetts.
Killinite.—Crystalline foliated. Cleavage along a prism
of 135°. H. = 4; G. = 2·65. Greenish-gray, yellow or
brownish-green. B.B. melts difficultly to a white porous
enamel. Chem. com. 2 $\ddot{A}$l $\ddot{S}i^3$ + $\dot{R}$ $\ddot{S}i^3$ + 3 $\dot{H}$, in which R
is potash, lime, magnesia, iron protoxide, and lithia. Killi-
ney near Dublin, with spodumene.

13. Pollux.—$\ddot{A}$l $\ddot{S}i^3$ + $\dot{R}$ $\ddot{S}i^3$ + $\dot{H}$.
Tesseral; faces of cube and icositetrahedron. Mostly
massive, with mere traces of cleavage; fracture conchoidal.
H. = 5·5...6·5; G. = 2·87...2·89. Transparent; splendent
vitreous. Colourless. B.B. melts on thin edges to an
enamel-like porous glass, colouring the flame reddish-yellow.
Soluble in warm h. acid. Chem. com. 44·03 silica, 15·97
alumina, 0·68 lime, 0·68 iron peroxide, 34·07 cæsium
oxide, 3·84 soda, and 2·40 water. Elba, with castor.

14. Zygadite.—$\ddot{S}i$, $\ddot{A}$l, $\dot{L}i$(?).
Triclinic, in macles like albite. H. = 5·5; G. = 2·51.

Subtranslucent; vitreous.   Reddish ·or yellowish white.
Andreasberg.   Probably a variety of albite, and no lithia.

15. AMORPHOUS FELSPAR.

Hyaline substances, with no regular structure, and
rather rocks than minerals.

**(a.) OBSIDIAN.—Compact in globular grains or masses.
Fracture conchoidal; brittle.   H. = 6...7 ; G. = 2·2...2·6.
Semitransparent to translucent on the edges; vitreous.
Black, gray, green, red, and brown, or striped and spotted.
B.B. melts to a foamy mass, a glass or enamel.   Chem.
com. indeterminate, but 70 to 80 silica, 6 to 12 alumina,
3 to 10 soda, 3 to 6 potash, 1 to 7 lime, 1 to 2 magnesia,
and 1 to 6 iron peroxide.   Streams or detached masses
near volcanoes, as Iceland, Lipari Islands, Milo, Santorin,
Teneriffe, Mexico, and Hungary.

**(b.) PUMICE.—Porous, vesicular, or fibrous.   Fracture
conchoidal or flat; very brittle.   White, gray, yellow, brown,
or black.   H. = 5 ; G. in powder = 2·19...2·2 ; in masses
swims on water.   B.B. melts more or less easily to a white
enamel.   Chem. com. like obsidian, of which it seems a
peculiar state.   Andernach on the Rhine, Lipari, and Ponza
Islands.   Used as a polishing material.

(c.) PEARLSTONE.—Roundish concentric globules imbedded in a vesicular basis.   Fracture conchoidal; very
brittle.   H. = 6 ; G. = 2.2...2·4.   Pearly.   Reddish, bluish,
or ash gray; also yellow, red, or brown in stripes or spots.
B.B. melts to a white fungus-like mass.   Chem. com.
indefinite, or a mixture of felspar and opal, with 2 to 4 per
cent water.   Hungary, Siberia, Mexico.   *Sphærulite*, small
spherical concretions in pearlstone in Hungary and Mexico,
and in pitchstone in Arran and Meissen.

*(d.) PITCHSTONE.—Compact, slaty, or in concentric
scaly concretions.   Fracture conchoidal; splintery.   H. =
5·5...6 ; G. = 2·2...2·3.   Subtranslucent to opaque; resinous.
Gray, green, yellow, red, brown, black.   B.B. melts to a
porous glass or gray enamel.   Chem. com. indefinite; but

64 to 76 silica, 11 to 14 alumina, 1 to 3 lime, 1 to 6 soda, 0 to 6 potash, 0 to 7 magnesia, 1 to 4 iron peroxide, and 5 to 9 water. Beds or veins at Tokai, Kremnitz, Schemnitz in Hungary, Meissen, Saxony, Newry in Ireland, and Arran in Scotland. The basis of that from Arran is, according to Zirkel, a nearly colourless glass containing crystals of quartz, felspar, and hornblende.

FAMILY III.—SCAPOLITE.

Crystallisation tetragonal or hexagonal (prehnite rhombic). Cleavage more or less perfect. H. = 5...6, or a little more in prehnite; G. 2·6...3. All fusible and soluble in acids, and gelatinise. Chem. com. anhydrous silicates of alkalies or lime, and of alumina. They are generally transparent or translucent. Colourless, but often with green or yellow tinge and resinous lustre. They resemble the felspars both in aspect and composition, and occur chiefly in volcanic or in plutonic rocks, but are rather rare.

*16. SCAPOLITE, $\{$ $\ddot{Al}^2 \ddot{Si}^3 + 3 (\dot{C}a, \dot{N}a) \ddot{Si}$, *or*
    Wernerite. $\{$ $[2 Al^2 O^3 . 3 Si O^2 + 3 (RO . Si O^2)]$.
Tetragonal; P 63^b 42'. Crystals $\infty P \infty$. P . ∞P, often long prismatic; also massive and granular or columnar. Cleavage, $\infty P \infty$ rather perfect, ∞P less perfect. H. = 5...5·5 ; G. = 2·6...2·8. Transparent or translucent ; vitreous, pearly, or resinous. Colourless, but pale gray, green, yellow, or red. B.B. melts with effervescence to a vesicular glass ; in the closed tube many show traces of fluorine ; with solution of cobalt become blue ; soluble in h. acid. Chem. com. about 49 silica, 28 alumina (with iron peroxide) and 23 lime (with soda) ; but analyses vary widely, and some come nearer 43 sil., 37 al., and 20 lime ; others 42 sil., 32 al., and 26 lime. The silica ranges from 40 to 60, alumina 16 to 36, iron peroxide 1 to 8, lime 3 to 24, soda to 9 and potash to 7 per cent. Arendal, Tunaberg, Pargas, Bolton in Massachusetts, and Governeur in New York. Easily known by its indistinct rectangular cleavage, the resinous lustre on fracture surfaces, and its action before blowpipe.

Meionite and *Mizzonite* from Somma; *Nuttalite* from Bolton; *Glaucolite* from near Lake Baikal; *Strogonowite* from the Slüdänka; *Ersbyite* from Pargas; and *Couzeranite* from Couzeran in the Pyrenees, pitch black, blackish-blue, or gray, are only varieties. So also the *Porcelain Spar* or *Passauite* from near Passau, which forms porcelain earth when decomposed.

Barsowite.—Granular or compact, with one distinct cleavage. Translucent on the edges; pearly. Snow-white. Gelatinises in warm h. acid, and dif. fusible. Barsowski, in Ural, is similar.

17. DIPYR.—$3 \ddot{\textrm{Al}} \ddot{\textrm{Si}} + 4 (\dot{\textrm{Ca}}, \dot{\textrm{Na}}) \ddot{\textrm{Si}}^{\textrm{s}}$.
Tetragonal; P 64° 4′ in rounded eight-sided prisms. Cleavage, prismatic distinct. H. = 6; G. = 2.6...2.7. Translucent on the edges; vitreous, whitish or reddish. B.B. becomes opaque, and melts readily to a white vesicular glass. Slightly affected by acids. Chem. com. 55.7 silica, 25.1 alumina, 9.1 lime, and 10.1 soda. Mauléon, and Castillon in the Pyrenees.

*18. NEPHELINE, $\left\{ \begin{array}{l} \ddot{\textrm{Al}} \ddot{\textrm{Si}} + 4 (\dot{\textrm{Na}}, \dot{\textrm{K}}) \ddot{\textrm{Si}}, \textit{ or} \\ [\textrm{Al}^{\textrm{s}} \textrm{O}^{\textrm{s}} . 2 \textrm{ Si O}^{\textrm{s}} + \textrm{RO . Si O}^{\textrm{s}}] . \end{array} \right.$
Elæolite.

Hexagonal; P 88° 10′. Crystals, ∞P . 0P, and ∞P. 0P. P (*M, P, z,* Fig. 108); embedded, or in druses; also massive granular. Cleavage, basal and prismatic imperfect. Fracture conchoidal or uneven. H. = 5.5...6; G. = 2.58...2.64. Transparent or translucent; vitreous and resinous on fracture. Colourless or white (nepheline); or more opaque, dull resinous, and green, red, or brown (elæolite). B.B. melts difficultly (nepheline), or easily with slight effervescence (elæolite), into a vesicular glass. Soluble and gelatinises in h. acid. Chem. com. 41.2 silica, 35.3 alumina, 17 soda, 6.5 potash, with 0.2 to 2 lime, 0.5 to 1.5 iron peroxide,

Fig. 108.

and under 2 water. Nepheline at Monte Somma, Capo di Bove, Katzenbuckel in the Odenwald, Aussig, and the Lausitz. Elæolite in the zircon syenite at Laurvig, Fredriksvärn, Brevig, and Miask.

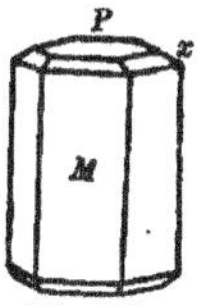

Davine, long prismatic, $\frac{1}{2}$ P 51° 46′. G. = 2.43. Seems only nepheline, with about 13 carbonate of lime. Vesuvius and Somma.

19. CANCRINITE.—2 $(\ddot{Al}\ \ddot{Si} + \dot{Na}\ \ddot{Si}) + \dot{Ca}\ \ddot{C}$.

Hexagonal ; massive and columnar. Cleavage, prismatic perfect. H. = 5...5·5 ; G. = 2·42...2·46. Translucent or transparent ; resinous, on cleavage vitreous or pearly. Green, yellow, and rose-red. B.B. melts to a white vesicular glass. Soluble with effervescence in h. acid. Chem. com. 2 atoms nepheline and 1 carbonate of lime, with about 36 silica, 30 alumina, 18 soda, and 15 carbonate of lime. Miask, and Litchfield in Maine.

20. GEHLENITE.—$(\ddot{Al}, \ddot{Fe})\ \ddot{Si} + (\dot{Ca}, \dot{Mg}, \dot{Fe})^3\ \ddot{Si}$.

Tetragonal ; P 59°. Crystals, 0P. ∞P∞, thick tabular or short prismatic. Cleavage, basal rather perfect, prismatic traces. H. = 5.5...6 ; G, = 2·9...3·1. Translucent on the edges ; dull resinous. Mountain, leek, or olive green, to liver-brown. B.B. melts difficultly in thin fragments. Gelatinises with h. acid. Chem. com. 31·4 silica, 20 to 24 alumina, 3 to 6 iron peroxide, 35 to 38 lime, 0 to 4 magnesia, 0 to 1·7 iron protoxide, and 1 to 3 water. Mount Monzoni in the Fassa valley.

21. HUMBOLDTILITE.—$(\ddot{Al}, \ddot{Fe})\ \ddot{Si}+2\ (\dot{Ca}, \dot{Mg}, \dot{Na}, \dot{K})\ \ddot{Si}^2$.

Tetragonal ; P 65° 30′ ; 0P. ∞P∞, tabular or short prismatic. Cleavage, basal perfect. H. = 5...5·5 ; G.= 2·91...2·95. Translucent on the edges ; vitreous or resinous. Yellowish-white, honey-yellow, and yellowish-brown. B.B. melts easily to a light or blackish coloured glass. Gelatinises with h. acid. Chem. com. about 40 silica, 32 lime, 6 to 7 magnesia, 2 to 4 soda, 0·3 to 1·5 potash, 6 to 11 alumina, and 4 to 10 iron peroxide. Vesuvius and Capo di Bove. *Melilite, Somervillite,* and *Zurlite* are identical. *Sarkolite,* from Vesuvius, is similar.

*22. PREHNITE, $\{\ddot{Al}\ \ddot{Si} + 2\ \dot{Ca}\ \ddot{Si} + \dot{H},\ or$
Koupholite. $\{[Al^2O^3 . SiO^2 + 2 (CaO . SiO^2) + H^2O]$.

Rhombic ; ∞P 99° 56′, 3P̄ ∞33° 0′, ⅔P̄∞ 126° 40′. Crystals 0P . ∞P (Fig. 109), or ∞P (*m*) . 0P (*P*) . ∞P̆∞ (*l*) .

$3\breve{P}\infty$ (*o*) (Fig. 110), tabular or short prismatic, in druses, fan-shaped or cock's-comb groups. Also granular or spherical, reniform and fibrous. Cleavage, basal distinct, ∞P imperfect. H. = 6...7 ; G. = 2·8...3·0. Transparent or

Fig. 109.

translucent on the edges ; vitreous, on 0P pearly. Col ourless, but mostly greenish-white, olive, apple, or leek green, also yellow or reddish. When heated becomes polar-electric. B.B. melts easily, with much intumescence, to a porous enamel. Soluble in con. h. acid, but only gelatinises perfectly when pre- viously ignited or fused. Chem. com. 43·6 silica, 24·9 alumina, 27·1 lime, and 4·4 water (but with 0·1 to 7 peroxide of iron and manganese). Cape of Good Hope ; Bourg d'Oisans in Dauphiné : Ratschinges and Fassa in Tyrol ; Friskie Hall and Campsie, Dumbartonshire ; Hartfield Moss,

Fig. 110.

Renfrewshire ; Corstorphine Hill, the Castle Rock, and Salisbury Craigs, near Edinburgh ; Mull ; Skye ; and Dal- nabo, near Glengairn, Aberdeenshire.

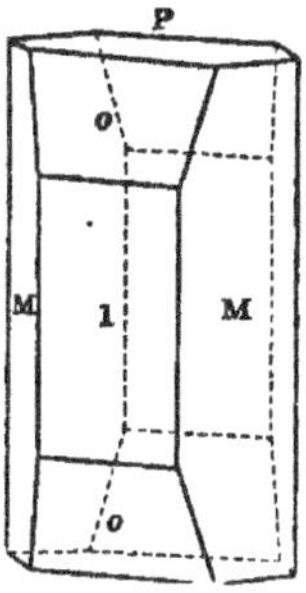

Prehnitoid, like prehnite, but scarce affected by h. acid. Wexio in Sweden.

23. KARPHOLITE.—$\ddot{A}l\ \ddot{S}i + Mn\ \ddot{S}i + 2\ \dot{H}$.

Rhombic ; radiating or stellated and acicular. H = 5...5·5 ; G. = 2·9...3. Translucent ; silky. Straw to wax yellow. B.B. intumesces and forms an opaque brown glass. Scarcely affected by acids. Chem. com. 37 silica, 30·6 alumina, 21·6 manganese protoxide, 10·8 water, with iron protoxide and fluoric acid. Schlaggenwald and Wippra in the Harz.

24. The following are doubtful :—

(*a.*) *Kirwanite.*—Spheroidal ; radiating fibrous. H. = 2 ; G. = 2·9. Opaque ; dark olive-green. B.B. becomes black, and partially fuses. Chem. com. 40·5 silica, 11·14 alumina, 23·9 iron protoxide, 19·8 lime, and 4·4 water. Mourne Mountains, Ireland.

Neurolite. — Fine columnar.   H. = 4·5 ; G. = 2·47.
Translucent or opaque.   Greenish-yellow.   B.B. infusible,
but becomes snow-white and pulverulent.   Chem. com. 73
silica, 17·4 alumina, 3·3 lime, 1·5 magnesia, and 4·3 water.
Stamstead in Lower Canada.

FAMILY IV.—HALOID STONES.

These minerals are so named from their resemblance to
salts.   Their crystallisation is rhombic or monoclinic.
H. = 4...6 ; G. = 2·3...3·1.   Soluble in acids.   Generally
infusible, or with difficulty.   Most colour the B.B. flame
bluish-green from phosphoric acid, being compounds of this
acid with alumina, in some also with magnesia or iron protoxide.   Are brightly-coloured minerals, of blue, green, or
yellow tints.   Most contain water, and do not form constituents of rocks.

25. LAZULITE, Blue Spar.—$\ddot{Al}^2\, \overset{..}{\ddot{P}} + (Mg, \dot{Fe})^2\, \overset{..}{\ddot{P}} + 2\,\dot{H}.$
Monoclinic ; C. = 88° 2′, ∞P 91° 30′, P 99° 40′,—P 100°
20′ ; crystals pyramidal, tabular or prismatic, but rare ;
usually massive or granular.   Cleavage, prismatic, ∞P imperfect ; fracture uneven, splintery.   H. = 5...6 ; G. = 3...3·1.
Translucent on the edges ; vitreous.   Indigo, smalt, or
other shades of blue inclining to green or white ; streak
white.   In closed tube yields water and loses its colour.
B.B. intumesces, but does not melt.   With cobalt solution
assumes a fine blue colour.   Scarcely affected by acids till
after ignition, when almost wholly soluble.   Chem. com.
44·1 phosphoric acid, 31·7 alumina, 9 to 12 magnesia,
2 to 10 iron protoxide, 1 to 4 lime, and 5·7 water.   Werfen
in Salzburg, Vorau (*Voraulite*) and Kreiglach in Styria,
Brazil, Georgia, and North Carolina.

*26. CALAITE, Turquoise.—$\ddot{Al}^2\, \overset{..}{\ddot{P}} + 5\,\dot{H}.$
Massive, reniform, or stalactitic.   Fracture conchoidal.
H. = 6 ; G. = 2·6...2·8.   Opaque or translucent on the
edges ; dull or waxy.   Skye-blue, greenish-blue, rarely
green ; streak greenish-white.   In the closed tube yields
water, decrepitates violently, and becomes black.   B.B. in-

fusible, but colours the flame green.   Soluble in acids.
Chem. com. 47 alumina, 32·5 phosphoric acid, and 20·5
water, but mixed with phosphate of iron and copper.
Silesia, Lausitz, and Voigtland.   Oriental turquoise, in
veins, at Meschid near Herat ; in pebbles in Khorazan,
Bucharia, and Syrian desert.   Takes a fine polish, and is
valued as an ornamental stone.   *Variscite* seems identical.

27. FISCHERITE.—$\ddot{A}l\ \ddot{P} + 8\ \dot{H}$.
Rhombic ; $\infty P\ 118°\ 32'$, mostly in crusts or indistinct
six-sided prisms. H. = 5 ; G. = 2·46. Transparent ; vitreous ;
green.   Slightly soluble in h. or n., wholly in s. acid, and on
heating becomes white or partly black.   Chem. com. 42
alumina, 29 phosphoric acid, 29 water, with a little lime
and copper oxide.   Nischnei Tagilsk.
Peganite.—Probably rhombic; $\infty P\ 127°$ nearly ; in very
small prismatic crystals or thin crusts.   Emerald, grass-
green, or white.   H. = 3...4 ; G. = 2·49...2·54. Chem. com.
like fischerite, but 6 $\dot{H}$.   Strigis in Saxony.   *Berlinite*
and *Trolleite* from Westana, and *Evansite*, colourless or
bluish-white, from Hungary, are other phosphates of alumina
with water.

*28. WAVELLITE, $\begin{cases} \ddot{A}l^3\ \ddot{P}^2 + 12\ \dot{H}, \text{ or} \\ [3\ Al^2\ O^3 . 2\ P^2O^5 + 12\ H^2O]. \end{cases}$
      Lasionite.
Rhombic; $\infty P\ 126°\ 25'$, $\bar{P}\infty\ 106°\ 46'$; crystals $\infty P\infty$
$(P) . \infty P\ (d) . \bar{P}\infty\ (o)$ (Fig. 111) ; but generally small, acicular, and in hemispherical radiated fibrous masses.   Cleavage,
along ∞P and $\bar{P}\infty$ rather perfect.   H. = 3·5...4 ; G. = 2·3...
2·5.   Translucent ; vitreous.   Colourless, but generally
yellowish or grayish, sometimes green or blue.   In
closed tube yields water.   B.B. in the forceps
colours the flame weak bluish-green ; on charcoal intumesces, and becomes snow-white. Soluble
in acids.   Chem. com. 38·0 alumina, 35·3 phosphoric acid, and 26·7 water ; but generally traces
of fluoric acid (2 per cent).   Beraun in Bohemia, Amberg
in Bavaria, Barnstaple in Devonshire, St. Austle in Cornwall, near Clonmel, Cork, and Portrush, Ireland, and in

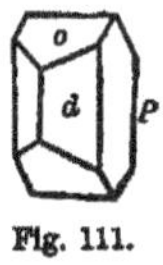

Fig. 111.

the Shiant Isles in Scotland ; also in New Hampshire and Tennessee.

29. WAGNERITE.—$\dot{M}g^3\overset{...}{P} + Mg\,F.$

Monoclinic ; C. = 63° 25′, ∞P 57° 35′. Cleavage, prismatic and orthodiagonal imperfect. Fracture conchoidal or splintery. H. = 5...5·5 ; G. = 3·0...3·2. Translucent or transparent ; resinous. Wine or honey yellow and white. B.B. fuses with great difficulty in thin splinters to a dark greenish-gray glass. Chem. com. 43·3 phosphoric acid, 11·4 fluorine, 37·6 magnesia, and 7·7 magnesium ; but with 3 to 4·5 iron protoxide, and 1 to 4 lime. Very rare ; Werfen in Salzburg.

30. AMBLYGONITE. — $\overset{...}{A}l^5\overset{...}{P}^3 + (\dot{L}i,\,\dot{N}a)^5\,\overset{...}{P}^3 + \pm l\,F^3$ + (Li, Na) F.

Triclinic ; crystals very rare, most coarse granular. Cleavage 0P pearly, meeting two others at 105° and 87° 40′. Fracture uneven and splintery. H. = 6 ; G. = 3...3·1. Translucent ; vitreous. Grayish or greenish-white to pale mountain-green. In closed tube yields water, sometimes corroding the glass. B.B. fuses very readily to a transparent glass, opaque when cold. Finely pulverised it is slowly soluble in acids. Chem. com. 47·9 phosphoric acid, 34·5 alumina, 6·9 lithia, 6 soda, and 8·3 fluorine. Penig, Arendal, Montebras, also Hebron and Paris in Maine. *Montebrasite*, with no soda, is perhaps distinct.

FAMILY V.—LEUCITE.

Tesseral ; H. = 5...6 ; G. = 2·2...2·5. All fusible, except leucite, and all soluble and mostly gelatinise in hydrochloric acid. They are silicates of alumina and of alkalies (or lime), often with chlorine, sulphur, or sulphuric acid. Their colours are white, gray, or often blue. Generally occur imbedded in volcanic rocks.

**31. LEUCITE.— $\begin{cases} \overset{...}{A}l\,\overset{..}{S}i^3 + \dot{K}\,\overset{..}{S}i,\ or \\ [Al^2O^3 \,.\, 3\,SiO^2 + K^2O \,.\, SiO^2]. \end{cases}$

Tesseral ; only 2O2 (Fig. 6). The crystals generally single. Cleavage, hexahedral very imperfect. Fracture

conchoidal. H. = 5·5...6 ; G. = 2·4...2·5. Transparent to
translucent on the edges ; vitreous, inclining to resinous.
Colourless, but grayish, yellowish, or reddish-white or gray ;
streak white. B.B. infusible ; with cobalt solution becomes
blue. Soluble in h. acid, without gelatinising. Chem.
com. 54·9 silica, 23·6 alumina, and 21·5 potash. Abundant in
the lavas of Vesuvius, the tufas near Rome, and the peperino
of Albano ; also at the Kaiserstuhl, and near Lake Laach.
Readily distinguished from analcime, by its infusibility
and by never showing faces of the cube.

32. SODALITE.—3 ($\dot{A}$l $\ddot{S}$i + $\dot{N}$a $\ddot{S}$i) + Na Cl.
Tesseral ; ∞O (Fig. 3) ; massive and granular. Cleav-
age, ∞O more or less perfect. Fracture conchoidal or
uneven. H. = 5·5 ; G. = 2·13...2·29. Translucent ; vitreous,
inclining to resinous. White, gray, and rarely green or
blue. B.B. becomes white and fuses easily alone, sometimes
intumescing to a clear glass ; with difficulty in borax. Gelatinises with acids. Chem. com. 37 silica, 31·8 alumina,
19·2 soda, 4·7 sodium, and 7·3 chlorine, but in the green
sodalite from Vesuvius only 2·55 chlorine. Greenland,
Vesuvius, Ilmen Hills, Brevig and Fredriksvärn in Norway,
and Litchfield in Maine.

*33. HAUYNE.—2 ($\dot{A}$l $\ddot{S}$i + $\dot{N}$a $\ddot{S}$i) + $\dot{C}$a $\ddot{S}$.
Tesseral ; chiefly ∞O, but more common in grains.
Cleavage ∞O more or less perfect. H.=5...5·5 ; G.=2·4...2·5.
Semi-transparent or translucent ; vitreous or resinous.
Azure or skye-blue ; streak bluish-white. B.B. decrepi-
tates violently, and melts to a bluish-green vesicular glass.
Soluble and gelatinises in h. acid. Chem. com. 34·2 silica,
28·5 alumina, 11·5 soda, 4·3 potash, 10·4 lime, and 11·1
sulphuric acid. Vesuvius, Mount Vultur near Melfi, the
Campagna of Rome, and Niedermendig near Andernach.

34. NOSEAN.—3 ($\dot{A}$l $\ddot{S}$i + $\dot{N}$a $\ddot{S}$i) + $\dot{N}$a $\ddot{S}$.
Tesseral, like hauyne, but oftener granular. H. = 5·5 ;
G. = 2·28...2·40. Translucent ; vitreous to resinous. Ash
or yellowish gray, sometimes blue, brown or black. B.B.
becomes paler, and melts on the edges to a vesicular glass.

Soluble in acids. Chem. com. 36 silica, 31 alumina, 25 soda, and 8 sulphuric acid; but with 1 to 1·5 lime and 0·6 chlorine. Lake Laach and Rieden, near Andernach, on the Rhine. Zirkel says occurs in all phonolites in microscopic crystals. *Skolopsite,* granular, smoke-gray and reddish-white; G. = 2·53; is very similar. Kaiserstuhl.

35. ITTNERITE.—$\ddot{A}l$ $\ddot{S}i$ + $(\dot{N}a, \dot{C}a)$ $\ddot{S}i$ + 2 $\dot{H}$.

Tesseral, but only coarse granular. Cleavage, dode-cahedral distinct; fracture imperfect conchoidal. H. = 5·5; G. = 2·37...2·40. Translucent; resinous. Smoke, ash, or dark bluish-gray. In the closed tube yields much water. B.B. fuses, with much effervescence and sulphur-eous smell, to a vesicular opaque glass. Soluble, and gelatinises in con. h. acid. Chem. com. by Whitney's analysis, 35·69 silica, 29·14 alumina, 5·64 lime, 12·57 soda, 1·20 potash, 4·62 sulphuric acid, 1·25 chlorine, 9·83 water and loss. Kaiserstuhl near Freiburg. Probably altered nosean.

*36. LAPIS-LAZULI, Lasurstein.

Tesseral; ∞O, but rarely distinct; generally massive and fine granular. Imperfect dodecahedral cleavage. H. = 5·5; G. = 2·38...2·42. Translucent on the edges; dull resinous or vitreous. Ultramarine or azure blue; streak light blue. B.B. fuses readily to a white porous glass. In h. acid the powder is dissolved and gelatinises, evolving sul-phuretted hydrogen. Chem. com. by Varrentrapp's ana-lysis, 45·50 silica, 5·89 sulphuric acid, 31·76 alumina, 9·09 soda, 3·52 lime, 0·86 iron, 0·42 chlorine, 0·95 sulphur, 0·12 water. Near Lake Baikal, China, Thibet, and Tartary, also in Monte Somma and Chili. It is used for ornamental purposes, and the preparation of ultramarine-blue. The colour both in it and the hauyne seems caused by some compound of sulphur, probably with soda. A mode of pre-paring the artificial colour was discovered by Chr. Gmelin.

37. EUDIALITE.—6 $\dot{R}$ $\ddot{S}i^2$ + $\dot{R}$ $\ddot{Z}r$.

Hexagonal-rhombohedral. R 73° 30'; also massive and granular. Cleavage, basal distinct. H. = 5...5·5;

G. = 2·84...3·0. Semitranslucent or opaque ; vitreous. Peach-blossom to brownish-red ; streak white. B.B. fuses easily to a light green opaque glass. Gelatinises in h. acid. Chem. com. about 50 silica, 16·5 zirconia, and $\dot{R} = 13$ soda, 11 lime, 8·5 protoxide of iron with manganese, and 1·4 chlorine. Greenland ; Brevig ; and Magnet Cove in Arkansas.

**FAMILY VI.—ZEOLITE.

Crystallisation chiefly rhombic and monoclinic ; also hexagonal, tetragonal, and tesseral. H. = 3·5...6, or mostly scratched by steel ; G. = 2·0...3·0. Mostly hyaline and white ; rarely red, gray, or yellow coloured. Cleavage generally distinct. All yield water in closed tube ; all fusible B.B., mostly easily and often intumescing ; all soluble in acids, and mostly gelatinise or deposit silica. They are hydrated silicates of alkalies, or alkaline earths, mostly with silicates of alumina, but rarely contain magnesia. Some mineralogists regard the water as basic, in union with silica, and Kenngott gives the formula in that form, thus—

Analcime = $[(Na^2O \cdot Al^2O^3) \ 2 \ SiO^2 + 2 \ (H^2O \cdot SiO^2)]$.
Natrolite = $[(Na^2O \cdot Al^2O^3) \ 2 \ SiO^2 + 2 \ H^2O \cdot SiO^3]$.
Stilbite = $[CaO \cdot Al^2O^3 + 6 \ (H^2O \cdot SiO^2)]$.

and the others similar. They are generally found in amygdaloidal cavities or fissures of trap or plutonic rocks, apparently as deposits from water percolating through them, and thus probably products of decomposing felspars. Never form constituents of rocks. Natrolite, Scolezite, Thomsonite, and the connected varieties, are marked by their needle-like radiating forms ; Stilbite and Heulandite by their broad foliated, pearly cleavage.

**38. ANALCIME.— $\begin{cases} \ddot{A}l \ \dot{S}i^2 + \dot{N}a \ \dot{S}i + 2 \ \dot{H}, \ or \\ [Al^2O^3 . 3 \ SiO^2 + Na^2O . SiO^2 + 2 \ H^2O]. \end{cases}$

Tesseral ; crystals 2O2, seldomer ∞O∞ . 2O2 (Fig. 112), in druses ; also granular. Cleavage hexahedral, very imperfect ; fracture uneven. H. = 5·5 ; G. = 2·1...2·25.

Transparent to translucent on the edges; vitreous. White, grayish, greenish, yellowish, or reddish white; also flesh-

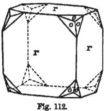

Fig. 112.

red, and very rarely leek-green. B.B. melts quietly to a clear vesicular glass. Completely soluble and gelatinises in h. acid. Chem. com. 54·4 silica, 23·4 alumina, 14·1 soda, and 8·1 water, with occasionally a little potash or lime. Seisser Alp in Tyrol, and in Siebenburg; Cyclopean Islands, Sicily; the Vicentine, Norway, Faroe, Iceland, Nova Scotia; also Giant's Causeway; and Glenfarg, Salisbury Crags, Dumbarton, Hebrides, and other parts of Scotland. *Cuboit*, and the *Cluthalite*, are varieties.

*39. NATROLITE, { Äl S̈i² + N̈a S̈i + 2 Ḧ, *or*
Mesotype. { [Al²O³ . 2 SiO³+Na²O . SiO³+2 H²O].
Rhombic; ∞P 91°, P polar edges 143° 20′, and 142° 40′, middle edge 53° 20′; crystals, ∞P.P (Fig. 113), fine prismatic, acicular or fibrous, and radiating. Cleavage, ∞P perfect. H. = 5...5·5; G. = 2·17...2·26. Pellucid; vitreous. Colourless or grayish-white, but some yellow, seldom red or brown. Is *not* pyroelectric. B.B. becomes obscure and melts quietly to a clear glass colouring the flame yellow. Gelatinises in h. acid. Chem. com. 47·2 silica, 27 alumina, 16·3 soda, and 9·5 water, with a little lime and iron oxides. Clermont in Auvergne, Alpstein in Hessia, Hohentwiel in Swabia, Norway; in Scotland, as in Mull, Canna, and near Tantallon Castle; in Ireland at Glenarm and Portrush; also in Nova Scotia, and other countries. *Bergmannite*, *Radiolite*, and *Lehuntite*, are varieties; also *Galactite*, H. = 4·5, with 4 lime and 10·5 water. Glenfarg, Kilpatrick, and Bishopstown.

Fig. 118.

**40. SCOLEZITE, Needlestone, Äl S̈i² + C̈a S̈i + 3 Ḧ.
Monoclinic; C. = 89° 6′, ∞P 91° 35′, P 144° 20′; crystals, ∞P . P . – P, prismatic or acicular. Twin crystals very common, united by a face of ∞P°∞, and one

face with feathery striæ (Fig. 114); also massive and radiating. Cleavage, ∞P rather perfect. H. = 5...5·5; G. =
2·2...2·3. Pellucid; vitreous, fibrous varieties silky.
Snow-white, grayish, yellowish, and reddish white.
Distinctly pyro-electric. B.B. bends and twists
in a vermicular manner, and melts easily to a
porous glass. In h. acid gelatinises; also soluble
in oxalic acid, leaving oxalate of lime. Chem.
com. 45·8 silica, 26·2 alumina, 14·3 lime, and 13·7
water. Very fine on Staffa, also Mull and Skye; at
Berufiord in Iceland; in Faroe, in Tyrol, Auvergne, and
India.

Fig. 114.

The following are either varieties of, or closely allied to,
Scolezite or Natrolite :—

Mesolite, with 4 to 6 soda and 10 to 14 water; Storr and
Talisker, Skye; Kinross; Edinburgh; Giant's Causeway, and
Iceland, is perhaps a mixture of natrolite and scolezite.
Harringtonite, compact, earthy, snow-white; Portrush in
Ireland. *Antrimolite*, white, fibrous, and opaque. G. =
2·096; H. = 3·75. Antrim. *Poonahlite*, rhombic prisms
of 92° 20′, otherwise like scolezite, from Poonah in Hindostan. *Brevicite*, radiated, massive, white, reddish-gray, or
dark red ; Brevig. *Mesole* or *Faröelite*, radiating, fibrous;
transparent, pearly; white, yellow, or gray. H. = 3·5. G.
= 2·35. B.B. fuses with effervescence to a frothy enamel.
Chem. com. 41·3 silica, 28·4 alumina, 11·5 lime, 5·7 soda,
and 13·2 water. Faroe, Schonen; Storr, Uig, and Portree
in Skye. The last is perhaps a distinct species.

**41. THOMSONITE, } 2 $(\ddot{A}l \ \ddot{S}i + (\ddot{C}a, \ \dot{N}a) \ \ddot{S}i) + 5 \ \dot{H}$, *or*
　　Comptonite. 　} $[R \ Al^2 \ Si^2 \ O^8 + 5 \ aq.]$—*Rams.*

Rhombic ; ∞P 90° 40′, usually ∞P∞ ∞P̄∞ P∞
or *M, T, s* (Fig. 115), terminating in an extremely
obtuse dome *x*P∞ (*i*) of 177° 23′, like the basis
with the plane broken. In druses, fan-shaped
or radiated. Cleavage, macrodiagonal and brachydiagonal equally perfect. H. = 5...5·5 ; G. = 2·3
...2·4. Translucent, but often obscure ; vitreous, some-

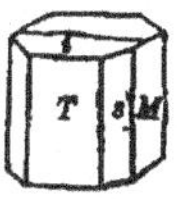

Fig. 115.

K

times pearly. White. B.B. intumesces, becomes opaque, and fuses with difficulty to a white enamel. Soluble and gelatinises in h. acid. Chem. com. 37·1 silica, 31·7 alumina, 17·3 lime but with 3 to 7 soda, and 13·9 water. Vesuvius, Sicily, Bohemia, Tyrol, Iceland, Faroe, Scotland (Lochwinnoch, Kilkpatrick Hills, St. Cyrus in Kincardineshire), and Nova Scotia. *Chalilite* and · *Scoulerite* are varieties, Antrim.

**42. STILBITE, $\{$ $\ddot{A}l \ \ddot{S}i^3 + \dot{C}a \ \ddot{S}i^3 + 6 \ \dot{H}$, *or*
   Desmine. $\{$ $[Al^2 O^3 3 Si O^3 + Ca O . 3 Si O^3 + 6 H^2 O]$.
   Rhombic; P polar edges, 119° 16', and 114°; crystals, $\infty \bar{P} \infty$ (*M*) . $\infty \bar{P} \infty$ (*T*) . P (*r*) . 0P (*P*) (Fig. 116), broad pyramidal, very often fascicular or diverging; also radiat-

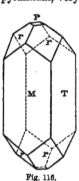

Fig. 116.

ing or broad columnar, or macled. Cleavage, brachydiagonal T very perfect. H. = 3·5...4; G. = 2·1...2·2. Translucent, or only on the edges; vitreous; pearly on *T*. White, red, gray, yellow, and brown. B.B. intumesces greatly, and melts to a white porous enamel. Decomposed by c. h. acid, leaving slimy silica. Chem. com. 57·5 silica, 16·4 alumina, 8·9 lime with 1 to 3 soda or potash, and 17·2 water. Andreasberg in the Harz, Kongsberg and Arendal, Iceland, Faroe, and the Vendayah mountains in Hindostan; Scotland, Talisker and Storr in Skye, Kilpatrick, Kilmalcolm, and Arran. *Sphærostilbite* and *Hypostilbite* are related species. *Ædelforsite*; fibrous or columnar; H. = 6; G. = 2·6; is a stilbite with two atoms less water, or a laumonite mixed with quartz. Ædelfors in Sweden.

**43. HEULANDITE.—$\ddot{A}l \ \ddot{S}i^3 + \dot{C}a \ \ddot{S}i^3 + 5 \ \dot{H}$.
   Monoclinic; C. = 63° 40', P∘∞ 50° 20'; crystals $\infty P^∘ \infty$. $\infty P^∘ \infty$. $P^∘ \infty$. 0P. 2P (*M, N, P, T, z*) (Fig. 117); mostly tabular, rarely prismatic; in druses or radiated lamellar. Cleavage, clinodiagonal very perfect; brittle.

H. = 3·5...4 ; G. = 2·1...2·2. Transparent to translucent on the edges ; vitreous or pearly. White, but often flesh or brick red, and yellowish or hair brown.   B.B. exfoliates, intumesces, and melts to a white enamel.   Soluble in h. acid, leaving slimy silica. Chem. com. 59·1 silica, 16·9 alumina, 9·2 lime, and 14·8 water.   Arendal, Kongsberg, Andreasberg, Fassa Valley, Iceland, Faroe, Nova Scotia, New Jersey, and the Vendayah Mountains, Hindostan ; at Campsie, in Skye,   Fig. 117. and other parts of Scotland. *Beaumontite* is the same ; Baltimore.

44. BREWSTERITE.—$\ddot{A}$l $\dot{S}$i³ + ($\frac{2}{3}$ $\dot{S}$r + $\frac{1}{3}$ $\dot{B}$a) $\dot{S}$i² + 5 $\dot{H}$.
Monoclinic ; C. = 86° 20' ; crystals short prismatic, of several vertical prisms, bounded by an extremely obtuse clinodome (172°) (Fig. 118), are mostly small. Cleavage, clinodiagonal very perfect. H. = 5...5·5 ; G. = 2·12...2·2 (or 2·4).   Pellucid ; vitreous or pearly.   White, gray, yellow, brown, or green.   B.B. froths, intumesces, and fuses   Fig. 118. to a porous glass. Soluble in h. acid, and gelatinises. Chem. com. 54·3 silica, 15·0 alumina, 10·1 strontia, 7·4 baryta with 1·3 lime, and 13·1 water ; and thus with all the three alkaline earths.   Strontian in Scotland, Giant's Causeway, Freiburg in the Bresgau, and the Pyrenees.

45. EPISTILBITE.—$\ddot{A}$l $\dot{S}$i³ + $\dot{C}$a $\dot{S}$i³ + 5 $\dot{H}$.
Rhombic ; ∞P (*M*) 135° 10', $\bar{P}$∞ (*t*) 109° 46', $\bar{P}$∞ (*s*) 147° 40' ; in long prismatic crystals (Fig. 119).   Macles united by a face of ∞P ; also massive and granular. Cleavage, brachydiagonal very perfect. H. = 3·5 ...4 ; G. = 2·3...2·4.   Pellucid ; vitreous or pearly. Colourless or white.   B.B. melts with intumescence to a porous enamel. Soluble without gelatinising, but after ignition is insoluble. Chem. com. 59 silica, 17·5 alumina, 9 lime, with   Fig. 119. 1·5 soda, and 14·5 water, or like heulandite.   Iceland and Faroe ; also in Skye and Nova Scotia.

46. APOPHYLLITE.— $\begin{cases} 8 \ (\dot{C}a \ \ddot{S}i^2 + 2 \ \dot{H}) + KF, \ or \\ [4 \ (Ca \ O.2 \ Si \ O^3 + 2 \ H^2 \ O) + KF]. \end{cases}$

Tetragonal; P about 120° 30′, but 1° less or more; crystals P. ∞P∞ (P, *m*) (Fig. 120) and 0P, are pyramidal, or

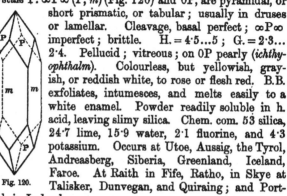

short prismatic, or tabular; usually in druses or lamellar. Cleavage, basal perfect; ∞P∞ imperfect; brittle. H. = 4·5...5; G. = 2·3... 2·4. Pellucid; vitreous; on 0P pearly (*ichthyophthalm*). Colourless, but yellowish, grayish, or reddish white, to rose or flesh red. B.B. exfoliates, intumesces, and melts easily to a white enamel. Powder readily soluble in h. acid, leaving slimy silica. Chem. com. 53 silica, 24·7 lime, 15·9 water, 2·1 fluorine, and 4·3 potassium. Occurs at Utoe, Aussig, the Tyrol, Andreasberg, Siberia, Greenland, Iceland, Faroe. At Raith in Fife, Ratho, in Skye at

Fig. 120.   Talisker, Dunvegan, and Quiraing; and Portrush in Ireland.

Gyrolite, spherical radiated concretions, with 50·7 silica, 1·48 alumina, 33·24 lime, 0·18 magnesia, and 14·18 water; Storr in Skye, seems a variety. Also *Xylochor* from Iceland.

47. OKENITE.—$\dot{C}a \ \ddot{S}i^2 + 2 \ \dot{H}.$

Rhombic; ∞P 122° 19′; usually fine columnar or fibrous. H. = 5; G. = 2·28...2·36. Pellucid; slightly pearly. Yellowish to bluish-white. B.B. froths up and melts to an enamel. In powder easily soluble in h. acid, leaving gelatinous flakes; after ignition insoluble. Chem. com. 56·6 silica, 26·4 lime, and 17 water; or apophyllite without the fluoride. On Disco Island, Faroe, and Iceland.

48. PECTOLITE.—$4 \ \dot{C}a \ \ddot{S}i + \dot{N}a \ \ddot{S}i^2 + \dot{H}.$

Monoclinic, but mostly spheroidal, radiating, and columnar. H = 5; G. = 2·74...2·9. Translucent on the edges; slightly pearly. Grayish-white or yellowish. B.B. melts easily to a white enamel-like glass. Soluble in h. acid, leaving flaky silica; after ignition gelatinises perfectly. Chem. com. 54·2 silica, 33·7 lime, 9·4 soda, and

2·7 water. Monte Baldo, Monte Monzoni in Tyrol. In Scotland at Talisker in Skye, near Ballantrae, white, fibrous, and nearly three feet long; Kilsyth (*Stellite*), Ratho, Corstorphine, and Castle Rock, Edinburgh. Resembles wollastonite in form and composition, the soda replacing the lime and the water from decomposition.

49. LEVYNE.—$\ddot{A}l\ \ddot{S}i^3 + \dot{C}a\ (\ddot{K},\ \dot{N}a)\ \ddot{S}i + 4\ \dot{H}$.

Hexagonal-rhombohedral; R 79° 29′; crystals, 0R. R − ½R, thick tabular, in perfect intersecting macles (Fig. 121). H. = 4; G. = 2·1...2·2. Chem. com. 44·5 silica, 23·8 alumina, 10·7 lime, 1·6 potash, 1·4 soda, and 17·4 water. Otherwise like chabasite. Faroe, Glenarm, Storr in Skye, and Hartfield Moss in Renfrewshire.

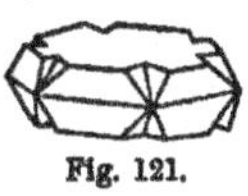

Fig. 121.

50. CHABASITE, Lime-Ch.—$\ddot{A}l\ \ddot{S}i^3 + \dot{C}a\ (\dot{N}a,\ \ddot{K})\ \ddot{S}i + 6\ \dot{H}$.

Hexagonal-rhombohedral; R 94° 46′; R mostly alone but also with −½R and −2R (Fig. 122). Intersecting macles very common; crystals in druses and striated. Cleavage, R rather perfect. H. = 4...4·5; G. = 2...2·2. Transparent to translucent; vitreous. Colourless, grayish, yellowish, reddish to flesh-red. B.B. fuses to a finely porous enamel. Soluble in h. acid, leaving slimy silica. Chem. com. 47·3 silica, 20·3 alumina, 11·1 lime (with 0 to 2·5 soda and 0·2 to 3 potash) and 21·3 water. Faroe, Iceland, Greenland, Aussig in Bohemia, Giants' Causeway, Kilmalcolm in Renfrewshire, in Skye, and other places in Scotland. *Glottalite* of Thomson, from near Port-Glasgow, seems chabasite. *Phacolite*, with rather less silica and more alumina, is a variety; Leipa in Bohemia.

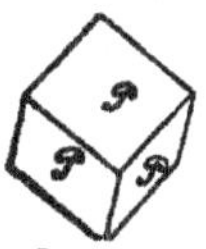

Fig. 122.

51. GMELINITE, Soda } $\ddot{A}l\ \ddot{S}i^3 + \dot{N}a\ (\dot{C}a,\ \ddot{K})\ \ddot{S}i + 6\ \dot{H}$.
    Chabasite. }

Hexagonal; P 80° 13′; crystals P . 0P . ∞P (Fig. 123). The faces of P striated parallel to their polar edge; those of the prism horizontally. Cleavage, ∞P distinct. Gelatinises with h. acid ; otherwise like chabasite. Chem. com.

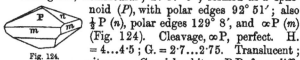

47·6 silica, 19·7 alumina, 12 soda (with 3 to 5 lime, and 0·4 to 2 potash) and 20·7 water. Talisker in Skye, Glenarm in Antrim, Vicenza. *Lederite*, with only 9 per cent water, seems a variety ; Cape Blomidon, Nova Scotia.

Fig. 123.

52. FAUJASITE.—2 $\ddot{A}l$ $\ddot{S}i^3$ + $(\dot{C}a, \dot{N}a)^3$ $\ddot{S}i^3$ + 18 $\dot{H}$.

Tesseral ; octahedrous. Fracture uneven ; brittle. H. = 7. G. = 1·923. Transparent ; vitreous or adamantine. White or brown. B.B. intumesces and fuses to a white enamel. Soluble in h. acid. Chem. com. 46 silica, 17 alumina, 5 lime, 5 soda, and 27 water. Kaiserstuhl.

53. EDINGTONITE.—4 $\ddot{A}l$ $\ddot{S}i^3$ + 3 $\dot{B}a$ $\ddot{S}i$ + 12 $\dot{H}$.

Tetragonal, hemihedral ; P. 87° 9′ ; formed as a sphenoid (*P*), with polar edges 92° 51′ ; also $\frac{1}{2}$P (*n*), polar edges 129° 8′, and ∞P (*m*) (Fig. 124). Cleavage, ∞P, perfect. H. = 4...4·5 ; G. = 2·7...2·75. Translucent ; vitreous. Grayish-white. B.B. fuses difficultly to a colourless glass. Chem. com. 37·3 silica, 23·7 alumina, 26·5 baryta, and 12·5 water (*analysis*). Kilpatrick Hills, Dumbartonshire.

Fig. 124.

**54. HARMOTOME, $\Big\{$ $\ddot{A}l$ $\ddot{S}i^3$ + $\dot{B}a$ $\ddot{S}i^3$ + 5 $\dot{H}$, *or*

Cross-stone. $\Big\{$ [BaO . Al² O³ + 5 (H²O . Si O²)].

Rhombic ; P polar edges 119° 4′ and 121° 6′ (or 120° 1′ and 120° 42′), and ∞P 88° 14′ ; crystals, ∞$\bar{P}$∞ (*q*). ∞$\bar{P}$∞ (*o*).P . $\bar{P}$∞ , short prismatic. Generally in perfectly intersecting macles (Fig. 125). (Now thought monoclinic and the macles of four crystals.) Cleavage, macrodiagonal and brachydiagonal imperfect ; brittle ; fracture uneven. H. = 4·5 ; G. = 2·3...2·5. Translucent ; vitreous. Colourless, but white, gray, yellow, brown, or red. B.B. fuses rather difficultly but quietly to a clear glass. Soluble, but not readily, in h. acid, with deposition of silica. Chem. com.

Fig. 125.

46·5 silica, 15·9 alumina, 23·7 baryta (with 1 to 3 lime and 1 to 2·5 potash), and 13·9 water.   Andreasberg, Kongsberg, Oberstein.   Strontian (*Morvenite*) ; Old Kilpatrick, Campsie Hills, and Corstorphine, Scotland.

55. PHILLIPSITE.—$\ddot{A}l\ \ddot{S}i^3 + (\dot{C}a,\ \dot{K})\ \ddot{S}i + 5\ \dot{H}$.
Rhombic ; P polar edges 119° 18′ and 120° 42′. Forms, macles, and other characters, like harmotone. G. = 2·15...2·20.   B.B. fuses easily with slight intumescence ; gelatinises in h. acid. Chem. com. 48·6 silica, 20·2 alumina, 7·3 lime, 6·2 potash, and 17·7 water.   Giessen, Marburg, Cassel, Iceland, and the Giants' Causeway.

56. HERSCHELITE.—$\ddot{A}l\ \ddot{S}i^2 + (\dot{N}a,\ \dot{K},\ \dot{C}a)\ \ddot{S}i + 3\ \dot{H}$.
Hexagonal (or rhombic?) ;. P polar edges, 124° 45′ ; crystals ∞P . 0P . H. = 4·5 ; G. = 2·06. Translucent ; pearly ; white.   B.B. fuses readily to a white enamel.   Chem. com. 48·5 silica, 20·1 alumina, 9·2 soda, 4·6 potash (with 0·2 to 5 lime), and 17·6 water.   Aci Reale and Palagonia in Sicily.   Richmond, near Melbourne, Australia, but with 46 silica, 22 alumina, 7·1 lime, 5·5 soda, 0·7 potash, and 19 water.

57. ZEAGONITE.—$\ddot{A}l\ \ddot{S}i^2 + (\dot{C}a,\ \dot{K})\ \ddot{S}i + 4\ \dot{H}$.
Rhombic ; P polar edges 120° 37′ and 122° 44′ ; crystals single or in groups.   H. = 5, on angles and edges = 7 or more ; G. = 2·213.   Transparent ; vitreous.   Colourless, white, or bluish. B.B. becomes white, falls down, shines, and melts to a clear glass.   Capo di Bove.

58. GISMONDINE, Abrazite.—$\ddot{A}l\ \ddot{S}i + \dot{C}a\ (\dot{K})\ \ddot{S}i + 4\ \dot{H}$.
Tetragonal (or rhombic?) ; P 92° 30′ ; crystals, P or with ∞P∞, in groups. Cleavage, P. imperfect. H. = 5, on edges and angles = 6 ; G. = 2·265.   Semitransparent to translucent ; vitreous.   Grayish-white to pale-red.   B.B. intumesces, becomes opaque, and melts to a white enamel. Chem. com. 35 silica, 29 alumina, 15·7 lime (with 2·8 potash), and 20·3 water.   Vesuvius, Aci Castello, and Capo di Bove.

59. LAUMONITE.—$\ddot{A}l\ \ddot{S}i^3 + \dot{C}a\ \ddot{S}i + 4\ \dot{H}.$

Monoclinic; $C. = 80°\ 42',\ \infty\ P\ 86°\ 15',\ \infty\ P : -P°\infty$ (or $M : P)\ 113°\ 30'$; crystals (Fig. 126) prismatic, also columnar. Cleavage, prismatic perfect; clinodiagonal in traces; rather brittle. $H. = 3...3\cdot5$; $G. = 2\cdot2...2\cdot3$. Pellucid; vitreous; on cleavage pearly. White, grayish, yellowish, and reddish. In the air soon decomposed. B.B. intumesces and melts easily to a white enamel, which becomes clear in a stronger heat. Soluble and gelatinises in h. acid. Chem. com. $50\cdot9$ silica, $21\cdot9$ alumina, $11\cdot9$ lime, and $15\cdot3$ water. Huelgoët, in Brittany, Eule near Prague, Fahlun, Iceland, Faroe, Snizort and Storr in Skye, Dumbarton, and other parts of Scotland, and in North America.

Fig. 126.

60. LEONHARDITE.—$\ddot{A}l\ \ddot{S}i^3 + \dot{C}a\ \ddot{S}i + 3\ \dot{H}.$

Monoclinic; $\infty P\ 83°\ 30',\ \infty\ P : -P°\infty\ 114°$; crystals, prismatic, and grouped in bundles; also granular and columnar. Cleavage, ∞P very perfect, basal imperfect. Very friable. $H. = 3...3\cdot5$; $G. = 2\cdot25$. Translucent on the edges; pearly; yellowish-white. B.B. exfoliates, froths, and melts easily to a white enamel. Becomes opaque, and decomposes quickly in the air. Chem. com. $53\cdot7$ silica, $22\cdot4$ alumina, $12\cdot2$ lime, and $11\cdot7$ water. Schemnitz. *Caporcianite*, reddish-gray, fibrous and radiating, from Caporciano, Tuscany, is identical.

**FAMILY VII.—MICA.

Crystallisation monoclinic or rhombic, and hexagonal or rhombohedral. Cleavage mostly very perfect in one direction (basal), and thin laminæ flexible. Pellucid, with a strong, often pearly or semimetallic lustre. $H. = 2...3$, more rarely $1...6$; $G. = 2\cdot5...3$. B.B. mostly fusible. Are silicates of alumina, with silicates of potash, magnesia, lithia, and protoxides of iron and manganese, with or without water. Lime is rare, or almost wanting. They are mostly constituents of the plutonic or volcanic rocks.*

* Neither the optical nor crystallographical characters of the micas, Nos. 67 to 71, are well determined. All magnesia micas were formerly regarded as monoaxial and hexagonal, but some now appear to be binaxial,

** 61. MUSCOVITE, Potash-Mica, Phengite, Binaxial-Mica.

$3 \; \ddot{A}l \; \ddot{S}i + \dot{K} \; \ddot{S}i^3, \; or$
$[Al^2O^2 . SiO^2 + RO . SiO^2]. — Rams.$

Rhombic. Crystals chiefly rhombic or six-sided tables, with ∞P 120° and 60° nearly. Imbedded, or in druses; also scaly, foliated, or lamellar. Macles rather rare. Cleavage, basal highly perfect; sectile, and in thin laminæ elastic. H. = 2...3; G. = 2·8...3·1. Pellucid in various degrees; optically binaxial; metallic-pearly, on some faces vitreous. Colourless, but white, gray, green, red, brown, black, and rarely yellow. In closed tube usually yields water, with traces of fluorine. B.B. loses its transparency, and fuses to an obscure glass or white enamel. Not affected by h. or s. acids. Chem. com. very variable, but by second formula [RO = $\frac{1}{3}$ K²O, $\frac{2}{3}$ H²O] 45·1 silica, 38·6 alumina, 11·8 potash, and 4·5 water. The analyses give also peroxides of iron (or protoxide) and manganese, with traces of lime, magnesia, and soda, and most also 1 per cent or under of fluorine. The green micas (*Fuchsite*) also 4 to 6 chrome oxide. Abundant as a constituent of granite, gneiss, mica-slate, and other rocks. Large plates in Norway, Sweden, and especially in Siberia, often a yard in diameter, and used for windows, but become white on exposure. Fine crystals, Vesuvius, St. Gotthardt, Pargas, Arendal, Utoe, Fahlun, Kimito, Cornwall, and Aberdeenshire.

Damourite.—H. = 1·5; soluble in sulph. acid, leaving silica, from Pontivy in Brittany; *Margarodite* from Connecticut and Ireland; *Didrimite* from Zillerthal, are only mica, as water appears to occur in all varieties as an essential constituent. *Paragonite* or mica-slate, from St. Gotthardt, is similar, but contains 8·5 soda, and B.B. infusible.

*62. LEPIDOLITE, Lithia-Mica.

Monoclinic or rhombic; physical characters like potash-mica, but colour often rose or peach-blossom red. In

with the angle between the axes small; in biotite under 5°, often 0° to 1° or 2°; in phlogopite, 5° to 20°. The crystallisation of the potash mica and lepidolite is most probably rhombic. The chem. com. also is not well represented by any general formula.

the closed tube shows evident fluorine reaction. B.B. melts *very easily* with effervescence to a colourless, brown, or rarely black magnetic glass, colouring the flame *red*. Imperfectly soluble in acids, wholly so after fusion. Chem. com. very uncertain. Analyses give 40 to 52 silica, 20 to 34 alumina, 0 to 27 iron peroxide, 0 to 5 manganese peroxide, 5 to 10 potash, 2 to 6 lithia, 4 to 8 fluorine, and 0 to 2 soda. Part of the iron is probably the protoxide and most show also water. Rammelsberg regards the fluorine as replacing part of the oxygen, both in the bases and acids. Penig and Zinnwald, Saxony, Rozena, Moravia (contains rubidium), Paris and Hebron in Maine ; St. Michael's Mount, Cornwall ; Loch Fine, Ballachulish (in limestone), Portsoy (in serpentine), Scotland. Sometimes used as an ornamental stone and for preparing lithia.

**63. BIOTITE, Magnesia- $\begin{cases} \ddot{A}l\ \ddot{S}i + (Mg, \dot{K}, \dot{F}e)^3\ \ddot{S}i,\ or \\ \ddot{R}^2\ \ddot{S}i^3 + m\dot{R}^3\ \ddot{S}i. \end{cases}$
Mica.

Hexagonal, rhombohedral ; R 62° 56′ ; crystals mostly tabular, rarely short prisms. Cleavage, basal very perfect ; sectile ; in thin plates elastic. H. = 2·5...3 ; G. = 2·85... 2·9. Transparent, but often only in very thin plates (and generally monoxial) ; metallic, pearly. Usually dark-green, brown, or black ; streak greenish-gray or white. B.B. difficultly fusible to a gray or black glass. Completely soluble in con. s. acid, leaving white pearly plates of silica. Chem. com. very variable. In the second formula (*Rams.*) $\ddot{R}$ is alumina and iron per-oxide, $\dot{R}$ magnesia, iron protoxide, potash and water, whilst $m = 2, 3, 4$ or 6. Most characteristic is the large amount of magnesia and iron. Analyses give 37 to 44 silica, 13 to 22 alumina, 2 to 27 iron peroxide, 10 to 30 magnesia, 0 to 10 potash, 0 to 2 fluorine, and 1 to 3 water. Pargas, Bodenmais, Monroe in New York, Greenland, near Aberdeen, and in other parts of Scotland. *Rubellan*, brownish-red, Bohemia and Saxony, is a decomposed variety. *Phlogopite*, yellow or copper red from limestone, New York and Canada, also a magnesian mica, but the crystals rhombic and binaxial.

64. LEPIDOMELANE.—$(\ddot{\text{Al}}, \ddot{\text{Fe}})\ \ddot{\text{Si}} + (\ddot{\text{Fe}}, \dot{\text{K}})\ \ddot{\text{Si}}.$

Hexagonal, small six-sided tables. Cleavage, basal perfect; rather brittle. H. = 3 ; G. = 3·0. Highly vitreous; opaque and raven-black; or translucent and leekgreen; streak mountain-green. B.B. becomes brown, and fuses to a black magnetic bead. Soluble easily in h. acid, leaving pearly scales of silica. Chem. com. 35 to 37 silica, 12 to 17 alumina, 24 to 27 iron peroxide, 1 to 12 iron protoxide, 4 to 9 potash, 3 to 5 magnesia, 0·5 to 1 lime, 1 to 2 manganese protoxide, with 4 to 7 water. Thus a magnesian mica with much iron—common in the granite of Ireland and Persberg, Sweden.

65. CHLORITOID.—$\dot{\text{Fe}}\ \ddot{\text{Si}} + \ddot{\text{Al}}\ \dot{\text{H}}.$

Granular, foliated. Cleavage, in one direction perfect; brittle. H. = 5·5...6; G.= 3·55. Opaque; weak pearly. Blackish-green; streak greenish-white. B.B. infusible, but becomes darker and magnetic. Not affected by acids. Chem. com. 23·8 silica, 40·6 alumina, and 28·5 iron protoxide, and 7·1 water, but generally 3 to 4 per cent magnesia. Kosoibrod in the Ural, Tyrol, and in Canada (chloritoid slate.) *Sismondine*, St. Marcel in Piedmont, is similar; and *Masonite*, from Rhode Island.

66. OTTRELITE.—$\ddot{\text{Al}}^2\ \ddot{\text{Si}}^3 + 3\ (\ddot{\text{Fe}}, \ddot{\text{Mn}})\ \ddot{\text{Si}} + 3\ \dot{\text{H}}.$

Monoclinic (?) in thin hexagonal tables. Cleavage, parallel to the lateral faces, rather perfect. Scratches glass. G. = 4·4. Translucent; vitreous. Greenish or blackish gray. B.B. melts difficultly on the edges to a black magnetic globule. Powder soluble in warm s. acid. Chem. com. 43·9 silica, 24·3 alumina, 17·0 iron protoxide, 8·5 manganese protoxide, and 6·3 water. In gray clay-slate at Ottrez in Belgium; Pyrenees.

CHLORITE.—The minerals (67 to 70) formerly thus named are now divided into several species, but there is much confusion in the names, increased by their close agreement in chemical and physical characters. Kenngott gives for the whole, including also kämmererite, $[\text{RO}.2\ddot{\text{H}}\text{O}+2(\text{RO}.\text{Si O}^3)]$, or $\dot{\text{R}}\ \dot{\text{H}} + 2\dot{\text{R}}\ \ddot{\text{Si}}$,—R being chiefly magnesia replaced in part

by iron protoxide, and the silicate $\dot{M}g$ $\ddot{S}i$ also replaced in part
by alumina = Al O . Al O². All have cleavage basal highly
perfect ; laminæ flexible, but not elastic ; thin plates transparent or translucent ; pearly on the basis. Green, but
red by light transmitted transverse to the chief axis. In
closed tube yield water,

**67. CHLORITE   } 2 $\dot{R}$ $\ddot{S}i$ + $\dot{R}^2$ $\ddot{A}l$ + 3 $\dot{H}$, *or*
(Ripidolite, *G. Rose*). } [2 (2 RO. Si O⁵) +Al² O³. 3 H⁴ O].
Hexagonal ; P 106° 50' ; crystals tabular of 0P . ∞$\check{P}$,
or 0P. P (Fig. 127), often in comb-like or other groups ;

generally foliated and scaly. H. = 1...1·5. G.
= 2·78...2·96. Leek to blackish green ; streak
greenish-gray.   B.B. exfoliates ; difficultly
fusible on thin edges to a black glass ;
soluble in con. sul. acid. Chem. com. when 4 $\dot{R}$,

Fig. 127.

=3 $\dot{M}g$ + $\dot{F}e$, =26·3 sil., 21·8 al., 25·5 mag., 15·0 $\dot{F}e$, and 11·5 water.
=2 $\dot{M}g$ +2$\dot{F}e$, =24·6 ... 20·1 ... 15·9 ... 28·5 ... 10·9 ...

but the analyses variable. Common in the Alps, Scandinavia, the Ural, the Harz, Cornwall, Cumberland, Wales ;
Portsoy, Glen Tilt, Jura, and other parts of Scotland.

68. PENNINE.—4 $\dot{M}g$ $\ddot{S}i$ + $\dot{M}g^3$ $\ddot{A}l$ + 5$\dot{H}$.

Hexagonal, rhombohedral ; R 65°28' (64° 30'Kenngott).
Crystals chiefly very acute rhombohedrons, with or without
the basis, and in groups or druses. Lustre somewhat
resinous.   H. = 2...3 ; G. = 2·6...2·77. Streak, greenish-
white.   B.B. exfoliates, becomes white, and fuses on the
edges to a white enamel. Completely soluble in warm s.
acid. Chem. com. 33·6 silica, 14·4 alumina, 39·4 magnesia,
and 12·6 water ; but with 5 to 6 iron protoxide replacing
magnesia. Zermatt in Valais, Schwarzenstein in Tyrol,
Ala in Piedmont, and Mauleon in the Pyrenees. *Leuchten-
bergite*, yellowish-white, from Slatoust, is the same.

69. CLINOCHLORE, Ripidolite } 3 $\dot{M}g$ $\ddot{S}i$+$\dot{M}g^3$ $\ddot{A}l$+4 $\dot{H}$.
        (Chlorite, *G. Rose*). }
Monoclinic ; C. = 76° 4' ; ∞P 121° 28', 0P : P 113° 59',
0P : ∞P 192° 8'. Crystals − 2P . P . 4P^c ∞ . 0P (*n*,
m, *t*, *P*, Fig. 128). Macles common ; also in groups

and druses. Lustre somewhat vitreous or resinous. H.
= 2...3 ; G. = 2·6...2·8. B.B. becomes white,
and fuses on thin edges to a grayish-yellow
enamel. Chem. com. 30·3 silica, 17·3 alumina, 40·3 magnesia, and 12·1 water, but in
most 3 to 4 iron protoxide, and some peroxide of iron and chrome. Traversalla in Piedmont, West Chester in Pennsylvania, Achmatowsk in Ural, and Leugast in Bavaria (massive).

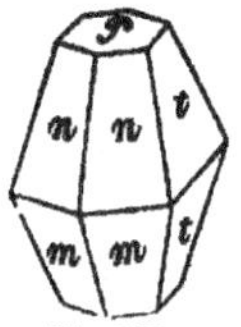

Fig. 128.

Epichlorite, Metachlorite, Helminth, Delessite, and *Grengesite,*
are other chlorite-like minerals.

70. KÄMMERERITE.—3 $\dot{M}g \ddot{S}i + \ddot{A}l \ddot{S}i + 5 \dot{H}$.

Hexagonal ; P 140° 16′, and P : OP = 105° 52′, crystals
OP . ∞ P tabular and prismatic ; but usually massive and
foliated. Cleavage, basal perfect. Sectile, flexible. H.
= 1·5...2 ; G. = 2·6...2·76. Translucent ; pearly. Violet-
blue, reddish, or greenish. Feels greasy. B.B. exfoliates
without fusing. Chem. com. 37·0 silica, 14·2 alumina, 1·0
chrome oxide, 31·5 magnesia, 1·5 lime, 1·5 iron protoxide,
and 13·0 water in that from Bissersk. Varieties from
Lake Atkul, Siberia, and Texas in Pennsylvania, give 5
chrome oxide, and agree with chlorite.

Rhodochrome.— Massive, fine scaly, splintery fracture.
H. = 2·5...3 ; G. = 2·668. Greenish-black, in fine splinters
peach-blossom red. Tino in Greece, the Ural, Styria, and
near Baltimore.

Tabergite from Taberg ; *Vermiculite,* in fine scales,
twisting up B.B., from Millbury, Mass. ; and *Loganite,* from
Canada, are closely allied.

Pyrosclerite, massive (but rhombic ?). Cleavage, in two
directions at right angles, the one perfect, the other imperfect ; fracture uneven, splintery. Sectile. H. = 3 ; G.
= 2·7...2·8. Translucent ; dull, or weak pearly. Apple,
emerald, or grayish green. B.B. fuses with difficulty to a
gray glass. With borax forms a chrome-green glass.
Chem. com. like kämmererite, and probably identical.
Elba. *Chanikrite* found with it is similar, but with 12
lime.

**71. TALC.—$\dot{M}g^3\ddot{Si}^4+\dot{H}$, *or* [3 $(MgO.SiO^3)+H^2O.SiO^3$].
Rhombic, or monoclinic.   Rarely found in six-sided or
rhombic tables.   Generally massive, granular, or scaly.
Cleavage, basal very perfect.   Soft, sectile, and flexible, in
thin plates.   H. = 1 ; G.= 2·6...2·8.   Transparent in thin
plates, and optically binaxial ; pearly or resinous.   Colourless, but generally greenish or yellowish-white, to apple,
leek, or olive green.   Feels very greasy.   B.B. emits a
bright light, exfoliates, and hardens (H.=6), but is infusible ;
with cobalt solution becomes red.   Not soluble in h. or s.
acid before or after ignition.   Chem. com. 63·5 silica,
31·7 magnesia, and 4·8 water ; but analyses give 57 to 63
silica, 0 to 4·7 alumina, 30 to 35 magnesia, 0 to 2·3 iron
protoxide, with traces of lime and nickel oxide, and 2 to 6
water.   Greiner in Tyrol, Sala, Fahlun, the Pyrenees, Unst
in Zetland, Cairnie in Aberdeenshire, and many parts of
the Scottish Highlands (talc-slate).   Used as crayons ; also
for forming crucibles and porcelain.

Steatite.—Massive.   Gray, red, yellow, or green.   B.B.
melts in fine splinters to a white enamel ; but in other
respects acts like talc, of which it seems only a compact
variety.   Briançon, Wunsiedel, the Lizard Point, Cornwall,
Portsoy, and near Kirkcaldy, Scotland.   Savage nations
cut the steatite into culinary utensils.   *Potstone* is a mixture of talc, chlorite, and other minerals.

72. PYROSMALITE.—$(\dot{F}e, \dot{M}n)^4\ddot{Si}^3 + 2\dot{H}$.

Hexagonal ; P 101° 34' ; crystals $\infty P.0P$, tabular ;
also granular.   Cleavage, basal perfect, ∞P imperfect ;
brittle.   H. = 4...4·5 ; G. = 3·0...3·2.   Translucent to
opaque ; resinous, or metallic pearly.   Liver-brown to
olive-green.   B.B. fuses to a black magnetic globule.
Wholly soluble in c. n. acid.   Chem. com. 35·5 silica, 27·5
iron protoxide, 21·5 manganese protoxide, 8 chloride of
iron or manganese, replacing protoxide, and 7·5 water.
Rare.   Nordmark in Sweden.

73. CRONSTEDTITE,
   Chloromelan. $\Big\}\ddot{F}e\ddot{Si} + (\dot{F}e, \dot{M}g)^3\ddot{Si} + 3\dot{H}$.

Rhombohedral, chiefly radiated, columnar.   Cleavage,

basal perfect; thin laminæ elastic.   H. = 2·5 ; G. = 3·3
...3·5.   Opaque or translucent; highly vitreous.   Raven-
black; streak dark-green.   B.B. intumesces, and melts
on the edges slowly to a steel-gray globule.   Gelatinises
with h. or s. acid.   Chem. com. 22 silica, 29 iron peroxide,
39 iron protoxide (with 1 manganese protoxide and 4 magnesia), and 10 water.   Przibram ; Huel Maudlin, Cornwall ; and Conghonas do Campo in Brazil (*Sideroschisolite*).

74. STILPNOMELAN.—$(\dot{F}e\ \dot{M}g)^3\ (\ddot{S}i,\ \ddot{A}l)^3 + 2\ \dot{H}.$

Massive or radiating-foliated.   Cleavage, one very perfect ; rather brittle.   H. = 3...4 ; G. = 3...3·4.   Opaque ;
vitreous, inclining to pearly.   Greenish-black ; streak greenish.   B.B. fuses with difficulty to a black shining globule.
Imperfectly decomposed by acids.   Chem. com. 45·3 silica,
6·9 alumina, 38·3 iron protoxide (with 2 to 3 magnesia),
and 9·5 water.   Zuckmantel, Silesia, and Wielburg, Nassau.

75. CLINTONITE, Seybertite, ⎱
    Holmesite, Chrysophane.   ⎰ $5\ \dot{R}\ \ddot{S}i + 6\ \dot{R}\ \ddot{A}l.$

Hexagonal or rhombic in six-sided tables, or massive
and foliated.   Cleavage, very perfect in one direction, traces
in another.   H. = 4·5...5·5 ; G. = 3 to 3·16.   Translucent ;
pearly on the cleavage.   Wax-yellow or reddish-brown.
Soluble in con. h. acid.   B.B. infusible alone, but some
become white and colour the flame yellow.   Chem. com.
20 silica, 39 alumina, 3·5 iron peroxide, 21 magnesia, and
13·5 lime ; but also some soda, potash, and (2 or less) zirconia.   Amity, New York.

Disterrite, Brandisite, from Monzoni, in Tyrol ; H. = 5 on
basis, 6...6·5 on the prism ; when fresh blackish-green, but
reddish-brown after exposure ; *Xanthophyllite* from Slatoust ;
and *Groppite,* coarse foliated ; H. = 2·5 ; G. = 2·73 ; rose
or brown red ; Gropptorp in Sweden ; are closely allied.

76. MARGARITE, Pearl- ⎱
    mica, Emerylite.   ⎰ $\ddot{A}l^2\ \ddot{S}i + (\dot{C}a,\ \dot{N}a,\ \dot{M}g)\ \ddot{S}i + \dot{H}.$

Rhombic ; rarely in six-sided tables ; generally granular
foliated.   Cleavage, one very perfect.   Thin plates slightly
elastic.   H. = 3·5...4·5 ; G. = 3·0.   Translucent ; pearly.

Snow-white, reddish-white, or pearl-gray. B.B. intumesces and difficultly fusible. Soluble in acids. Chem. com. 30·1 silica, 51·2 alumina, 11·6 lime, 2-6 soda, 0·5 to 3 magnesia, and 4·5 water. Sterzing in Tyrol; Asia Minor and Greece, with emery; and in Pennsylvania. *Diphanite*, in hexagonal prisms, bluish-white; B.B. fuses to an enamel; from the Ural; is nearly allied.

Euphyllite.—Like mica, but less readily cleavable. H. = 4 ; G. = 3. Pellucid; bright pearly; colourless. B.B. exfoliates with a bright light, and fuses on the edges. Contains 40 silica, 42 alumina, 1·4 iron peroxide, 1·4 lime, 3·3 potash, 5 soda, and 5·5 water. Unionville, Pennsylvania.

77. PYROPHYLLITE.—$\ddot{A}l \ddot{S}i^4 + \dot{H}$.

Rhombic (?), but radiated, columnar, or foliated. Cleavage very perfect; flexible; sectile. H. = 1 ; G. = 2·8...2·9. Translucent; pearly. Light verdigris-green to yellowish-white. B.B. swells up with many twistings to a white infusible mass. Partially soluble in sulphuric acid. Chem. com. 67 silica, 28 alumina, and 5 water, with 0·1 to 4 magnesia and lime. Ural, Spaa, Morbihan, Westana in Sweden, Carolina, and Brazil.

78. ANAUXITE.—$\ddot{A}l \ddot{S}i^4 + 3 \dot{H}$.

Granular, with a very perfect cleavage in one direction. H. = 2...3 ; G. = 2·2...2·4. Translucent on the edges; pearly. Greenish-white. B.B. becomes white and fuses on thin edges. Chem. com. 60·5 silica, 26 alumina, and 13·5 water. Bilin in Bohemia.

79. PHOLERITE, Nacrite.—$\ddot{A}l \ddot{S}i^2 + 2 \dot{H}$.

In minute six-sided tables, in fan-like groups; usually fine scaly. H. = 0·5...1 ; G. = 2·35...2·6. Glimmering or pearly. Snow or yellowish white. B.B. infusible, with cobalt solution blue. Chem. com. 46·3 silica, 39·8 alumina, and 13·9 water, but often impure. Thus a crystalline form of kaolin. Common in mineral veins and clay-ironstone of the coal formation, as at Fins in the Allier dept., Mons, Freiberg, and Pennsylvania.

80. ROSELLAN, Poly- } $\ddot{A}l^2 \ddot{S}i^2 + (\dot{K}, \dot{C}a, \dot{M}g) \ddot{S}i + 2 \dot{H}.$
    argite, Rosite.

Small grains, with perfect cleavage. H. = 2·5 ; G. = 2·72. Translucent ; splendent ; fine rose-red. B.B. fuses with difficulty to a white slag. Chem. com. 45 silica, 35 alumina, 6·6 potash, 3·6 lime, 2·45 magnesia, and 6·5 water. Aker and Tunaberg in Sweden.

**FAMILY VIII.—SERPENTINE.

Massive or rhombic. H. = 1...4, rarely more ; G. = 2·3...3·0. Often compact or fibrous ; most feel greasy. Colour often green or yellow, with resinous lustre. B.B. not or difficultly fusible. Mostly soluble in acids. Chem. com. generally hydrated silicates of magnesia, partly re-placed by protoxide of iron. Occur in plutonic or altered rocks ; the serpentine often in large masses or beds.

**81. SERPENTINE. $\begin{cases} \dot{M}g^3 \ddot{S}i^2 + 2 \dot{H} = 2 \dot{M}g \ddot{S}i + \dot{M}g \dot{H}^2, or \\ [3 \; MgO \; . \; 2 \; SiO^2 + 2 \; H^2O]. \end{cases}$

Crystallisation uncertain ; generally massive, and granu-lar or fibrous. Fracture flat-conchoidal, uneven, or splintery. Sectile and slightly brittle. H. = 3...3·5 ; G. = 2·5...2·7. Translucent to opaque ; dull resinous. Green, gray, yellow, red, or brown, often in spots, stripes, or veins ; streak white, shining. Feels greasy, but does not adhere to the tongue. In the closed tube yields water and becomes black. B.B. becomes white, and fuses with much difficulty on thin edges. Soluble in h. or easier in s. acid. Chem. com. 43·5 silica, 43·5 magnesia, and 13 water, but with 1 to 8 iron protoxide, and also carbonic acid, bitumen, and chrome oxide.

Varieties are—1*st*, Noble Serpentine, brighter coloured and more translucent ; 2*d*, Picrolite or fibrous (H. = 3·5... 4·5) ; 3*d*, Common or compact ; 4*th*, Chrysotile (*Baltimorite, Metaxite*), in fine asbestiform fibres, easily separated, with a metallic or silky lustre. G. = 2·219. Common in Nor-way, Sweden, North America, the Lizard Point in Cornwall, in Shetland, Portsoy, Ballantrae, and many parts of Scotland. The chrysotile, at Reichenstein in Silesia, the Vosges Mountains, and North America. Serpentine is often a product of decomposition or pseudomorph of various minerals, as augite, hornblende, olivine, spinel, garnet, etc. It forms whole rocks and mountains, is manufactured into various ornamental articles, and used for preparing magnesia.

Marmolite, with cleavage in two directions, and probably monoclinic, from the serpentine of Hoboken, in New Jersey, and other parts of North America, also in Finnland, agrees nearly in characters and chem. com. 3 $\ddot{Mg} \ddot{Si}$ + 2 $\dot{Mg} \dot{H}^2$, with serpentine.

82. ANTIGORITE.

Very thin, straight laminæ. H. = 2·5 ; G. = 2·62. Transparent or translucent. Green, with brown spots ; streak white. B.B. very thin edges fuse to a yellowish-brown enamel. Chem. com. 41 silica, 3 alumina, 6 iron protoxide, 37 magnesia, and 13 water. Antigorio in Piedmont, probably serpentine.

83. HYDROPHITE.—($\dot{Mg}$, $\dot{Fe}$)⁴ $\ddot{Si}^3$ + 4 $\dot{H}$.

Massive or fibrous. Fracture uneven. H. = 3...4 ; G. = 2·65. Mountain-green ; streak lighter. B.B. infusible. Chem. com. 39·5 silica, 24·6 iron protoxide, 20·5 magnesia, and 15·4 water, but with some alumina and (2 to 4) manganese protoxide. Taberg in Sweden, and New York.

84. PICROSMINE.—2 $\dot{Mg} \ddot{Si}$ + $\dot{H}$.

Rhombic, but massive. Cleavage, $\infty \breve{P} \infty$ perfect ; less so in other directions. Very sectile. H. = 2·5...3 ; G. = 2·5...2·7. Translucent or opaque ; vitreous, but pearly on $\infty \breve{P} \infty$. Greenish-white, gray, or blackish-green ; streak colourless. Yields a bitter odour when breathed on (hence the name). In closed tube gives water and blackens. B.B. becomes white and hard (= 5). Chem. com. 55·8 silica, 36·1 magnesia, and 8·1 water. Presnitz in Bohemia, and the Greiner in Tyrol.

Monradite. — Massive, foliated, translucent, and yellowish-gray. H. = 6 ; G. = 3·267. Has nearly the same composition, but with half the water. B.B. infusible. Bergen, Norway.

Picrophyll.—Dark-green, foliated. G. = 2·73 ; H. = 2·5. B.B. infusible, but becoming white. Is similar or altered augite. Sala.

85. VILLARSITE.—$2 \dot{M}g^2 \ddot{S}i + \dot{H}$.

Rhombic ; crystals P . 0P, meeting at 136° 32′ ; often in macles of three ; also granular. Fracture uneven. H. = 3 ; G. = 2·9...3·0. Translucent. Greenish or grayish-yellow. B.B. infusible ; decomposed by acids. Chem. com. 41 silica, 53 magnesia, with 3 or 4 iron protoxide and 2 or 3 manganese protoxide, and 6 water. Traversella in Piedmont.

86. SPADAITE.—$\dot{M}g^3 \ddot{S}i^4 + 4 \dot{H}$.

Only massive, with splintery fracture. Sectile. H. = 2·5. Translucent ; weak resinous. Red ; streak white. B.B. fuses to an enamel-like glass ; soluble in con. h. acid, leaving slimy silica. Chem. com. 57 silica, 32 magnesia, and 11 water. Capo di Bove, near Rome.

87. GYMNITE, Deweylite.—$\dot{M}g^4 \ddot{S}i^3 + 6 \dot{H}$.

Only massive. H. = 2...3 ; G. = 1·9...2·2. Semi-translucent ; resinous. Pale or dirty orange-yellow. B.B. becomes dark brown, and fuses on very thin edges. Chem. com. 41 silica, 36 magnesia, and 23 water. Bare Hills near Baltimore, and Tyrol.

88. BRUCITE, Nemalite.—$\dot{M}g \dot{H}$.

Rhombohedral ; R 82° 22′ ; crystals also 2R and 0R ; also foliated or columnar. Cleavage, basal very perfect. Sectile ; fine laminæ flexible. H. = 2 ; G. = 2·3...2·4. Translucent ; pearly. Colourless, or grayish and greenish-white. B.B. infusible ; easily soluble in acids. Chem. com. 69 magnesia and 31 water, but after exposure often contains carbonic acid and effervesces. *Nemalite* is a fine fibrous variety with silky lustre. Swinaness in Unst, Hoboken in New Jersey, and Beresowsk in the Ural.

**FAMILY IX.—HORNBLENDE.

Monoclinic mostly. Distinct cleavage in several directions. H. = 4...6, but generally 5, or scratch with knife ; G. = 2·5...4·0, but mostly high. Mostly coloured, ranging from white, through green (rarely brown), to black. Lustre vitreous, in some silky or metallic pearly. Soluble, but not very readily, in acids; and more or less easily fusible. Chem. com. anhydrous silicates and aluminates of lime, magnesia, iron protoxide, more sparingly of soda, yttria, and manganese protoxide. The chief species are essential constituents of the igneous rocks, and form by their decomposition highly fertile soils.

N.B.—Hornblende and Augite rather represent groups of mineral substances than single species. They are best distinguished, when imperfectly formed, by the cleavage and angles of the prisms.

**89. HORNBLENDE, $\begin{cases} \dot{R} \ddot{S}i = [RO . SiO^3], \textit{or} \\ 6 \dot{R} \ddot{S}i + \dot{R}^2 \ddot{S}i^3. \end{cases}$
    Amphibole.

Monoclinic ; C = 75° 10′, ∞P 124° 30′, P 148° 30′. The crystals short and thick, or long and thin prismatic, formed especially by ∞P (*M*) and ∞P°∞ (*x*), and bounded on the ends chiefly by 0P and P (*r*) (Fig. 129). Macles common, with the chief axis the twin axis. Very often . radiated, fibrous or columnar, or granular. Cleavage, prismatic along ∞P $124\frac{1}{2}$° very perfect, orthodiagonal and clinodiagonal very imperfect. H. = 5...6 ; G. = 2·9...3·4. Pellucid in all degrees ; vitreous, but sometimes pearly or silky. Colourless ; white, but usually some shade of gray, yellow, green, brown, or black. B.B. fuses, generally intumescing and boiling, to a gray, green, or black glass. Those containing most iron are most fusible, and are also partially soluble in hydrochloric acid, which scarcely affects the others. Chem. com. very variable ; the silica is partly replaced by alumina, specially in the green or black varieties ; $\dot{R}$ is chiefly $\dot{M}g$, $\dot{C}a$ and $\dot{F}e$. The lime is the most constant element,

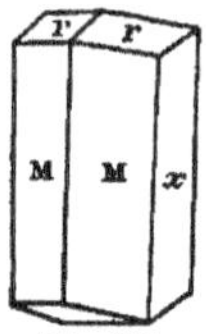

Fig. 129.

in most from 10 to 12, magnesia and iron protoxide replace each other, the one increasing as the other diminishes. With 4 S̈i and Ṙ = 2 Ṁg + 1 Ċa + 1 F̈e, the average com. is 53·6 silica, 17·8 magnesia, 12·5 lime, and 16·1 iron protoxide ; but analyses give 40 to 60 silica, 0 to 17 alumina, 0 to 30 magnesia, 0 to 15 lime, 0 to 36 iron protoxide (or peroxide), 0 to 4 manganese protoxide, 0 to 8 soda, 0 to 3 potash, and 0 to 1·5 fluorine, with a little water.

The more remarkable varieties are —

1. *Tremolite, Grammatite,* or *Calamite.*—3 Ṁg S̈i + Ċa S̈i, with 58·35 silica, 28·39 magnesia, and 13·26 lime. White, gray, green, in long prismatic crystals, often striated longitudinally. Pearly or silky ; semitransparent or translucent. B.B. fuses readily to a white or nearly colourless glass. Sweden, the Alps, Pyrenees, Silesia, Siberia, North America, Cornwall, Cumberland, Glen Tilt, Glenelg, Tiree, Portsoy, Aberdeenshire, and Unst.

2. *Actinolite, Actinote,* or *Strahlstein.*—Colour green, inclining to black, gray, or brown. Translucent, or only on the edges. Long prismatic crystals, or radiated columnar masses. B.B. melts to a greenish or blackish enamel. Sweden, Tyrol, North America, Glenelg, Isle Oronsay, Loch Shin, and Aberdeenshire.

3. *Asbestus, Amianthus,* and *Byssolite.*— Fine fibrous. White, gray, or green. The fibres often easily separable, elastic, and flexible. Savoy, Tyrol, Corsica, and Unst. *Rock-cork,* felt-like, and swims on water ; Saxony, Sweden, Portsoy and Leadhills in Scotland. *Rock-leather,* flat and flexible ; Leadhills, Buck of Cabrach in Aberdeenshire, and Strontian ; and *Rock-wood,* near Sterzing, in the Tyrol.

4. *Hornblende.*—Green or black, seldomer brown or gray. G. = 3·1...3·3. B.B. Fuses rather easily to a yellow, greenish, or black enamel. Three varieties are distinguished. (*a.*) The noble or *Pargasite,* pale celadine or olive-green, and strong pearly or vitreous lustre ; at Pargas in Finland, Tyrie in Scotland. (*b.*) Common hornblende, dark leek or blackish green, opaque ; streak greenish-gray. A constituent of many rocks, as in Norway, the Alps, and Scottish Highlands (Ballater, Ben Lair, East Rona). (*c.*) Basaltic,

foliated, with bright even cleavage, opaque, velvet-black; streak gray or brown. Generally contains alumina (9 to 15) and much (5 to 11) iron peroxide; and Zirkel says often numerous microscopic grains of magnetite. In basalt and volcanic rocks; Etna, Vesuvius, the Rhine, Bohemia.

5. *Anthophyllite.*—Said rhombic and a distinct species, but very doubtful. Clove-brown to leek-green, translucent, radiating, and columnar; pearly on cleavage planes. B.B. very difficultly fusible. In it the lime is chiefly replaced by protoxide of iron. Kongsberg and Modum, Norway, Greenland, and the United States.

Arfvedsonite. — Massive and granular. Pure black, opaque; streak grayish-green. Cleavage, very perfect along a prism of 123° 55′. G. = 3·44; H. = 6. Fusible in fine splinters in the flame of a candle. B.B. intumesces much, and melts to a black magnetic globule. Not soluble in acids. Chem. com. about 50 silica, 14 to 26 iron perox-ide, 24 to 12 iron protoxide, and 8 to 10 soda, with some alumina, lime, and magnesia. Greenland, Frederiksvarn in Norway, and Arendal.

Uralite.—Dark-green or greenish-black, with the form of augite, otherwise like hornblende. The Ural. Is a pseudomorph.

**90. Augite,⎱ Ṙ S̈i, = (Ca, Ṁg, Ḟe) S̈i, *or*
 Pyroxene. ⎰ [RO . Si O², = Ṙ Si O³ + Ṙ⁵ O³].

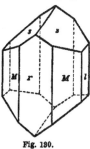
        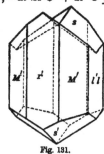

  Fig. 130.   Fig. 131.

 Monoclinic; C. = 74° 11′, ∞P 87° 6′, P (*s* to *s*) 120° 48′—P 131° 30′, 2P 95° 48′. Crystals, ∞P (M) . ∞P°∞ (*r*).

∞ P°∞ (*l*) . P (*s*) . (Fig. 130) ∞P . 2P . 0P . 3P . ∞P°∞ and ∞P°∞ . ∞P°∞ . P°∞ . ∞P, almost always prismatic, imbedded, or attached ; also granular, columnar, and scaly. Macles (Fig. 131) common.   Cleavage, prismatic along ∞P (with angles of 87° 6′ and 92° 54′), generally rather imperfect ; orthodiagonal and clinodiagonal imperfect. H. = 5... 6 ; G. = 3·0...3·5.   Pellucid in all degrees ; vitreous ; in some pearly on ∞P°∞.   Colourless, and white, but usually gray, green, or black.   B.B. generally fusible ; imperfectly soluble in acids.   Chem. com. generally

		Silica.	Lime.	Magnesia.	Iron.
a.	Magnesia-augite............	56·22	25·54	18·24	...
b.	Magnesia-iron-augite......	52·72	23·81	8·50	14·97
c.	Iron-augite	49·06	22·29	...	28·65

Analysis gives 47 to 56 silica, 20 to 25 lime, 5 to 15 magnesia, 1 to 20 iron protoxide, with 0 to 3 manganese protoxide, and 0 to 8 alumina.   The alumina, chiefly found in very dark green or black augites, may in some be a mixture, in others replace either silica or part of the silicate [Al O . Al O^2 = RO . SiO^2].

The more important varieties are—

1. *Diopside.*—Grayish or greenish white, to pearl-gray or leek-green ; streak white.   Crystallised or broad columnar, or concentric lamellar.   Transparent to translucent on the edges.   Not affected by acids.   B.B. fuses to a whitish semitransparent glass.   Chem. com. chiefly lime 26, and magnesia 18·5, with 55·5 silica.   Mussa Alpe (*Mussite*) and Ala (*Alalite*) in Piedmont, Schwarzenstein in the Tyrol ; the Alps, Scandinavia, Finnland, Ural, and North America.

2. *Sahlite, Malacolite.*—Green, rarely yellow, brown or red ; streak white.   Translucent, or only on the edges ; vitreous, inclining to pearly.   Seldom crystallised, mostly columnar or lamellar.   B.B. melts to a dark-coloured glass, Fassathal (*Fassaite*), Piedmont, Arendal, Philipstadt in Sweden ; Lake Baikal (*Baikalite*) ; near Lake Lherz in the Pyrenees (*Lherzolite*) ; Sahla, Sweden ; Glentilt, Glenelg, Tiree in Scotland ; Tyrol, and North America.   *Coccolite* is a distinct granular sahlite or augite.

3. *Augite.*—Leek-green, greenish-black, or velvet-black, rarely brown ; streak greenish-gray.   Vitreous to resinous ; translucent or opaque.   Only slightly affected by acids. B.B. fuses to a black, often magnetic glass.   An essential component of many rocks, basalt, dolerite, clinkstone, and augite porphyry, in Germany, Auvergne, Vesuvius, and Scotland.   Augite crystals in basalt often contain very many microscopic crystals and glasses ; also pores with fluid carbonic acid.   *Jeffersonite*, from Sparta, New Jersey, with 4 zinc oxide, is a variety ; also *Polylite.*

4. *Amianthus.*—Some asbestiform minerals and rock-cork are augite, but the greater number hornblende.

5. *Breislackite.*—Fine yellowish or brown woolly crystals. Vesuvius, and Capo di Bove near Rome.

Hornblende and augite agree so closely in crystalline forms and chemical composition, that it has sometimes been proposed to unite them in one species.   They, however, differ too widely to justify their union.   Hornblende is more fusible, and ranges lower in specific gravity (hornblende from 2·931 to 3·445 ; augite, 3·195 to 3·525). Though both possess a cleavage parallel to their vertical prisms, yet these differ in angular dimensions.   Hornblende 124° 12′; augite 87° 6′.   They also occur in distinct geognostic positions.   Hornblende in rocks containing quartz or free silica, and mostly with minerals that are neutral compounds of silica, as orthoclase and albite ; augite in rocks that do not contain free silica, and mostly with minerals that are not neutral silicates, as labradorite, olivine, and leucite.   Hence there are two distinct series of massive or igneous rocks ; the hornblende series, including granite, syenite, diorite, diorite-porphyry, and red porphyry ; and the augite series or hypersthene rock, gabbro, dolerite, nepheline rock, augite-porphyry, and leucite porphyry.

91. NEPHRITE, Jade.—Ṙ S̈i̇
Compact ; fracture coarse splintery. Very tenacious. H. = 6...6·5 ; G. = 2·9...3·0. Translucent, dull, or resinous. Leek-green, to greenish-white or blackish-green.   Feels

slightly greasy. B.B. becomes white and melts with difficulty to a gray mass. Chem. com. 58 to 59·5 silica, 23 to
26 magnesia, 10·5 to 14·6 lime, but with 1 to 3 protoxide
of iron and 1 to 2·5 water. China and the East, also in
New Zealand. Compact varieties of hornblende or augite.
Cut into ring-stones or amulets.

92. DIALLAGE.—($\dot{C}$a, $\dot{M}$g, $\dot{F}$e) $\ddot{S}$i.
Like augite, and only a variety, with very perfect cleavage in the clinodiagonal, a metallic pearly lustre, and gray
or pinchbeck-brown colour. B.B. melts easily to a grayish
or greenish enamel. Chem. com. 50 to 53 silica, 1 to 5
alumina, 15 to 23 magnesia, 11 to 20 lime, and 5 to 12
manganese protoxide. Constituent of the gabbro. Baste
in the Harz, Silesia, the Alps, Apennines, and Ural. *Va-
nadine-bronzite*, containing soda and vanadic acid, and *Dia-
clasite*, are similar.

93. HYPERSTHENE, Paulite.—($\dot{M}$g, $\dot{F}$e) $\ddot{S}$i.
Rhombic; ∞P 86° 30′ and 93° 30′. Granular or disseminated. Cleavage, brachydiagonal very perfect, prismatic ∞P distinct, macrodiagonal very imperfect. H. = 6 ;
G. = 3·3 ... 3·4. Opaque or translucent on thin edges ;
vitreous or resinous, but metallic-pearly on the cleavage
planes, of which one is copper-coloured, two silvery. Pitch-
black and grayish-black ; streak greenish-gray, or pinchbeck-
brown, inclining to copper-red. Not affected by acids. B.B.
melts more or less easily to a greenish-black glass, often
magnetic. Chem. com. generally 46 to 58 silica, 0 to 4
alumina, 11 to 26 magnesia, 1 to 5 lime, 13 to 34 iron
protoxide, 0 to 6 manganese protoxide. Paul's Island
(*Paulite*), Labrador, and Greenland. Crystals occur in
sanadine bombs at Lake Laach (*Amblystegite*), and in
meteorites of Breitenbach. Hypersthene rock in Norway,
Elfdal in Sweden, Cornwall, the Harz, and Canada. Zirkel says that the hypersthene rock of the Cuchullins, Skye,
is gabbro of plagioclase (triclinic felspar), diallage, and
olivine.

**94. ENSTATITE, Bronzite.—$\dot{M}$g ($\dot{F}$e) $\ddot{S}$i = [Mg O.Si O^3].
Rhombic ; ∞P 93° and 87°; crystals ∞$\bar{P}$∞ . ∞$\bar{P}$∞ pris-

matic. Usually embedded, or indistinct granular masses.
Cleavage, macrodiagonal very perfect, prismatic ∞P distinct,
brachydiagonal imperfect. H. = 4·5...5·5 ; G. = 3·1...3·3.
Translucent, or only on the edges ; vitreous or pearly on
the more perfect cleavage-planes. Colourless, grayish or
greenish white, yellowish or brown. Not affected by acids.
B.B. almost infusible. Chem. com. 60 silica and 40 magnesia, but with 6 to 8 iron protoxide, 1 to 2 alumina, and
1 or 2 water. In olivine and serpentine rocks in
Moravia, the Harz (Baste), and Pyrenees. Bronzite, with
∞P 86°, partially decomposed varieties of yellow or brown
colour, with distinct pinchbeck-brown metallic lustre. Scotland, on Deveron near Huntly, Glentilt, and in Skye.

95. BASTITE, } $\dot{M}g\ (\ddot{F}e,\ \dot{C}a),\ \ddot{S}i\ (\ddot{A}l,\ \ddot{G}r,\ \ddot{F}e) + \dot{H}.$
    Schillerspar. }
Monoclinic, or rhombic ; only granular and foliated.
Cleavage, one very perfect, meeting another less so at 87°.
Fracture uneven, splintery. H. = 3·5...4 ; G. = 2·6...2·8.
Translucent on thin edges ; metallic pearly ; green, inclining to yellow, or brown. Imperfectly soluble in h., wholly
in s., acid. B.B. becomes magnetic, and fuses in very thin
splinters. Chem. com. 43 silica, 26 magnesia, 2·7 lime, 7·4
iron protoxide, 3·3 iron peroxide, 2·4 chrome oxide, 1·7
alumina, and 12·4 water. Baste in the Harz. Probably an
altered enstatite.

96. RHODONITE, Manganese-spar.—$\dot{M}n\ \ddot{S}i.$
Triclinic, but chiefly massive or granular. Cleavage,
∞P∞ and 0P meeting at 87° 38' perfect. Brittle. H. =
5...5.5 ; G. = 3·5...3·7. Translucent ; vitreous or partly
pearly. Dark rose-red, bluish-red, or reddish-brown. Not
affected by acids. B.B. fusible. Chem. com. 45·8 silica
and 54·2 manganese protoxide, with 3 to 5 lime, and 0 to
6 iron protoxide. St. Marcel, Langbanshytta, Katharinenburg, the Harz, and New Jersey. The *Bustamite*, pale-
greenish or reddish-gray, with 14 lime, Mexico ; *Fowlerite*,
New Jersey, with 7 to 11 iron protoxide ; and *Paisbergite*,
Sweden, are varieties. *Hydropite, Photicite, Allagite,* and
Horn-manganese, mere mixtures.

97. WOLLASTONITE, Tabular-spar.—$\dot{C}a$ $\ddot{S}i$.

Monoclinic; C. = 84° 30′, ∞$\ddot{P}$ 87° 18′. Very rarely crystallised, mostly broad prismatic or laminar. Cleavage, along 0P and ∞P^o∞ perfect, but planes uneven or rough; meet at 95° 23′. H. = 4·5...5; G. = 2·8...2·9. Translucent; vitreous, or pearly on cleavage. White, inclining to gray, yellow, red, or brown; streak white. Phosphoresces with heat or friction; gelatinises in hydrochloric acid. B.B. difficultly fusible to a semitransparent glass. Chem. com. 51·7 silica and 48·3 lime, but with 0 to 2 magnesia, and 0 to 2 iron protoxide. Bannat, Finnland, Sweden, North America, Ceylon, Capo di Bove, Monaltrie in Aberdeenshire, and the Castle Rock at Edinburgh.

98. ACMITE.—2 $\ddot{F}e$ $\ddot{S}i^2$ + 3 $\dot{R}$ $\ddot{S}i$.

Monoclinic. Crystals long, often acute-pointed, prisms. Cleavage like augite, ∞P (86° 56′) H. = 6...6·5; G. = 3·4 ...3·6. Nearly opaque; vitreous. Brownish or greenish black; streak greenish-gray. Imperfectly soluble in acids. B.B. fuses easily to a black magnetic glass. Chem. com. 52 silica, 30 iron peroxide, 5 iron protoxide, and 13 soda, but with 1 to 3 manganese peroxide, and also 3 to 4 titanic acid. Eger and Porsgrund in Norway.

99. BABINGTONITE.—9 ($\dot{C}a$, $\ddot{F}e$, $\dot{M}n$) $\ddot{S}i$ + $\ddot{F}e$ $\ddot{S}i^2$.

Triclinic; crystals very low eight-sided prisms (Fig. 132), small, attached; $g : h = 90°\ 24′$; $M : P = 87°\ 27′$; $M : t = 112°\ 12′$. Cleavage, basal (P) very perfect, also along t. H. = 5·5...6; G. = 3·4...3·5. Thin laminæ translucent. Splendent vitreous; black. Not affected by acids. B.B. fuses easily with effervescence to a black magnetic bead. Chem. com. 50·7 silica, 11 iron peroxide, 10·3 iron protoxide, 7·7 manganese protoxide, and 20·3 lime, in the Arendal specimens; one from Nassau gave about 17 of peroxide, with only 11 protoxides. Arendal, Nassau, Zetland, and Governeur, New York.

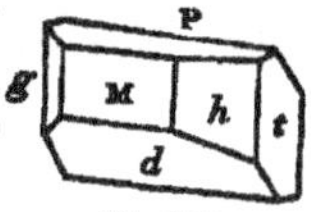

Fig. 132.

100. SORDAWALITE.—$\ddot{A}l$ $\ddot{S}i^2$ + 4 ($\dot{M}g$, $\dot{F}e$) $\ddot{S}i$ + 2$\dot{H}$.

Massive. Fracture conchoidal; brittle. H. = 4...4·5 ;

G. = 2·55...2·62. Opaque; resinous or vitreous. Brownish-black or blackish-green; streak liver-brown. B.B. fuses to a black globule. Chem. com. 50·7 silica (with 2·68 phosphoric acid), 14 alumina, 19·6 iron protoxide, 10·9 magnesia, and 4·8 water. Sordawala in Finnland.

101. KROKYDOLITE.—$3 \dot{F}e \ddot{S}i + (\dot{N}a, \dot{M}g) \ddot{S}i^{2} + 2\dot{H}$.

Very fine, easily separable, but tough, elastic fibres. H. = 4; G. = 3·2...3·3. Translucent; silky, or dull. Indigo-blue; streak lavender-blue. B.B. fuses easily to a black magnetic glass. Chem. com. 50·3 silica, 35·0 iron protoxide, 2·2 magnesia, 6·7 soda, and 5·8 water. Orange River in South Africa, Stavern in Norway, and Greenland.

102. PYRALLOLITE.

Monoclinic; prismatic; usually columnar or granular. Cleavage, basal and hemidomatic, meeting at 94° 36′ distinct. Fracture uneven, splintery; rather brittle. H. = 3·5 ...4; G. = 2·55...2·60. Opaque, or translucent on the edges; resinous, or pearly. Greenish-white, asparagus-green, and yellowish-gray. B.B. becomes black, then white, and fuses with very much difficulty. Chem. com. silicate of magnesia with a little silicate of lime, water, and bituminous matter. Storgard, Finnland. Probably decomposed augite or hornblende.

103. ISOPYRE.—$(\ddot{A}l, \ddot{F}e)^{2} \ddot{S}i^{3} + 3 \dot{C}a \ddot{S}i$ (?).

Brittle; fracture conchoidal. H. = 5·5...6; G. = 2·90... 2·95. Opaque; vitreous. Grayish or velvet-black, sometimes with red spots; streak pale greenish-gray. Imperfectly soluble in acids. B.B. fuses to a magnetic globule. Chem. com., by Turner's analysis, 47·09 silica, 13·91 alumina, 15·43 lime, 20·07 iron peroxide, 1·94 copper oxide. St. Just near Penzance, Calton Hill, Edinburgh (?).

104. TACHYLITE.—$\ddot{A}l \ddot{S}i^{2} + 3 (\dot{F}e, \dot{C}a, \dot{M}g, \dot{M}n, \dot{N}a, \dot{K}) \ddot{S}i$.

Conchoidal. H. = 6·5; G. = 2·52. Opaque; vitreous or resinous. Velvet, brownish, or greenish black; streak dark gray. B.B. fuses very easily to an opaque glass; soluble in h. acid. Vogelsberg (*Hyalomelan*) near Dransfeld, Munden, and Iceland. Seems a vitreous basalt.

FAMILY X.—CLAYS.

Amorphous, earthy, variously-coloured masses. H. = 1 ...5, but generally low or 1...3 ; G. = 1...3, but often about 2. Many have a shining streak, adhere to the tongue, feel greasy, and fall down in water. Some then form a ductile paste and are used for pottery. These are slightly affected by acids (under 25 per cent of mass, soluble). They are chiefly silicates of alumina, with about 10 to 12 per cent water. Others with 20 to 25 per cent water, and a considerable proportion of iron, lime, or alkaline matter, are far more soluble in acids, do not become plastic, and in the fire become misshapen or fuse ; but often combine with grease or oil to an earthy soap. Many are thus of great economic importance. They scarcely form true species, but are mostly indefinite mixtures or mere products of the decomposition of rocks and minerals.

*105. KAOLIN,⎰ $\ddot{A}l\ .\dot{S}i^2 + 2\ \dot{H}$, *or*
Porcelain-earth.⎱ $[H^2O\ .\ Al^2O^3 + H^2O.\ 2\ SiO^2]$.

Massive in beds and veins. Fracture uneven ; fine-earthy, very soft, sectile, and friable. H. = 1 ; G. = 2·2. Opaque, dull. White or gray, inclining to blue, green, yellow, or red. Feels meagre, not greasy, when dry, and plastic when wet. B.B. infusible. Not affected by h. acid, but decomposed by warm s. acid, leaving silica. Chem. com. very variable, but approximates to 46 silica, 40 alumina, and 14 water. Chiefly a product of the decomposition of orthoclase, or of granite, porphyry, and other rocks containing this mineral. Pholerite or Nacrite (No. 79 above) is the crystalline form of the same compound. Cornwall and Devonshire in Britain, Limoges in France, Meissen in Saxony, are some of the chief European localities for the kaolin used in manufacturing porcelain.

*106. CLAY.

Clays are merely varieties of kaolin, mixed with quartz-sand, carbonate of lime, magnesia, the oxyhydrates of iron and manganese, or other substances. Usually they contain 40 to 50 silica, 30 alumina, 13 to 20 water, about 4 iron peroxide, with lime and potash. In the fire they are infusible, burn hard. Generally they are compact and friable, of white, yellow, red, blue, gray, or brown colours. Their spec. gr. varies from 1·8 to 2·7. Varieties are—*Pipe-clay*, grayish or yellowish white, with a greasy feel, adheres strongly to the tongue; and when wet is very plastic and tenacious, and in the fire burns white. Abundant in Devonshire, and in the Trough of Poole in Dorsetshire ; in France, Belgium, and Germany. Used for manufacturing tobacco-pipes and similar articles. *Potters' clay*, red, yellow, green, or blue, becoming yellow or red when burnt; more easily fused than the former, and often effervesces with acids. That used in the potteries in England comes chiefly from Devonshire. *Loam*, coarser and more impure, with more sand, and consequently less plastic. *Shale* or *slate-clay*, grayish-black, and much mixed with bituminous or carbonaceous matter. *Bituminous shale*, known by its shining resinous streak. *Black chalk*, with more carbon, leaves a black mark on paper. *Iron-clay* contains much peroxide of iron, is reddish-brown, and forms the basis of many amygdaloids and porphyries.

107. ROCK-SOAP, Bergseife.
Compact. Fracture earthy or conchoidal ; sectile. H. = 1...2. Streak resinous. Colour pitch-black and bluish-black. Feels very greasy ; writes, but does not soil. Adheres strongly to the tongue, and falls to pieces in water. Chem. com. 44 to 46 silica, 17 to 26 alumina, 6 to 10 iron peroxide, 13 to 25 water. Arnstedt, Cassel, Bilin, and Isle of Skye. Used for crayons by painters, and for washing cloth.

108. PLINTHITE.
Compact ; earthy. H. = 2...3 ; G. = 2·34. Brick-red or brownish-red. Does not adhere to the tongue. B.B. becomes black, but is infusible. Chem. com. 30·9 silica, 20·8 alumina, 26·1 iron peroxide, 2·6 lime, and 19·6 water. Antrim in Ireland. *Erinite*, from the same place, is similar.

109. GREEN-EARTH, Seladonite.
Massive, forming crusts. Fracture, fine earthy ; sectile.
H. = 1...2 ; G. = 2·8. Opaque ; streak shining. Green.
Feels greasy. B.B. fuses to a black magnetic glass ; not
affected by acids. Chem. com. about 51 silica, 7 alumina,
21 iron protoxide, 6 magnesia, 6 potash, 2 soda, and 7
water. Common in the trap rocks of Faroe, Iceland,
Scotland, and other countries ; that used in the arts chiefly
from Monte Baldo near Verona, and Cyprus.

110. GLAUCONITE.
Small round green grains like gunpowder, with dull
resinous lustre. B.B. difficultly fusible to a black, weakly
magnetic slag ; completely soluble in warm con. h. acid.
Chem. com. essentially a hydrous silicate of iron protoxide
and potash, but with 43 to 57 silica, 5 to 17 alumina, 19
to 27 iron protoxide, 5 to 15 potash, 1 to 4 magnesia, 0 to
3 lime, and 7 to 13 water. The greensand of England,
France, Germany, and North America. In New Jersey
forms a valuable manure.

111. YELLOW-EARTH.—$(\ddot{F}e, \ddot{A}l)^2 \ddot{S}i^3 + 4 \dot{H}$.
Fracture fine earthy or slaty. H. = 1...2 ; G. = 2·2.
Ochre-yellow. Greasy ; adheres slightly to the tongue,
and pulverises in water. B.B. infusible, but becomes red ;
partially soluble in h. acid. A mixture of silicate of
alumina, peroxide of iron, and water. Harz, France, and
Scotland. Used as a coarse pigment.

112. PALAGONITE.—$(\ddot{A}l, \ddot{F}e)^2\ddot{S}i^3 + 3(\dot{C}a, \dot{M}g, \dot{N}a)\ddot{S}i + 10 \dot{H}$.
Amorphous ; fracture conchoidal. H. = 4...5 ; G. = 2·4
...2·6. Translucent ; resinous to vitreous. Wine-yellow
to brown. Like resin. B.B. fuses readily to a magnetic
bead. Easily soluble in acid. Palagonia in Sicily, Iceland,
Galapagos, Nassau, and Cassel.

113. HALLOYSITE.—$\ddot{A}l \ddot{S}i + 4 \dot{H}$.
Reniform ; H. = 1·5...2·5 ; G. = 1·9...2·1. Semitranslucent, and more so when moist. White, inclining to blue,

green, or yellow. Adheres slightly to the tongue. B.B. infusible ; soluble in c. s. acid. Chem. com. nearly 41·5 silica, 34·4 alumina, and 24·1 water. Liege, Tarnowitz, Thiviers in France ; Eifel (*Lenzinite*) ; Scotland (*Tuesite*).

*114. FULLER'S-EARTH, Walkerde.

Fracture uneven, slaty, or earthy ; H. = 1...1·5 ; G. = 1·8...2·0. Opaque ; dull, but streak resinous. Green, gray, or white. Very greasy ; scarcely adheres to the tongue. Falls down in water, but does not become plastic. That from Reigate in Surrey contains 53 silica, 10 alumina, 9·75 iron peroxide, 1·25 magnesia, 0·5 lime, and 24 water. It is used in preparing cloth,—the best for this purpose being found in England, as at Reigate, Maidstone in Kent, Woburn in Bedfordshire, etc. ; also near Maxton in Scotland, in Saxony, Bohemia, and Styria.

115. ALLOPHANE.—$\ddot{A}l\ \ddot{S}i + 5\ \dot{H}$.

Botryoidal and reniform. Fracture conchoidal, brittle. H. = 3 ; G. = 1·8...2. Pellucid ; vitreous. Pale-blue, white, green, or brown. B.B. intumesces and becomes white, but does not fuse ; gelatinises in acids. Chem. com. often near 24·3 silica, 40·4 alumina, and 35·3 water ; occasionally with 2 to 3 oxides of iron or copper and 2 to 4 carbonate of lime or magnesia. Charlton near Woolwich, Baden, Bonn, and Saalfield.

116. SCHRÖTTERITE.—$\ddot{A}l^2\ \ddot{S}i + 8\ \dot{H}$.

Amorphous. Conchoidal. H. = 3...3·5 ; G. = 2. Greenish, yellowish, or with brown spots. B.B. infusible, but burns white ; gelatinises in h. acid. Freienstein in Styria.

117. BOLE.

Earthy, in nests and veins. Conchoidal. H. = 1...2 ; G. = 2·2...2·5. Opaque, or translucent on the edges ; dull resinous ; streak shining. Brown, yellow, or red. Feels greasy ; some adhere strongly to the tongue, others not at all. In water crackle and fall to pieces. B.B. harden, and generally fuse to an enamel ; in acids are more or less soluble. Chem. com. hydrous silicates of alumina and iron peroxide in various proportions. Dransfield, Clermont,

Auvergne, the trap rocks of the Hebrides and other parts of Scotland, and Ireland. That from Stolpen (*Stolpenite*), gives a mere trace of iron but 4 of lime. *Sinopite*, red, from Asia Minor, is supposed to be the Sinopian earth of antiquity. *Fettbol*, from Freiberg, and *Ochran*, of a yellow colour, are infusible B.B.

118. TERATOLITE.

Fracture uneven, or earthy; $H. = 2.5...3$; $G. = 2.5$. Opaque; dull. Lavender-blue to plum-blue, often with reddish-white veins and spots. Feels rough and meagre. B.B. infusible. Schuler's analysis gave 41·66 silica, 22·85 alumina, 12·98 iron peroxide, 3·04 lime, 2·55 magnesia, 0·93 potash, 1·68 manganese peroxide, 14·20 water ($= 99.89$). Planitz near Zwickau; the *Terra miraculosa Saxoniæ* of old authors.

119. KOLLYRITE.—$\ddot{Al}^2 \ddot{Si} + 10 \dot{H}$.

Compact. Fracture even or fine-earthy. $H. = 1...2$; $G. = 2.0...2.15$. Semitranslucent or opaque; dull. Snow-white, rarely reddish, greenish, or yellowish. Feels greasy, and adheres strongly to the tongue. B.B. infusible; gelatinises imperfectly with acids. Chem. com. 14 silica, 46 alumina, and 40 water. Schemnitz, Pyrenees, and Saxony. *Scarbroite*, from Scarborough, is similar, but with more (48) water.

120. LITHOMARGE, Steinmark.

Kaolin-like substances, and perhaps mere varieties; in general compact, earthy, or pseudomorphous. $H. = 2.5...3.0$; $G. = 2.4...2.6$. Opaque, or dimly translucent; dull. White, yellow, or red. Feel greasy, and adhere more or less to the tongue. Landshut, Clausthal, and the Harz. Similar are *Carnat*, fine red; and *Myelin*, pale yellow or red, and reniform, both from Rochlitz in Saxony: *Melopsite*, yellowish or greenish white, from Neudeck in Bohemia. Also *Miloschin*, or *Serbian*. Conchoidal, or earthy; $H. = 2$; $G. = 2.13$. Indigo-blue to celadine-green. Contains 2 to 4 chrome oxide. Rudnaïk in Servia. Is a mixture.

M

121. KEROLITE.—$4 \dot{M}g \ddot{S}i + \ddot{\ddot{A}}l \ddot{S}i + 15 \dot{H}.$

Reniform. Uneven, conchoidal, or splintery; rather brittle. $H. = 2...3$; $G. = 2\cdot3...2\cdot4.$ Translucent; dull resinous. White, inclining to gray, yellow, green, or red. Feels greasy, but does not adhere to the tongue. B.B. infusible. Frankenstein in Silesia.

122. AGALMATOLITE, Figure-stone, Pagodite. $\left.\right\}$ $4 \ddot{\ddot{A}}l \ddot{S}i^2 + \dot{K} \ddot{S}i^2 + 3 \dot{H}.$

Massive or slaty. Fracture splintery; rather sectile. $H. = 2...3$; $G. = 2\cdot8...2\cdot9.$ Translucent, or only on the edges; dull or glimmering. Green, gray, red, and yellow. Feels somewhat greasy, but does not adhere to the tongue. B.B. burns white and fuses slightly on very thin edges; soluble in warm s. acid. Chem. com. 55 silica, 33 alumina, 7·6 potash, and 4·4 water. But others vary much, and are probably distinct. China, where it is cut into various works of art; also Nagyag in Hungary, and Saxony. *Cimolite*, pure white clay from Argentiera and Milo, used for cleaning cloth, is similar.

123. SOAPSTONE, Saponite.

Massive; sectile and very soft. $H. = 1\cdot5$; $G. = 2\cdot26.$ White, or light-gray, yellow, and reddish-brown; streak shining. Feels greasy, and writes feebly; does not adhere to the tongue. B.B. fuses to a colourless porous glass; soluble in s. acid. Chem. com. various, but about 44 silica, 7 alumina, 29 magnesia, and 20 water. Lizard Point and St. Clear in Cornwall, and Dalarne in Sweden (*Piotine*).

124. ONKOSIN.—$2 \ddot{\ddot{A}}l \ddot{S}i^2 + (\dot{K}, \dot{M}g) \ddot{S}i^2 + 2 \dot{H}.$

Fracture uneven or splintery; sectile. $H. = 2$; $G. = 2\cdot8.$ Translucent; slightly resinous. Apple-green or brown. B.B. intumesces and fuses; soluble in s. not in h. acid. Salzburg.

125. PIPESTONE.—$(\ddot{\ddot{A}}l, \ddot{F}e) \ddot{S}i^2 + (\dot{N}a, \dot{C}a, \dot{M}g) \ddot{S}i + \dot{H}.$

Compact; fracture earthy; sectile. $H. = 1\cdot5$; $G. = 2\cdot6.$ Opaque, dull. Grayish-blue, black, or red (*Catlinite*). B.B. infusible. Used by the North American Indians for pipes.

126. MEERSCHAUM.—$2 \dot{M}g^2 \ddot{S}i^3 + 3 \dot{H}$.

Fracture fine earthy ; sectile. H. = 2...2·5 ; G. = 0·8...
1·0 (when moist nearly 2). Opaque, dull. Streak slightly
shining. Yellowish and grayish white. Feels rather
greasy, and adheres strongly to the tongue. B.B. contracts
becomes hard, and fuses on the edges ; soluble in h. acid,
leaving silica. Chem. com. 62·6 silica, 28·3 magnesia, and
9·1 water ; but others give also 0·7 to 2·7 carbonic acid,
and 14 hygroscopic water. Asia Minor, Greece, near
Madrid and Toledo ; Morvia and Wermeland (*Aphrodite*,
G. = 2·21). Chiefly used in forming heads for tobacco-
pipes.

127. PIMELITE.—$2 \ddot{A}l \ddot{S}i + 3 \dot{M}g \ddot{S}i + 10 \dot{H}$.

Fracture conchoidal ; H. = 2·5 ; G. = 2·3 or 2·7. Translucent ; dull resinous. Colour apple-green ; streak yellowish-white. Feels greasy. B.B. fuses to a slag only on
thin edges. With borax shows reaction for nickel (3 per
cent nickel oxide). Silesia.

128. DERMATIN.—$(Mg, \dot{F}e) \ddot{S}i + 2 \dot{H}$.

Reniform ; H. = 2·5 ; G. = 2·136. Resinous. Colour
blackish-green ; streak yellowish-white. Does not adhere
to the tongue. B.B. cracks and becomes black. Waldheim
in Saxony.

*FAMILY XI.—GARNET.

Chiefly tesseral ; H. = 6...7·5 ; G. = 3·1...3·8. All
fusible ; and all soluble in acids, but not readily, or only after
ignition. Most are highly coloured, and. often with fine
gem-like lustre ; but rarely transparent, in general only
translucent or opaque. Are mostly anhydrous silicates of
alumina and the earths, coloured by oxides of iron, manganese, and chrome.

Occur imbedded, or in veins and druses, in the older
crystalline rocks, but rarely as essential constituents.

**129. GARNET.—$\begin{cases} \dot{R}^3 \ddot{S}i^2 + \ddot{R} \ddot{S}i = \\ [3 \ RO \ . \ 2 \ SiO^2 + R^2O^3 . \ SiO^2]. \end{cases}$

Tesseral ; most common forms ∞O (Fig. 3), and 2O2,

(Fig. 6). These are often combined (Figs. 18 and 19). Also granular or compact. Cleavage dodecahedral, but very imperfect ; fracture conchoidal, or uneven and splintery. $H. = 6\cdot5...7\cdot5$; $G. = 3\cdot5...4\cdot3$. Pellucid in all degrees ; vitreous or resinous. Rarely colourless or white ; generally red, brown, black, green, or yellow. B.B. in general fuse easily to a glass, black or gray in those containing much iron, green or brown in the others, and often magnetic ; imperfectly soluble in h. acid, some wholly, after long digestion, leaving the silica in powder. Chem. com. exceedingly variable, but generally form two series, according as $\dot{R}$ is chiefly alumina or chiefly iron peroxide : and these are again divided according as $\dot{R}$ is more especially lime, iron protoxide, magnesia, or similar bases.

The more important varieties are :—

(1.) *Almandine*, or *Noble Garnet.*—Columbine-red, inclining to violet, blood-red, or reddish-brown ; streak white ; transparent or translucent ; sometimes magnetic. Is an iron-alumina garnet, $\ddot{Fe}^3 \ddot{Si}^2 + \ddot{Al} \ddot{Si}$, with 36 silica, 21 alumina, and 43 iron protoxide. Common in the primary rocks, in crystals, or rarely forming beds and veins. The finest are from Pegu, Ceylon, and the East. Large crystals at Fahlun, Arendal, Kongsberg, the Tyrol, the Ural, and in North America. It is common in the mica-slates of Perth, Inverness, and Zetland ; in granite at Rubislaw, Aberdeen. Used as an ornamental stone.

(2.) *Manganese-alumina Garnet;* $\dot{R} = \dot{M}n$; reddish-brown ; Spessart, Sweden.

(3.) *Lime-alumina Garnets.*—$\dot{C}a^3 \ddot{Si}^2 + \ddot{Al} \ddot{Si}$, with 40 silica, 23 alumina, and 37 lime. To these belong—

(a.) *Grossular.*—White to olive-green, and translucent. Wilui River, Siberia, the Ural, and Tellemark in Norway.

(b.) *Cinnamon-stone, Hessonite,* or *Kaneelstein.*—Hyacinth-red to honey or orange yellow, and transparent or translucent. Ceylon and Wermeland. *Romanzowite,* Kimito in Finnland, is similar. When polished, this variety is often named hyacinth.

(c.) *Common Lime-garnet.*—Red, brown, yellow, or green,

and with part at least of the alumina replaced by iron peroxide. Abundant in Piedmont, Vesuvius, the Ural, and
North America.

(4.) *Magnesia-garnet.*—$\dot{R}$, chiefly magnesia; opaque, resinous; coal-black. G. = 3·157. Arendal.

(5.) *Iron-garnets.*—$\dot{C}a^3 \ddot{S}i^2 + \ddot{F}e \ddot{S}i$, with 35 silica, 32
iron peroxide, and 33 lime. G. = 3·7...4·0. More difficultly
fusible and more easily soluble in h. acid than the others.

(*a.*) *Common Iron-garnet, Rothoffite, Allochroite.*—Sub-
translucent or opaque. Green, brown, yellow, or black,
with white, gray, or yellow streak. Sweden and Arendal.

(*b.*) *Melanite.*—Black; opaque; in thin splinters trans-
lucent. Streak gray; slightly magnetic. Albano near
Frascati, Vesuvius, France, Lappmark. *Pyreneite,* near
Barèges in the Pyrenees.

(*c.*) *Colophonite.*—Yellowish-brown to pitch-black, also
yellow or red; resinous; streak white. G. = 3·43. Arendal.

(6.) *Uwarowite,* or *Chrome-garnet.*—Emerald-green; vitreous; streak greenish-white. Translucent, or only on the
edges, with $\ddot{R}$, principally chrome-oxide (= 22). G. = 3.4;
H. = 7·5. B.B. infusible. Bissersk and Kyschtimsk in the
Ural, India, and California.

130. PYROPE.—$(\dot{M}g, \dot{F}e, \dot{C}a, \dot{M}n)^3 \ddot{S}i^2 + \ddot{A}l \ddot{S}i.$

Tesseral, but crystals (cubes) rare and indistinct; generally in roundish grains. Cleavage not perceptible; fracture conchoidal. H. = 7·5; G. = 3·7...3·8. Transparent
or translucent; vitreous. Dark-hyacinth to blood-red. B.B.
becomes black and opaque, but regains its colour and transparency on cooling; fuses with difficulty to a black glass;
not soluble in acids, partially after fusion. Chem. com.
41·35 silica, 22·35 alumina, 15 magnesia, 9·94 iron protoxide, 5·29 lime, 4·17 chrome-protoxide, and 2·58 manga-
nese-protoxide (*Moberg*). Zöblitz in Saxony, Meronitz and
Mittelgebirge in Bohemia, and Elie in Fife (Elie rubies).
Valued as a gem.

131. HELVINE.—$\begin{cases} \dot{M}n \ S + 3 \ \dot{R}^3 \ \ddot{S}i, \ or \\ \dot{M}n \ S + \dot{R}^3 \ \ddot{S}i^2 + \ddot{G}l \ \ddot{S}i. \end{cases}$

Tesseral and tetrahedral; $\frac{O}{2}$ or $\frac{O}{2} . - \frac{O}{2}$ (Fig. 133). Em-

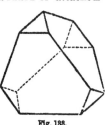

Fig. 133.

bedded or attached. Cleavage, octahedral imperfect. H. = 6...6·5 ; G. = 3·1 ... 3·3. Translucent on the edges ; resinous. Wax-yellow, siskin-green, or yellowish-brown. B.B. in the red, flame fuses with intumescence to a yellow obscure pearl; soluble in h. acid, evolving sulphuretted hydrogen, and gelatinises. Chem. com. 34 silica, 10 glucina, 8 iron protoxide, 43 manganese protoxide, and 5 sulphur. Schwarzenberg in Saxony, and near Modum in Norway. *Danalite*, flesh-red or gray, from Cape Ann and near Gloucester in Massachusetts, is nearly allied.

**132. IDOCRASE, Vesuvian. $\begin{cases} 3 \ (\dot{C}a, \ \dot{M}g)^3 \ \ddot{S}i + 2 \ \ddot{A}l \ \ddot{S}i^3, \ or \\ 6 \ \dot{R}^3 \ \ddot{S}i + \ddot{A}l^3 \ \ddot{S}i^3 - Rams. = \\ [6 \ (2RO.SiO^2) + 2Al^2O^3.3SiO^2]. \end{cases}$

Tetragonal ; P 74° 27'. Crystals of ∞P (*d*) . ∞P∞ (*m*) . P (*c*) . 0P (*p*) (Fig. 134) ; also P∞ (*o*) (56° 29') and many others (Fig. 135) ; but angles slightly variable. Prismatic, with faces striated; more rarely tabular or pyramidal. Also columnar or granular. Cleavage, prismatic along ∞P∞ and ∞P, but imperfect ; fracture uneven, splintery. H. = 6·5 ; G. = 3·35...3·45 (or 4·0). Pellucid; vitreous or resinous. Yellow, green, brown, almost black, rarely azure-blue ; streak white. B.B. fuses easily with intumescence to a yellowish-green or brown glass ; partially soluble in h. acid, after fusion wholly, and gelatinises. Chem. com. 37 to 39 silica, 14 to 18 alumina, 7 iron peroxide (or protoxide), 33 to 35 lime, and 2 to 3 magnesia, with 1 to 2 water. In the second formula the iron is taken as the protoxide. Vesuvius, Wilui

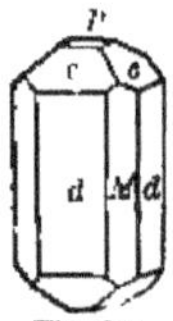

Fig. 134.

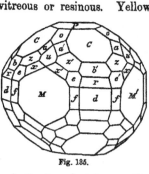

Fig. 135.

River in Siberia, Mussa-alp in Piedmont, Egg in Norway, Wicklow in Ireland, Monaltrie in Aberdeenshire, and near Broadford in Skye, in Scotland.

Gahnite, Loboite, Gökumite, from Gökum; *Frugardite,* from Finnland; *Egeran,* from near Eger; *Cyprine,* from Tellemark, Norway (azure-blue or green, contains copper, and B.B. melts easily in the inner flame to a red pearl); *Xanthite,* from Amity in New York—seem only idocrase.

Used as an ornamental stone, the brown being named hyacinth, the green chrysolite, but not highly valued.

*133. EPIDOTE, Pistazite, Thallite.
$\begin{cases} 2\ (\ddot{A}l,\ \ddot{F}e)\ \ddot{S}i^{3} + 3\ \dot{C}a^{3}\ \ddot{S}i,\ or \\ [3\ (Al^{2}\ O^{3}\ .\ Si\ O^{3} + CaO\ .\ Si\ O^{2}) + \\ \quad CaO\ .\ H^{2}O]. \end{cases}$

Monoclinic; C. = 89° 27′, ∞P°∞ (*M*), ∞P°2 63° 1′, P°∞ (*T*) 64° 36′, –P (*n*) 70° 25′, –P∞ (*r*) 63° 42′, as in Fig. 132 after Mohs, but Marignac and most recent authors choose another position with C. = 64° 36′, when *T* = ∞P°∞, *M* = 0P, *r* = P°_∞∞, and *n* = P, with ∞P 70°. Crystals horizontal, prismatic, and often complex

Fig. 136.

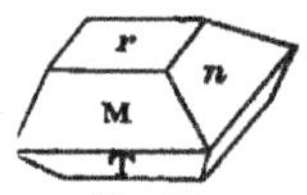

with many partial forms. Generally in druses; the faces often striated. Macles united by *T*; also columnar, granular, or compact. Cleavage, *M* very perfect, along *T* rather perfect. Meet at 115° 24′. Fracture conchoidal, uneven, or splintery. H. = 6...7; G. = 3·2...3·5. Pellucid in all degrees; vitreous, on cleavage adamantine. Especially green (*Pistazite*), yellow, and gray; rarely red and black. B.B. fusible, and swells up to a dark-brown slag. Strongly ignited, or after fusion, all are soluble in h. acid, and gelatinise. Chem. com. variable, but, according to Kenngott and Ludwig, the second above with 38·3 silica, 27·4 alumina, 8·5 iron peroxide, 23·9 lime, and 1·9 water in those from Switzerland; in those from Arendal, Bourg d'Oisans, and Sulzbach, with 37·2 silica, 21·3 alumina, 16·5 iron peroxide, 23·1 lime, and 1·9 water, the last basic. Arendal, Dauphiné, the Alps (Mont Blanc), Pyrenees, Greenland, the Ural, and North America. In Scotland, in syenite in Zetland, in gneiss in Sutherland, in trap in Mull and Skye, in quartz in Rona, in clay-slate in Arran, and in porphyry in Arran and Glencoe. *Puschkinite* from the Ural, *Withamite* from Glencoe, in minute bright-red crystals; and *Bucklandite*, in small black crystals, from Achmatowsk in Ural, are varieties; also *Piedmontite* or *Manganese-epidote.*—With much manganese-peroxide (14 to 20). Dark violet-blue or reddish-black; streak cherry-red. H. = 6·5; G. = 3·4. B.B. melts easily to a black glass. St. Marcel.

133*a*. ZOISITE.

Rhombic according to Descloizeaux; with ∞P 116° 16′ to 117° 5′, ∞P̃2 145° 28′, and other forms. Cleavage, brachydiagonal very perfect. But chiefly in large indistinct, embedded crystals, strongly striated, or foliated and columnar. H. = 6 ; G. = 3·2...3·4 White, yellowish, or brownish-gray. B.B. intumesces and forms a white or yellow porous mass, and on the edges fuses to a clear glass. Chem. com. like epidote, with 42 silica, 32 alumina, and 26 lime, and a little (2 to 7) iron oxide and magnesia. Is thus either a dimorphous form, or, as others think, monoclinic and a variety of epidote. Sterzing, Tyrol, Sau Alpe in Carinthia, the Ural, and Connecticut. *Thulite*, rose or peach-blossom red, from Souland in Norway, is similar.

* 134. AXINITE.— $\begin{cases} (\ddot{A}l, \ddot{B}) \ddot{S}i + 2 (\dot{C}a, \dot{F}e) \ddot{S}i, \ or \\ [R^2O^3. SiO^3 + 2 (RO . SiO^2)]. \end{cases}$

Triclinic. Crystals usually very unsymmetrical (Figs. 137 and 138), with *u* to *P* = 135° 31′, *u* to *r* = 115° 38′,

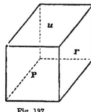

Fig. 137.

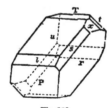

Fig. 138.

P to *r* = 134° 45′; attached singly, or in druses. Also laminar or broadly radiated. Cleavage, distinct along planes truncating the sharp edges between *P* and *u* and *P* and *r*. H. = 6·5...7 ; G. = 3·2...3·3. Pellucid; vitreous.

Clove-brown, inclining to smoke-gray or plum-blue, but often cinnamon-brown in one direction, dark violet-blue in a second, and pale olive-green in a third (*trichroism*). B.B. colours flame green; intumesces and fuses easily to a dark-green glass, becoming black in the ox. flame; not soluble in h. acid till after ignition, when it gelatinises. Chem. com. 45·9 silica, 5·9 boracic acid, 17·5 alumina, 9·3 iron (with manganese) protoxide, and 21·4 lime. Bourg d'Oisans in Dauphiné, Botallack and other mines in Cornwall, Kongsberg, Arendal, Nordmark in Sweden, Pyrenees, St. Gotthard, Tyrol, Thum in Saxony (*Thummerstein*), the Ural, and North America.

135. GLAUCOPHANE.—$2\ \ddot{A}l\ \ddot{S}i^3 + 9\ \dot{R}\ \ddot{S}i$.

Rhombic or monoclinic, only indistinct, thin, four or six sided prismatic crystals, or granular. Cleavage, prismatic distinct; fracture conchoidal. H. = 5·5; G. = 3·1. Translucent or opaque; vitreous or pearly. Gray, indigo-blue, or bluish-black. B.B. becomes yellowish-brown, and fuses readily to an olive-green glass; partly soluble in acids. Chem. com. 56·5 silica, 12·2 alumina, 10·9 iron protoxide, 0·5 manganese protoxide, 8 magnesia, 2·3 lime, and 9·3 soda. Island of Syra. Similar are—   •

Wichtyne.—Massive; black. B.B. fuses to a black enamel; not affected by acids. Wichtis in Finnland. *Violan.* — Massive; opaque, resinous. Dark violet-blue. B.B. fuses easily to a clear glass. St. Marcel in Piedmont.

FAMILY XII.—CYANITE.

Triclinic or rhombic, often in long prismatic forms. H. = 5...7·5; G. = 2·9...3·8. B.B. infusible; insoluble in acids. Some show fine colours and high vitreous lustre. They are chiefly anhydrous silicates of alumina. Occur especially in the crystalline strata.

**136. CYANITE, Disthene.—$\ddot{A}l\ \ddot{S}i = [Al^2O^3 . SiO^2]$.

Triclinic. Generally broad prismatic lengthened crystals (Fig. 139) formed by two faces (*M, T*) *M* : *T* 106° 15′, *M* : *i* 145° 41′, *P* : *M* 93° 15′. Macles common, united by *M*. Also even, curved, or radiated. Cleavage, along the prisms very (or less) perfect; brittle. H. = 5 on cleavage-planes, on other faces = 7; G. 3·5...3·7. Pellucid, vitreous; on cleavage pearly. Colourless, or blue, gray, green, yellow, or red. Not affected by acids. B.B. infusible. Chem. com. 36·9 silica, and 63·1 alumina. St. Gotthardt, Tyrol (*Rhætizite*), Pontivy in France, Bohemia, Nigg near Aberdeen, Botriphnie in Banffshire, and Hillswick in Zetland.

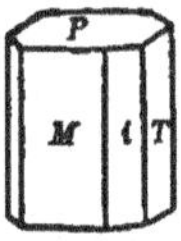

Fig. 139.

137. SILLIMANITE.—$\dddot{\text{Al}}\,\ddot{\text{Si}}$, *or* $\dddot{\text{Al}}^3\,\ddot{\text{Si}}^2$.

Rhombic, ∞P 111°. Crystals long and slender; also fibrous or columnar. Cleavage, macrodiagonal highly perfect. H. = 7...7·5; G. = 3·2...3·26. Translucent, resinous, on cleavage vitreous. Grayish-brown, clove, or hair-brown. B.B. infusible; not affected by acids. Chem. com. like andalusite. Chester and Norwich in Connecticut, Tvedestrand in Norway. *Monrolite*, from Monroe, New York; *Xenolite*, Finnland; *Bucholzite*, *Fibrolite*, and *Bamlite*, from Bamle, in Norway, seem the same; *Wörthite*, an altered variety.

*138. ANDALUSITE.—$\dddot{\text{Al}}\,\ddot{\text{Si}}$, *or* $\dddot{\text{Al}}^3\,\ddot{\text{Si}}^2$.

Rhombic; ∞P 90° 50′, $\bar{\text{P}}\infty$ 109° 4′. Crystals ∞P . 0P, or with $\bar{\text{P}}\infty$ (*M*, *P*, *o*) (Fig. 140); prismatic, attached or embedded; also columnar, or granular. Cleavage, ∞P rather indistinct; traces along $\infty\breve{\text{P}}\infty$, $\infty\bar{\text{P}}\infty$ and $\bar{\text{P}}\infty$. Fracture uneven, splintery. H. = 7...7·5; G. = 3·1...3·2. Pellucid; vitreous. Gray, green, red, or blue. B.B. infusible; not affected by acids. Chem. com. in most like cyanite, but in some 39·6 silica and 60·4 alumina, with 1 to 2 iron peroxide. Andalusia, Lisens in Tyrol, Penig in Saxony, Westford in Massachusetts, Litchfield in Connecticut; and Botriphnie in Banffshire, Huntly and Tyrie in Aberdeenshire, and Killiney Bay in Wicklow.

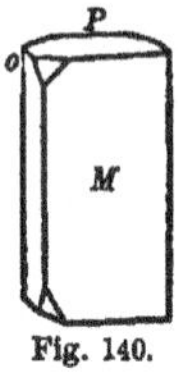

Fig. 140.

N.B.—Assuming $\dddot{\text{Al}}\,\ddot{\text{Si}}$ as the true formula for cyanite, sillimanite, and andalusite, then this substance is trimorphous.

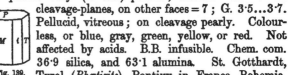

Chiastolite.—H. = 5...5·5 ; G. = 3·0. Dirty or pale gray, yellow, or red. Occurs imbedded in clay-slate, and often appears like four crystals separated by a black cross (Fig. 141). Fichtelgebirge, Brittany, the Pyrenees, Sierra Morena, Wolfscrag near Keswick, and on Skiddaw in Cumberland ; _{Fig. 141.} near Balahulish in Argyleshire, Boharm in Banffshire, and in Wicklow.

*139. STAUROLITE, Staurotide.—(Äl, F̈e) S̈i + (F̈e, M̈g) S̈i.

Rhombic ; ∞ 128° 42′, P̄∞ 70° 46′. Crystals ∞P (*M*). ∞P̄∞ (*o*) . 0P (*p*). Macles very common, like Figs. 142 or 143. Cleavage, brachydiagonal perfect, traces along ∞P;

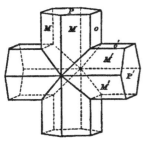

Fig. 142.

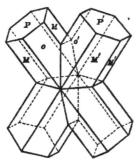

Fig. 143.

fracture conchoidal, or uneven and splintery. H. = 7 ; G. = 3·5...3·8. Translucent or opaque ; vitreous, inclining to resinous. Reddish to blackish brown ; streak white. B.B. infusible ; not affected by h., partially by s., acid. Chem. com. of a pure variety about 30 silica, 48·5 alumina, with 5·5 iron peroxide, and 12·5 iron protoxide, with 3·5 magnesia, but analyses vary greatly from microscopic mixture with other minerals. A specimen from Aberdeenshire contained quartz, brookite, magnetite, and mica. St. Gotthardt and Greiner in Tyrol, Finisterre, Pyrenees, Spain, the Ural, and in North America ; in Scotland, Bixeter Voe in Zetland, near Huntly, Aberdeenshire, and the Hebrides.

140. DIASPORE.—Äl Ḣ, *or* [Al²O³ . H²O].

Rhombic ; ∞P 129° 47′, broad, indistinct prisms, chiefly

of ∞P̆∞ , bounded by the curved faces of P (Fig. 144). Usually thin foliated or broad radiated. Cleavage, brachydiagonal highly perfect ; very brittle. H. = 6 ; G. = 3·3...3·4. Pellucid ; vitreous ; pearly on ∞P̆∞ . Colourless, but generally yellowish or greenish white ; also violet-blue.

Fig. 144.

Insoluble in acids. B.B. infusible, but some decrepitate into small white scales. Chem. com. 85 alumina and 15 water. Rare. Ural and Schemnitz, Broddbo and St. Gotthardt.

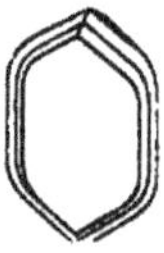

141. HYDRALGILITE.—Äl Ḣ³, *or* [Al²O³ . 3 H²O].

Monoclinic ; in six-sided tables of 0P . ∞P . ∞P̆°∞ , or granular scaly. Cleavage, basal very perfect. H. = 2·5... 3 ; G. = 2·3...2·4. Translucent ; vitreous ; pearly on 0P. Colourless, but greenish or reddish white. Slowly soluble in warm acids. B.B. exfoliates, and gives out a strong light, but is infusible. Chem. com. 65·5 alumina and 34·5 water. Near Slatoust in the Ural. Stalactitic, greenish or grayish white (*Gibbsite*); Richmond, Massachusetts, Villa Rica in Brazil.

142. PERICLASE.—Ṁg.

Tesseral, minute octahedrons or cubes. Cleavage hexahedral perfect. H. = 6 ; G. = 3·6...3·75. Transparent ; vitreous. Dark-green. B.B. infusible ; powder soluble in acids. Chem. com. magnesia, with 5 to 8 protoxide of iron. Monte Somma.

FAMILY XIII.—GEMS.

All very hard, H. = 7...9, or scratch quartz, except a few = 6, which are scarcely true gems ; G. = 2·6...4·7, but mostly high in the finest. Insoluble in acids, and infusible B.B. in the true gems. These have a high lustre, brilliant colours, and take a fine polish, and are therefore much valued. They are, however, rare, and generally small. Chem. com. variable, but mostly simple. Chiefly occur in the older igneous or metamorphic rocks.

*143. ZIRCON.—Żr Śi = [Zr O². Si O²].

Tetragonal; P 84° 20′.   Crystals, ∞P.P, often with 3 P 3; also ∞P∞.P, or ∞P∞ (*s*).∞P (*l*).P (*P*).3 P 3 (*x*).ᵗ. P∞ (*t*).4 P 4 (*y*).5 P 5 (*z*) (Fig. 145), chiefly prismatic or pyramidal, and in rounded
grains.   Cleavage, along P and ∞P,
both rather imperfect; fracture conchoidal or uneven.   H. = 7·5; G. =
4·0...4·7.   Transparent to opaque;
vitreous, often adamantine.   Rarely
white, generally gray, yellow, green,
or frequently red and brown.   B.B.
loses its colour, but is infusible; not
affected by any acid except con. s.
acid, after long digestion.   Chem. com.

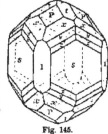

Fig. 145.

66·3 zirconia, and 33·77 silica, with 0 to 2 iron peroxide
as colouring matter.   Southern Norway, Ilmen Mountains,
Arendal, Sweden, Carinthia, Tyrol, Ceylon, and North
America; in Scotland, Strontian, and Scalpay in Harris.

The colourless varieties are sold for diamonds.   The
more brilliantly coloured are named hyacinth.

144. MALAKON.—3 Żr Śi + Ḣ.

Tetragonal; P. 83° 30′.   Crystals, like zircon.   H. = 6;
G. = 3·9...4·1.   Opaque; resinous or vitreous.   Internally
bluish-white, but on the surface mostly brownish, reddish,
yellowish, or blackish.   Chem. com. zircon, with 3 per cent.
water; probably not essential.   Hitterö in Norway (*Malakon.*)   *Œrstedtite* from Arendal, and *Tachyaphaltite* from
Krageroe, are probably altered zircon.

*145. SPINEL.—Ṁg Äl = [Mg O . Al² O²].

Tesseral; O alone or predominating, ∞O and 3O3.
Macles united by a face of O (Fig. 146); also in grains or
fragments.   Cleavage, octahedral imperfect; fracture conchoidal.   H. = 8; G. = 3·4...4·1.   Transparent to opaque;
vitreous.   Red, blue, green, and black; streak white.   B.B.
infusible and unchanged.   Chem. com. 72 alumina and 28
magnesia; but some with a little iron protoxide or per-

oxide, and the red varieties 1 to 5 chrome. Varieties are—

Spinel or *Spinel ruby*, rose-red (*Balas ruby*), yellow or orange-red (*Rubicelle*), violet (*Almandine ruby*) or brown; G. = 3·52; from Ceylon, Ava, and the East. Much prized as ornamental stones. *Sapphirine.*—Pale sapphire-blue to greenish or reddish blue; G. = 3·4...3·7; with 4 per cent iron protoxide; Aker in Sweden, Greenland, and North America. *Pleonaste*, dark green or blue and black; G. = 3·65...3·8; with 8 to

Fig. 146.

20 iron protoxide; Candy in Ceylon (*Candite* or *Zeilanite*). Monte Somma, Monzoni, Arendal, Bohemia (*Hercynite*), the Ural, and New York. *Chlorospinel*, grass-green, with a yellowish-white streak; G. = 3·59; Slatoust in the Ural.

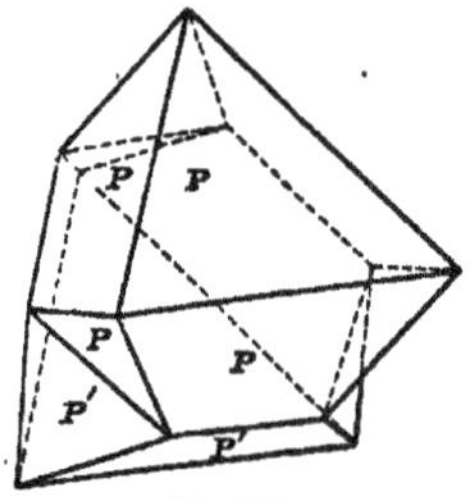

146. AUTOMOLITE, Gahnite.—Żn Äl.
Tesseral; O, alone or with ∞O, also cubes and macles like Fig. 146. Cleavage, O perfect; brittle, with conchoidal or splintery fracture. H. = 7·5...8; G. = 4·3...4·9. Opaque or translucent on the edges; vitreous, inclining to resinous. Dark leek-green to blackish green and blue; streak gray. B.B. unchanged; not affected by acids or alkalis. Chem. com. 56 alumina and 44 zinc oxide, but with 4 to 6 protoxide of iron, and 2 to 5 magnesia. Fahlun, Broddbo, Haddam in Connecticut, and Franklin in New Jersey. *Dysluite*, yellowish-brown, with manganese, from Sterling, Massachusetts; and *Kreittonite*, brown, from Bodenmais, are similar.

*147. CORUNDUM.—Äl = [Al² O²].
Hexagonal, rhombohedral; isomorphous with the peroxides of iron and chrome; R 86° 4'. Crystals chiefly of ∞P2 (*s*), OR (*o*), R (*P*), are pyramidal (Fig. 147), prismatic (Fig. 148), or rhombohedral. Macles common, united by a face of R. Cleavage, rhombohedral along R, and basal more or less perfect. Extremely tough, and difficultly frangible. H. = 9; G. = 3·9...4·2. Transparent

or translucent; vitreous, or pearly on OR. Colourless and white, but generally blue, red, yellow, brown, or gray. B.B.

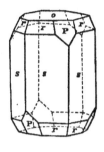

Fig. 147.　　　　Fig. 148.

unchanged. Chem. com. alumina, with a minute proportion of peroxide of iron or other colouring matter.

Varieties are:—(1.) *Sapphire*, highly transparent, very imperfect cleavage and conchoidal fracture; colourless, blue (*Salamstein*), seldomer green, yellow, red (*Oriental rubies*), or brown; Ceylon, Ava, Pegu, Miask, Slatoust, Bilin in Bohemia, and Expailly in Auvergne. (2.) *Corundum*, rough crystals or foliated, less transparent and duller colours; Malabar, Ceylon, Ava, Canton in China, Siberia, St. Gotthardt, and Piedmont. Some (*Asteria* or *star sapphire*) show a bright opalescent star of six rays. Recently crystals (one of 300 lbs. weight) of gray corundum with blue sapphire in the interior at Macon in North Carolina. (3.) *mantine spar*, with distinct cleavage, hair-brown, and adamantine; Gellivara, Ural, Malabar, and North America. (4.) *Emery*, compact, dimly translucent, and gray or indigoblue; Asia Minor near Smyrna, Naxos, Spain, Saxony, and Greenland. Sapphire and rubies are highly valued as ornamental stones; emery as a polishing material.

148. TOPAZ.— $\begin{cases} 5 \ddot{Al} \ddot{Si} + (Al F^3 + Si F^2), \textit{ or} \\ [5 (Al^2 O^3 . Si O^2) + Al^2 F^6. Si F^4]. \end{cases}$

Rhombic; ∞P (*M*) 124° 17′, $2\breve{P}\infty$ (*n*) 92° 42′, $\infty\breve{P}2$ (*l*) 93° 14′, P (*o*), and numerous other forms. Crystals always prismatic (Fig. 149), often hemimorphic, and the prisms finely striated ; also granular. Cleavage, basal very perfect, traces in other directions, especially M and l in the

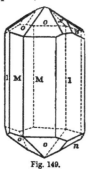

Fig. 149.

Scottish varieties ; fracture conchoidal or uneven. H. = 8 ; G. = 3·4...3·6. Transparent to translucent on the edges ; vitreous. Colourless, but yellowish, reddish, or greenish white, honey-yellow, hyacinth-red, and asparagus-green. Becomes electric from heat or friction. B.B. infusible. Not affected by h. acid, but by long digestion in s. acid gives traces of fluorine. Chem. com. essentially $\ddot{A}l\ \ddot{S}i$ with part of the oxygen replaced by fluorine ; or nearly 33·16 silica, 56·70 alumina, and 17·50 fluorine (= 107·36). Brazil, Siberia, Ceylon, New Holland, Peru, Connecticut, Bohemia, Saxony, and Cornwall (St. Michael's Mount), Mourne Mountains in Ireland, Cairngorm Mountains in Aberdeenshire (one crystal nineteen ounces). The common or coarse columnar named *Pyrophysalite*, at Finbo, and Broddbo near Fahlun. Topaz is valued as an ornamental stone. The purest from Brazil, when cut in facets like the diamond, closely resemble it in lustre and brilliance, but are easily known by their electricity.

Pycnite, Schorlite. — Massive. H. = 7.5 ; G. = 3·49... 3·54. Translucent ; vitreous. Straw-yellow to reddish-white. Variety of topaz. Altenberg in Saxony, and Schlaggenwald and Zinnwald, Durango in Mexico.

149. LEUCOPHANE.—6 $\dot{C}a\ \ddot{S}i + 3\ \ddot{G}l^2\ \ddot{S}i + 2\ Na\ F$.

Rhombic ; ∞P about 91° ; but crystals rare. Cleavage, basal perfect. H. = 3·5...4 ; G. = 2·97. In thin splinters pellucid and almost colourless ; in thicker pieces wine-yellow or olive-green ; vitreous or resinous. B.B. fuses to a pale violet-blue bead. *Melinophane* is a variety. Both near Brevig in Norway.

150. CHRYSOBERYL, Cymophane.—$\ddot{G}l\ \ddot{A}l$.

Rhombic ; P with polar edges 86° 16′ and 139° 53′.

Crystals of $\infty\bar{P}\infty$ (*M*) $\infty\bar{P}\infty$ (*T*) . $\bar{P}\infty$ (*i*), or this with ∞P2 (*s*), and also with P (*o*) (Fig. 150), are short and broadly columnar, or thick tabular with vertical striæ. Macles very common, united by a face of $\bar{P}\infty$. Cleavage, brachydiagonal imperfect, macrodiagonal more so; fracture conchoidal. H. $= 8.5$; G. $= 3.68...3.8$. Transparent or translucent; vitreous, sometimes resinous. Greenishwhite, leek-green, olive-green, and greenishgray; sometimes with a bluish opalescence, or beautiful trichroism. B.B. infusible; not affected by acids. Chem. com. 80 alumina, and 20 glucina with 3 to 4 protoxide of iron. Brazil, Ceylon, India, Haddam in Connecticut, and Ural.

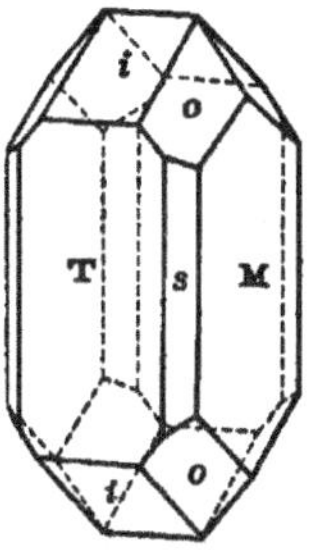

Fig. 150.

151. Euclase.—2 $\dot{\text{G}}$l $\ddot{\text{S}}$i $+\dot{\text{H}}$ $\ddot{\text{Al}}$.

Monoclinic; C. $= 79°$ 44'; ∞P$^{\circ}$2 (*S*) 115°, 3P$^{\circ}$3 (*t*) 105° 49'. Crystals specially of ∞P$^{\circ}$2 . ∞P$^{\circ}\infty$. (*T*) . 3P$^{\circ}$3, and many other forms (Fig. 151). Cleavage, clinodiagonal highly perfect, less so in other directions. Very brittle and fragile; fracture conchoidal. H. $= 7.5$; G. $= 3.0...3.1$. Transparent; splendent vitreous. Pale mountain-green, passing into

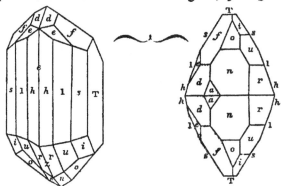

Fig. 151.

yellow, blue, or white. B.B. intumesces, becomes white, and melts in thin splinters to a white enamel. Not affected by acids. Chem. com. about 42 silica, 35 alumina, 18 glucina, and 6 water. Peru and Brazil, and Southern Ural, but very rare.

*152. EMERALD, BERYL.—$\ddot{A}l\ \ddot{S}i^3 + 3\ \dot{G}l\ \ddot{S}i$.

Hexagonal; P 59° 53'.   Crystals of ∞P . 0P, and ∞ P . 0P . P (*M, P, x*, Fig. 152), are prismatic, generally with vertical striæ.   Cleavage, basal rather perfect, ∞P imperfect. H. = 7·5...8 ; G. = 2·6...2·8.   Transparent or translucent ; vitreous.   Colourless or white, but generally green, sometimes very brilliant, also yellow, and smalt-blue.   B.B. melts with difficulty on the edges to an obscure vesicular

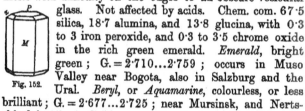

Fig. 152.

glass.   Not affected by acids.   Chem. com. 67·5 silica, 18·7 alumina, and 13·8 glucina, with 0·3 to 3 iron peroxide, and 0·3 to 3·5 chrome oxide in the rich green emerald.   *Emerald*, bright green ;   G. = 2·710...2·759 ;   occurs in Muso Valley near Bogota, also in Salzburg and the Ural.   *Beryl*, or *Aquamarine*, colourless, or less brilliant ; G. = 2·677...2·725 ; near Mursinsk, and Nertschinsk in Siberia, Salzburg and Brazil ; in the United States, where at Grafton, between the Connecticut and Merimac, crystals 4 to 6 feet long, and weighing 2000 to 3000 lbs., occur ; Mourne Mountains in Ireland ; Mount Battoch and Cairngorum in Scotland.   *Common beryl* at Fahlun in Sweden, Fossum in Norway, Limoges in France, Rabenstein in Bavaria ; Nigg Bray and Rubislaw near Aberdeen (*Davidsonite*).   Emerald and beryl are much valued as precious stones.   Known from quartz by face P.

153. PHENAKITE.—$\dot{G}l^2\ \ddot{S}i$.

Hexagonal and tetartohedral ; R 116° 36'.   Crystals R . ∞P2, or ∞P2 . $\frac{3}{4}$P2 . R. (*n, s, P*, Fig. 153). Macles with parallel axes and intersecting.   Cleavage, R and ∞P2 not very distinct ; fracture conchoidal.   H. = 7.5...8 ; G. = 2·97.   Transparent or translucent ; vitreous.   Colourless, and wine-yellow or brown when fresh, but soon lost on exposure.   B.B. infusible ; not affected by acids.

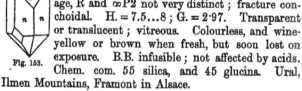

Fig. 153.

Chem. com. 55 silica, and 45 glucina.   Ural, Ilmen Mountains, Framont in Alsace.

•154. CORDIERITE, $\left\{\begin{array}{l}\ddot{A}l^2\ \ddot{S}i^3\ +\ 2\ (\dot{M}g,\ \dot{F}e)\ \ddot{S}i,\ or \\ [2\ Al^3\ O^3\ .\ 3\ Si\ O^2\ +\ 2\ (MgO\ .\ SiO^2].\end{array}\right.$
Iolite, Dichroite.

Rhombic; $\infty P\ 119°\ 10'$, middle edge of $P\ 95°\ 36'$.
Crystals $\infty P\ (T)$. $\infty \bar{P}\infty\ (l)$. $0P\ (M)$, and this with $\infty \bar{P}\infty$
(k), $\infty \bar{P}3\ (d)$, $\bar{P}\infty\ (n)$, and $\frac{1}{2}P\ (s)$ (Fig. 154); short, prismatic. Cleavage, $\infty \bar{P}\infty$; rather distinct, traces along $\bar{P}\infty$;
fracture conchoidal or uneven. H. = 7...

7·5 ; G. = 2·5...2·7. Transparent or translucent ; vitreous, inclining to resinous.
Colourless, but chiefly dark blue, or violet,
green, brown, yellow, and gray, often with
distinct trichroism, on 0P blue, on $\infty \bar{P}\infty$
gray, and on $\infty \bar{P}\infty$ yellowish. B.B. fuses
difficultly to a clear glass ; slightly
affected by acids. Chem. com. 48 to 51
silica, 29 to 33 alumina, 8 to 13 magnesia, 1 to 12 iron protoxide, and 0 to
1·5 manganese protoxide. Cabo de Gata

Fig. 154.

in Spain, Bodenmais (*Peliom*), Orrijerfvi (*Steinheilite*), Norway, Sweden, Greenland, North America, and Siberia.
Small rolled masses of an intense blue colour and transparent, found in Ceylon, are the *Sapphire d'Eau* or *Luchs-
sapphir* of the jewellers.

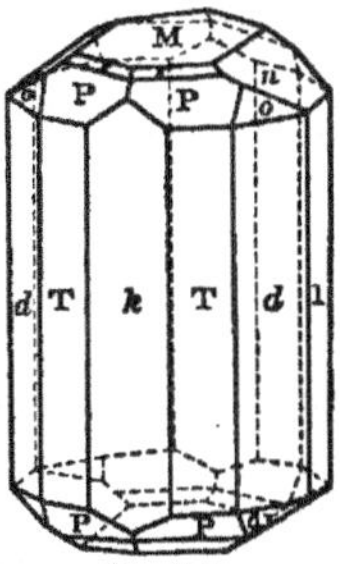

The following substances seem cordierite altered, or with
2 to 6 atoms water :—

(*a.*) *Bonsdorfite, Hydrous Iolite*, greenish-brown or dark
olive-green ; near Åbo. (*b.*) *Esmarkite, Chlorophyllite*, large
prisms or foliated, green or brownish ; near Brevig in Norway, Unity in Maine, and Haddam in Connecticut. (*c.*)
Fahlunite, Triclasite, compact, greenish-brown or black foliated ; H. = 2·5...3 ; G. = 2·5...2·8 ; Fahlun. (*d.*) *Huronite*,
granular ; pearly, yellowish-green ; H = 3·3 ; G. = 2·86.
Infusible and insoluble ; Lake Huron. (*e.*) *Weissite*, kid-
ney-shaped and ash-gray or brown ; Fahlun and Lower
Canada. (*f.*) *Pyrargillite*, indistinct embedded crystals,
black passing into brown or red, dull resinous lustre ; H.
= 3·5 ; G. = 2·5 ; Helsingfors. (*g.*) *Pinite*, crystallised, or
massive and laminar, with imperfect cleavage ; H. = 2...3 ;

G. = 2·7...2·9 ; semitranslucent or opaque, dull or **resinou**
and dirty-gray, green, or brown ; B.B. fuses to **a glas**
sometimes clear, at other times dark-coloured ; **Auvergne**
Schneeberg, Penig in Saxony, in the Harz, Cornwall, **Aber**
deenshire, the United States, and Greenland (*Gieseckite*)
Oosite from Geroldsau in Baden, snow-white, opaque, **fragile**,
is similar. (*h.*) *Gigantolite* ; H. = 3·5 ; G. = 2·8...2·9 ;
opaque, dull resinous, and greenish-gray or brown. B.B.
intumesces slightly, and fuses easily to a greenish slag ;
Tammela in Finnland. (*i.*) *Praseolite*, lamellar and green ;
Brevig in Norway.

**155. Tourmaline, $\left\{ \begin{array}{l} n\ddot{R}\,\ddot{S}i + \dot{R}^{3}\,\ddot{S}i = \\ [n(R^{2}\,O^{3}\,.\,Si\,O^{2})+3RO\,.\,Si\,O^{2}]. \end{array} \right.$

Schorl.

Rhombohedral ; R 133° 10'. Crystals of 0R (*k'*), $-\frac{1}{2}R$
(155°), R (*P*), — 2R (103° 3') (*o*), ∞P2 (*s*), and ∞R (*l*),
usually long prismatic, striated, and often as if broken.
They are remarkable for hemimorphism, ∞R appearing as
a trigonal prism (Figs. 155, 156); also radiating, columnar,

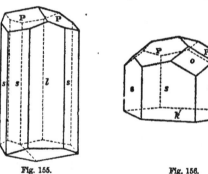

Fig. 155.   Fig. 156.

or fibrous. Cleavage, R and ∞P2 both imperfect; fracture conchoidal or uneven. H. = 6·5...7·5 ; G. = 3...3·3.
The black opaque, the others pellucid ; vitreous. Colourless, but gray, yellow, green, blue, red, brown, and most
frequently black. Often several colours in layers perpendicular, or parallel to the axis. By friction acquires positive, by heat polar electricity ; powder white, often mag-

netic. B.B. some fuse, others only intumesce, and some both fuse and intumesce. Powder not soluble in h., only imperfectly in s. acid. Chem. com. very complex, but, according to Rammelsberg, with much general agreement. They. all contain water chemically combined, also fluorine from 0·3 to 0·8 per cent (seldom more, 1·2 ; seldomer less), and the iron only as the protoxide. They are all one-third silicates (Drittelsilicate), but in two divisions :—

$$\text{I.} = 3\,\ddot{\text{R}}\,\ddot{\text{S}}\text{i} + \text{R}^{2}\,\ddot{\text{S}}\text{i} \text{ with } 3\,\ddot{\text{R}} = 2\,\ddot{\text{A}}\text{l} + \ddot{\text{B}}$$

$$\text{II.} = 8\,\ddot{\text{R}}\,\ddot{\text{S}}\text{i} + \text{R}^{3}\,\ddot{\text{S}}\text{i} \text{ with } 8\,\ddot{\text{R}} = 6\,\ddot{\text{A}}\text{l} + 2\,\ddot{\text{B}}$$

and $\dot{\text{R}}$ consisting of $\dot{\text{M}}$g, $\dot{\text{C}}$a, $\dot{\text{F}}$e, $\dot{\text{M}}$n, and of $\dot{\text{N}}$a, $\dot{\text{K}}$, $\dot{\text{L}}$i, and $\dot{\text{H}}$ in variable proportions.

I. is by far the more common, and includes the yellow, brown, and (apparently) black varieties. They contain 32 to 34 alumina, and some yellow or brown varieties are almost free from (1 per cent or less), others, the black, contain much (5 to 17 per cent) iron peroxide.

II. includes the colourless, pale green, and transparent varieties, or noble tourmaline, with no iron, or almost none, also very little manganese and magnesia, and 42 to 44 alumina ; also lithia in determinable amount (to 1·2).

Isomorphous mixtures of the two divisions occur, and even parts of the same crystal vary in composition as in colour. Analyses give boracic acid 7 to 13, magnesia 1 to 15, lime 1·6 or less, soda 1 to 2·4, potash under 1, and water 1 to 3.

Black varieties are the most common, and known as *Schorl*, the red as *Rubellite*, the colourless as *Achroite*.

The finest transparent varieties or noble tourmalines come from Ceylon, Siberia, and Brazil. The dark blue or *Indicollite* occurs chiefly in Utoe. Large crystals of the dark opaque varieties occur in Greenland, Arendal, the Tyrol, and various parts of North America. In England, Bovey in Devonshire and St. Just in Cornwall are well-known localities ; and in Scotland large prisms, often curved or broken, abound in the granite of Aberdeenshire.

Tourmaline is not much valued as a gem, the colours being rarely pure. *Zeuxite* seems only tourmaline.

*156. CHRYSOLITE, Olivine, Peridot. $\left\{ \begin{array}{l} (\dot{M}g, \dot{F}e)^2\ \ddot{S}i = \\ [2\ \dot{R}O . SiO^3]. \end{array} \right.$

Rhombic; ∞P (n) 130° 2′, $\bar{P}\infty$ (d) 76° 54′, $2\bar{P}\infty$ (k) 80° 53′; also $\infty\bar{P}\infty$ (M), $\infty\bar{P}\infty$ with P (p), 0P (Fig. 157). The crystals are frequently prismatic and embedded; also massive and granular. Cleavage, $\infty\breve{P}\infty$ rather distinct;

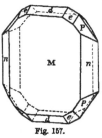

Fig. 157.

fracture conchoidal. H. = 6·5...7; G. = 3·3...3·5. Transparent or translucent; vitreous. Olive-green, also yellow and brown, rarely colourless. B.B. infusible, except some with much iron; soluble and gelatinising in acids. Chem. com. 38 to 43 silica, 43 to 51 magnesia, 8 to 18 iron protoxide, with a little manganese. *Chrysolite* is the fine green, transparent and crystallised varieties from the East, Esne in Egypt, and Brazil. *Olivine*, the darker and less pellucid, from Vesuvius, Unkel on the Rhine, the basalts of Germany, and the trap of Arthur Seat and other parts of Scotland; also in meteoric iron, as in the mass found by Pallas in Siberia, and in that of Otumpa in South America. Used as an ornamental stone, but not much valued.

The following seem varieties or mixtures :—

Fosterite, colourless, from Monte Somma; and *Boltonite*, greenish or bluish gray, from Bolton, Massachusetts, have only 2 to 3 iron protoxide.

Hyalosiderite.—Brown or yellow, very ferruginous (30 $\dot{F}e$) and metallic-looking; H. = 5; G. = 2·875; in other respects like olivine; Kaiserstuhl in the Breisgau. *Chusite, Limbelite*, and *Tautolite*; Lake Laach. *Batrachite*, greenish-gray or white, translucent; Rizoni Mountain, Tyrol. *Monticellite*, transparent, colourless, or yellowish; but ∞P 133° 6′, 2 P∞ 82°, is probably distinct; Vesuvius.

Fayalite.—Crystalline, columnar and foliated, but often as if fused. Greenish or pitch-black, brownish or brass-yellow, with a resinous metallic lustre. H. = 6·5; G. = 4·0 ...4·15. Partly soluble in h. acid. Chem. com. $\dot{F}e^2\ \ddot{S}i$

with 29·4 silica, 70·6 iron protoxide, but 2 to 8 manganese protoxide. Fayal and Mourne Mountains.

Knebellite.—Massive, opaque, gray, green, brown, or red. Chem. com. 32·5 silica, 32 iron protoxide, and 35 manganese protoxide. Ilmenau and Dannemora.

Tephroite.—Granular, with two cleavages at right angles. H. = 5·5 ; G. = 4...4·12. Lustre adamantine. Ash-gray, with reddish-brown tarnish. Chem. com. 70 manganese protoxide and 30 silica. Franklin and Sparta, New Jersey.

157. CHONDRODITE, Maclurite, Brucite, $\big\}$ $\dot{\text{M}}\text{g}^{s}$ $\ddot{\text{Si}}^{s}$.
　　　　　　　　Humite.

Rhombic ; P middle edge 156° 38′, polar edges 131° 34′ and 54° 28′, but crystals often monoclinic in character or indistinct ; chiefly in round grains or granular. Cleavage indistinct ; fracture imperfect conchoidal. H. = 6·5 : G. = 3·15...3·25. Transparent or translucent ; lustre vitreous or resinous. Yellow, red, brown, green, and almost black ; streak white or yellowish. B.B. infusible, or only on very thin edges ; decomposed by acids. Chem. com. silicate of magnesia, with part of the oxygen replaced by fluorine in various proportions, but without influence on the forms. Von Rath finds three types of crystals with two axes constant, the third varying as 7 : 5 : 9. The chondrodite of Pargas belongs to the second type, the Humite mostly to the third, the first and second being rare on Vesuvius. He gives for types I., II., III., from Vesuvius, silicium 17·24, magnesium 36·94, fluorine 2·57, oxygen 43·25 ; in type II., from Sweden, silicium 17·00, magnesium 36·43, fluorine 4·94, oxygen 41. Chondrodite occurs at Pargas in Finnland, Åker and Gullsjö in Sweden, Sparta in New Jersey, and Orange County in New York ; also in Saxony, and on Loch Ness in Scotland. *Humite* on Monte Somma.

FAMILY XIV.—METALLIC STONES.

Crystallisation predominantly rhombic ; some tesseral or monoclinic ; but many massive, or products of decomposition, and thus rather metallic clays or rocks. The crystalline species are rather hard,—H. = 5·5...6·5 ; and with

G. $= 3·6...5·6$. Those with high specific gravity are mostly infusible B.B., the others fusible. Most are soluble in acids, often gelatinising. They are chiefly silicates, with a metallic base, and thus an intermediate group between the true stones and the metallic ores. Often opaque, and black or brown and yellow. They occur especially in the igneous and metamorphic rocks, or in metallic veins, and chiefly those of Scandinavia and the Ural.

*158. LIÉVRITE, Yenite, $\begin{cases} \ddot{\text{F}}\text{e }\ddot{\text{Si}} + 3 \,(\dot{\text{Fe}}\,\dot{\text{Ca}})^{\text{s}}\,\ddot{\text{Si}} + \dot{\text{H}} = \\ [\text{Fe}^{\text{s}}\,\text{O}^{\text{s}}\,.\,\text{SiO}^{\text{s}} + 3\,(2\,\text{RO}\,.\\ \text{SiO}^{\text{s}}) + \text{H}^{\text{s}}\text{O.}] \end{cases}$
Ilvaite.

Rhombic; P (o), polar edges $139°\ 30'$ and $117°\ 27'$, ∞P $112°\ 38'$, $\overline{\text{P}}\infty$ (d) $112°\ 49'$ ∞P2 (s) $106°\ 15'$. Crystals

(Fig. 158), are long prismatic and vertically striated; also radiated columnar or fibrous. Cleavages several, all imperfect; brittle. H. $= 5·5...6$; G. $= 3·9...4·2$. Opaque, resinous or imperfect metallic. Brownish or greenish black; streak black. B.B. fuses easily to a black magnetic globule; soluble in h. acid, forming a yellow jelly. Chem. com. $29·3$ silica, $19·6$ iron peroxide, $35·2$ iron protoxide, $13·7$ lime, and $2·2$ water. Rio in Elba, Fossum, Kupferberg, Rhode Island, and Greenland. *Wehrlite*, iron-black, with greenish-gray streak, and B.B. difficultly fusible, is a variety; Hungary.

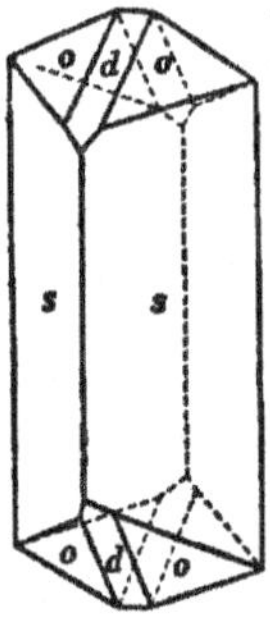

Fig. 158.

159. HISINGERITE, Thraulite.—$\ddot{\text{F}}\text{e}^{\text{s}}\,\ddot{\text{Si}}^{\text{s}} + 2\,\dot{\text{Fe}}\,\ddot{\text{Si}} + 10\,\dot{\text{H}}$. Reniform, or in crusts. H. $= 3·5...4$; G. $= 2·6...3$. Opaque; resinous. Brownish or bluish black; streak liver or yellowish brown. B.B. fuses with difficulty; soluble in acids, leaving slimy silica. Chem. com. very various, but $32·5$ silica, $33·5$ iron peroxide, $15·1$ iron protoxide, and 19 water, in the *Thraulite* from Bodenmais. Also Gillinge, Rydarhyttan in Sweden, and Breitenbrun (*Polyhydrite*).

160. ANTHOSIDERITE.—$\ddot{\text{F}}\text{e}^{\text{s}}\,\ddot{\text{Si}}^{\text{s}} + 2\,\dot{\text{H}}$. Fine fibrous or flower-like; very tough. H. $= 6·5$; G. $= 3$. Opaque or translucent; silky. Ochre-yellow to

yellowish-brown. B.B. becomes reddish-brown, then black, and fuses with difficulty. Soluble in h. acid. Chem. com. 61 silica, 35 iron peroxide, and 4 water. Minas Geraes.

161. NONTRONITE.—$\ddot{F}e\ \ddot{S}i^2 + 5\ \dot{H}$.

Massive. Fracture uneven. H. = 2...3 ; G. = 2...2·3. Opaque; dull or glimmering; streak resinous. Straw-yellow, yellowish-white, or siskin-green. B.B. decrepitates, becomes black and magnetic, but without fusing; soluble, and gelatinises in warm acids. Chem. com. nearly 43 silica, 36 iron peroxide, and 21 water, with 3·5 alumina and 2 magnesia. Nontron in France, Harz, and Bavaria.

Chloropal is similar, but B.B. brown and infusible. Unghwar in Hungary, and near Passau. *Pinguite*, sectile ; H. = 1 ; feels greasy ; and B.B. fuses on the edges ; is also a silicate of iron oxides with water; Wolkenstein in Saxony, near Zwickau, and Suhl.

162. CHLOROPHÆITE.—$(\ddot{F}e,\ \dot{M}g)^3\ \ddot{S}i^4 + 18\ \dot{H}$.

Massive. Cleavage in two directions ; fracture con-choidal, earthy ; very soft and sectile. G. = 2·02. When first exposed translucent and pistacio or olive-green, but soon changes to brown or black, and opaque. B.B. melts to a black glass. Chem. com. of a specimen from Faroe, 32·85 silica, 22·08 iron protoxide, 3·44 magnesia, and 41·63 water. Scuir More in Rum, Faroe, and Iceland ; also in Fife, and near Newcastle.

163. THORITE.—$\ddot{T}h\ \ddot{S}i + 2\ \dot{H}$.

Tesseral, but crystals rare. Massive. Fracture con-choidal ; hard and brittle. G. = 4·63...4·8. Opaque; splendent, vitreous. Reddish-brown, or black clouded with red ; streak dark-brown. B.B. infusible; gelatinises with h. acid. Chem. com. essentially 73·4 thorina, 16·8 silica, and 9·8 water, but combined with very many other substances : lime, iron, manganese, magnesia, uranium, lead, tin, potash, soda, and alumina. Near Brevig. *Orangite* seems a variety with less water. Very rare ; Brevig.

164. EULYTINE.—$\ddot{B}i^3\ \ddot{S}i^2$.

Tesseral and tetrahedral ; $\dfrac{202}{2}$ and $-\dfrac{202}{2}$. The crystals (like Fig. 9) very small, and often with curved faces. Cleavage very imperfect; fracture conchoidal. H. = 4·5... 5; G. = 5·9...6·1. Transparent and translucent; adamantine. Clove-brown, yellow, gray, or white; streak white or gray. B.B. fuses readily with intumescence to a brown bead, leaving a yellow ring on the charcoal; decomposed by h. acid, forming gelatinous silica. Chem. com. 16·2 silica and 83·8 bismuth peroxide, but with phosphoric acid and iron peroxide. Schneeberg, and Bräunsdorf near Freiberg.

Hypochlorite or *Green Iron-earth*, from Schneeberg, reniform or fine earthy; and siskin or olive green. H. = 6; G. = 2·9...3. B.B. infusible. Insoluble. Is a mixture of silicate of iron and bismuth with phosphate of alumina. *Hypochlorite* from Bräunsdorf, is chiefly silica 88 per cent, with phosphate of iron and antimony.

165. GADOLINITE. $\begin{cases} (\dot{Y}, \dot{C}e, \dot{F}e)^3 \ddot{S}i, \; and \\ (\dot{Y}, \dot{G}l, \dot{F}e, \dot{L}a)^3 \ddot{S}i. \end{cases}$

Monoclinic; C. = 89° 28′, ∞P 116°, P 120° 56′; (but Rhombic, with ∞P = 105° 52′, Von Rath, etc.) Crystals rare and indistinct. Cleavage very indistinct, or none; fracture conchoidal or splintery. H. = 6·5...7; G. = 4·0...4·4. Opaque or translucent on the edges; vitreous, often resinous. Black; streak greenish-gray. B.B. the conchoidal (vitreous) varieties incandesce vividly, intumesce, but do not fuse; the splintery varieties form cauliflower-like ramifications, but do not incandesce; gelatinises in h. acid. Chem. com. uncertain, but 25 to 29 silica, 36 to 51 yttria, 10 to 15 protoxide of iron, 5 to 17 protoxide of cerium with lanthanium, and 0 to 12 glucina. The cerium protoxide and glucina seem not to occur together. Hitteroe in Norway, Ytterby, Broddbo, and Finbo near Fahlun.

166. ALLANITE, Cerin, Orthite.—$\ddot{R}^3 \ddot{S}i^3 + \ddot{R} \ddot{S}i.$

Monoclinic, like epidote, but distinct crystals rare (Fig. 159), mostly columnar, or granular. Cleavage imperfect; fracture conchoidal or uneven. H. = 6; G. = 3·4...3·8. Opaque or translucent in thin splinters; imperfect metallic, to vitreous or resinous. Black inclining to green or brown;

streak greenish or brownish-gray. B.B. froths, and melts easily to a black or brown scoria or glass, often magnetic ; gelatinises with h. acid. Chem. com. very variable, but similar to garnet (*Rams.*), with 30 to 35 silica, 12 to 18 alumina and iron peroxide, whilst Ṙ. includes protoxides of cerium (11 to 24), lanthanium (2 to 8), iron (4 to 21), and manganese (0 to 3·5), with lime (2 to 12), yttria (0·3 to 4), and magnesia (0·4 to 5). *Allanite* occurs in Greenland, and at Hitteroe, the Jotun Fjeld, Snarum, and near Schmiedefeld in Thuringia ; also Bradford

Fig. 159.

and Bethlem, Pennsylvania and Franklyn, New Jersey. *Cerin* at Rydderhyttan ; *Orthite* at Finbo, Fahlun, Arendal, and Krageroe. *Bucklandite,* from Lake Laach and Arendal, is orthite.

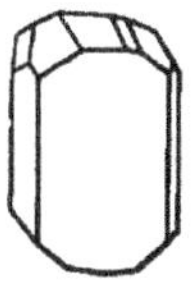

Pyrorthite, with carbonaceous and other matter ; *Uralorthite,* from the Ilmen Mountains, containing more alumina ; *Bodenite,* from Boden, Saxony ; and *Bagrationite,* from Achmatofsk, are only varieties.

· 167. TSCHEFFKINITE.

Massive. Fracture flat conchoidal. H. = 5…5·5 ; G. = 4·5. Opaque ; vitreous, splendent. Velvet-black ; streak dark-brown. B.B. intumesces greatly, becomes porous, and often incandesces ; in the strongest white heat fuses to black glass ; gelatinises with warm h. acid. Chem. com. 21 silica, 20 titanic acid, 11 iron protoxide, 45 peroxides of cerium, lanthanium, and didymium, and 4 lime and magnesia. Ilmen Mountains near Miask.

168. CERITE.—(Ċe, Ṙ)² S̈i + Ḣ.

Hexagonal ; 0P . ∞P, in low six-sided prisms, but very rare. Generally fine granular, almost compact. Cleavage, traces ; fracture uneven, splintery ; brittle. H. = 5·5 ; G. = 4·9…5. Translucent on the edges, or opaque ; dull, adamantine, or resinous. Clove-brown, cherry-red, or pearl-gray ; streak white. B.B. infusible, but becomes dirty yellow ; soluble in h. acid, leaving gelatinous silica. Chem. com. 20·5 silica, 73·5 protoxide of cerium (with didymium and lanthanium), and 6 water, with iron protoxide and lime. Bastnaes near Ridderhyttan.

169. TRITOMITE.—$\ddot{S}i$, $\dot{C}e$, $\dot{L}a$, $\dot{C}a$, $\dot{H}$.

Tesseral in tetrahedrons. Fracture conchoidal; brittle. H. = 5·5 ; G. = 4·16...4·7. Vitreous ; translucent on the edges. Dark-brown. B.B. swells and cracks ; soluble in acids. Lamoe near Brevig.

170. PYROCHLORE.—[5 R Nb^2 O^s + 4 R (Ti, Th) O^s + 4 Na Fl].

Tesseral ; O. Cleavage octahedral ; brittle ; fracture conchoidal. H. = 5 ; G. = 4·0...4·4. Opaque or translucent ; resinous. Dark reddish-brown, or almost black, some crystals ruby-red and transparent ; streak pale-brown. B.B. becomes yellow and fuses with much difficulty into a blackish-brown slag ; the fine powder soluble in con. s. acid. Chem. com. very complex, but Ramelsberg gives the above formula for the Miask variety (R = Ce, Ca, Mg, Fe), in which he found 53·19 niobic acid, 10·47 titanic acid, 7·56 thoria (acid), 7·00 cerium protoxide, 14·21 lime, 0·22 magnesia, 1·84 iron protoxide, 5·01 soda, and 3·06 fluorine. But those from Brevig and Fredriksvärn differ, and contain uranium protoxide. Also occurs on Kaiserstuhl and at Chesterfield, Massachusetts (*Microlite*).

Pyrrhite, small orange-yellow octahedrons ; H. = 6 ; is a niobate of zirconia, with iron and uranium. Mursinsk and Azores.

171. OERSTEDTITE.

Tetragonal ; P 84° 26′, like zircon. H. = 5·5; G. = 3·629. Opaque or translucent on the edges ; adamantine vitreous. Reddish-brown. B.B. infusible. Forchhammer found 19·71 silica, 2·61 lime, 2·05 magnesia, 1·14 iron protoxide, 68·96 titaniate of zirconia, 5·53 water. Arendal.

172. KEILHAUITE, Yttrotitanite. } $5(\dot{C}a\ \dot{Y})(\ddot{S}i,\overset{..}{Ti}) + (\overset{..}{Al},\overset{..}{Fe})(\ddot{S}i,\overset{..}{Ti})^s$.

Monoclinic ; C. = 58°, ∞P = 114°. Cleavages, along − 2 P intersecting at 138°. H. = 6...7 ; G. = 3·5...3·7. Translucent ; vitreous or resinous. Blackish-brown ; by transmitted light reddish ; streak grayish-yellow. B.B. fuses easily with effervescence to a black shining slag ; with borax forms a blood-red glass in the red. flame ; in powder

soluble in h. acid. Chem. com. 29·7 silica, 28·7 titanic
acid, 21·1 lime, 10·8 yttria, 6·2 alumina, and 6·5 iron
peroxide. Near Arendal.

173. WöHLERITE.

Monoclinic ; C. = 70° 45′, ∞P 90° 14′, but crystals
rare. Cleavage clinodiagonal distinct ; fracture conchoidal.
H. = 5...6 ; G. = 3·41. Translucent ; vitreous or resinous.
Yellow, inclining to red or brown. B.B. fuses to a yellowish
glass ; easily soluble in warm con. h. acid, depositing silica
and niobic acid. Analysis—30·62 silica, 14·47 niobic acid,
15·17 zirconia, 3·67 iron and manganese protoxide, 26·19
lime, and 7·78 soda. Fredriksvärn (*Eukolite*), and Brevig
in Norway.

ORDER II.

SALINE STONES.

COMPRISES minerals which, in external aspect and composition, resemble (or are) the salts of the chemist. With a few exceptions, as rock-salt and fluor-spar, they are combinations of the second order of two oxygen compounds. The acid component is one of the common acids,—the carbonic, sulphuric, boracic, or phosphoric acid,—not silica or alumina, as in the first order. They are almost all crystallised, and predominantly in rhombic or monoclinic forms, but some rhombohedral or tesseral. Their hardness is low; one 7, a few about 5, most lower. G. = 1·5...4·7. All are soluble in acids, except the sulphates (three); more than half in water. B.B. all fusible or decompose. Many of them are products of decomposition. Occur rather in veins than as components of rocks, and then generally constitute the whole mass.

**FAMILY I.—CALC-SPAR.

Generally rhombohedral in crystals and cleavage. H. = 3...4·5; G. = 2·6...3·4, becoming higher as the metallic element increases. They are soluble and often effervesce in acids; and become caustic or alkaline when burned. They form a series of closely-related compounds of carbonic acid with lime, magnesia, and isomorphous bases, as the protoxide of iron. Are generally white and translucent, with a vitreous or pearly lustre.

**174. CALCITE, CALC-SPAR, Calcareous Spar. $\dot{C}a \ddot{C}, = [CaO . CO^2]$.

Hexagonal and rhombohedral; R 105° 5′ (Fig. 160); the forms and combinations exceeding those of any other mineral. Among them are more than 40 rhombohedrons, especially $-\frac{1}{2}R$ 135°, R, $-2R$ 79°, and 4R 66°, with 0R and ∞R as limiting forms; eighty-five distinct scalenohedrons, as R3,

R2, and $\frac{1}{4}$R2; and the second hexagonal prism ∞P2, whilst

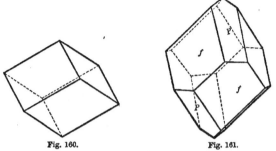

Fig. 160.   Fig. 161.

hexagonal pyramids are among the rarer forms. Some of the most usual combinations are ∞R. $-\frac{1}{2}$R (*c, g*, Fig. 164); or $-\frac{1}{2}$R. ∞R, very frequent; also ∞R. 0R; likewise $-$2R. R (*f, P*, Fig. 161); R3. ∞R. $-$2R; R5 (*y*). R3 (*r*). R (*P*). 4R (*m*). ∞R (*C*) (Fig. 162); and many others, several hundred distinct combinations being known.

Macles are not uncommon, especially with the systems of axes parallel (Figs. 163, 164), and others conjoined by a

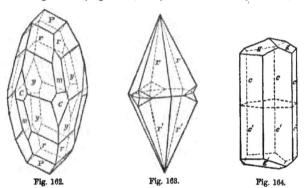

Fig. 162.   Fig. 163.   Fig. 164.

face of R with the chief axes almost at right angles, 89° 8′ (Fig. 82); or by a face of $-\frac{1}{2}$R, in which the chief axes form an angle of $127\frac{1}{2}$° ; and usually many times repeated, so that the centre crystals appear in lamellæ not thicker than paper (Fig. 81). Also occurs granular, lamellar, parallel or radiated fibrous, compact and earthy. Cleavage, rhombohedral along R very perfect and easily obtained, so that the conchoidal fracture is rarely observable ; brittle. H. = 3 ; G. = 2·6...2·8 ; pure transparent crystals = 2·72. Pellucid in all degrees. Very distinct double refraction. Lustre vitreous, but several faces resinous, and OR pearly. Most frequently colourless or white, but often gray, blue, green, yellow, red, brown, or black; streak grayish-white. B.B. infusible, but becomes caustic and emits a bright light. Effervesces, and is entirely soluble in h. or n. acid. The fine powder, ignited on platina-foil over the spirit-lamp, forms a somewhat connected mass, and even adheres to the platina. Chem. com. of the purest varieties, carbonate of lime, with 44 carbonic acid and 56 lime, or 40 calcium, 12·2 carbon, and 47·8 oxygen; but usually contains magnesia and protoxide of iron or of manganese. Remarkable specimens of the crystallised variety, or proper calc-spar, are found in Andreasberg and other parts of the Harz (six-sided prisms), Freiberg, Tharand, Maxen, Alston Moor in Cumberland (flat rhombic crystals), and in Derbyshire (pale yellow transparent pyramids).

Certain varieties are distinguished, as—Iceland spar, remarkable for its transparency and double refraction, occurs massive in a trap rock in that island. *Slate spar*, thin lamellar, often with a shining white pearly lustre, and greasy feel; Wicklow in Ireland, Glen Tilt in Scotland, and Norway. *Aphrite*, fine scaly, from Hessia and Thuringia. *Marble* is the massive crystalline variety of this mineral, produced by igneous action on compact limestone. Paros, Naxos, and Tenedos furnished the chief supply to the Grecian artists ; Carrara, near the Gulf of Genoa, to those of modern times. Some of the coloured marbles of the ancients were impure limestones, as the *Cipollino*, zoned with green talc or chlorite ; and *Verde antique*, mixed with green serpentine. *Ruin marble* shows irregular markings like ruins ; Val d'Arno (Florentine marble), and Bristol (Cotham marble). *Lucullite*, from Egypt, and *Anthraconite*, from Kilkenny in Ireland, are black from carbon. *Luma-*

chello, from Bleiberg in Carinthia, exhibits beautiful iridescent colours from fossil shells, sometimes deep-red or
orange (*Fire marble*).

Limestone occurs in all formations under various names,
as *Oolite*, egg or roë-stone, round concretions, with a concentric structure like the roe of fish ; *Pisolite*, or peastone,
similar structure; *Chalk*, soft earthy: *Lithographic stone*,
yellowish and compact, from Solenhofen ; and *Marl*, calcareous matter more or less mixed with clay.　*Tufa*, or
calcareous tufa, generally a recent deposit from calcareous
springs, has often a loose friable texture, but at other times
is hard and compact ; and in the neighbourhood of Rome
forms the common building-stone or *Travertino*.　The sandstone of Fontainebleau is carbonate of lime ($\frac{1}{3}$) mixed with
quartz sand ($\frac{2}{3}$), and occasionally crystallising in rhombohedrons.

This mineral is employed in many ways—the coarser
varieties when burnt to drive off the carbonic acid, as lime,
for mortar, manure, tanning ; as a flux in melting iron and
other ores, or in preparing glass, and for similar purposes;
the finer, as marbles, for sculpture, architecture, and ornamental stonework ; the chalk for writing, whitewashing,
or producing carbonic acid.

Plumbocalcite.—Cleavage, 104° 53′.　White and pearly;
softer than calc-spar ; but G. = 2·824.　Contains 2·3 to
7·8 carbonate of lead.　Wanlockhead and Leadhills, Scotland.

**175. DOLOMITE, Bitter $\{$Ċa Ö + Ṁg Ö. =
　　　　　Spar.　　　$\{$[Ca O . CO² + Mg O . CO²].

Hexagonal-rhombohedral ; R 106° 15′—20′ ; most frequent form R ; also R and $-\frac{1}{2}$R, or 0R, ∞R, and 4R.
The rhombohedrons often curved and saddle-shaped ; also
granular or compact, often cellular and porous.　Cleavage,
rhombohedral along R.　H. = 3·5...4·5 ; G. = 2·85...2·95.
Translucent ; vitreous, but often pearly or resinous.　Colourless or white, but frequently pale-red, yellow, or green.
B.B. infusible, but becomes caustic, and often shows traces
of iron and manganese.　Fragments effervesce very slightly
or not at all in hydrochloric acid ; the powder is partially

o

soluble, or wholly when heated; the very fine powder ignited on platina-foil for a few minutes over a spirit-lamp *continues* pulverulent, but intumesces slightly during ignition. Chem. com. 54·3 carbonate of lime, and 45·7 carbonate of magnesia (30 lime and 22 magnesia), but generally carbonate of lime with more than 20 per cent carbonate of magnesia, and less than 20 per cent carbonate of iron.

Varieties are—*Dolomite*, massive, granular, easily divisible, white; *Rhomb* or *Bitter-spar*, larger grained, or distinctly crystallised and cleavable, often inclining to green; and *Brown-spar* and *Pearl-spar*, in simple crystals or in imitative forms, of colours inclining to red or brown, more distinct pearly lustre, and under 10 per cent carbonate of iron. Traversella in Piedmont, St. Gotthardt, Gap in France, Alston in Cumberland, in Derbyshire, and at Leadhills and Charlestown in Scotland. Greenish, macled; Miemo in Tuscany (*Miemite*), and Tharand in Saxony (*Tharandite*). *Gurhofian*, from Gurhof in Austria, is white and compact.

The massive and compact varieties are very common, and valued as building-stones (cathedral of Milan, York Minster, and the new houses of Parliament). The Parian marble, and also the Iona marble in the Hebrides, have been supposed to belong to this species.

Predazzite.—Granular and white; is a mixture with brucite. Predazzo in Tyrol.

176. Breunnerite, Giobertite.—$\dot{\text{M}}\text{g} \ddot{\text{C}} = [\text{Mg O . CO}^2]$.

Hex.-rhombohedral; R 107° 10′—30′; as yet only R; and granular or columnar. Cleavage, R very perfect, with straight faces. H. = 4...4·5; G. = 2·9...3·1. Transparent or translucent on the edges; highly vitreous. Colourless, but often yellowish-brown, or blackish-gray. B.B. infusible, but generally becoming gray, or black and magnetic; soluble in acids, often only when pulverised and warmed. Chem. com. essentially carbonate of magnesia, with 51·7 carbonic acid and 48·3 magnesia, but often mixed with 8 to 17 carbonate of iron or manganese. Tyrol, St. Gotthardt, Harz, Fassathal; also Unst in Zetland.

Mesitine-spar, splendent, yellow, lenticular crystals; G. = 3·35...3·4; Traversella in Piedmont; and *Pistomasite;* G. = 4·4; Salzburg; are similar.

177. MAGNESITE.—$\dot{M}g\,\ddot{C}$.

Reniform or massive. H. = 3...5; G. = 2·85...2·95. Sub-translucent or opaque; streak shining. Snow-white, grayish, or yellowish-white, and pale-yellow. Adheres slightly to the tongue. B.B. and with acids acts like breun-nerite, of which it is only a chemical pure and compact variety. Tyrol, Norway, North America.

178. HYDROMAGNESITE.—$\dot{M}g^4\,\ddot{C}^3 + 4\,\dot{H}$.

Monoclinic; ∞P 88° nearly. Crystals small, rare; also massive. H. = 1·5...3; G. = 2·14...2·18. Vitreous or silky. White. B.B. infusible; soluble with efferves-cence in acids. Chem. com. 36·2 carbonic acid, 44 mag-nesia, and 19·8 water. Moravia, Kumi, Hoboken in New Jersey, and Texas in Pennsylvania. *Lancasterite* from Pennsylvania, and *Hydromagnocalcite,* a yellow sinter from Vesuvius, are similar.

**179. ARRAGONITE, Needle Spar, Flos-ferri.—$\dot{C}a\,\ddot{C}$.

Rhombic; ∞P 116° 10′, $\breve{P}$∞ 108° 27′. The most common combinations are ∞$\breve{P}$∞ (*h*), ∞$\breve{P}$ (*M*) . P∞ (*k, P*), generally long prismatic (like Fig. 165, and the separate

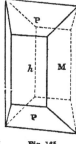
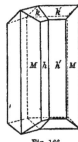

Fig. 165.   Fig. 166.   Fig. 167.

crystals in Fig. 166); ∞$\breve{P}$∞ . ∞P . 0P, generally short prismatic; 6$\breve{P}$⅓ . ∞ P . $\breve{P}$∞, acute pyramidal. But simple crystals are rare, from the great tendency to form macles, conjoined by a face of ∞P, and repeated (Figs. 166, 167). Also columnar, fibrous, and in crusts, stalactites, and other forms. Cleavage, brachydiagonal distinct, also ∞P and P̄∞ imperfect; fracture conchoidal or uneven. H. = 3·5 ...4; G. = 2·9...3 (massive 2·7). Transparent or translucent; vitreous. Colourless, but yellowish-white to wine-yellow, reddish-white to brick-red; also light-green, violet-blue, or gray. In the closed tube, before reaching a red heat, it swells and falls down into a white coarse powder, evolving a little water. A portion of this powder heated in the forceps, B.B., colours the flame carmine-red when strontia is present; on charcoal it becomes caustic. With acids acts like calc-spar. Chem. com. carbonate of lime, occasionally mixed with (0·1...4) carbonate of strontia. Valencia, Molina, and in Arragon; Leogang in Salzburg, and Antiparos. *Flos-ferri*, coralloid, in the iron mines of Styria. *Satin-spar*, fine fibrous silky, at Dufton; stalactitic in Buckinghamshire, Devonshire, coast of Galloway, and Leadhills; also deposited as tufa by the Carlsbad and other hot springs.

Arragonite is most readily distinguished from calc-spar by falling to pieces at a low temperature, and by its less distinct and prismatic cleavage.

Tarnowitzite contains 2 to 4 carbonate of lead. Tarnowitz in Silesia.

**Family II.—Fluor-Spar.

Crystallisation tesseral, hexagonal, or rhombic. H. = 4 ...5, in one 7; G. = 2·9...4·7, but mostly about 3. All soluble in acids, and mostly fusible or altered by heat. Those containing fluorine, when warmed with concentrated sulphuric acid, evolve vapours that corrode glass; those with phosphoric acid, when moistened with sulphuric acid, colour B.B. the flame green.

**180. Fluorite, Fluor-spar.—Ca F, *or* [Ca F²].

Tesseral; the most common form is the cube ∞O∞, then the octahedron O, and the rhombic dodecahedron ∞O; but many other forms occur in combinations. Macles are

common; also coarse granular, columnar, or compact and
earthy. Cleavage, octahedral perfect; fracture conchoidal;
brittle. $H. = 4$; $G. = 3\cdot1...3\cdot2$. Pellucid in all degrees;
vitreous. Colourless, but generally very various, and beautiful shades of yellow, green, blue, and red; often two or
more in one specimen. Many varieties phosphoresce when
heated (*Chlorophane*, with a bright green light). B.B. decrepitates, often violently, phosphoresces and fuses in thin
splinters to an opaque mass; slowly soluble in h. or nitric
acids, readily in s. acid, with evolution of hydrofluoric acid.
Chem. com. neutral fluoride of calcium, containing $48\cdot7$
fluorine, and $51\cdot3$ calcium ($= 72$ lime). Fluor-spar is a
very common mineral, chiefly in veins, as with tin ores in
Saxony, Bohemia, Cornwall; with silver at Freiberg,
Marienberg, Kongsberg; with lead in Derbyshire (near
Castletown), Cumberland (Alston Moor), Northumberland,
and Ireland. It is rare in Scotland, but in greenstone
near Gourock, in granite near Ballater in Aberdeenshire, on
the Avon in Banffshire, and in Sutherlandshire. In Derbyshire it occurs in large crystalline masses either with concentric colours or of a rich translucent blue (*Blue John*),
and is wrought into various ornamental articles. Fluor-
spar is chiefly used as a flux in reducing metallic ores,
especially iron and copper; also for etching on glass.

181. YTTROCERITE.
Very similar to fluor-spar. Granular, crystalline, or in
crusts. Cleavage imperfect. $H. = 4...5$; $G. = 3\cdot4...3\cdot5$.
Translucent or opaque; weak vitreous lustre. Violet-blue
to gray or white. B.B. infusible on charcoal alone, and
evolves fluorine when heated with s. acid. Chem. com.
fluorides of calcium, cerium, and yttrium, in variable proportions. Finbo and Broddbo near Fahlun, Massachusetts,
and Amity in New York.

182. FLUOCERITE.—$Ce\ F + Ce^2\ F^3 = [Ce\ F^2 + Ce^2\ F^4]$.
Hexagonal; $0P . \infty P$. $H. = 4...5$; $G. = 4\cdot7$. Opaque
or translucent on the edges; lustre weak. Pale brick-red
or yellowish; streak yellowish-white. In the closed tube
gives out fluorine. B.B. infusible. Chem. com. $82\cdot64$

peroxide of cerium, 1·12 yttria, and 16·24 hydrofluoric acid, *Berzelius.* Finbo and Broddbo.

183. FLUOCERINE.—$Ce^2 F^3 + \ddot{\Theta} \dot{H}$.

Massive, with traces of cleavage; fracture conchoidal. H. = 4·5. Opaque; vitreous or resinous. Yellow, inclining to red or brown; streak. brownish-yellow. B.B. infusible. Analysis, 84·21 peroxide of cerium, 10·85 hydrofluoric acid, and 4·95 water. Finbo. *Bastnesite*, from Bastnaes, 2 ($\dot{L}a$, $\dot{C}a$) $\ddot{C} +$ Ce F, with 20·2 carbonic acid, 46·2 lanthanium oxide, 3·8 cerium protoxide, 21·1 cerium, and 8·7 fluorine, is similar.

184. CRYOLITE.—3 Na F + $Al^2 F^3$, *or* [3 Na F + Al F^3].

Triclinic, but crystals very small, and resemble a combination of the cube and octahedron. Mostly indistinct crystalline or granular. Cleavage, one perfect, two others less so, the three nearly at right angles; brittle. H. = 2·5 ...3; G. = 2·9...3. Translucent, and after immersion in water almost transparent; vitreous, but on 0P rather pearly. Colourless and snow-white, but often grayish, yellowish, or reddish. B.B. fuses very easily (even in the flame of a candle) to a white enamel; in open tube shows traces of fluorine; partially soluble in h. acid; wholly so in s., with evolution of fluorine. Chem. com. 54 fluorine, 13 aluminium, and 33 sodium. Ivigtok, Arksutfiord, in South Greenland, Miask in Ural. Used for preparations of soda and alumina, and as an ore of aluminium.

Pachnolite, small rhombic prisms in druses of cryolite, has nearly half the sodium replaced by calcium, and 9 water. ·

185. CHIOLITE.— $\begin{cases} 3 \text{ Na F} + 2 \text{ Al}^2 \text{ F}^3 = \text{A.} \\ 2 \text{ Na F} + \text{Al}^2 \text{ F}^3 = \text{B.} \end{cases}$

Tetragonal, in minute pyramids, with middle edge 111° 44'; ∞P 124° 22'; mostly granular. Cleavage, P rather perfect. H. = 4. Resinous. White. Very easily fusible (more so than cryolite), colouring the flame deep yellow; evolves fluoric acid. Chem. com. twofold; one variety (A) with G. = 2·8...2·9, containing 18·6 aluminium, 23·4 sodium, and 58 fluorine; the second (B), with G. = 3·0...3·1, containing 16·4 aluminium, 27·8 sodium, and 55·8 fluorine. Miask in Siberia. B has been named *Nipholite;* and a similar mineral, but with calcium, 7 per cent, for part of the sodium, *Arksutite*, occurs with the cryolite.

Fluellite.—Small, white, transparent, rhombic pyramids; polar edges 109° 6′ and 82° 12′, middle 144°. Consists essentially of fluorine and aluminium. Stenna-gwyn in Cornwall.

Prosopite.—Crystals like datholite. H. = 4·5. Vitreous. Colourless and transparent. Scheerer found 42 alumina, 32 fluoride of calcium, 11 fluoride of silicium, and 15 water. Altenberg; Schlackenwald (?).

186. HOPEITE.

Rhombic; ∞P̆2, 82° 20′; P with polar edges 106° 36′ and 140°. Cleavage, macrodiagonal perfect. H. = 2·5...3; G. = 2·76...2·85. Vitreous or pearly. Grayish-white. B.B. melts to a clear globule, tinging the flame green; soluble in acids without effervescence. Chem. com. oxide of zinc and cadmium, with phosphoric (or boracic ?) acid, and much water. Rare. Altenberg near Aix la Chapelle.

*187. APATITE.— $\begin{cases} 3 \ \dot{C}a^3 \overset{..}{P} + Ca \ (Cl, F), \textit{ or} \\ [3 \ (3 \ Ca \ O . P^3 O^5) + Ca \ (Cl^2, F^2)]. \end{cases}$

Hexagonal and pyramidal-hemihedric; P 80° 26′; the

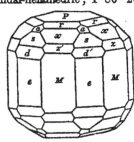

Fig. 168. Fig. 169.

most common forms are ∞P (*M*), ∞P2 (*e*), 0P (*P*), P (*x*); the basis 0P seldom wanting. The crystals (Figs. 168, 169) are short prismatic or thick tabular, and often striated vertically. Also granular, fibrous, or compact. Cleavage, prismatic and basal both imperfect; fracture conchoidal or uneven and splintery; brittle. H. = 5; G. = 3·1...3·25

Transparent to opaque; vitreous, but resinous on the cleavage-planes and fracture. Colourless and white, but generally light green, gray, blue, violet, or red. In powder phosphoresces with heat. B.B. fusible in thin splinters with much difficulty to a colourless, translucent glass; moistened with sulphuric acid it colours the flame green; soluble in nitric or h. acid. Chem. com. phosphate of lime (89 to 92·3), with chloride (to 11) or fluoride (to 7·7) of calcium, or both. Disseminated in granite, gneiss, mica, and hornblende slates, and trap rocks. Also in beds and veins. In tin mines in Saxony, Bohemia, St. Michael's Mount, St. Agnes, and Botallack in Cornwall; in granite, Bovey Tracey in Devonshire, Caldbeck Fell in Cumberland, near Cromarty, and in Aberdeenshire; also at St. Gotthardt, the Tyrol, and Krageroe, Hammond and Edenville in New York, and Elmsley, Canada. *Moroxite*, opaque greenish-blue from Arendal. *Asparagus-stone*, translucent, wine-yellow crystals, from the Zillerthal in Tyrol. *Phosphorite*, massive, from Logrosan in Estremadura.

Magnesia-apatite, from Kussinsk in the Ural, contains 7·74 magnesia.

188. HERDERITE, Allogonite.—$\ddot{A}l$, $\dot{C}a$, $\ddot{P}$, F.

Rhombic; P polar edges 77° 20′ and 141° 16′, $\infty\bar{P}$ 115° 53′. Cleavage, $\infty\bar{P}\infty$ and $\infty\breve{P}$ imperfect; fracture conchoidal. H. = 5; G. = 2·9...3·0. Translucent; vitreous, inclining to resinous. Yellowish or greenish white. B.B. difficultly fusible to a white enamel; moistened with s. acid colours the flame green; soluble in warm h. acid. Ehrenfriedersdorf in Saxony, but extremely rare.

189. CHILDRENITE.—2 $(\dot{F}e, \dot{M}n)^4 \ddot{P} + \ddot{A}l^2 \ddot{P} + 15 \dot{H}$.

Rhombic; polar edges 101° 43′, 130° 10′, middle 98°

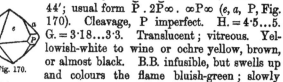

Fig. 170.

44′; usual form $\breve{P} . 2\breve{P}\infty . \infty P\infty$ (e, a, P, Fig. 170). Cleavage, P imperfect. H. = 4·5...5. G. = 3·18...3·3. Translucent; vitreous. Yellowish-white to wine or ochre yellow, brown, or almost black. B.B. infusible, but swells up and colours the flame bluish-green; slowly soluble in warm h. acid. Chem. com. 30·7 iron protoxide, 9 manganese protoxide, 14·5 alumina, 29 phosphoric acid, and 17 water. Tavistock in Devonshire, Crinnis in Cornwall, and Callington in Cumberland.

190. XENOTIME.—$\ddot{Y}^3 \overset{\cdots}{P}$.

Tetragonal; P 82°. Crystals P . ∞P. Cleavage, ∞P. H. = 4·5 ; G. = 4·4...4·55. Translucent in thin splinters ; resinous. Yellowish or reddish-brown, and flesh-red ; streak paler. B.B. infusible. Chem. com. 62 yttria, and 38 phosphoric acid, but some with 8 to 11 cerium prot-oxide. Lindesnaes and Hitteroe in Norway, Ytterby, Sweden, and Georgia, U.S., and (*Wiserin*) St. Gotthard.

191. BORACITE.— $\begin{cases} 2\ \ddot{M}g^3\ \ddot{B}^4 + Mg\ Cl,\ or \\ [2\ (3\ Mg\ O\ .\ 4\ B^3\ O^3) + Mg\ Cl^2]. \end{cases}$

Tesseral, and hemihedral; ∞O∞ , ∞O (Fig. 171), and $\dfrac{O.}{2}$

Cleavage, octahedral very imperfect ; fracture conchoidal ; brittle. H. = 7 ; G. = 2·9...3. Trans-parent, or translucent on the edges. Vitreous or adamantine. Colourless or white, often grayish, yellowish, or greenish. Becomes polar electric by heat. B.B. fuses with difficulty to a clear yellowish bead, which on cooling forms a white opaque mass of needle-like crystals ; at same time colours

Fig. 171.

the flame green ; soluble in h. acid. Chem. com. 62·5 boracic acid, 26·9 magnesia, 7·9 chlorine, and 2·7 magnesium. Lüneberg and Segeberg in Holstein ; Stass-furt.

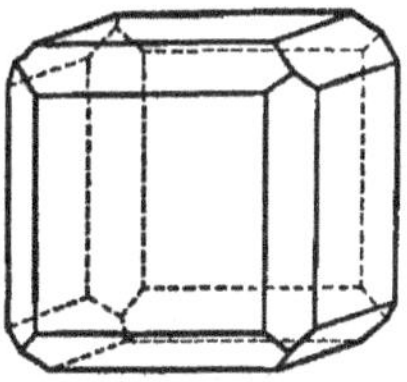

Stassfurtite.—In very minute prismatic crystals. White. Chem. com. same as boracite, and thus perhaps dimorphous. Stassfurt in Germany.

Rhodizite agrees in most characters with boracite ; only H. = 8 and G. = 3·3...3·42. B.B. fuses difficultly on the edges, colouring the flame first green, then green above and red below, and at last in some varieties all red. Chem. com. borate of lime. Mursinsk in Siberia.

192. HYDROBOROCALCITE.—$\dot{C}a \ddot{B}^2 + 6 \dot{H}$.

Delicate snow-white crystals, with 19 lime, 46 boracic acid, and 35 water. Iquique in Peru.

193. HYDROBORACITE.—$\dot{C}a^2 \ddot{B}^3 + \dot{M}g^2 \ddot{B}^3 + 12 \dot{H}$.

Radiating and foliated like gypsum. H. = 2 ; G. = 1·9 ...2. Translucent. White, but partly red. B.B. melts easily, tinging the flame green ; easily soluble in warm acids. Chem. com. 13·52 lime, 10·57 magnesia, 49·58 boracic acid, and 26·33 water. Caucasus. A similar mineral with soda in place of magnesia is found in Peru.

*194. DATHOLITE, Borate of Lime. } $\dot{C}a \ddot{B} + \dot{C}a \ddot{S}i^2 + \dot{H}$, *or* [Ca B Si H O²].

Monoclinic ; C. = 89° 51′, $\infty \check{P}$ (*f*) 76° 38′, $\infty P^\circ 2$ (*g*) 115° 22′, – P (*P*) 120°, – 2P°∞ (*a*) 45° 8′, $\infty P^\circ \infty$ (*s*), 2P°∞ (*o*) (Fig. 172); or rhombic with *b* : *f* 90°, *b* : *a* 135° ; *b* : *c* 141° 9′, and *f* : *g* 160° 39′ ; also coarse granular. Cleavage, orthodiagonal and ∞P very imperfect ; fracture

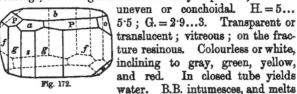

Fig. 172.

uneven or conchoidal. H. = 5... 5·5 ; G. = 2·9...3. Transparent or translucent ; vitreous ; on the fracture resinous. Colourless or white, inclining to gray, green, yellow, and red. In closed tube yields water. B.B. intumesces, and melts easily to a clear glass, colouring the flame green ; the powder gelatinises in h. acid. Chem. com. 38·1 silica, 21·6 boracic acid, 34·7 lime, and 5·6 water. Arendal, Utoe, Andreasberg, Seisser Alpe, Sonthofen (*Humboldtite*) ; Toggianna in Modena ; also Salisbury Crags, Corstorphine Hill, Glen Farg in Perthshire, and near Dunnotar ; Connecticut and New Jersey.

Botryolite.—Fine fibrous, botryoidal or reniform, snow-white ior hair-brown ; otherwise, and in chem. com., like datholite, but with two atoms water. Arendal.

FAMILY III.—HEAVY SPAR.

Crystallisation rhombic specially. H. = 3...4·5 ; G. = 3·2...4·7, but mostly 3·6...4·5. Transparent or translucent ; colourless or coloured red, yellow, blue, or green. Soluble in acids, except barytes and celestine. B.B. fusible or decompose. Those containing baryta colour the flame yellowish-green ; those with strontia carmine-red, best seen when moistened with h. acid. The sulphates fused with soda and then moistened leave a black stain on silver.

**195. BARYTES, Heavy Spar.—$\dot{\text{B}}\text{a}\,\ddot{\text{S}}. = [\text{Ba O . SO}^3]$.

Rhombic $\bar{\text{P}}\infty$ (*g*) 78° 20′, $\breve{\text{P}}\infty$ (*f*) 105° 22′, $\infty\breve{\text{P}}2$ (*d*) 77° 44′; also $\infty\bar{\text{P}}\infty$ (*c*) (Figs. 173, 174, 175, but in a different position, *d d* being placed vertical). The crystals show very many forms and combinations, and are tabular or columnar, often in druses or groups ; also foliated, fibrous, granular, or compact. Cleavage, brachydiagonal per-

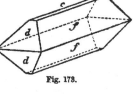

Fig. 173.

fect, along $\bar{\text{P}}\infty$ less perfect ; basal traces. H. = 3...3·5 ; G. = 4·3 ... 4·7 (4·48). Transparent to translucent ; vitreous or resinous. Colourless and white, but generally reddish-white,

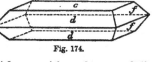

Fig. 174.

or flesh-red, yellow, gray, bluish, greenish, or brown. B.B. decrepitates violently, and fuses very difficultly, or only on the edges, colouring the flame yellowish-green ; not soluble in acids. Chem. com. 34·3 sulphuric acid, and

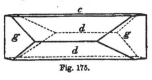

Fig. 175.

65·7 baryta, but occasionally with 1 to 15 sulphate of strontia. Very common, chiefly in veins, either alone or accompanying ores. Crystals at Dufton, Bohemia, Felsobanya and Kremnitz in Hungary, Auvergne, and United States. Columnar at Freiberg. The radiated from near Bologna, or the *Bolognese stone*, phosphoresces in the dark. Massive or *Cawk* from Derbyshire and Staffordshire ; in Scotland at Leadhills, Braid Hills near Edinburgh, the

Pentlands and Cheviots, and Arran, where mined as a white pigment.

Lime Barytes, from Freiberg, Strontian, and Derbyshire, seems a mixture with sulphate of lime; crystals, tabular, in rosettes and other groups. G. = 4·0...4·3.

Hepatite. — Dark-gray, from carbonaceous matter; Kongsberg. *Allomorphite*, scaly, white and pearly, near Rudolstadt, agrees essentially with barytes.

196. DREELITE.—Ċa S̈ + 3 Ḃa S̈.

Rhombohedral; R 93°. Cleavage, R imperfect. H. = 3...4; G. = 3·2...3·4. Lustre dull; on cleavage pearly. White. B.B. fuses to a white vesicular glass; effervesces with h. acid, but only partially dissolves. Chem. com. 61·73 sulphate of baryta, 14·27 sulphate of lime, 8·05 carbonate of lime, 9·71 silica, 2·40 alumina, 1·52 lime, 2·31 water. Nuissière near Beaujeu.

*197. WITHERITE.—Ḃa C̈, *or* [Ba O . CO²].

Rhombic; ∞P (*M*) 118° 30′, 2 P̃∞ (*P*) 112° (Fig. 176). Crystals not common, and often have quite a hexagonal aspect; macles like arragonite. More common spherical, botryoidal, or reniform, with radiated columnar texture. Cleavage, ∞P distinct, 2 P̃∞ and ∞P̃∞ imperfect; frac-

Fig. 176.

ture uneven. H. = 3...3·5; G. = 4·2...4·3. Semi-transparent or translucent; vitreous, or resinous on the fracture. Colourless, but generally yellowish or grayish. B.B. fuses easily to a transparent globule, opaque when cold; on charcoal boils, becomes caustic and sinks into the support; soluble with effervescence in nitric or h. acid. Chem. com. 22·3 carbonic acid and 77·7 baryta. Alston Moor and Hexham in Northumberland; also in Styria, Salzburg, Hungary, Sicily, Siberia, and Chili.

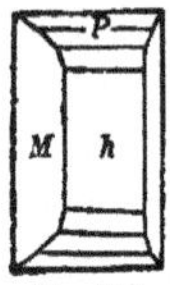

198. ALSTONITE.—Ḃa C̈ + Ċa C̈.

Rhombic, like witherite; ∞P 118° 50′, 2 P̃∞ 111° 50′; usual combination P . 2 P̃∞ . ∞P, resembling a hexagonal pyramid. Cleavage, ∞P and ∞P̃∞ rather distinct. H. = 4...4·5; G. = 3·65...3·76. Translucent; weak resinous.

Colourless or grayish-white. Chem.-com. 66 carbonate of baryta and 34 carbonate of lime, thus identical with the baryto-calcite. Fallowfield near Hexham, and Alston Moor.

199. BARYTO-CALCITE.—$\dot{B}a\,\ddot{C} + \dot{C}a\,\ddot{C}$.

Monoclinic ; C. = 69° 30′ ; ∞P (*b*) 84° 52′, P (*m*) 106° 54′, P°∞ (*h*) 61° (Fig. 177); also columnar and granular. Cleavage, P perfect, P°∞ less perfect. H. = 4 ; G. = 3·6...3·7. Transparent or translucent ; vitreous, inclining to resinous. Yellowish-white. B.B. infusible, but becomes opaque and caustic. Chem. com. like alstonite, Alston Moor.

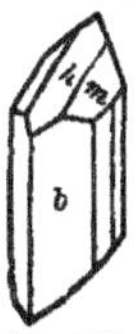

Fig. 177.

*200. CELESTINE.—$\dot{S}r\,\ddot{S} = [Sr\ O\ .\ S\ O^{\bullet}]$.

Rhombic ; forms like barytes and anglesite ; $\bar{P}\infty$ (*o*) 104° 8′, $\bar{P}\infty$ (*M*) 75° 58′. Usual combinations $\bar{P}\infty\,.\,\bar{P}\infty\,.\,\infty\bar{P}\infty$, or this with ∞P2 (*d*) (Fig. 179, also 178, but in another position) ; also columnar and foliated ; or fibrous, fine granular or compact. Cleavage, macrodiagonal perfect ; along $\bar{P}\infty$ less perfect. H. = 3...3·5 ; G. = 3·9...4. Transparent or translucent ; vitreous or resinous. Colourless, but usually bluish-white to indigo-blue, and rarely reddish or yellowish. B.B. decrepitates and fuses easily to a milk-white globule ; colours the flame carmine-red. Distinguished from barytes by a splinter after ignition in the inner flame, being moistened with h. acid, and held in the blue border of the flame of a candle, colouring this of a lively purple-red.

Fig. 178.

Scarcely affected by acids. Chem. com. 43·6 sulphuric acid, and 56·4 strontia, but often some baryta or lime. Sulphur mines of Girgenti and other parts of Sicily, Herrengrund in Hungary, Bex, Salzburg, Monte Viale near Verona, and Meudon and Montmartre near Paris ;

Fig. 179.

in England near Bristol, and Knaresborough ; in Scotland at Inverness, Tantallon Castle, Calton Hill. Used for strontium preparations, and red-light in fireworks.

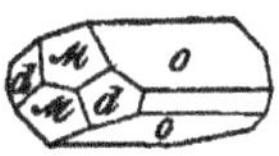

Baryto-celestine.—Radiating columnar or foliated. Bluish-white ; very brittle and friable. H. = 2·5 ; G. = 3·92. B.B.

difficultly fusible.   Chem. com. 2 Ṡr S̈ + Ḃa S̈, with 36 strontia, and 23 baryta.   Diamond Island in Lake Erie, Kingstown in Upper Canada, and Binnenthal.

*201. STRONTIANITE.—Ṡr C̈ = [Sr O . CO³].

Rhombic ; ∞P 117° 19′, P̄∞ 108° 12′.   Crystals (Fig. 180) and macles like arragonite ; also broad columnar and fibrous.   Cleavage, prismatic along ∞P (*M*) and 2 P̄∞ (*P*) (69° 16′) imperfect.   H. = 3·5 ;   G. = 3·6...3·8.   Translucent or transparent ; vitreous or resinous on fracture.   Colourless, but often light asparagus or apple-green, more rarely

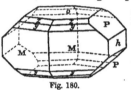

grayish or yellowish.   B.B. fuses in a strong heat only on very thin edges ; intumesces in cauliflower-like forms, shines brightly, and colours the flame red ; easily soluble with effervescence in acids.

Fig. 180.

Paper moistened with the solution in h. acid burns with a carmine-red flame.   Chem. com. 30 carbonic acid and 70 strontia, but often contains carbonate of lime (6 to 8).   Leogang in Salzburg, Bräunsdorf in Saxony, Hamm in Westphalia, the Harz ; at Schoharie and other parts of the United States (*Emmonite*); Strontian in Argyleshire, Leadhills, Yorkshire, and Giant's Causeway.   ·It is used to produce red fire in pyrotechnic exhibitions.

Stromnite or *Barystrontianite.*—Yellowish-white, semi-translucent, faint pearly lustre.   H. = 3·5 ; G. = 3·7.   Contains 68·6 carbonate of strontia, 27·5 sulphate of baryta, and 2·6 carbonate of lime.   Stromness in Orkney.

FAMILY IV.—GYPSUM.

Crystallisation rhombic or monoclinic.   H. = 2...3, or less, many yield to the nail.   G. = 2·2...2·9, or also low. All, except the sulphates, soluble in acids, some in water ; also fusible in general.   Mostly translucent and colourless, but often coloured by mixtures.

**202. GYPSUM.—Ċa S̈ + 2 Ḣ, *or* [Ca O . SO³ + 2H² O].
Monoclinic ;   C. = 80° 57′ ;   the most common forms

are ∞P 111° 30′, P 138° 40′, –P 143° 30′, and ∞P°∞.
Two common combinations are ∞P (f). ∞P°∞ (P).—P
(l) (Fig. 181), and this with P. Lenticular
crystals often occur; macles frequent (Fig.
83 above); also granular, compact, fibrous,
scaly, or pulverulent. Cleavage, clinodiagonal very perfect, along P much less perfect; sectile, thin plates flexible. H. = 1·5
...2 (lowest on P); G. = 2·2...2·4. Transparent or translucent; vitreous, on cleavage
pearly or silky. Colourless and snow-white,
but often red, gray, yellow, brown, and more
rarely greenish or bluish. In the closed
tube yields water. B.B. becomes opaque

Fig. 181.

and white; exfoliates and fuses to a white enamel, which is
alkaline; soluble in 400 to 500 parts of water, scarcely
more so in acids. Chem. com. 46·5 sulphuric acid, 32·6
lime, and 20·9 water.

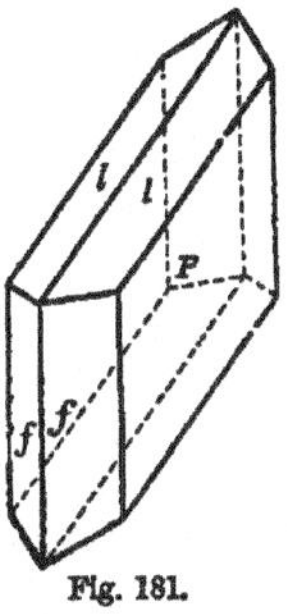

Gypsum is a very common mineral, often in nests or
reniform masses in clay or marl. Transparent crystals, or
Selenite, occur in the salt mines of Bex in Switzerland, of
the Tyrol, Salzburg, and Bohemia, in the sulphur mines of
Sicily, at Lockport in New York, in the clay of Shotover
Hill near Oxford, at Chatley near Bath, and many other
localities. Fibrous gypsum at Ilfeld in the Harz, and Matlock in Derbyshire. Compact gypsum at Volterra in Tuscany (*Alabaster*), and in whole beds in many parts of Germany, France, Italy, and England, often with rock-salt.

The finer varieties, or *Alabaster*, are cut into various
ornamental articles. Plaster of Paris, used for casts and
other works of art, is formed by calcining gypsum at a
temperature below 300° Fahr., and grinding it down to a
fine powder, which forms a paste that soon hardens by
absorbing the water driven off by the heat.

*203. ANHYDRITE, Karstenite.—$\dot{C}$a $\ddot{S}$ = [Ca . O . S O⁷].

Rhombic; ∞P 90° 4′, $\breve{P}\infty$ 96° 30′. Crystals 0P. $\infty\bar{P}\infty$
. $\infty\bar{P}\infty$. ∞P, but rare; chiefly granular, or almost compact
or columnar. Macles rare. Cleavage, macrodiagonal and

brachydiagonal both very perfect, basal perfect.   H. = 3...
3·5 ; G. = 2·8...3·0.   Transparent or translucent ; vitreous ;
on $\infty \bar{P} \infty$ pearly.   Colourless or white, but often blue, red,
or gray ; streak grayish-white.   In closed tube gives no
water.   B.B. fuses difficultly to a white enamel ; with fluor
spar fuses readily to a clear globule, which becomes opaque
when cold, and, on continuation of the heat, intumesces
and becomes infusible ; very slightly soluble in water or
acids.   Chem. com. 58·75 sulphuric acid and 41·25 lime.

The crystalline, or *Muriacite*, occurs in the salt mines of
Bex, Hall in Tyrol, and Aussee in Styria ; also Sulz, Stassfurt, and Bleiberg.   Compact at Ischel in Austria, Berchtesgaden, Eisleben, and the Harz.   Granular, or *Vulpinite*,
near Bergamo.   The contorted, or *Gekrösstein*, chiefly at
Wieliczka and Bochnia.

204. POLYHALITE.—2 $\dot{C}a \overset{..}{S} + \dot{M}g \overset{..}{S} + \dot{K} \overset{..}{S} + 2 \overset{..}{H}$.
Rhombic ; ∞P 115° ; mostly columnar or fibrous.
Cleavage, ∞P imperfect.   H. = 3·5 ; G. = 2·7...2·8.   Translucent ; pearly or resinous.   Colourless, but generally pale
red, seldom gray.   Weak bitter, and slightly saline taste.
Soluble in water, leaving gypsum.   B.B. fuses on charcoal
to an opaque reddish bead, becoming white when cold.
Chem. com. sulphate of lime 45, of magnesia 20·5, of potassa
29, and water 5·5.   Ischel, Aussee, and Berchtesgaden.

205. GLAUBERITE, Brongniartin.—$\dot{N}a \overset{..}{S} + \dot{C}a \overset{..}{S}$.
Monoclinic ; C. = 68° 16′ ; ∞P 83° 20′, —P 116° 20′.
Crystals 0P.—P, or with ∞P (*P, f, M*, Fig. 182).   Cleavage,
basal perfect, along ∞P traces.   H. = 2·5...3 ; G. = 2·75...

Fig. 182.

2·85.   Translucent ; vitreous to resinous.
Colourless, but yellowish or grayish white,
yellow, or red.   Taste slightly saline and bitter.   B.B. decrepitates violently, and melts to
a clear glass ; decomposed by water, which
removes the sulphate of soda.   Chem. com. 51
sulphate of soda, and 49 sulphate of lime.   Villarubia in
Spain, Vic, Berchtesgaden ; near Brugg in Aargau, Aussee
and Ischel in Austria, and Tarapaca in Peru, with 1 to 5
boracic acid.

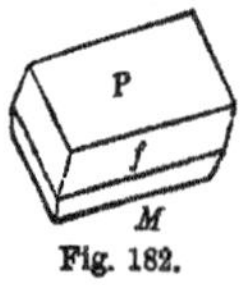

206. ALUNITE,⎱ 3 $\ddot{A}l\ \ddot{S} + \dot{K}\ \ddot{S} + 6\ \dot{H}$, *or*
   Alumstone. ⎰ [$K^2O . SO^3 + 3\,(Al^2\,O^3 . SO^3) + 6\ H^2\,O$].

  Rhombohedral; R. 89° 10'. Crystals, R, or R . 0R

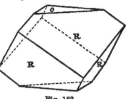

Fig. 183.

(Fig. 183); also fine granular, earthy, or compact. Cleavage, basal rather perfect. H. = 3·5 ...4 ; G. = 2·6...2·8. Translucent; vitreous, on 0R pearly. Colourless and white, but grayish, yellowish, or reddish. B.B. decrepitates; infusible alone; but becomes blue with cobalt solution. Soluble in warm con. s. acid, not in h. acid. Chem. com. 37·2 alumina, 11·3 potash, 38·5 sulphuric acid, and 13 water. Bereghszasz in Hungary, Tolfa, Lipari Islands, Auvergne, and Milo.

Jarosite; dark yellow or brown, is isomorphous, and chem. com. similar, but $\ddot{F}e$ for $\ddot{A}l$. Spain, Saxony, and Mexico.

  207. ALUMINITE, Websterite.—$\ddot{A}l\ \ddot{S} + 9\ \dot{H}$.

  Reniform, and very fine scaly or fibrous. Fracture earthy; sectile or friable. H. = 1 ; G. = 1·7. Opaque ; dull or glimmering; snow-white or yellowish-white. In closed tube yields much water. B.B. emits sulphurous fumes, the remainder being infusible; easily soluble in h. acid. Chem. com. 29·8 alumina, 23·2 sulphuric acid, and 47 water. Newhaven in Sussex; Eperney, Auteuil, and Lunel Vieil in France; Halle and Morl in Prussia. *Felsö-banyite* from Hungary, in rhombic tables, is similar.

  208. PHARMACOLITE.—⎰ $\dot{C}a^3\ \ddot{A}s + 6\ \dot{H}$, *or*
                       ⎱ [2 Ca O . $As^2\,O^3$ + 6 H^2 O].

  Monoclinic ; C. = 65° 4'; ∞P 117° 24', − P 139° 17'. Crystals prismatic ; often acicular or capillary, or radiated fibrous crusts. Cleavage, clinodiagonal very perfect ; sectile and flexible. H. = 2...2·5 ; G. = 2·6...2·8. Translucent; vitreous ; pearly or silky. Colourless and white, but red or green. Yields water in the closed tube. B.B. fuses to a white enamel; in the inner flame on charcoal gives arsenic fumes, and fuses to a semitranslucent grain, colouring the flame blue; easily soluble in acids. Chem.

P

com. 51 arsenic acid, 25 lime, and 24 water.   Andreasberg, Riechelsdorf, Biber, Joachimsthal, Markirchen, and Wittichen.

Picropharmacolite contains magnesia.   *Roselite*, vitreous ; rose-red.   B.B. with borax forms a deep-blue glass.   Chem. com. arsenic acid, oxide of cobalt, lime, magnesia, and water.   Schneeberg in Saxony.

209. HAIDINGERITE.—$\overset{..}{Ca}{}^2 \overset{...}{As} + 3\,\overset{.}{H}$.

Rhombic ; ∞P 100°.   Cleavage very perfect ; sectile, flexible.   H. = 2...2·5 ;   G. = 2·8...2·9.   Otherwise like pharmacolite.   Chem. com. 85·68 arseniate of lime and 14·32 water.   Joachimsthal.

210. BERZELIITE.—$\overset{..}{Ca}{}^3 \overset{...}{As} + \overset{..}{Mg}{}^3 \overset{...}{As}$.

Massive, with traces of cleavage.   Brittle.   H. = 5.5 ; G. = 2·52.   Translucent on the edges ; resinous.   Honey-yellow or yellowish-white.   B.B. infusible, but becomes gray ; soluble in nitric acid.   Contains also 2 to 4 manganese protoxide.   Longbanshytta in Sweden.

211. STRUVITE, Guanite.—$(\overset{.}{NH}{}^4 O, \overset{.}{Mg}{}^3) \overset{...}{P} + 12\,\overset{.}{H}$.

Rhombic ; $\bar{P}\infty$ 63° 7′, $\bar{P}\infty$ 95°.   Cleavage, brachy-diagonal perfect.   H. = 1·5...2 ;   G. = 1·66...1·75.   Transparent or opaque ; vitreous.   Colourless, but yellow or brown.   In the closed tube yields water and ammonia. B.B. fuses to a white enamel ; soluble in h. acid, and very slightly in water.   Chem. com. 29·9 phosphoric acid, 16·3 magnesia, 10·6 ammonia, and 44 water.   Under St. Nicolai church at Hamburg, and in guano from Africa.

*FAMILY V.—ROCK-SALT.

Crystallisation monoclinic and rhombic, some tesseral or hexagonal.   H. = 1...3, but most about 2 ; G. = 1·5... 3, but generally 2.   All soluble in water, and B.B. fusible or decompose.   When pure, mostly colourless, white, translucent, and vitreous.   They are chiefly products of decomposition, and occur especially in the rainless regions, or in lakes not communicating with the sea.   Occasionally form beds or masses in the strata.   Many are valuable in the arts, or used as medicine, and then produced artificially.

**212. ROCK-SALT.—Na Cl.

Tesseral ; almost always cubes.   Generally granular and

fibrous. Cleavage, hexahedral very perfect; fracture conchoidal; rather brittle; yields slightly when scratched with the nail. H. = 2; G. = 2·1...2·2. Transparent or translucent; vitreous. Colourless or white, but often coloured red, yellow, gray, and rarely blue. Taste saline. In the closed tube decrepitates, and yields a little water. B.B. on charcoal fuses and partly evaporates, partly sinks into the support. With soda fuses to a clear mass, colouring the flame yellow. Very soluble in water. Chem. com. 60·7 chlorine and 39·3 sodium, but often with various impurities.

This important mineral is very widely disseminated, either in thick masses, with clay, anhydrite, and gypsum, or as an efflorescence, covering extensive tracts of country. The most celebrated European deposits occur at Wieliczka and other parts of Galicia, in Hungary, Siebenburg, Moldavia, Styria, Salzburg (Hallein), in Tyrol (Hall); also in Bavaria, Wurtemburg, Switzerland (Bex), and Spain, especially at Cardona. In England the chief deposits are in Cheshire, as at Northwich. In Ireland near Belfast. As an efflorescence it is most abundant on the sandy plains in Brazil, at the foot of the Atlas Mountains in Africa, in Abyssinia, in Arabia, and in the Steppes round the Caspian Sea and Lake Aral. Also as a sublimation among the lavas of Vesuvius and other volcanoes. Dissolved in the water of the ocean, salt lakes, and springs. Used for food, medicine, manures, a flux in melting ores, and in many manufactures. In 1871 the produce of the United Kingdom was 1½ million tons, worth £753,000.

Sylvine, or chloride of potassium, with 52·4 potassium and 47·6 chlorine, found as a sublimation on Vesuvius, and in the rock-salt of Hallein and Berchtesgaden, agrees in most characters with rock-salt (G. = 1·9...2).

213. CARNALLITE.—2 Mg Cl + K Cl + 12 $\dot{\text{H}}$.

Rhombic; P middle edge 107° 20′, ∞P 118° 37′; mostly massive and granular. Conchoidal fracture. H. = 2...2·5; G. = 1·6. Colourless, but generally more or less red from iron peroxide. Deliquesces in the atmosphere, and B.B. fuses very easily, colouring the flame pale violet. Chem. com. 34·2 chloride of magnesium, 26·9 chloride of potassium, and 38·9 water; but also traces of rubidium and cæsium. Stassfurt, Kalusz in Galicia, and Manan in Persia. *Tachydrite*, a yellow, pellucid, very soluble salt, found in anhydrite at Stassfurt, has a similar chem. com., except chloride of calcium (21·4) instead of chloride of potassium. Crystals said to be rhombohedral.

*214. ALUM.— $\begin{cases} \dot{R}\ \ddot{S} + (\ddot{Al},\ \ddot{Fe})\ \ddot{S}^3 + 24\ \dot{H} = \\ [RO . R^3 O^3 . 4\ SO^3 . 24\ H^2O]. \end{cases}$

Tesseral; O, sometimes with $\infty O \infty$ and ∞O. Generally fibrous crusts, or as an efflorescence. Cleavage, octahedral imperfect; fracture conchoidal. H. = 2...2·5; G. = 1·75...1·9. Translucent. Colourless and white. Taste sweetish astringent. Easily soluble in water. B.B. generally evolves sulphurous fumes.

(*a.*) *Potash-alum*, with $\dot{R} = \dot{K}$, and 33·7 sulphuric acid, 10·9 alumina, 9·9 potash, and 45·5 water. In the closed tube fuses, intumesces, and yields much water. In the Silurian alum-slates of Sweden, Norway, and Scotland; the coal formation, Hurlet and Campsie in Scotland; the lias near Whitby; in the brown coals of Hessia and the Rhine; and in the volcanic formations of the Lipari Islands, Sicily, and the Azores.

(*b.*) *Ammonia-alum*, with $\dot{R} = NH^4\ O$, and about 4 per cent ammonia and 48 water. In the closed tube it forms a sublimate of sulphate of ammonia. Tschermig in Bohemia.

(*c.*) *Soda-alum*, with $\dot{R} = \dot{N}a$, and 7 soda and 48 water. Like potash-alum, but more easily soluble. Near Mendoza in South America, the Solfatara at Naples, and Milo.

(*d.*) *Magnesia-alum.*—$\dot{R} = \dot{M}g$ with $\dot{M}n$. Translucent and silky, but soon changes in the air. South Africa, Iquique in Peru (*Pickeringite*).

(*e.*) *Iron-alum* (*Feather-alum*), with $\dot{R} = \ddot{F}e$. Hurlet near Paisley, Mörsfield in Rhenish Bavaria, Krisuvig in Iceland (*Hversalt*).

215. VOLTAITE.—3 ($\ddot{F}e$, $\dot{K}$) $\ddot{S}$ + 2 ($\ddot{F}e$, $\ddot{Al}$) $\ddot{S}$ + 12 $\dot{H}$.

Tesseral. Black, brown, or green; greenish-gray streak. Like alum, but more difficultly soluble in water, and with 4 to 5 potash, and 2 to 5 alumina. Solfatara of Pozzuoli.

216. ALUNOGENE, Hair-salt.—$\ddot{Al}\ \ddot{S}^3$ + 18 $\dot{H}$.

Capillary or acicular, in crusts or reniform masses. H. =

$1\cdot5...2$; G. $= 1\cdot6...1\cdot7$. Silky. White, inclining to green or yellow. Tastes like alum. B.B. in closed tube intumesces, yields much water, and is infusible. Chem. com. 36 sulphuric acid, $15\cdot4$ alumina, $48\cdot6$ water. Volcanoes of South America, in coal and brown coal in Germany, and on old walls.

217. MIRABILITE, Glauber-salt.—Na $\ddot{S}$ + 10 $\dot{H}$.

Monoclinic; C $= 72°$ $15'$; ∞P(o) $86°$ $31'$, P(n) $93°$ $12'$. Crystals predominantly 0P and ∞P°∞ (M, T, Fig. 184); but generally efflorescent crusts. Cleavage, orthodiagonal very perfect; fracture conchoidal. H. $= 1\cdot5...2$; G. $= 1\cdot4...1\cdot5$. Pellucid and colourless; taste cool, saline, and bitter; decomposes readily in the atmo-

Fig. 184.

sphere, and falls into powder. B.B. fuses very easily, and sinks into the charcoal; colours the flame yellow. Chem. com. $19\cdot2$ soda, $24\cdot8$ sulphuric acid, and 56 water.

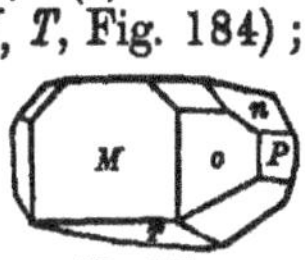

As an efflorescence in quarries, on old walls, or on the earth; in the water of lakes and springs in Russia and Egypt, and on Vesuvius in lava. Used in medicine, and in preparing glass and soap.

The following, Nos. 218-226, form a sub-family of *Metallic salts* or *Vitriols*:—

*218. MELANTERITE, Green or ⎱ Fe $\ddot{S}$ + 7 $\dot{H}$ =
   Iron Vitriol, Copperas. ⎰ [Fe O . SO³ + 7 H³O].

Monoclinic; C $= 75°$ $45'$; ∞P (f) $82°$ $22'$, $-$ P (P) $101°$ $34'$, P°∞ (o) $67°$ $30'$ (Fig. 185); chiefly stalactitic, reniform, or in crusts. Cleavage, basal very perfect, prismatic less so. H. $= 2$; G. $= 1\cdot8...1\cdot9$. Translucent, rarely transparent; vitreous. Leek or mountain green, often with a yellow coating; streak white. Taste sweetish astringent. Very soluble. B.B. becomes brown, then black and magnetic. Chem. com. 26 protoxide of iron, 29 sulphuric acid, and 45 water. Bodenmais, Rammelsberg in the Harz, Fahlun, Schemnitz,

Fig. 185.

Bilin, and Hurlet near Paisley. Used in dyeing, in manufacturing ink, Prussian blue, and sulphuric acid.

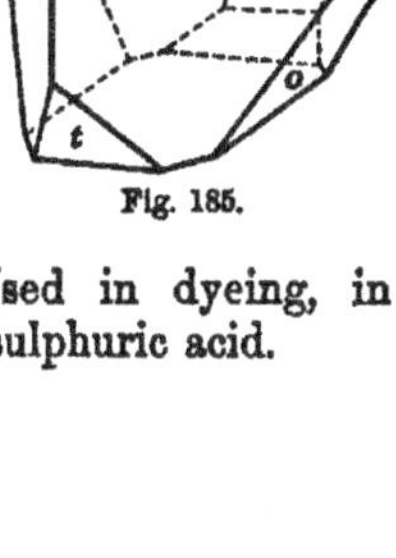

219. BOTRYOGENE, } $\ddot{Fe}^3 \ddot{S}^2 + 3 \ddot{Fe} \ddot{S}^2 + 36 \dot{H}$ (?).
    Red vitriol. }

Monoclinic ; C. = 62° 26'; ∞P 119° 56'.   Crystals small and short prismatic ; more common botryoidal and reniform.   Cleavage, ∞P rather distinct.   H. = 2...2·5 ; G. = 2...2·1.   Translucent ; vitreous.   Hyacinth-red, orange-yellow, and yellowish-brown ; streak ochre-yellow. Taste slightly astringent.   Partially soluble in water, leaving a yellow ochre.   Chem. com. sulphates of the protoxide and peroxide of iron (48), with 31 water, and about 21 per cent sulphates of magnesia and lime ; the two latter considered mixtures by Berzelius.   Fahlun in Sweden.

Römerite from the Harz seems the same.

220. COPIAPITE.—$\ddot{Fe}^3 \ddot{S}^3 + 13 \dot{H}$.

Six-sided tables, but crystal system uncertain ; also granular.   Cleavage perfect.   Translucent ; pearly.   Yellow. Chem. com. 34 iron peroxide, 42 sulphuric acid, and 24 water.   Copiapo in Coquimbo in Chili.   Also radiated fibrous masses ; dirty greenish-yellow, incrusting the former. Contain 32 sulphuric acid, and 37 water ; but both are probably mixtures.   To these may be added—

Fibroferrite, also from Chili.   *Yellow Iron-ore*, from the brown coal at Kolosoruk in Bohemia and Modum in Norway.   Both are reniform, or compact and earthy.   H. = 2·5 ...3 ; G. = 2·7...2·9.   Colour ochre-yellow.   Not soluble in water, with difficulty in hydrochloric acid.

Apatelite, reniform earthy, yellow, from Auteuil near Paris, is similar ; also *Vitriol ochre* from Fahlun ; and *Misy*, from Rammelsberg in the Harz, containing sulphates of iron, copper, zinc, and other metals, a product of decomposition.

221. COQUIMBITE.—$\ddot{Fe} \ddot{S}^3 + 9 \dot{H}$.

Hexagonal ; P 58°.   Crystals 0P, with ∞P and P ; usually granular.   Cleavage, ∞P imperfect.   H. = 2...2·5 ; G. = 2...2·1.   White, also brown, yellow, red, and blue. Taste astringent.   Chem. com. 28·5 iron peroxide, 42·6 sulphuric acid, and 28·9 water.   Copiapo in Chili, and Calama in Bolivia.

222. TECTIZITE.—$\ddot{\text{Fe}}$, $\ddot{\text{S}}$, $\dot{\text{H}}$.

Rhombic; dimensions unknown. H. = 1·5...2 ; G. = 2 nearly. Vitreous or resinous. Clove-brown. Saxony near Schwarzenberg, and at Bräunsdorf.

*223. CYANOSE, Blue } $\dot{\text{Cu}}$ $\ddot{\text{S}}$ + 5 $\dot{\text{H}}$ =
Vitriol. } [Cu O . SO³ + 5 H²O].

Triclinic. Crystals very unsymmetric ; $\infty\bar{\text{P}}\infty$ (*n*) to $\infty\bar{\text{P}}\infty$ (*r*), forms an angle of 79° 19'; P' (*P*) to ∞P' (*T*) 127° 40', to $\infty\bar{\text{P}}\infty$ (*n*) 120° 50', to $\infty\bar{\text{P}}\infty$ (*r*) 103° 27', and ∞ P' (*T*) to ∞'P (*M*) 123° 10' (Fig. 186). More often stalactitic, reniform, or as an incrustation. Cleavage, along ∞P', and ∞'P very imperfect ; fracture conchoidal. H. = 2·5 ; G. = 2·2...2·3. Translucent; vitreous. Blue. Taste very nauseous. Readily soluble in water, from which metallic copper is precipitated by iron. B.B. on charcoal, especially with soda, is easily reduced to metallic copper. Chem. com. 32 protoxide of copper, 32 sulphuric acid, and 36 water.

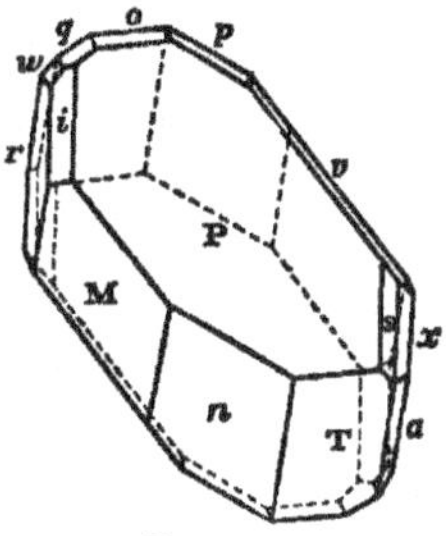

Fig. 186.

Abundant in the water of some mines, as in the Harz, Hungary, Tyrol, Fahlun, in Anglesea, Cornwall, and Wicklow. Also on the lava of Vesuvius. Used in dyeing, and in forming blue and green pigments.

*224. GOSLARITE, White } $\dot{\text{Zn}}$ $\ddot{\text{S}}$ + 7 $\dot{\text{H}}$ =
Vitriol. } [Zn O . SO³ + 7 H²O].

Rhombic ; ∞P 90° 42', isomorphous with epsomite ; ∞P . $\infty\bar{\text{P}}\infty$. P (*M, o, l*, Fig. 187). Mostly granular, or stalactitic, reniform and encrusting. Cleavage, brachydiagonal perfect. H. = 2...2·5 ; G. = 2...2·1. Pellucid ; vitreous. White, inclining to gray, yellow, green, or red. Taste nauseous astringent. Chem. com. 28·2 zinc oxide, 27·9 sulphuric acid, and 43·9 water. Rammelsberg in the Harz, Fahlun, Schemnitz, Holywell in Flintshire, and in Cornwall. Used in dyeing and medicine.

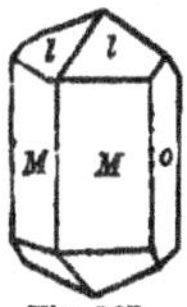

Fig. 187.

225. BIEBERITE, Cobalt Vitriol.—$\dot{C}o \ \ddot{S} + 7 \ \dot{H}$.

Monoclinic ; similar to melanterite ; usually stalactitic, or an efflorescence. Pale rose-red. Taste astringent. Chem. com. 20 cobalt oxide, 4 magnesia, 29 sulphuric acid, and 47 water. Bieber near Hanau, and Leogang. *Morenosite* is a similar nickel vitriol, fibrous and emerald-green, with 27 nickel-oxide. Riechelsdorf, and near Lake Huron.

226. JOHANNITE.—Uran Vitriol.

Monoclinic ; C. $= 85°\ 40'$; ∞P 69°. Crystals similar to trona (Fig. 190), but very small and rare. H. $= 2...2·5$; G. $= 3·19$. Semitransparent ; vitreous. Bright grass-green. Chem. com. a hydrous sulphate of uranium protoxide. Joachimsthal and Johann-Georgenstadt.

*227. NATRON.— $\begin{cases} \dot{N}a \ \ddot{C} + 10 \ \dot{H}, \ or \\ [Na^2 \ O \ . \ CO^2 + 10 \ H^2 \ O]. \end{cases}$

Monoclinic ; C. $= 57°\ 40'$. Crystals artificial (Fig. 188); with ∞P (M) 79° 41', P (P) 76° 28'. Cleavage, orthodiagonal distinct. H. $= 1...$ 1·5 ; G. $= 1·4 ... 1·5$. Pellucid ; vitreous. Colourless or grayish-white. B.B. melts easily, colouring the flame yellow. Chem. com. 22 soda, 15 carbonic acid, and 63 water ; but mixed with chloride of sodium, and other salts. Only as an efflorescence on the ground or rocks (lava of Vesuvius and Etna) in various countries, Hungary, Egypt, Tartary, and in mineral springs and lakes. Used in the manufacture of soap, in dyeing, bleaching, and medicine.

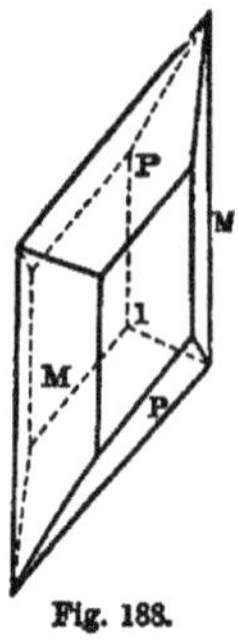

Fig. 188.

228. THERMONATRITE. $\begin{cases} \dot{N}a \ \ddot{C} + \dot{H}, \ or \\ [Na^2 \ O \ . \ CO^2 + H^2 \ O]. \end{cases}$

Rhombic ; $\infty \bar{P}$ 2 (d) 107° 50', $\bar{P}\infty$ (o) 83° 50'; with $\infty \bar{P} \infty$ (P) in rectangular tables (Fig. 189). Cleavage, brachydiagonal perfect. H. $= 1·5$; G. $= 1·5...1·6$. Colourless. B.B. like natron, but does not melt. Chem. com. 50·1 soda, 35·4 carbonic acid, and 14·5 water. Natron lakes of Lagunilla in Colombia, of Lower Egypt, and of the steppes between the Ural and Altai.

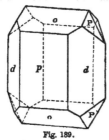

Fig. 189.   Fig. 190.

229. TRONA, Urao.—$\overset{.}{N}a^2 \overset{..}{C}^3 + 4 \overset{.}{H}$.

Monoclinic. Crystals 0P, $\infty P^\circ \infty$ (103° 15′), P (*M, T, n*, Fig. 190). Cleavage, orthodiagonal perfect. H. = 2·5... 3; G. = 2·1...2·2. Transparent to translucent; colourless. Does not decompose in the air. Taste alkaline. Chem. com. 38 soda, 40 carbonic acid, and 22 water. Fezzan and Barbary (*Trona*), Lagunilla (*Urao*).

230. GAYLUSSITE.—$\overset{.}{N}a \overset{..}{C} + \overset{.}{C}a \overset{..}{C} + 5 \overset{.}{H}$.

Monoclinic; C. = 78° 27′; ∞P 68° 51′, P 110° 30′. Cleavage, ∞P imperfect; fracture conchoidal. H. = 2·5; G. = 1·9...1·95. Transparent; vitreous; colourless. Slowly and partially soluble in water. B.B. fuses readily to an opaque bead. Chem. com. 34·5 carbonate of soda, 33·6 carbonate of lime, 30·4 water, with 1·5 clay. Lagunilla.

*231. BORAX, Tinkal.—$\overset{.}{N}a \overset{..}{B}^2 + 10 \overset{.}{H}$.

Monoclinic; C. = 73° 25′; ∞P 87°, P 122° 34′; almost isomorphous with augite. Twin crystals frequent. Cleavage, clinodiagonal perfect; ∞P less distinct; fracture conchoidal, rather brittle. H. = 2...2·5′; G. = 1·7...1·8. Pellucid; resinous. Colourless, but yellowish, greenish, and grayish-white. Taste feebly alkaline and sweetish. B.B. intumesces greatly, becomes black, and melts to a transparent bead, colouring the flame yellow, or, with sulphuric acid, green; soluble in 12 parts of cold water. Chem. com. of the pure salt, 16·4 soda, 36·5 boracic acid, and 47·1 water; but often with 2 phosphoric acid or other impurities. Shores of salt lakes in Thibet and Nepal; in

California, and near Potosi. Borax is prepared from this mineral, and is used for blowpipe experiments, in preparing fine glass, in medicine, and for dyeing.

*232. SASSOLINE.—$\ddot{\text{B}} + 3$ H, *or* [B^3 O^3 + 3 H^2 O].

Triclinic; 0P : ∞$\tilde{\text{P}}$∞ 75° 30′; usually fine scaly six-sided tables, or fibrous, and stalactitic. Macles frequent. Cleavage, basal very perfect; sectile and flexible. H. = 1 ; G. = 1·4...1·5. Translucent; pearly. Grayish or yellowish white. Taste acidulous and slightly bitter. Feels greasy. Easily soluble in boiling, less so in cold water. Froths up and melts in the candle flame to a hard transparent glass, colouring the flame green. Chem. com. 56·3 boracic acid, and 43·7 water. Vulcano in the Lipari Islands, hot springs of Sasso near Sienna, and lagoni of Tuscany.

*233. NITRE, Saltpetre.—$\begin{cases} \dot{\text{K}} \; \ddot{\text{N}}, \; or \\ [\text{K}^2 \text{O} + \text{N}^2 \text{O}^5 = \text{KNO}^5]. \end{cases}$

Rhombic; ∞P (*M*) 118° 49′, 2$\tilde{\text{P}}$∞ (*P*) 70° 55′, $\tilde{\text{P}}$∞ 109° 52, ∞$\tilde{\text{P}}$∞ (*h*) (Fig. 191); isomorphous with arra-

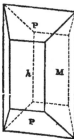

Fig. 191.

gonite. In nature only occurs acicular, capillary, or pulverulent. Cleavage indistinct; fracture conchoidal. H. = 2 ; G. = 1·9...2·0. Semitransparent; vitreous or silky. Colourless, white, or gray. Taste saline and cooling. Deflagrates when placed on hot charcoal; and B.B. on platina wire melts very easily, colouring the flame violet. Chem. com. 46·6 potash and 53·4 nitric acid, but always more or less mixed. In the limestone caves of many countries, Hungary, Spain, India. Used for producing nitric acid, in glass-making, medicine, and the manufacture of gunpowder.

234. NITRATINE.—$\dot{\text{Na}} \; \ddot{\text{N}}$ *or* [Na^2 O + N^2 O^5].

Rhombohedral; R = 106° 30′, isomorphous with dolomite. Cleavage rather perfect. H. = 1·5...2 ; G. = 2·1 ...2·2., Translucent or transparent, with very distinct double refraction; vitreous. Colourless, or grayish and yellowish-white. Taste saline and cooling. Deflagrates on hot charcoal. B.B. fuses on platina wire, colouring the flame yellow. Chem. com. 36·6 soda, and 63·4 nitric acid, but mixed with common salt and other substances. Tarapaca in Chili. Used in the arts as a substitute for nitre; but deliquesces in the air.

235. NITROCALCITE. — $\dot{C}a \ddot{N} + \dot{H}$.
Fibrous or pulverulent. White or gray. Translucent. Taste sharp and bitter. Readily soluble in water, and deliquesces in the air; melts slowly on burning charcoal, with slight detonation. Chem. com. 30·8 lime, 59·3 nitric acid, and 9·9 water. Limestone caves of Kentucky; on old walls and limestone rocks.

236. NITROMAGNESITE.—$\dot{M}g \ddot{N} + \dot{H}$.
In the same places, and similar to nitrocalcite. Taste bitter. Chem. com. 24 magnesia, 65 nitric acid, and 11 water.

*237. SAL-AMMONIAC.—N H⁴ Cl, *or* [Am Cl].
Tesseral; O, also $\infty O\infty$, ∞O, and 3O3. In crusts, stalactites, and earthy or pulverulent. Cleavage, O imperfect; fracture conchoidal. H. = 1·5...2; G. = 1·5...1·6. Pellucid; vitreous. Colourless, but gray or yellow, rarely green, brown, or black. Taste saline and pungent. B.B. volatilises without fusing; on copper wire colours the flame bluish-green. Chem. com. (32 per cent ammonia, or) 33·6 ammonium, and 66·4 chlorine. Chiefly occurs as a sublimate on active volcanoes, Vesuvius, Etna, the Solfatara, Vulcano, and Iceland; also near ignited coal-seams, Newcastle, and Scotland. Used in medicine, dyeing, and various metallurgic operations.

238. MASCAGNINE.—N H³ $\ddot{S}$ + $\dot{H}$.
Rhombic; ∞P 121° 8', $\bar{P}\infty$ 107° 40'; ∞P . $\infty\bar{P}\infty$. P (Fig. 192); but chiefly in crusts and stalactites. Cleavage rather perfect; sectile. H. = 2...2·5; G. = 1·7...1·8. Pellucid, vitreous. Colourless, white or yellowish. Taste pungent and bitter; easily soluble, and deliquesces. B.B. decrepitates, melts, and volatilises. Chem. com. 25·9 ammonia, 60·5 sulphuric acid, and 13·6 water. Near volcanoes, as Etna, Vesuvius, the Solfatara, the Lipari Islands, in the lagoni near Sienna, and in ignited coal-beds, as at Bradley in Staffordshire.

Fig. 192.

239. ARCANITE, Glaserite.—$\dot{K}\ddot{S}$.

Rhombic; acute pyramids, with ∞P 120° 24′, $2\breve{P}\infty$, 0P, and other forms; but dimorphous and also rhombohedral, with R 88° 14′. Mostly in crusts, or pulverulent. Cleavage, basal imperfect. H. = 2·5...3; G. = 2·7. Pellucid; vitreous or resinous. Colourless or white. Taste saline, bitter. B.B. decrepitates, fuses, and becomes hepatic. Chem. com. 54 potash, and 46 sulphuric acid. Lavas of Vesuvius and other volcanoes.

*240. THENARDITE.—$\dot{N}a\ddot{S}$.

Rhombic; acute pyramids P, with 0P and ∞P, in crusts and druses. Cleavage, basal rather perfect; fracture uneven. H. = 2·5; G. = 2·6...2·7. Pellucid, vitreous. White. Taste feebly saline. B.B. colours the flame deep yellow, and fuses. Chem. com. 43·82 soda, and 56·18 sulphuric acid. Salinas d'Espartinas near Aranjuez, and Tarapaca. Used for preparing soda.

241. LÖWEITE.—$2\,(\dot{N}a\ddot{S} + \dot{M}g\ddot{S}) + 5\,\dot{H}$.

Tetragonal, but only compact; cleavage, basal distinct. H. = 2·5...3; G. = 2·376. Vitreous. Yellowish-white to flesh-red. Taste slightly saline. Chem. com. 20 soda, 13 magnesia, 52 sulphuric acid, and 15 water. Ischl.

*242. EPSOMITE, Epsom-salt. $\begin{cases} \dot{M}g\ddot{S} + 7\,\dot{H} = \\ [\text{Mg O} \cdot \text{SO}^3 + 7\,\text{H}^2\,\text{O}]. \end{cases}$

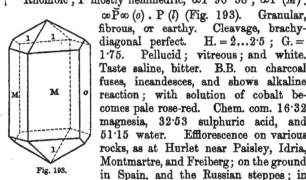

Rhombic; P mostly hemihedric, ∞P 90° 38′; ∞P (M). $\infty\breve{P}\infty$ (o) . P (l) (Fig. 193). Granular, fibrous, or earthy. Cleavage, brachydiagonal perfect. H. = 2...2·5; G. = 1·75. Pellucid; vitreous; and white. Taste saline, bitter. B.B. on charcoal fuses, incandesces, and shows alkaline reaction; with solution of cobalt becomes pale rose-red. Chem. com. 16·32 magnesia, 32·53 sulphuric acid, and 51·15 water. Efflorescence on various rocks, as at Hurlet near Paisley, Idria, Montmartre, and Freiberg; on the ground in Spain, and the Russian steppes; in mineral waters, as at Epsom in Surrey (Epsom salts), Said-

Fig. 193.

schütz and Seidlitz in Bohemia. Used in medicine and in preparing magnesia.

243. KIESERITE, Martinsite.—$\dot{M}g \ddot{S} + \dot{H}$.

Rhombic, but chiefly massive. G. = 2·52. Pellucid; grayish-white. Slowly soluble in water. Chem. com. 29 magnesia, 58 sulphuric acid, and 13 water. In beds at Stassfurt.

244. BLÖDITE, Astrakanite.—$(\dot{M}g \; \dot{N}a) \ddot{S} + 2 \dot{H}$.

Monoclinic; C. = 100° 43'; ∞P2 = 112° 55' in prismatic crystals, or efflorescent. H. = 3·5; G. = 2·2. Transparent. White or red. Chem. com. 47·9 sulphuric acid, 8·5 soda, 12 magnesia, and 21·5 water. Salt lakes on the Volga near Astrakan, Ischl, Stassfurt, and near Mendoza in South America.

Reussin from Seidlitz similar, but a mixture. *Kainite* from Stassfurt, and Kalusz in Galicia, fine granular, yellow or light-gray masses, is chiefly sulphates of magnesia and potash with water, but analyses vary much, and probably a mixture.

ORDER III.

SALINE ORES.

RESEMBLE the saline stones both in external characters and chemical composition, forming almost a parallel series, with metallic oxides in place of the earthy bases. Lime or magnesia occasionally occur in more or less extent, and the acid element is one of the common acids of the chemist. Crystallisation in the carbonates is often rhombohedral, in the others monoclinic or rhombic. Other systems only occur in rare cases.

Hardness is not high, mostly 3...4, in a few as high as 5, or as low as 2. Their specific gravity is high, from the metallic element in their composition; mostly from 3...4 in the salts of iron or copper, and from 5...7 or 8 in the salts of lead and some others. They are almost all soluble in acids, and the carbonates effervesce. B.B. mostly fusible, decomposed, or reduced, and with fluxes form coloured glasses characteristic of the different metals. They are mostly translucent, rarely transparent. Their lustre is often pearly or vitreous. Some are white, others are coloured, and these colours are now characteristic of the metal as the essential element.

*FAMILY I.—THE SPARRY IRON ORES.

Crystallisation and cleavage rhombohedral. H. = 3·5... 5; G. = 3·3...4·5. They are all soluble in acids, and often effervesce. B.B. they are all infusible, but decomposed, and leave a magnetic residue, or show reactions of metals. The colours are white, but often with a brown, yellow, or red tinge, especially when weathered. They chiefly occur in veins.

**245. SIDERITE, Sparry Iron, $\Big\}$ $\dot{F}e \ddot{C} = [FeO . CO^2]$.
Sphärosiderite, Chalybite.

Hexagonal and rhombohedral; R 107°.   Chiefly R, often curved, saddle-shaped, or lenticular, occasionally 0R, $-\frac{1}{2}$R, ∞R, −2R, ∞P2.   Frequently fine or coarse granular, more rarely botryoidal or reniform (*Sphærosiderite*). Cleavage, rhombohedral along R perfect. Brittle. H. = 3·5...4·5 ; G. = 3·7...3·9.   Translucent in various degrees, becoming opaque when weathered ; vitreous or pearly. Rarely white, generally yellowish-gray or yellowish-brown, changing to red or blackish-brown on exposure. B.B. infusible, but becomes black and magnetic ; with borax and salt of phosphorus shows reaction for iron ; with soda usually for manganese.   In acids soluble with effervescence. Chem. com. carbonate of iron, with 62·1 protoxide of iron and 37·9 carbonic acid, but usually 0·5 to 10, or even 25 protoxide of manganese, 0·2 to 15 magnesia, and 0·1 to 2 lime.   In beds or masses, in Styria, Carinthia, and Westphalia ; in veins in Anhalt and the Harz ; also in the Pyrenees, and the Basque provinces of Spain, as near Bilboa. In crystals at Joachimsthal, Freiberg, Klausthal, Beeralstone in Devonshire, Alston Moor in Cumberland, and in many of the tin mines of Cornwall.

Clay ironstone, gray, blue, brown, or black, G. = 2·8... 3·5 ; H. = 3·5...4·5, is an impure variety.   It occurs chiefly in slate-clay or marls, in layers or nodular masses, especially in the coal formation of Britain, Belgium, and Silesia. These ores contain 50 to 85 per cent carbonate of iron, and yield 25 to 42 metal.   The Lanarkshire blackband contains 70 carbonate of iron, 23 carbonaceous matter, 7 of silica, alumina and lime, and yields 33·7 iron.   In 1871 England produced 4,379,370 tons ; Wales, 1,087,809 ; and Scotland, 1,160,000 ; or, in all, 6,627,179 tons pig-iron, worth at the place of production about seventeen millions sterling.

Junkerite, from Brittany, is a mere variety. *Oligon spar* contains 20 per cent or more manganese protoxide ; *Sideroplesite,* from Salzburg, 10·4 magnesia.

Ankerite.—R 106° 12′, but mostly massive and granular.   G. = 2·9...3·1 ; otherwise like siderite.   Contains 51 carbonate of lime, 12 to 33 carbonate of magnesia, 12 to 36 carbonate of iron, and 0 to 3 carbonate of manganese protoxide. Styria. Used as an ore or flux.

246. DIALOGITE, Red Manganese.—$\dot{M}n \ddot{C}$.

Hexagonal, rhombohedral; R 106° 56'; R and $-\frac{1}{2}$R, sometimes 0R and ∞P 2. Crystals often curved, lenticular, or saddle-shaped; also spherical, reniform, and columnar or granular. Cleavage, R perfect. H. = 3·5...4·5; G = 3·3... 3·6. Translucent; vitreous or pearly. Rose-red to flesh-red; streak white. B.B. decrepitates and becomes gray or black, but is infusible; with borax reaction for manganese; the powder soluble with effervescence in warm h. acid. Chem. com. 62 manganese protoxide and 38 carbonic acid, but usually mixed with carbonates of lime 0 to 13, magnesia 0 to 7, or iron 0 to 15. Freiberg, Schemnitz, Kapnik, Nagyag, Elbingerode, and near Sargans. At the latter, also hydrated, and fibrous silky (*Wiserite*); compact in Hessia and Glendree, Ireland.

247. MANGANOCALCITE.—$(\dot{M}n, \dot{C}a, \dot{F}e) \ddot{C}$.

Rhombic; in prisms like arragonite, and bears the same relation to dialogite that arragonite does to calc-spar. H. = 4...5; G. = 3·03. Red or reddish-white; vitreous. Schemnitz.

248. LANTHANITE.—$\dot{L}a \ddot{C} + 3 \dot{H}$.

Rhombic; ∞P 92° 46'; small tabular crystals; usually granular or earthy. Cleavage basal. H. = 2; G. = 2·7. Dull or pearly. White or yellowish. B.B. becomes brown-ish-yellow; soluble in acids with effervescence. Chem. com. 21 carbonic acid, 55 lanthanium oxide, and 24 water. Bastnaes in Sweden, Lehigh in Pennsylvania.

249. PARISITE.—$\dot{C}e \ddot{C}$, Ca F, $\dot{H}$.

Hexagonal; P 164° 58'. Cleavage, basal very perfect. H. = 4·5; G. = 4·35. Vitreous; on the cleavage-planes pearly. Brownish-yellow inclining to red. B.B. infusible and phosphoresces. Chem. com. 23·5 carbonic acid, 42·5 protoxide of cerium, 8·2 lanthanium oxide, 9·6 didymium oxide, 2·8 lime, 10·1 fluoride of calcium, and 2·2 fluoride of cerium. Emerald mines of the Musso Valley in New Granada, Ural.

*250. SMITHSONITE, Calamine.—$\dot{Z}n\ \ddot{C} = [Zn\ O\ .\ CO^2]$.

Hexagonal-rhombohedral; R 107° 40'; R, 4R, and R3. The crystals generally small, obtuse-edged, and rounded. Usually reniform, stalactitic, and laminar or granular. Cleavage, R perfect but curved; fracture uneven conchoidal; brittle. H. = 5; G. = 4·1...4·5. Translucent or opaque; pearly or vitreous. Colourless, but often pale grayish-yellow, brown, or green. B.B. becomes white, on charcoal forms a ring, yellow when hot, white when cold; soluble in acids with effervescence; also in solution of potash. Chem. com. 64·8 zinc oxide, and 35·2 carbonic acid, but with protoxide of iron 2 to 3, or of manganese 3 to 7, lime 1 to 2, or magnesia 0 to 3.

This mineral occurs in beds or veins in the crystalline and stratified rocks. It is most common in limestone, and is often associated with calc-spar, quartz, blende, and ores of iron and lead. Chessy near Lyons, Altenberg near Aix-la-Chapelle, Brillon in Westphalia, Tarnowitz in Silesia, Hungary, Siberia; also Mendip in Somersetshire, Matlock in Derbyshire, Wanlockhead and Leadhills in Scotland; compact at Alston Moor. Zinc is obtained chiefly from this mineral. In Silesia also cadmium.

Varieties are—*Kapnite*, with 15 to 37 per cent of iron protoxide. *Zinc-bloom*, reniform, earthy, pale-yellow, and shining streak; seems a mere product of decomposition. Bleiberg and Raibel in Carinthia. *Herrerite*, green, with 3 to 4 per cent copper oxide; from Mexico.

*251. GALMEI, Electric $\begin{cases} \dot{Z}n^3\ \ddot{S}i + \dot{H} = \\ [2\ Zn\ O\ .\ Si\ O^3 + H^2\ O]. \end{cases}$
      Calamine.

Rhombic, and hemimorphic; $2\ \bar{\breve{P}}\ 2\ (P)$ with polar edges 101° 35', and 132° 26'; $\infty P\ (d)$ 103° 50', $\bar{P}\infty\ (o)$ 117° 14', $\breve{P}\infty\ (l)$ 128° 55'; common form $\infty\breve{P}\infty\ (s)$. $\infty P\ .\ \bar{P}\infty$ (Fig. 194). Also columnar, fibrous, granular, and earthy. Cleavage, prismatic along ∞P very perfect, along $\bar{P}\infty$ perfect. H. = 5; G. = 3·3...3·5. Transparent to translucent; vitreous and pearly. Colourless or white, but often light gray, also yellow, green, brown, and blue; becomes electric by heat. B.B. decrepitates slightly, but is infusible, with cobalt solution blue and partly green; readily soluble in acids, and gelatinises. Chem. com. 25 silica, 67·5 zinc oxide, and 7·5 water. With calamine, as at Raibel and Bleiberg in Carinthia, Aix-la-Chapelle, Iserlohn, Tarnowitz, and Nertschinsk; Pennsylvania and Virginia; also Mendip Hills, Matlock in Derbyshire, and Wanlockhead. Used as an ore of zinc.

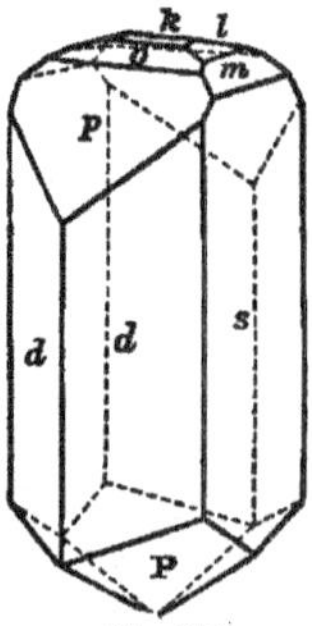

Fig. 194.

252. WILLEMITE, Troostite.—$\ddot{Z}n^2\ddot{S}i$. Rhombohedral; R 128° 30'. ∞R. R; also granular and reniform. Cleavage, basal rather perfect, ∞R imperfect; brittle. H. = 4·5; G. = 4·1...4·2. Translucent or transparent; dull resinous. White, yellowish, or brown. B.B. in closed tube yields no water, otherwise like galmei. Chem. com. 73 zinc oxide and 27 silica, with 0 to 9 protoxide of manganese, 0 to 5 iron protoxide, and 0 to 3 magnesia. Aix-la-Chapelle, Liege, Raibel, also Sterling and Franklin in New Jersey.

FAMILY II.—IRON SALTS.

Crystallisation predominantly rhombic or monoclinic. H. = 2...5·5; G. = 2·2...4·0. They are all soluble in acids, and many easily. B.B. all fusible, and also often easily so. Their colours are often brown, or dark blue and dark green; the streak yellow or red. They are chiefly phosphates or arseniates of iron. The phosphates B.B., moistened with sulphuric acid, colour the flame bluish-green. The arseniates B.B. in the reducing flame, or with carbonate of soda, evolve odour of arsenic.

*253. VIVIANITE, Blue $\begin{cases} \dot{F}e^3\overset{...}{P} + 8\dot{H} = \\ [3\,Fe\,O\,.\,P^2\,O^5 + 8\,H^2\,O]. \end{cases}$ Iron.

Monoclinic; C. = 75° 34', ∞P 108° 2', P 120° 26', P∞ 54° 40'. Crystals prismatic (Fig. 195); also spherical or reniform, and fibrous or earthy. Cleavage, clinodiagonal, very perfect; thin laminæ flexible. H. = 2; G. = 2·6...2·7.

Translucent or transparent; vitreous, or bright pearly on cleavage. Indigo-blue to blackish-green; streak bluish-white, but soon becomes blue on exposure. The white earthy variety also changes to blue in the air; the dry crushed powder is liver-brown. In the closed tube yields much water, intumesces, and becomes spotted with gray and red. B.B. on charcoal becomes red, and then fuses to a gray, shining, magnetic granule; easily soluble in h. or nitric acid; becomes black in warm solution of potash. Chem. com. the colourless vivianite is a hydrous phosphate of iron protoxide, with 43 iron protoxide, 28 phosphoric acid, and 29 water; but after exposure part of the water is exchanged for oxygen, and to six molecules of the above one of $(\overset{...}{Fe}{}^3\,\overset{..}{P}{}^2 + 8\,\overset{.}{H})$ is added, when it acquires a blue colour, and contains 29 phosphoric acid, 33·1 iron protoxide, 12·2 iron peroxide, and 25·7 water. Transparent indigo-coloured crystals at St. Agnes in Cornwall, and Allentown and Imleytown in New Jersey, Earthy in Cornwall, Styria, North America, Greenland, and New Zealand, and in peat mosses in Northern Germany, Sweden, Norway, and the Zetland Isles. Used as a pigment. *Mullicite* and *Anglarite* are varieties.

Fig. 195.

Beraunite.—Radiated; red or brown; streak ochreyellow; from Beraun, Bohemia, is a decomposed product. *Kakoxene*, yellow and silky, from Zbirow in Bohemia, is also similar.

254. DUFRÉNITE, Green Iron Earth.—$2\,\overset{...}{Fe}{}^3\,\overset{...}{P} + 5\,\overset{.}{H}$.

Rhombic; ∞P about 123°; spherical or reniform. Cleavage brachydiagonal; very brittle. H. = 3...3·5; G. = 3·3 ...3·4. Translucent on the edges, or opaque; shining or dull. Dirty, leek, or blackish green; streak siskin-green. B.B. fuses readily to a porous, black, non-magnetic globule; soluble in h. acid. Chem. com. 63 iron peroxide, 28 phosphoric acid, and 9 water. Westerwald, Hirschberg, and Limoges. *Kraurite* is the same.

255. TRIPLITE.—$(\overset{.}{Fe},\,\overset{.}{Mn})^3\,\overset{..}{P} + R\,F$.

Monoclinic (?); only granular. Cleavage, in two directions at right angles; fracture conchoidal. H. = 5...5·5;

G. = 3·6...3·8. Translucent or opaque; resinous. Chestnut or blackish brown; streak yellowish-gray. B.B. on charcoal fuses easily, with strong intumescence, to a black magnetic globule; soluble in a. acid, with reaction of fluorine. Chem. com. iron and manganese protoxides, with 33 phosphoric acid and 7 or 8 fluorine. Limoges, Schlaggenwald.

256. ZWIESELITE, Eisenapatit.—$(\ddot{F}e, \ddot{M}n)^s \ddot{P} + \ddot{F}e \ F.$

Rhombic, but only massive. Cleavage, basal rather perfect, two others imperfect. H. = 4·5...5; G. = 3·95...4. Brown; streak yellow. B.B. decrepitates and fuses easily. Chem. com. like triplite, and identical or isomorphous. Zwiesel in Bavaria. *Alluaudite*, clove-brown, from Chanteloube, near Limoges, is altered triplite.

257. TRIPHYLINE.—$(2 \ \dot{F}e + \dot{L}i) \ \ddot{P}.$

Rhombic; ∞P 133°; chiefly granular. Cleavage, basal perfect, prismatic and diagonal imperfect. H. = 5; G. = 3·6. Translucent on the edges; resinous. Greenish-gray with blue spots. B.B. fuses very easily to a dark steel-gray magnetic bead; easily soluble in h. acid. Chem. com. 45 phosphoric acid, 40 iron protoxide, 5·5 manganese protoxide, 7·5 lithia, and 2 magnesia. Bodenmais in Bavaria, Norwich in Massachusetts. *Tetraphyline* or *Perowskine*, from Tammela in Finland, is similar.

258. MONAZITE.—$(\dot{C}e, \dot{L}a)^s \ddot{P}.$

Monoclinic; C. = 76° 14′, ∞P 93° 23′; crystals (like Fig. 196), thick, tabular, or very short prismatic. Cleavage, basal perfect. H. = 5...5·5; G. = 4·9...5·25. Trans-

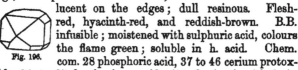
Fig. 196.

lucent on the edges; dull resinous. Flesh-red, hyacinth-red, and reddish-brown. B.B. infusible; moistened with sulphuric acid, colours the flame green; soluble in h. acid. Chem. com. 28 phosphoric acid, 37 to 46 cerium protoxide, 24 to 27 lanthanium oxide (18 thorina?), with 2 tin oxide, 1·5 lime, and some magnesia and manganese. Miask, Norwich in Connecticut (*Edwardsite*), and New Granada.

Monazitoid.—G. = 5·28; brown, with 18 phosphoric acid; probably a variety. Also *Eremite*, from N. America.

259. CRYPTOLITE.—$\dot{C}e^2\overset{...}{P}$.

Acicular crystals, embedded in apatite. G. = 4·6. Transparent. Pale wine-yellow. Powder soluble in con. s. acid. Wöhler found 73·70 cerium protoxide, 27·37 phosphoric acid, and 1·51 iron protoxide. Arendal.

260. HUREAULITE.—$(\dot{M}n, \dot{F}e)^5 \overset{...}{P}{}^2 + 5 \dot{H}$

Monoclinic; C. = 89° 27′, ∞P 61°; fracture conchoidal. H. = 3·5; G. = 3·2. Translucent; resinous. Reddish-yellow or brown. B.B. fuses easily to a black metallic globule; soluble in acids. Chem. com. 39 phosphoric acid, 8 iron protoxide, 42 manganese protoxide, and 12 water. Hureaux near Limoges.

Heterozite.—H. = 5; G. = 3·5. Opaque; vitreous or resinous. Dark-violet or blue to greenish-gray; streak violet-blue or crimson-red. Hureaux. Probably decomposed triphyline.

261. DIADOCHITE.—$\overset{...}{F}e \overset{...}{P}{}^2 + 4 \overset{...}{F}e \overset{...}{S} + 32 \dot{H}$.

Reniform and stalactitic. Fracture conchoidal. H. = 3; G. = 1·9...2·0. Resinous; vitreous. Yellow or yellowish-brown; streak white. B.B. intumesces and fuses on the edges to a black magnetic enamel. Chem. com. 36·7 iron peroxide, 14·8 phosphoric acid, 15·2 sulphuric acid, and 30·3 water. Grafenthal and Saalfeld in Thuringia.

262. DELVAUXENE, Delvauxite.—$\overset{...}{F}e^2 \overset{...}{P} + 24 \dot{H}$.

Massive and earthy. H. = 2·5; G. = 1·85. Reddish or blackish-brown or yellow. B.B. decrepitates, and fuses to a gray magnetic bead. In h. acid forms a brown solution. Chem. com. 35·8 iron peroxide, 48·3 water, and 15·9 phosphoric acid. Visé in Belgium. Perhaps only dufrenite with water. Delvauxene, from Leoben in Styria, with less water, is probably distinct.

263. PISSOPHANE.—$(\overset{...}{A}l, \overset{...}{F}e)^2 \overset{...}{S} + 15 \dot{H}$.

Stalactitic; fracture conchoidal; very easily frangible. H. = 2; G. = 1·9...2. Transparent or translucent; vitreous. Olive-green to liver-brown; streak greenish-white to pale yellow. B.B. becomes black; easily soluble in h. acid. Chem. com. 7 to 35 alumina, 10 to 40 iron peroxide, 12 sulphuric acid, and 41 water. Saalfeld and Reichenbach in Saxony.

Karphosiderite, reniform opaque, resinous, and straw-yellow, with a greasy feel, is related.   H. = 4·5 ; G. = 2·5. B.B. becomes red and fuses to a black magnetic bead ; consists of hydrous sulphate of iron.   Labrador.

264. PITTICITE, Iron Sinter.—$\ddot{F}e^3\,\ddot{S}^3 + 2\,\ddot{F}e\,\ddot{A}s + 24\,\dot{H}$.

Reniform and stalactitic ; brittle ; fracture conchoidal. H. = 2...3 ; G. = 2·3...2·5.   Translucent, or on the edges ; resinous, inclining to vitreous.   Yellowish, reddish, or blackish-brown, sometimes in spots or stripes ; streak light-yellow, or white.   B.B. on charcoal fuses easily, with effervescence and strong arsenical fumes, to a black magnetic globule ; easily soluble in h. acid to a yellow fluid. Chem. com. 35 iron peroxide, 26 arsenic acid, 14 sulphuric acid, and 24 water.   In many old mines, as Freiberg and Schneeberg.

265. SYMPLESITE.

Monoclinic, like gypsum ; in very fine prismatic crystals or groups.   Cleavage perfect.   H. = 2·5 ;   G. = 2·957. Transparent or translucent ; vitreous, pearly on the cleavage.   Pale indigo to celadine-green, with bluish-white streak.   B.B. emits arsenic odours, becomes black and magnetic, but does not fuse.   Chem. com. arseniate of iron protoxide with water.   Lobenstein in Reuss, Lölling.

266. SCORODITE, Neoctese.—$\ddot{F}e\,\ddot{A}s + 4\,\dot{H}$.

Rhombic ; P, with polar edges 103° 5′ and 114° 34′.

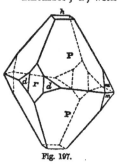
Fig. 197.

Crystals P (*P*) $\infty\bar{P}\infty$ and $\infty\breve{P}\infty$ (*r*) ; also 0P (*h*), $\infty\bar{P}$ 2 (*d*) 120° 10′, and 2 $\bar{P}\infty$ (*m*) 132° (Fig. 197) ; also columnar and fibrous.   Cleavage imperfect ; rather brittle.   H. = 3·5 ...4 ; G. = 3·1...3·2.   Translucent ; vitreous.   Leek-green to greenish-black, also indigo-blue, red, and brown.   In closed tube yields water and becomes yellow.   B.B. on charcoal fuses easily, emitting arsenic vapours, to a gray magnetic slag ; easily soluble in h. (not in nitric) acid, forming a brown

solution. Chem. com. 49·8 arsenic acid, 34·6 iron peroxide, and 15·6 water.   St. Austle in Cornwall, near Limoges
in France, Schwarzenberg, Lölling in Carinthia, Brazil, and
Siberia.

267. ARSENIOSIDERITE.—$\overset{\cdot\cdot}{C}a^{3} \overset{\cdots}{A}s + \overset{\cdots}{F}e^{3} \overset{\cdots}{A}s + 6 \overset{\cdot}{H}$.
Spherical and fibrous; friable, and leaves a mark on
paper. H. = 1...2; G. = 3·52...3·88.   Opaque; metallic
pearly.   Ochre-brown, becoming darker in the air; streak
brownish-yellow.   B.B. fuses easily, with reaction for iron
and arsenic.   Chem. com. 38 arsenic acid, 39 iron peroxide,
14 lime, and 9 water.   Romanêche near Màçon.

268. PHARMACOSIDERITE, Cube Ore.—$\overset{\cdots}{F}e^{4} \overset{\cdots}{A}s^{3} + 15 \overset{\cdot}{H}$.
Tesseral and tetrahedral; usually $\infty O \infty$, with $\dfrac{O}{2}$, or ∞O.

Cleavage, tesseral very imperfect; rather brittle. H. = 2·5;
G. = 2·9...3·0.   Semitransparent to translucent; adamantine
or resinous.   Olive to emerald green, honey-yellow, and
brown; streak straw-yellow.   Pyro-electric.   In closed
tube yields water and becomes red.   B.B. on charcoal fuses
easily to a steel-gray magnetic slag; easily soluble in acids.
Chem. com. 43 arsenic acid, 40 iron peroxide, and 17 water.
Huel Gorland, Huel Unity, and Carharrak in Cornwall;
Burdle Gill in Cumberland; also Lobenstein in Reuss,
Schwarzenberg in Saxony, North America; and the gold-
quartz of Australia.
Beudantite, rhombohedral; R 91° 18′.   H. = 3·5; G. = 4.
Vitreous; olive-green, streak greenish-yellow.   Chem. com.
oxides of iron and lead, with arsenic acid, phosphoric acid,
and water; but probably a mixture of pharmacosiderite
with sulphate of lead.   Horhausen in Nassau; Cork in
Ireland.

*FAMILY III.—COPPER SALTS.

Crystallisation generally rhombic and monoclinic. Hardness generally from 2...3·5, but a few as low as 1...2,
others 4...5. Gravity 2...4, but mostly 3...4. The colours
are predominantly green, and rarely blue. They are all

soluble in acids, and mostly easily so. Mostly fusible B.B. and on charcoal, when moistened with hydrochloric acid, the copper is known by colouring the flame blue. With soda they are reduced to metallic copper. They are, with a few exceptions, compounds of copper with one of the common acids, and some used as ores of that metal. They occur especially in veins.

269. DIOPTASE, Emerald Copper.—$\dot{C}u\ \ddot{S}i + \dot{H}$.

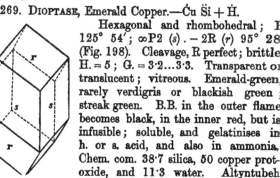

Hexagonal and rhombohedral; R 125° 54'; ∞P2 (*s*) . − 2R (*r*) 95° 28' (Fig. 198). Cleavage, R perfect; brittle. H. = 5; G. = 3·2...3·3. Transparent or translucent; vitreous. Emerald-green, rarely verdigris or blackish green; streak green. B.B. in the outer flame becomes black, in the inner red, but is infusible; soluble, and gelatinises in h. or s. acid, and also in ammonia. Chem. com. 38·7 silica, 50 copper protoxide, and 11·3 water. Altyntubeh in the Kirgis Steppe.

Fig. 198.

270. CHRYSOCOLLA, Copper-green.—$\dot{C}u\ \ddot{S}i + 2\ \dot{H}$.

Botryoidal, reniform, or investing; brittle; fracture conchoidal, and fine splintery. H. = 2...3; G. = 2·0...2·3; Translucent or semitransparent; weak resinous. Verdigris to emerald green or azure-blue; streak greenish-white. B.B. and with acids like dioptase. Chem. com. 34·83 silica, 44·94 copper protoxide, and 20·23 water. Saxony, Bavaria, Ural, Cornwall, Hungary, the Tyrol, Spain, the Harz (*Siliceous malachite*), Mexico, and Chili.

*271. AZURITE, Blue Copper. $\begin{cases} \dot{C}u^3\ \ddot{C}^2 + \dot{H} = \\ [3\ Cu\ O\ .\ 2\ CO^2 + H^2O]. \end{cases}$

Monoclinic; C. = 87° 39', ∞P (*M*) 99° 32', − P (*k'*) 106° 14'. Crystals 0P . ∞P . ∞P°∞ . − P, (or *h*, *M*, *s*, *k'*, in Fig. 199, but in another position); also radiated and earthy. Cleavage, clinodomatic (*P*) 59° 14', rather perfect; fracture conchoidal, or splintery. H. = 3·5...4·2; G. = 3·7 ...3·8. Translucent or opaque; vitreous. Azure-blue, the

earthy varieties (and streak) smalt-blue.   B.B. on charcoal
fuses and yields a grain of
copper; soluble with effervescence in acids and also in
ammonia.   Chem. com. 69·1
protoxide of copper, 25·7
carbonic acid, and 5·2 water.
Crystals at Chessy near
Lyons, in Siberia, Moldawa

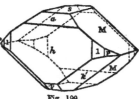

Fig. 199.

in the Bannat; Burra-Burra, Australia; also Redruth in
Cornwall, Alston Moor and Wanlockhead; massive in
Cornwall, Thuringia, the Harz, Hessia, and the Ural.
Common as a pseudomorph.   Valued as an ore of copper.

**272. MALACHITE. $\left\{ \begin{array}{l} \dot{C}u^2\ddot{C}+\dot{H}=[2\,CuO\,.\,CO^2+H^2O], or \\ [Cu\,O\,.\,H^2\,O + Cu\,O\,.\,CO^2]. \end{array} \right.$

Monoclinic; C. = 61° 50′, ∞P 104° 20′; crystals ∞P
(*M*). ∞P°∞ (*s*). 0P (*P*), in macles (Fig. 200).   In general
acicular, scaly, or reniform, stalactitic, and radiated fibrous.
Cleavage, basal and clinodiagonal very perfect.   H. = 3·5
...4; G. = 3·6...4·0.   Transparent or translucent on the
edges; adamantine, vitreous, silky or dull.   Emerald and
other shades of green; streak apple-green.   B.B. and with
acids, like azurite.   Chem. com. 71·8 copper protoxide.
(= 57·5 copper), 20 carbonic acid, and 8·2
water.   Crystalline at Rheinbreitenbach on the
Rhine, and Zellerfeld in the Harz; fibrous and
compact at Chessy in France, Siberia, the Ural,
Saalfeld in Thuringia, Moldawa in the Bannat,
Sandlodge in Zetland, Cornwall, Wales, and Ireland, and in North America, and Australia.

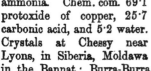

Fig. 200.

Frequent pseudomorph after copper and its ores; also
after calcite and cerussite.   It is a valuable ore of copper,
and the finer varieties are prized for ornamental purposes.

Lime-Malachite.—Reniform, botryoidal, and radiated
fibrous; brittle.   H. = 2·5.   Silky; verdigris-green.   B.B.
blackens and fuses to a black slag; soluble in h. acid,
leaving gelatinous gypsum.   Seems a hydrous carbonate of
copper and lime, with sulphate of lime and some iron.
Lauterberg in the Harz.   *Mysorine*, compact, blackish-

brown, and soft, G. = 2·62, is a mixture of a carbonate of copper with iron peroxide. Mysore in the East Indies.

273. AURICHALCITE.—2 Ċu C̈ + 3 Żn Ḣ.

Acicular. H. = 2. Translucent, pearly, and verdigris-green. B.B. on charcoal in the inner flame deposites zinc oxide, and with fluxes shows reaction for copper; soluble with effervescence in h. acid. Chem. com. 29·2 copper protoxide, 44·7 zinc oxide, 16·2 carbonic acid, and 9·9 water. Loktefskoi in the Altai; Matlock in Derbyshire.

Buratite, azure-blue, like aurichalcite, but perhaps mixed with lime. Loktefskoi, Chessy, and Volterra.

274. CHALCOPHYLLITE, { Ċu³ Äs + 23 Ḣ, *or*
   Copper-mica. { Ċu⁶ Äs + 12 Ḣ.

Hexagonal and rhombohedral; R 69° 48′. Crystals, 0R (*o*) . R (Fig. 201). Cleavage, basal very perfect; sectile. H. = 2; G. = 2·4...2·6. Translucent or transparent; vitreous inclining to adamantine; pearly on 0R. Emerald

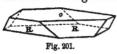

Fig. 201.

to grass or verdigris green; streak light-green. B.B. decrepitates violently, emits arsenical vapours, and fuses to a gray metallic grain; easily soluble in acids and ammonia. Chem. com. 49·6 copper protoxide, 18 arsenic acid, and 32·4 water; or 51·6 copper protoxide, 25 arsenic acid, and 23·4 water; but also 2 alumina and 1·5 phosphoric acid. Tingtang, Huel Gorland and Huel Unity Mines near Redruth; also Saida in Saxony, and Moldawa in the Bannat.

275. TIROLITE.—Ċu⁵ Äs + 5 Ḣ + Ċa C̈.

Rhombic (?); reniform, or radiating foliated. Cleavage, basal very perfect; sectile. Thin laminæ flexible. H. = 1·5...2; G. = 3...3·2. Translucent; pearly or vitreous. Verdigris-green to azure-blue; streak paler. B.B. decrepitates violently and fuses to a steel-gray bead; soluble in acids, evolving carbonic acid. Chem. com. 50·4 copper oxide, 29·1 arsenic acid, 9·1 water, and 11·4 carbonate of lime. Analyses give more water, and the carbonate of lime is essential. Falkenstein in Tyrol, in Hungary, Reichelsdorf,

Saalfeld, Piombino in Italy, in Asturia and at Linares in Spain, and Matlock in Derbyshire.

276. ERINITE.—$\dot{C}u^5 \ddot{A}s + 2 \dot{H}$.

Reniform and foliated; conchoidal fracture. H. = 4·5 ...5 ; G. = 4...4·1. Translucent on the edges; dull resinous. Emerald or grass green; streak similar. Chem. com. 59·9 copper protoxide, 34·7 arsenic acid, and 5·4 water. Said from Limerick, but probably Cornwall. *Cornwallite* is similar, but dark-green, and with 13 water or 5 $\dot{H}$. Cornwall.

277. LIROCONITE.—$\dot{C}u^8 \ddot{A}s + \ddot{A}l \ddot{A}s + 24 \dot{H}$.

Monoclinic; C. = 88° 33′; ∞P (*d*) 61° 31′, P°∞ (*o*) 74° 21′ (Fig. 202). Cleavage, prismatic imperfect. H. = 2... 2·5 ; G. = 2·8...3·0. Translucent; vitreous, or resinous on fracture. Azure-blue to verdigris-green; streak paler. In the closed tube does not decrepitate, but becomes green; then ignites and brown. B.B. on charcoal emits arsenical vapours and fuses; soluble in acids and ammonia. Chem. com. 36·6 copper protoxide, 11·9 alumina, 26·6 arsenic acid, and 24·9 water. Near Redruth ; also Herrengrund in Hungary.

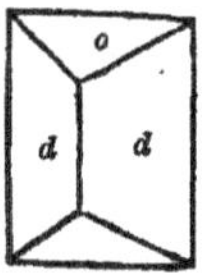

Fig. 202.

*278. OLIVENITE. $\begin{cases} \dot{C}u^4 (\ddot{A}s \ddot{P}) + \dot{H}, \ or \\ [4\ Cu\ O . As^2\ O^5 + H^2\ O.] \end{cases}$

Rhombic; ∞P (*r*) 92° 30′, $\breve{P}\infty$ (*l*) 110° 50′; $\infty\bar{P}\infty$ (*n*) (Fig. 203); also spherical and reniform, and columnar or fibrous. Cleavage (*r*) and (*l*) very imperfect. H. = 3 ; G. = 4·1...4·6. Pellucid in all degrees; vitreous, resinous, or silky. Leek, olive, or blackish green, also yellow and brown; streak olive-green or brown. B.B. in the forceps fuses easily to a dark-brown adamantine bead covered with radiating crystals; on charcoal detonates, emits arsenical vapours, and is reduced; soluble in acids and ammonia. Chem. com. 56·5 copper protoxide,

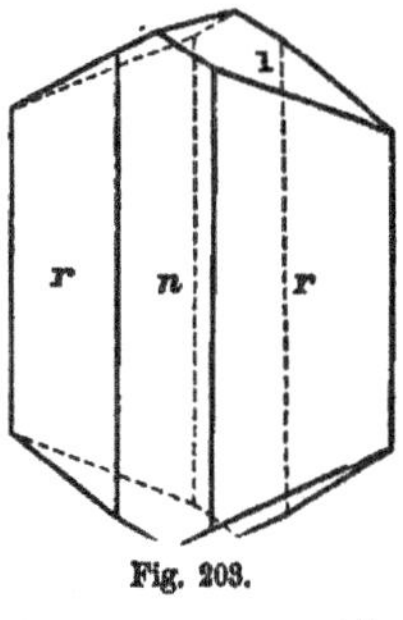

Fig. 203.

39·5 arsenic acid, and 4 water, but also 1 to 6 phosphoric acid. Carharrach, Tin Croft, Gwennap, and St. Day, in Cornwall; also Alston Moor, Thuringia, Tyrol, Siberia, Chili.

279. EUCHROITE.—$\dot{C}u^4 \ddot{As} + 7 \dot{H}$.

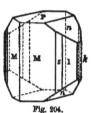

Fig. 204.

Rhombic; ∞P (M) 117° 20′, $\bar{P}\infty$ (n) 80° 52′, with $\infty\bar{P}2$ (l), and 0P (P),(Fig. 204). Cleavage M and n imperfect; rather brittle. H. = 3·5...4; G. = 3·35...3·45. Transparent or translucent; vitreous. Emerald or leek green; streak verdigris-green. B.B. in forceps fuses to a greenish-brown crystallised mass; easily soluble in nitric acid. Chem. com. 47 copper protoxide, 34 arsenic acid, and 19 water. Libethen in Hungary.

280. KLINOCLASE, Aphanese, Abichite.—$\dot{C}u^6 \ddot{As} + 3 \dot{H}$.

Monoclinic; C. = 80° 30′, ∞P 56°; also hemispherical radiated masses. Cleavage, basal highly perfect. H. = 2·5 ...3; G. = 4·2...4·4. Translucent or opaque; vitreous; pearly on the cleavage. Dark verdigris-green inclining to sky-blue; streak bluish-green. B.B. becomes black, and is reduced; soluble in acids and ammonia. Chem. com. 62·6 copper protoxide, 30·3 arsenic acid, and 7·1 water. Cornwall, Tavistock, and the Erzgebirge.

281. PHOSPHOROCHALCITE, Lunnite.—$\dot{C}u^6 \ddot{P} + 3 \dot{H}$.

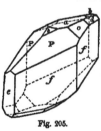

Fig. 205.

Monoclinic; crystals ∞P°2 (f) 38° 56′, P (P) 117° 49′, with 0P (a) and ∞P°∞ (e) (Fig. 205); usually small and indistinct, more common in spherical or reniform, and radiated fibrous masses. Cleavage, (e) imperfect; fracture uneven and splintery. H. = 5 ; G. = 4·1...4·3. Translucent, or on the edges; adamantine or resinous. Blackish, emerald, or verdigris green. B.B. decrepitates, or blackens and fuses to a black

globule; easily soluble in nitric acid or ammonia. Chem.
com. 70·8 copper protoxide, 21·2 phosphoric acid, and
8 water, but some arsenic acid, which occurs also in the
other phosp. of copper. Rheinbreitenbach, Nischne-Tagilsk,
and in Cornwall. *Dihydrite*, G. = 4·4 and 6 water, and
Copper-diaspore, seem varieties.

282. THROMBOLITE.—$\ddot{C}u^3 \ddot{\ddot{P}}^2 + 6 \dot{H}$.

Porodine. Fracture conchoidal; brittle. H. = 3...4;
G. = 3·38...3·40. Opaque; vitreous. Emerald, leek, or
dark green. B.B. colours the flame blue and then green;
on charcoal fuses easily. Chem. com. 45·1 phosphoric acid,
37·8 copper protoxide, and 17·1 water. Retzbanya.

283. LIBETHENITE.—$\dot{C}u^4 \ddot{\ddot{P}} + \dot{H}$.

Rhombic; ∞P (*u*) 92° 20', $\breve{P}\infty$ (*o*) 109° 52', and P .
(Fig. 206). Cleavage, brachydiagonal
and macrodiagonal imperfect. H. =
4; G. = 3·6...3·8. Translucent on
the edges; resinous. Leek, olive, or
blackish green; streak olive-green.
B.B., and with acids, like phosphorochalcite. Chem. com. 66 copper
protoxide, 30 phosphoric acid, and
4 water. Libethen in Hungary,
Tagilsk, and Gunnislake in Cornwall.

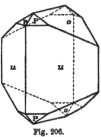

Fig. 206.

284. TAGILITE.—$\dot{C}u^4 \ddot{\ddot{P}} + 3 \dot{H}$.

Monoclinic but botryoidal, and radiating fibrous or
earthy. H. = 3; G. = 4·0. Emerald-green. Chem. com.
61·8 copper protoxide, 27·7 phosphoric acid, and 10·5
water. Nischne-Tagilsk, and near Hirschberg.

285. EHLITE.—$\dot{C}u^5 \ddot{\ddot{P}} + 3 \dot{H}$.

Rhombic; but botryoidal or reniform, and radiating
foliated, or compact. Cleavage in one direction perfect.
H. = 1·5...2; G. = 3·8...4·27. Translucent on the edges;
pearly on the cleavage. Verdigris-green; streak paler.
B.B. breaks violently into small fragments. Chem. com.
67 copper protoxide, 24 phosphoric acid, and 9 water.
Ehl on the Rhine, Nischne-Tagilsk, and Libethen. *Prasin*
is similar.

286. ATACAMITE.—Cu Cl + 3 Ċu Ḣ.

Rhombic; ∞P (M) 112° 25′, P̄∞ (P) 106° 10′, and
∞P̄∞ (h) (Fig. 207); also reniform and columnar or gra-

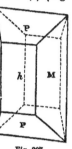

nular. Cleavage (h) perfect.   H. = 3...
3·5; G. = 3·7...3·9.   Semitransparent or
translucent on the edges; vitreous. Olive,
grass, or emerald green; streak apple-
green. B.B. fuses, and leaves copper;
easily soluble in acids. Chem. com. 55·85
copper protoxide, 14·86 copper, 16·61
chlorine, and 12·68 water; or 74·46 copper protoxide and 17·09 h. acid. Remo-
linos and Santa Rosa in Chili, Tarapaca
in Bolivia, Schwarzenberg, Burra-Burra,
Australia, and on the lavas of Ætna and

Fig. 207.

Vesuvius.   Used as an ore of copper.

Percylite, tesseral crystals, from Sonora, Mexico. Azure-
blue. Contains chlorides of lead and copper, with oxides of
lead and copper, and water.

287. VOLBORTHITE.—(Ċu Ċa)⁴ V̈ + Ḣ.

Hexagonal; small tabular crystals, 0P . ∞P, single or in
groups.   H. = 3 ; G. = 3·45...3·89.   Olive-green; streak
almost yellow. B.B. on charcoal fuses easily, and forms a
graphite-like slag, containing grains of copper; on platina
wire, with salt of phosphorus, forms a green glass; soluble
in nitric acids, and with water gives a brick-red precipitate.
Chem. com. 37 to 38 vanadic acid, 39·4 to 46 copper oxide,
18·5 to 13 lime, 3·6 to 5 water. Syssersk, Nischne-Tagilsk,
and Friedrichrode in Thuringia.

288. BROCHANTITE.—Ċu S̈ + 3 Ċu Ḣ.

Rhombic; ∞P 104° 32′, P̄∞ 152° 37′, and ∞P̄∞;
also reniform. Cleavage, brachydiagonal very perfect. H.
= 3·5...4; G. = 3·75...3·9.   Transparent or translucent;
vitreous. Emerald or blackish green; streak bright green.
B.B. on charcoal fuses, leaving copper; easily soluble in
acids. Chem. com. 70 copper protoxide, 18 sulphuric acid,
and 12 water. Rezbanya, Katharinenburg, and Roughton
Gill in Cumberland; also Krisuvig in Iceland (*Krisuvigite*).

289. LANGITE.—$\dot{C}u^4\,\ddot{S}+5\,\dot{H}$.

Rhombic ; $\infty P = 123°\ 44'$. Crystals, long tabular, mostly in macles. Cleavage, basal and brachydiagonal. H. $= 2\cdot5$; G. $= 3\cdot5$. Vitreous. Greenish-blue. Easily soluble in acids and ammonia. Chem. com. $65\cdot1$ copper protoxide, $16\cdot4$ sulphuric acid, and $18\cdot5$ water. Cornwall.

Warringtonite is similar ; also *Konigine* from Siberia.

290. URANITE, Lime-Uranite,
Autunite. Uran-Mica *in part.* $\Big\}\ (\dot{C}a + \ddot{U}^3)\ \ddot{\dddot{P}} + 8\,\dot{H}$.

Rhombic ; $\infty P = 90°\ 43'$, P middle edge $127°\ 32'$; thus nearly tetragonal, and crystals flat, tabular, and very like those of chalcolite. Cleavage, basal very perfect ; sectile. H. $= 1...2$; G. $= 3...3\cdot2$. Translucent ; pearly on 0P. Siskin-green to sulphur-yellow ; streak yellow. B.B. on charcoal fuses to a black semicrystalline mass ; with soda forms a yellow infusible slag ; in n. acid forms a yellow solution. Chem. com. $15\cdot5$ phosphoric acid, $62\cdot6$ uranium peroxide, $6\cdot1$ lime, and $15\cdot8$ water. Johann-Georgenstadt and Eibenstock in Saxony, Autun and Limoges in France, Chesterfield in Massachusetts, and Cornwall.

291. CHALCOLITE, Copper-
Uranite. $\Big\}\ (\dot{C}u + \ddot{U}^3)\ \ddot{\dddot{P}} + 8\,\dot{H}$.

Tetragonal ; P middle edge $142°\ 8'$, P∞ $128°\ 14'$. Crystals, 0P . P (o, P) (Fig. 208), or with ∞P. Cleavage, basal very perfect, and pearly lustre. Brittle. H. $= 2...$ $2\cdot5$; G. $= 3\cdot5...3\cdot6$. Grass to emerald or verdigris green ; streak apple-green. B.B. like uranite, but with soda yields a grain of copper. Chem. com. $15\cdot2$ phosphoric acid, 61 uranium peroxide, $8\cdot5$ copper protoxide, and $15\cdot3$ water. Johann-Georgenstadt, Eibenstock, Schneeberg, Bodenmais, near Baltimore, North America, and near Redruth, and St. Austle.

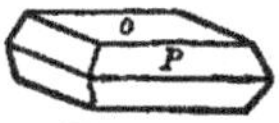

Fig. 208.

292. ZEUNERITE.—$(\dot{C}u^3 + \ddot{U}^6)\ \ddot{\dddot{A}}s^3 + 24\,\dot{H}$.

Tetragonal ; and in form, cleavage, colour, and H. like chalcolite. But G. $= 3\cdot2$. Chem. com. $15\cdot1$ arsenic acid, $55\cdot6$ uranium peroxide, $8\cdot7$ copper protoxide, $14\cdot5$ water, with 5·2 iron peroxide, and 1·2 lime. Neustädtel, Schnee-berg.

*293. ERYTHRINE, Cobalt-Bloom.—$\dot{C}o^3 \overset{...}{A}s + 8 \dot{H}$.

Monoclinic; $\infty P^\circ \infty$ (P) . $\infty P^\circ \infty$ (T) . $P\infty$ (M) (like Fig. 195), with $M : T = 55°$ $9'$; also $\infty P3$ (k), and P (l)

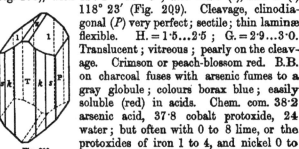

Fig. 209.

118° 23′ (Fig. 2Q9). Cleavage, clinodia-gonal (P) very perfect; sectile; thin laminæ flexible. H. = 1·5...2·5 ; G. = 2·9...3·0. Translucent ; vitreous ; pearly on the cleav-age. Crimson or peach-blossom red. B.B. on charcoal fuses with arsenic fumes to a gray globule ; colours borax blue ; easily soluble (red) in acids. Chem. com. 38·2 arsenic acid, 37·8 cobalt protoxide, 24 water ; but often with 0 to 8 lime, or the protoxides of iron 1 to 4, and nickel 0 to 9. Schneeberg, Saalfeld, Allemont, Riech-elsdorf, the Pyrenees, and Modum in Norway ; also Corn-wall, Alston in Cumberland, at Alva in Stirlingshire, and Tyndrum in Perthshire. Used in preparing blue colours.

Köttigite.—White or peach-blossom red incrustations of minute crystals like erythrine, with which it agrees, but the cobalt almost wholly replaced by zinc. Schneeberg.

Kobaltbeschlag, or *Earthy-encrusting Cobalt*, reniform, is a mixture of erythrine with arsenious acid.

Lavendulan.—Thin reniform lavender-blue crusts ; trans-lucent ; resinous or vitreous. H. = 2·5...3 ; G. = 2·95... 3·1. B.B. fuses very easily, colouring the outer flame blue. Consists of arsenic acid, protoxides of cobalt, nickel, and copper, with water. Annaberg.

294. ANNABERGITE, Nickel-ochre.—$\dot{N}i^3 \overset{..}{A}s + 8 \dot{H}$.

Monoclinic (?); in capillary crystals, also massive, earthy ; rather sectile. H. = 2...2·5 ; G. = 3...3·1. Dull or glis-tening. Apple-green or greenish-white ; streak greenish-white and shining. B.B. on charcoal fuses with arsenical vapours ; easily soluble in acids. Chem. com. 38·7 arsenic acid, 37·3 nickel protoxide, and 24 water, but with a little cobalt or iron. Andreasberg, Annaberg, Saalfeld, Riechels-

dorf, Joachimsthal, and Leadhills. Used in preparing blue
colours.

295. EMERALD-NICKEL, Zaratite.—$\overset{..}{Ni}\overset{..}{C} + 6\overset{.}{H}$.

Amorphous, reniform, and encrusting. H. = 3 ; G. =
2·6...2·7. Translucent ; vitreous. Emerald-green. B.B.
infusible, becomes black and shows reaction for nickel.
Effervesces and forms a green solution in acids. Chem.
com. 59·3 nickel protoxide, 11·7 carbonic acid, and 29
water. On chromite at Swinaness, Unst, Texas in Pennsylvania. Also Cape Ortegal, Spain, and Tyrol.

FAMILY IV.—LEAD-SALTS.

Crystallisation predominantly rhombic and monoclinic
in the lead compounds, but in some salts of other metals
tetragonal or hexagonal. Hardness moderate, generally
from 2...4·5, or about calc-spar. All have a high specific
gravity, or from 5·3...8,—this family including all minerals
without metallic lustre and aspect, with G. above 5·5.
They are all soluble in nitric acid, and form coloured solutions or precipitates. They are all easily fusible, and mostly
readily reduced alone, or with soda, to lead. They are
mostly compounds of lead, and the cerussite is an ore of
this metal. The others are not abundant, but often show
fine colours. Occur chiefly in veins and mines with other
ores of lead.

Lead B.B. on charcoal forms a greenish or sulphur-
yellow coating round the assay. Solutions in nitric acid
give, with sulphuric acid, a white precipitate, reduced B.B.;
and with chromate of potassa, a yellow precipitate.

**296. CERUSSITE, Lead Spar.—$\overset{.}{Pb}\overset{..}{C} = [Pb\ O\ .\ CO^?]$.

Rhombic ; isomorphous with arragonite and nitre ; ∞P
(*M*) 117° 14′, $\bar{P}∞$ 108° 13′, $2\bar{P}∞$ (*u*) 69° 18′; also 0P,
P (*t*), $\frac{1}{2}\bar{P}∞$ (*s*), ∞$\bar{P}∞$ (*l*), ∞$\bar{P}3$ (*e*) (Figs. 210, 211). Macles
are very common (Fig. 212); also granular or earthy.
Cleavage, ∞P and $2\bar{P}∞$ rather distinct ; fracture conchoidal ; brittle and easily frangible. H. = 3...3·5 ; G. =
6·4...6·6 (earthy 5·4). Transparent or translucent ; ada-

R

mantine or resinous. Colourless and often white, but also gray, yellow, brown, black, rarely green, blue, or red ; streak white. B.B. decrepitates violently, but easily fused and reduced ; soluble with effervescence in nitric acid.

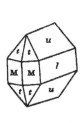 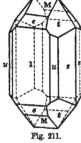 

Fig. 210.   Fig. 211.   Fig. 212.

Chem. com. 83·5 protoxide of lead and 16·5 carbonic acid. Very common at Przibram, Mies, and Bleistadt, Tarnowitz, Johann-Georgenstadt, Zellerfeld, Klausthal, Beeralston in Devonshire, St. Miniver's in Cornwall, Alston Moor, Keswick, Leadhills, and Wanlockhead, and many other places.

*297. ANGLESITE.—$\overset{..}{P}b\ \overset{..}{S} = [Pb\ O\ .\ SO^3]$.

Rhombic ; $\infty\breve{P}$ 103° 43′, P∞ 75° 35′. The crystals of many forms and combinations, are short prismatic, or pyramidal, or tabular; like Fig. 213 (but often placed in other positions). Cleavage, prismatic along ∞P and basal, neither very perfect; fracture conchoidal; very brittle. H. = 3 ;

G. = 6·2...6·35. Transparent or translucent ; adamantine or resinous. Colourless and white, but occasionally yellow, gray, brown, or blue; streak white. Decrepitates in candle; B.B. on charcoal fuses in the ox. flame to a milk-white

Fig. 213.   bead ; very difficultly soluble in acids, wholly in solution of potash. Chem. com. 73·7 lead protoxide and 26·3 sulphuric acid, in some with a little silver. Zellerfeld, Clausthal, Badenweiler, Siegen, Silesia, Linares, Phœnixville in Pennsylvania, Parys Mine in Anglesea, St. Ives in Cornwall, Derbyshire, Leadhills, and Wanlockhead. Compact (*Bleiglas*), Alston Moor in Cumberland.

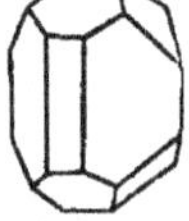

298. LEADHILLITE.—3 Ṗb C̈ + Ṗb S̈.

Rhombic; P middle edge 137°, ∞P 120° 20', 2P̄∞ 43° 12'. Crystals, 0P. ∞P. ∞P̄∞ (*c, m, a,* Fig. 214), mostly tabular; also macles. Cleavage, basal very perfect; slightly brittle.   H. = 2·5 ; G. = 6·26...6·44.   Transparent or translucent; resinous or adamantine, pearly on 0P. Yellowish-white, inclining to gray, green, yellow, or brown.   B.B. on charcoal intumesces, and becomes yellow, but again white when cold,

Fig. 214.

and easily reduced; soluble with effervescence in nitric acid, leaving sulphate of lead.   Chem. com. 72·6 carbonate and 27·4 sulphate of lead.   Leadhills, Taunton ; also Grenada and Nertschinsk.   *Maxite,* found with it at Iglesias, Sardinia, with 2 water, is probably the same.

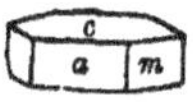

299. SUSANNITE.—3 Ṗb C̈ + Ṗb S̈.

Rhombohedral; R 72° 30'. Cleavage, basal perfect. H. = 2·5 ; G. = 6·55.   White, green, yellow, or brown. Otherwise like leadhillite.   Susannah Mine, Leadhills, Moldawa.   According to Kenngott, may be only triple macles of leadhillite, but G. higher.

300. LANARKITE.—Ṗb S̈ + Ṗb C̈.

Monoclinic; ∞P (*a*) 49° 50'. 0P : P°∞ (*b : c*) 59° 15' (Fig. 215). Cleavage, basal very perfect; sectile, thin laminæ flexible.   H. = 2...2·5; G. = 6·3...6·7. Transparent; resinous or adamantine; on 0P pearly. Greenish or yellowish white, inclining to gray ; streak white.   B.B. on char-

Fig. 215.

coal fuses to a white globule containing metallic lead ; partially soluble in n. acid with effervescence.   Chem. com. 53 sulphate and 47 carbonate of lead.   Leadhills, rare. Pisani says is nearly pure Ṗb S̈, and no effervescence.

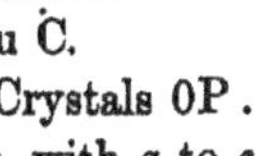

301. CALEDONITE.—3 Ṗb S̈ + 2 Ṗb C̈ + C̈u C̈.

Rhombic; ∞P 94° 47', P̄∞ 109° 38'.   Crystals 0P . ∞P̄∞. ∞P (*c, a, m,* Fig. 216) (or Monoclinic, with *a* to *c* 90° 30', and *a* to *m* 132° 32', *Schrauf*).   Cleavage, brachy-diagonal (*a*) distinct, two others (*m, c*) imperfect.   H. = 2·5 ...3 ; G. = 6·4.   Transparent or translucent; resinous.   Verdigris to mountain green ; streak greenish-white.   B.B. on charcoal easily reduced; soluble in nitric acid, leaving

Fig. 216.

sulphate of lead. The solution is greenish, and shows reaction for lead and copper. Chem. com. 55·8 sulphate of lead, 32·8 carbonate of lead, and 11·4 carbonate of copper. Leadhills, Red Gill in Cumberland, and Rezbanya.

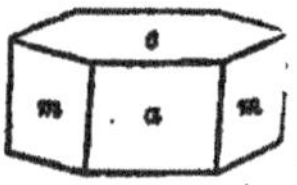

302. LINARITE.—$\dot{P}b\,\ddot{S} + \dot{C}u\,\dot{H}$.

Monoclinic; C. = 77° 27′, ∞P 61° 36′, 2P°∞ 52° 38′. Crystals ∞P°∞ . 0P, with the above or other forms; macles united by ∞P°∞ . Cleavage, orthodiagonal very perfect, basal less so; fracture conchoidal. H. = 2·5...3; G. = 5·2 ...5·45. Translucent; adamantine. Azure-blue; streak pale-blue. Chem. com. 75·7 sulphate of lead, 19·8 copper protoxide, and 4·5 water. Leadhills, Red Gill, Roughten Gill, Linares, and Nertschinsk.

303. PHOSGENITE, Corneous Lead, Cerasine. } $Pb\,Cl + \dot{P}b\,\ddot{C}$.

Tetragonal; P 113° 56′. Crystals short prismatic or sharp pyramidal. Cleavage, ∞P rather perfect; fracture conchoidal. H. = 2·5...3; G. = 6...6·2. Transparent or translucent; resinous adamantine. White, yellow, green, or gray. B.B. fuses easily to an opaque yellow globule, crystalline on cooling; soluble with effervescence in nitric acid. Chem. com. 51 chloride and 49 carbonate of lead. Very rare; Matlock and Cromford, Derbyshire, and Stottfield near Elgin in Scotland; Tarnowitz.

304. MENDIPITE, Berzelite.—Pb Cl + 2 $\dot{P}b$.

Rhombic; but chiefly massive. Cleavage, along ∞P 102° 36′ highly perfect; fracture conchoidal or uneven. H. = 2·5...3; G. = 7·0...7·1. Translucent; adamantine-pearly on the cleavage. Yellowish-white to straw-yellow and pale-red; streak white. B.B. decrepitates, fuses easily, and becomes more yellow; easily soluble in nitric acid. Chem. com. 40 chloride and 60 protoxide of lead = 85·8 lead, and 9·8 chlorine. Churchill in the Mendip Hills, and Brilon in Westphalia.

305. MATLOCKITE.—Pb Cl + Ṗb.

Tetragonal; P 136° 17'. Crystals, 0P . P . P∞, small, thin, tabular. Cleavage, basal indistinct; fracture uneven conchoidal. H. = 2·5; G. = 7·21 (*Greg.*), 5·39 (*Ram.*) Transparent or translucent; adamantine. Yellowish or greenish. B.B. decrepitates and fuses to a grayish-yellow globule. Chem. com. 55·6 chloride of lead, and 44·4 lead oxide. Cromford, on galena.

306. COTUNNITE, Cotunnia.—Pb Cl = [Pb Cl²].

Rhombic; ∞P 118° 38', P̄∞ 126° 44'. Small acicular crystals. Transparent; adamantine. White. H. = 2; G. = 5·238. B.B. on charcoal fuses easily, colours the flame blue, volatilises, forms a white ring, and leaves a little lead. Chem. com. 74 lead and 26 chlorine. Crater of Vesuvius after the eruption of 1822.

*307. PYROMORPHITE. $\begin{cases} 3 \text{ Ṗb}^{\textbf{.}} \overset{...}{\text{P}} + \text{Pb Cl} \\ = [3 (3\text{Pb O} . \text{P}^{\textbf{.}} \text{O}^{\textbf{.}}) + \text{Pb Cl}^{\textbf{.}}]. \end{cases}$

Hexagonal; P 80° 44'. Crystals ∞P . 0P, with ∞P2, or P (*M, P, x*) (Fig. 217), occasionally thicker in the middle, or spindle-shaped; also reniform or botryoidal. Cleavage, P very imperfect, ∞P in traces; fracture conchoidal or uneven. H. = 3·5...4; G. = 6·9...7·0. Translucent; resinous or vitreous. Colourless, but generally grass, pis-tacio, olive, or siskin green, and clove or hair brown. B.B. fuses easily, with a transitory igni-tion, to a crystalline granule; soluble in nitric acid and in solution of potash. Chem. com. 89·7 phosphate and 10·3 chloride of lead, but with 0 to 9 arseniate of lead, 0 to 11 phosphate of lime, and 0 to 1 fluoride of calcium. Przibram, Mies and Bleistadt in Bohemia, Zschopau, Clausthal, Poullaouen, Beresof, Phœnixville in Pennsylvania, and Mexico; also Cornwall, Derbyshire, Yorkshire, Durham, Cumberland, Wicklow, Stroutian, Leadhills, and Wanlockhead. *Miesite, Polysphærite,* and *Nussierite,* from near Beaujeu, are varieties.

Fig. 217.

*308. MIMETESITE.—3 Ṗb³ Äs + Pb CL

Hexagonal; P 81° 48'. Crystals, ∞P . 0P . P (Fig. 217), or P . 0P. Cleavage, P rather distinct, ∞P very imperfect;

fracture conchoidal or uneven. $H. = 3\cdot5...4\cdot0$; $G. = 7\cdot19...$
$7\cdot25$. Translucent. Colourless, but usually honey or wax yel-
low, yellowish-green, or gray. B.B. on charcoal fusible, but
less easily than pyromorphite, with strong arsenious vapours.
Chem. com. $90\cdot7$ arseniate and $9\cdot3$ chloride of lead; but
part of the arsenic occasionally replaced by phosphoric acid.
Johann-Georgenstadt, Zinnwald, Badenweiler, St. Prix in
France, Nertschinsk, and Zacatecas in Mexico; Huel Alfred
and Huel Unity in Cornwall, Roughten Gill and Dry Gill,
Cumberland ; Beeralston in Devonshire, and Leadhills.

Kampylite.—Orange-yellow ; $G. = 6\cdot8...6\cdot9$. Chem.
com. like mimetesite, but contains phosphate of lime and
chromate of lead. Alston in Cumberland and Badenweiler.

Hedyphane.—Crystalline masses with an imperfect hexagonal cleavage. $G. = 5\cdot4...5\cdot5$. Translucent; resinous
adamantine. White. Chem. com. like mimetesite, but 13
arseniate and $15\cdot5$ phosphate of lime. Langbanshytta.

309. PLOMBGOMME.—$\ddot{P}b^3 \ddot{P} + 6 \ddot{A}l \dot{H}^3$.
Reniform or stalactitic. Fracture conchoidal and splin-
tery. $H. = 4...4\cdot5$; $G. = 6\cdot3...6\cdot4$. Translucent; resinous.
Yellowish or greenish-white to reddish-brown. B.B. on
charcoal becomes opaque and white, intumesces, and partially fuses; soluble in nitric acid. Chem. com. 38 protoxide of lead, 35 alumina, 8 phosphoric acid, and 19 water;
but with 2 chloride of lead. Poullaouen and Nussiére near
Beaujeu. It much resembles gum-arabic.

310. BLEINIERITE.—$\dot{P}b$, $\ddot{S}b$, $\dot{H}$.
Reniform, spheroidal ; earthy, or encrusting. $H. = 4$;
$G. = 3\cdot9...4\cdot76$. Opaque ; dull resinous, or earthy. Gray,
brown, red, or yellow ; streak grayish or yellowish white.
B.B. on charcoal reduced with antimony fumes. Chem.
com. mixture of protoxide of lead (40 to 62), antimony
oxides (31 to 47), and water (6 to 12); some also contain
arsenic acid. Nertschinsk, Lostwithiel in Cornwall.

311. VANADINITE.—$3 \dot{P}b^3 \ddot{V} + Pb Cl.$
Hexagonal; $P\ 78° 46'$ to $80°$, like pyromorphite. H.
$= 3$; $G. = 6\cdot8...7\cdot2$. Opaque ; resinous. Yellow and
brown ; streak white. B.B. decrepitates violently, and on

charcoal fuses to a globule, which emits sparks and is reduced; in nitric acid forms a yellow solution; n. acid dropped on the crystals colours them first deep red, then bright yellow. Chem. com. 89·7 vanadiate, and 10·3 chloride of lead. Zimapan in Mexico, Beresof, and Wanlockhead.

312. DECHENITE.—$\dot{P}b\ \ddot{V}$.

Rhombic; P middle edge 91°, but mostly botryoidal or thin lamellar. H. = 3·5...4; G. = 5·81. Resinous; translucent on the edges. Red or reddish-yellow; streak yellow. B.B. fuses easily to a yellow bead, and on charcoal reduced to lead; easily soluble in nitric acid. Chem. com. 54·7 lead oxide, and 45·3 vanadic acid, but analysis gave 46 to 49 of the latter. Niederschlettenbach in Rhenish Bavaria. Kappel in Carinthia.

Descloizite.—Small rhombic crystals; olive-green to black; on fracture concentric yellow and brown zones. La Plata. Is probably identical.

Similar are—*Aræoxene*; botryoidal; red, with a brown tinge. Chem. com. vanadic acid, with 48·7 lead oxide, and 16·3 zinc oxide. Dahn on the Rhine.

Eusynchite.—Yellowish-red; opaque. B.B. melts easily to a lead-gray globule. Chem. com. 56 lead oxide, 23 vanadic acid, and 21 deutoxide of vanadium. Freiburg.

Eosite.—Minute tetragonal crystals, aurora red, with brownish orange-yellow streak. Show reaction for molydena, vanadium, and lead. Leadhills.

313. WULFENITE.—$\dot{P}b\ \ddot{Mo}$.

Tetragonal; P 131° 48'; 0P (*a*), $\frac{1}{4}$P (*b*), P, ∞P, and P∞ (Fig. 218). Cleavage, P rather perfect, basal imperfect; fracture conchoidal to uneven; rather brittle. H. = 3; G. = 6·3...6·9. Pellucid; resinous or adamantine. Colourless, but generally yellowish-gray,

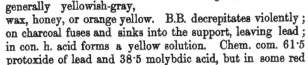

Fig. 218.

wax, honey, or orange yellow. B.B. decrepitates violently; on charcoal fuses and sinks into the support, leaving lead; in con. h. acid forms a yellow solution. Chem. com. 61·5 protoxide of lead and 38·5 molybdic acid, but in some red varieties chrome preponderates. Bleiberg and Windisch Kappel, Retzbanya, Badenweiler; Phœnixville in Pennsylvania, and Zacatecas.

314. SCHEELITINE, Stolzite.—Ṗb Ẅ.
Tetragonal and hemihedric; P 131° 25'. Crystals, 2 P. P . ∞P, spindle-shaped. Cleavage, P imperfect. H. = 3 ; G. = 7·9...8·1. Semitransparent or translucent ; resinous. Gray, brown, yellow, or green. B.B. fuses to a dark crystalline grain, with salt of phosphorus in red. flame to a blue glass ; soluble in nitric acid, with a yellow precipitate. Chem. com. 51·6 tungstic acid, and 48·4 protoxide of lead. Zinnwald ; Coquimbo ; and near Keswick.

315. CROCOISITE, Krokoit.—Ṗb Ċr.
Monoclinic; C.= 77° 27'; ∞P 93° 42' (M), – P 119° 12' (t), ∞P°2 (r) 56° 10', ∞P°∞ (g) (Fig. 219). Cleavage,

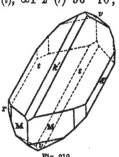
Fig. 219.

∞P rather distinct ; sectile. H. = 2·5...3 ; G. = 5·9...6·1. Translucent ; adamantine. Hyacinth or aurora red ; streak orange-yellow. B.B. decrepitates, blackens, and fuses on charcoal, the lower part being reduced ; with borax or salt of phosphorus in the ox. flame a green, in the red. flame a gray glass ; soluble in warm h. acid. Chem. com. 31 chromic acid, and 69 lead protoxide. Beresof, Mursinsk, and Nischne-Tagilsk in the Ural ; Congonhas do Campo in Brazil, Rezbanya, Moldawa, and Tarnowitz. Used as a pigment, but not permanent.

316. MELANOCHROITE, Phœnicochroite.—Ṗb³ Ċr².
Rhombic ; dimensions unknown. Cleavage imperfect. H. = 3...3·5 ; G. = 5.75. Translucent on the edges ; resinous or adamantine. Cochineal to hyacinth red ; streak brick-red. B.B. on charcoal fuses easily to a dark crystalline mass ; in the red. flame yields lead ; soluble in h. acid. Chem. com. 23 chromic acid, and 77 protoxide of lead. Beresof.

317. VAUQUELINITE.—$\dot{C}u^3 \ddot{C}r^2 + 2 \dot{P}b^3 \ddot{C}r^2$.

Monoclinic; C. = 67° 15′. Crystals 0P. − P. − P°∞ (or *P*, *f*, *h*), always macled (Fig. 220), the faces of 0P forming an angle of 134° 30′; also botryoidal or reni-form. H. = 2·5...3; G. = 5·5...5·8. Semi-translucent or opaque; resinous. Blackish or dark olive-green; streak siskin-green. B.B. on charcoal intumesces, froths up, and fuses to a dark-grey metallic globule surrounded by small grains of lead; in nitric acid forms a dark-green solution with a yellow re-sidue. Chem. com. 61 lead protoxide, 11 copper protoxide, 28 chromic acid. Beresof, Congonhas do Campo.

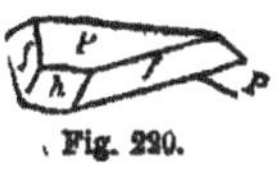

Fig. 220.

318. BISMUTHITE.—$\ddot{B}i^4 \ddot{C}^3 + 4 \dot{H}$.

Disseminated, investing, or acicular. Fracture conchoidal or uneven; very brittle. H. = 4...4·5; G. = 6·8...6·91. Opaque; dull vitreous. Gray, yellow, or green. B.B. de-crepitates, fuses very readily, and is reduced with efferves-cence; in h. acid it forms a deep-yellow solution. Chem. com. 90·1 bismuth oxide, 6·4 carbonic acid, and 3·5 water. Ullersreuth near Hirschberg, Schneeberg, and Johann-Georgenstadt; also Chesterfield in S. Carolina, where like cerussite.

Pucherite; minute rhombic crystals, ∞P.0P. Cleav-age, basal perfect. H. = 4; G. = 5·9...6·0. Vitreous; reddish-brown or red; streak yellow. B.B. decrepitates, fuses, and with soda yields bismuth. Easily soluble in acids. Chem. com. $\ddot{B}i \ddot{V}$, with 17 bismuth oxide, and 28 vanadic acid. Schneeberg in Saxony.

319. KERATE, Hornsilver.—Ag Cl.

Tesseral; chiefly ∞O∞; small or very small; also mass-ive. Fracture conchoidal; malleable and yields to the nail. H. = 1...1·5; G. = 5·5...5·6. Translucent; adaman-tine resinous; gray, occasionally bluish or greenish. B.B. fuses very easily to a gray, brown, or black bead, which in the inner flame is reduced; slightly affected by acids, and slowly soluble in ammonia. Chem. com. 75 silver and 25 chlorine, but with some (0 to 6) iron peroxide. Johann-Georgenstadt, Joachimsthal, Huelgöet, Kongsberg in Nor-way, Spain, and Cornwall; now chiefly from Mexico and Peru.

Carbonate of Silver (Selbite), ash-gray, massive, very soft, effervescing in nitric acid, and B.B. easily reduced, seems a mixture. Wolfach in Baden, and Real de Catorce in Mexico (*Plata azul*), a rich silver ore.

320. CALOMEL.—$Hg^2 Cl = [Hg\,Cl]$.
Tetragonal; P 135° 50′. Crystals like Fig. 120 above, but very small; sectile. H. = 1...2; G. = 6·4...6·5 (artificial 7·0). Translucent; adamantine. Grayish or yellowish-white. In the closed tube it sublimes as a white mass, and with soda yields mercury. B.B. on charcoal, when pure, wholly volatilises; in nitric acid not soluble, in h. acid partially. Chem. com. 15 chlorine and 85 mercury. Moschellandsberg in Rhenish Bavaria, also Idria and Almaden.

321. IODITE.—Ag I.
Hexagonal, but usually in thin flexible plates. Malleable. H. = 1...1·5; G. = 5·5...5·7. Translucent; resinous or adamantine. Pearl-gray, greenish or orange yellow. B.B. on charcoal becomes red, fuses easily, colouring the flame purple-red, and leaves a grain of silver. Chem. com. 54 iodine and 46 silver. Albarradon in Zacatecas; Arqueros in Chili, and Guadalajara in Spain.

322. COCCINITE.—Hg I.
Scarlet-red, easily fusible, and subliming; said to occur at Casas Viejas in Mexico, and to be used as a pigment. Chem. com. probably 44·3 mercury and 55·7 iodine, like the artificial salt, which crystallises in tetragonal pyramids.

323.—BROMITE.—Ag Br.
Tesseral; ∞O∞ and O. Crystals very small; also crystalline grains. H. = 1...2; G. = 5·8...6. Very splendent. Olive-green or yellow, with gray tarnish; streak siskin-green. B.B. very easily fusible; scarcely affected by acids. Chem. com. 57·5 silver and 42·5 bromine. San Onofre in the district of Plateros in Mexico (*Plata verde*), and used as an ore of silver.

324. EMBOLITE.—2 Ag Br + 3 Ag Cl.
Tesseral; ∞O∞ and O. H. = 1...1·5; G. = 5·8. Resinous or adamantine. Yellow or green. Chem. com. 67

silver, 20 bromine, and 13 chlorine. Chili, Mexico, and Honduras. Ore of silver.

325. ROMEITE, Romeine.—$\dot{C}a^3 \ddot{S}b \ddot{S}b$.

Tetragonal; P 110° 50′; consequently very like an octahedron. Scratches glass. G. = 4·6 ... 4·7. Honey-yellow or hyacinth-red. B.B. fuses to a blackish slag; not soluble in acids. Chem. com. 41·3 antimonic acid, 37·3 antimony oxide, and 21·4 lime, but with 2 to 3 manganese and iron protoxide. St. Marcel in Piedmont.

*326. SCHEELITE, Tungsten.—$\dot{C}a \ddot{W}.=[\text{Ca O . WO}^3]$.

Tetragonal and hemihedric; P 113° 52′; often alone. The usual combinations are P (*P*). 2P∞ (*n*), (Fig. 221). Crystals pyramidal or tabular. Cleavage, 2P∞ 130° 33′ rather perfect, along P and 0P less perfect. Fracture con-choidal and uneven. H. = 4 ... 4·5; G. = 5·9 ... 6·2. Translucent; resin-ous or adamantine. Colourless, but gray, yellow, or brown; streak white. B.B. fuses difficultly to a translucent glass; decomposed in h. or n. acid, leaving a yellow residue. Chem. com. 80·6 tungstic acid and 19·4 lime, but with 0 to 3 silica and 0 to 1·5 iron peroxide, or rarely copper protoxide when the mineral is green. Caldbeckfell near Keswick; Pen-gelly, Cornwall; at Zinnwald and Schlaggenwald; also in the gold mines of Salzburg and of Hungary;

Fig. 221.

Chili and Siberia; also in the Monroe Mines in Connecti-cut, where used in preparing tungstic acid, a very fine yellow pigment.

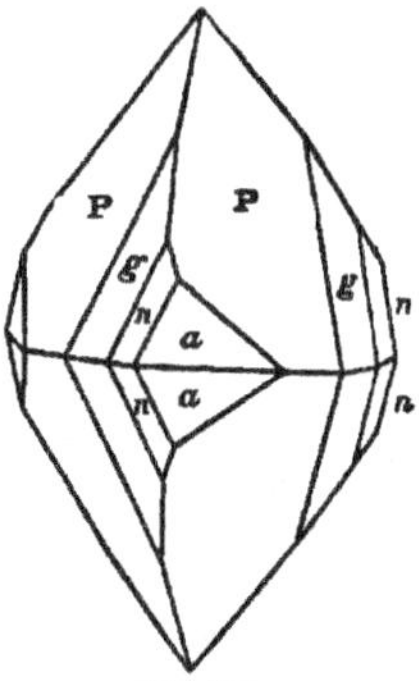

Order IV.

OXIDISED ORES.

CRYSTALLISATION often rhombic, then tesseral or tetragonal, less frequently hexagonal or rhombohedral. Hardness generally high, mostly equal to felspar, or 5...7. Gravity also high, or 4·0...7·0 or 8·0. They are generally soluble in acids, and solutions coloured. B.B. infusible, or very difficultly so. Chem. com. oxides of the metals alone or in combination. They are mostly opaque, with metallic lustre, and of black, brown, or dark-gray colours; streak mostly coloured and characteristic. Occur in beds, veins, or large masses, especially in the metamorphic and igneous rocks.

*FAMILY I.—OXIDISED IRON ORES.

Crystallisation tesseral, rhombohedral, or rhombic. H. = 5...6·5; G. = 3·4...6·5; crystalline species 4·5...5·3. Soluble in acids; solution green. B.B. infusible or very difficult, but become magnetic in the red. flame. With borax show reaction for iron. Colours black, brown, or red. Occur in beds, veins, or large masses, in the older rocks, and highly important as valuable ores. Also as rock constituents, and then causing decomposition.

**327. MAGNETITE, Magnetic Iron. $\begin{cases} \ddot{\text{Fe}} \ddot{\text{Fe}} = \\ [\text{Fe O . Fe}^2 \text{O}^3]. \end{cases}$
Tesseral; crystals chiefly octahedrons and rhombic dodecahedrons, or these combined with $\infty O \infty$, 2O2 and 2O. Faces of ∞O mostly striated in the long diagonal. Macles common, united by O (Fig. 222). Generally granular or almost compact; often in loose grains. Cleavage octahedral perfect or mere traces; fracture conchoidal or uneven; brittle. H. = 5·5...6·5; G. = 4·9...5·2. Opaque; lustre

metallic. Iron-black, or inclining to brown or gray; streak
black. Highly magnetic, and often
polaric as natural magnets. B.B.
becomes brown and non-magnetic,
and fuses with extreme difficulty;
powder soluble in h. acid. Chem.
com. 31 protoxide, and 69 peroxide of iron, or 72·4 iron and 27·6
oxygen, but some a little titanic
acid. Crystals at Traversalla in
Piedmont, Greiner in Tyrol, Kraubat
in Styria; large masses at Arendal

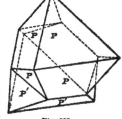

Fig. 222.

in Norway; Dannemora, Utoe, Norberg, Taberg in Sweden;
Kurunavara and Gellivara in Lapland; Nischne-Tagilsk,
Blagodat, and the Kaschkanar in the Ural; also the Harz,
Saxony, Bohemia, Silesia, Elba, and Spain; Mexico, Brazil,
and North America. In Cornwall near Redruth; in Scot-
land at Portsoy, Unst, and other places. Magnetite is the
most important ore of iron in Norway, Sweden, and
Russia.

*328. CHROMITE.—(Fe, Mg) (Ċr, A̤l) = [RO . R² O³].

Tesseral only in octahedrons; generally granular.
Cleavage, octahedral imperfect; fracture, imperfect conchoidal, or uneven. H. = 5·5; G. = 4·4...4·5. Opaque;
semi-metallic or resinous. Iron or brownish black; streak
yellowish or reddish brown. Sometimes magnetic. B.B.
infusible and unchanged, but the non-magnetic in the red
flame become magnetic; in borax forms an emerald-green
bead; scarcely affected by acids. Chem. com. 19 to 37
iron protoxide, 0 to 15 magnesia, 36 to 60 chrome peroxide
(or part protoxide), and 9 to 21 alumina, with 0 to 10
silica as a mixture. Saxony, Silesia, Bohemia, Styria
(Kraubat), Gassin in the Var dept. in France, Röraas in
Norway, Katherinenburg in the Ural, near Baltimore,
Chester in Massachusetts, and Hoboken; in Scotland in
great abundance in Unst and Fetlar in the Zetlands, at
Portsoy in Banff, and Tyndrum. It is often associated
with serpentine or granular limestone. Used in the preparation of various pigments.

329. FRANKLINITE.—(Ḟe, Żn, Ṁn) (F̈e, M̈n).

Tesseral; O and O . ∞O; also granular. Cleavage, octahedral, but very imperfect; fracture conchoidal or uneven; brittle. H. = 6...6·5 ; G. = 5·0...5·3. Opaque; imperfect metallic lustre. Iron-black; streak dark reddish-brown. B.B. infusible, but shines brightly and gives out sparks when strongly heated. On charcoal, with soda, a deposition of zinc; soluble in h. acid with strong extrication of chlorine. Chem. com. 66 to 69 iron and 15 to 18 manganese peroxides (or in part protoxides), and 10 to 27 zinc oxide. Franklin and Sterling in New Jersey.

Dysluite, from Sterling, N. J.; dark or yellowish brown; vitreous; G. = 4·5; contains 30 per cent alumina.

**330. HÆMATITE, Specular Iron.—F̈e = [Fe² O³].

Hexagonal and rhombohedral; R 86°. Crystals rhombohedric, prismatic or tabular, of R . 0R (Fig. 223), ⁴⁄₃P2 . R . ¼R (or *n*, *P*, *s*), (Fig. 224). Macles with parallel axes,

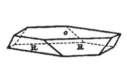

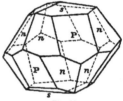

Fig. 223.   Fig. 224.

and mostly intersecting. Cleavage, R and 0R, but seldom distinct; fracture conchoidal or uneven; brittle. H. = 5·5 ...6·5; G. = 5·1...5·3. Opaque, or in very thin laminæ translucent and deep blood-red. Metallic; iron-black to steel-gray, but often tarnished, also red; streak cherry-red or reddish-brown. Some weak magnetic. B.B. in the red flame black and magnetic; slowly soluble in acids. Chem. com. 70 iron and 30 oxygen, but some contain oxide of titanium, chrome, or silica.

Specular Iron Ore, varieties with crystalline structure and high metallic lustre, includes *micaceous iron*, thin lamellar; and *red iron froth*, finer or scaly. The *Red Hæmatite* or

red iron ore, with inferior lustre, lower specific gravity
(4·5...4·9), and hardness (3...5), and deeper blood-red or
brownish-red colours ; comprises the *fibrous red iron*, reniform, botryoidal, and stalactitic, often with an irregular
concentric structure ; the *compact* and *ochrey* iron ores
more earthy or minute ; the *reddle* or red chalk, still
more earthy, and used as a drawing material ; and the
jaspery, columnar, and *lenticular clay iron,* mere impure
varieties.

Crystals, Elba, St. Gotthardt, Framont in the Vosges,
Arendal, Langbanshytta, Tilkerode in the Harz, Altenberg,
Capas in Brazil, Katherinenburg and Nischne-Tagilsk.
Micaceous, Zorge in the Harz, Tincroft in Cornwall, Tavis-
tock in Devonshire, Wales, Cumberland, and Birnam in
Perthshire ; also in Auvergne, on Vesuvius, Ætna, and
Stromboli. The *Red Hæmatite*, the Harz, Ulverstone in
Lancashire, St. Leonards near Edinburgh, near Ballater
and Allerg in Aberdeenshire, Arndilly on the Spey, and
many other parts of Britain. A most abundant ore of
iron.

Martite.—Tesseral, O, O . ∞O and O . ∞O∞ . H. = 6 ;
G. = 4·6...5·33. Iron-black ; streak reddish-brown. A
pseudomorph after magnetite, or a dimorphous form of
hæmatite. Brazil, Monroe in New York, Framont, and
Auvergne.

331. IRITE.—($\dot{\text{I}}$r, $\dot{\text{O}}$s, $\dot{\text{F}}$e) $\ddot{\text{I}}$r, $\ddot{\Theta}$s, $\ddot{\text{C}}$r).

Tesseral ; O ; but in fine iron-black scales, with strong
metallic lustre, which mark paper. G. = 6·506. Strongly
magnetic. B.B. fused with nitre gives out the odour of
osmium ; insoluble in acids. Chem. com. 62·86 peroxide
of iridium, 10·30 osmium protoxide, 12·50 iron protoxide,
13·7 chrome oxide. Ural, with platina.

**332. LIMONITE, Brown $\begin{cases} 2\ \ddot{\text{Fe}} + 3\ \dot{\text{H}} = \\ [2\ \text{Fe}^2\ \text{O}^3 . 3\ \text{H}^2\ \text{O}]. \end{cases}$
   Iron Ore.

Fine fibrous, in spherical, reniform, and stalactitic
masses ; also compact and earthy. H. = 4·5...5·5 ; G. = 3·4
...3·95. Opaque ; lustre weak silky, glimmering, or dull.
Colour brown, especially yellowish, clove, hair, and blackish-

brown, also yellow and green; streak yellowish-brown to ochre-yellow. In the closed tube yields water, and the powder becomes red. B.B. in the outer flame red on ignition; in the inner flame thin splinters fuse to a black magnetic glass. Chem. com. 85·6 peroxide of iron (=60 iron), and 14·4 water; but occasionally with silica, alumina, or phosphoric acid. Harz, Thuringia, Siegen near Bonn, Naussau, Styria, Carinthia, Pyrenees, Siberia, Brazil, and the United States; in Britain in Cornwall, at Clifton near Bristol, Sandlodge in Zetland, and in many other places. A valuable ore of iron, the iron usually uniting hardness with tenacity. *Stilpnosiderite, Lepidokrokite,* and *Yellow ochre* seem partly this mineral, partly götheite, or mixtures.

Bog-Iron Ore is also a hydrated oxide of iron, with no definite composition, and often containing thirty to fifty per cent of impurities. Phosphoric acid to 11 per cent. Occurs chiefly in bogs, meadows, and lakes, as in North Germany, Sweden, and Britain; especially the northern and western counties and islands of Scotland. Other deposits from springs contain two or three atoms water to one atom iron peroxide.

*333. GÖTHEITE, Pyrrho-siderite. $\left.\right\}$ $\ddot{Fe} + \dot{H} = [Fe^2 O^3 . H^2 O].$

Rhombic; P with polar edges 121° 5′ and 126° 18′, ∞P (*g*) 94° 53′, $\infty\bar{P}2$ (*d*) 130° 40′, $\bar{P}\infty$ (*b*) 117° 30′, with $\infty\breve{P}\infty$ (*M*) and P (*P*), (Figs. 225, 226); also columnar, fibrous,

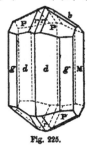

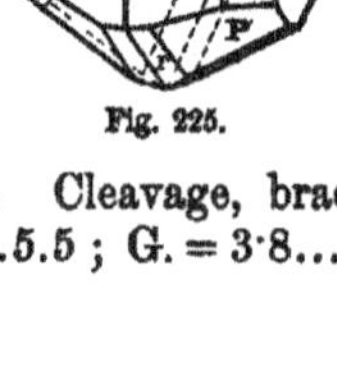

Fig. 225.

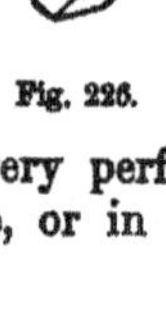

Fig. 226.

or scaly. Cleavage, brachydiagonal very perfect; brittle. H. = 5...5.5; G. = 3·8...4·4. Opaque, or in fine lamellæ

translucent and hyacinth-red; lustre adamantine or silky.
Colour yellowish, reddish, or blackish-brown; streak brownish or reddish yellow. In the closed tube the powder yields
water, and becomes reddish-brown. B.B. in the ox. flame
also brown; in the red. flame black and magnetic; difficultly fusible; soluble in h. acid, often leaving a little
silica. Chem. com. 90 peroxide of iron and 10 water, with
silica and manganese peroxide. Foliated, Eiserfeld near
Siegen. Crystals, Lostwithiel in Cornwall, and Clifton near
Bristol. Capillary, Przibram, Hüttenberg in Carinthia, and
Norway. Compact, Saxony, the Pyrenees, Ural, North
America, and many other localities. Often a pseudomorph
from pyrite.

Turgite, with 94·15 peroxide of iron and 5·85 water;
compact reddish-brown; G. = 3·54...3.74; Turginsk in the
Ural; is probably a mixture.

*334. ILMENITE, } Fe, Ti, *or*
    Titanitic Iron. } [Fe O . Ti O^2 + x Fe^2 O^3]—*Rams.*

Hexagonal and rhombohedral, isomorphous with hæmatite, but sometimes tetartohedral; R 86° (85° 40' to 86° 10').
Crystals tabular or rhombohedral, of 0R (*a*) and R, with
− ½R (*e*), − 2 R (*d*), and ½(½P 2 (*b'*), (Fig. 227). Also in
macles, granular or foliated, or in loose grains. Cleavage,
basal more or less perfect, and
rhombohedral R less distinct;
fracture conchoidal or uneven.
H. = 5 ... 6 ; G. = 4·66 ... 5.
Opaque; semimetallic. Iron-
black, often inclining to brown,
rarely to steel-gray; streak
black, or in some reddish-brown.

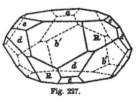

Fig. 227.

Slightly or not at all magnetic. B.B. infusible alone, but
with salt of phosphorus in the red. flame a red glass;
soluble, but often with much difficulty in h. acid. Chem.
com. peroxide of iron with 8 to 53 blue oxide of titanium.
Ilmen mountains ; Gastein in Salzburg (*Kibdelophan*) ; Eger-
sund in Norway; near Arendal (*Hystatit*) ; Menaccon in
Cornwall (*Menacconite*) ; Bourg d'Oisans in Dauphiné (*Crich-
tonite*) ; Massachusetts (*Washingtonite*).

s

Iserine, or magnetic iron sand, in cubes, octahedrons, and dodecahedrons, generally with rounded edges or in loose grains; strongly magnetic. In chemical action and composition it resembles ilmenite, but is perhaps only magnetite mixed with peroxide of titanium. Iserweise in Bohemia, the Eifel, Auvergne, near Rome and Naples; also in Northern Germany, Canada, and New Zealand; Cornwall, sands of the Don in Aberdeenshire, and Loch of Tristan in Zetland.

FAMILY II.—TIN ORE.

Crystallisation tetragonal, rhombic, or rarely monoclinic, with prismatic forms. Hardness 5·5...6·5 or 7. Gravity 3·4...4·3 in the titanium compounds; 4·6...8 in the remainder. Mostly not soluble, or very difficultly, in acids, and also B.B. very difficultly or not fusible. Colours dark, as black, brown, or red. Lustre resinous, semimetallic, or adamantine. Occur chiefly in the older crystalline strata, or in granite and syenite.

**335. CASSITERITE, Tin Ore.—$\ddot{S}n = [Sn\ O^{s}]$.

Tetragonal; P 87° 7′, P∞ 67° 50′. Crystals ∞P . P ; ∞P (*g*) . P (*s*) . ∞P∞ (*l*), or with P∞ (*P*), (Fig. 228); and also ∞P2 (*r*), and 3P¾ (*z*), (Fig. 229). Macles very com-

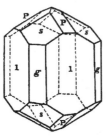
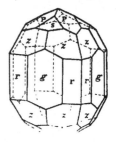

Fig. 228.   Fig. 229.

mon, combined by a face of P∞, with the chief axes 112° 10′ (Figs. 230, 231); also granular or fibrous (*wood tin*), or in rounded fragments and grains (*stream tin.*

Cleavage, prismatic along ∞P and ∞P∞, rather imperfect; brittle. H. = 6...7; G = 6·8...7·0. Translucent or opaque; adamantine or resinous. White, but usually gray, yellow, red, brown, and black; streak white, light-gray, or brown. B.B. in the forceps infusible; on charcoal, in the inner flame (more easily with soda), reduced to tin. Not affected by acids. Chem. com. 78·6 tin and 21·4 oxygen, but often mixed with peroxide of iron or manganese, tantalic acid, or

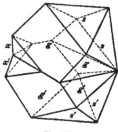

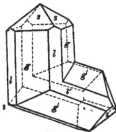

Fig. 230. Fig. 231.

silica. Cornwall, Bohemia, Saxony, Galicia in Spain, and Portugal; also Silesia, the Haute Vienne in France, Greenland, Sweden, Russia, North and South America, Malacca, Banca, and Queensland, Australia. The only ore of tin. The produce of the British mines in 1871 was 16,272 tons ore, yielding about 10,000 tons tin, worth 1½ million sterling, the average price being about £138 per ton. In the same year the Dutch mines produced 7500 tons.

Stannite.—Compact, brittle; H. = 6·75; G. = 3·5. Yellowish-white to yellow. Chem. com. 36·5 tin oxide with silica and alumina. A mixture with quartz. Cornwall.

*336. WOLFRAM.—(Fe, Mn) $\ddot{W}$ = [FeO, MnO . WO²].
Monoclinic; C. = 89° 22'; ∞P (r) 100° 37', $-\frac{1}{2}$P°∞ (t) 61° 54', P°∞ (u) 68° 6', ∞P∞ (M), (Fig. 232). Macles rather common, also columnar, laminar, or coarse granular. Cleavage, clinodiagonal very perfect; orthodiagonal imperfect; fracture uneven. H. = 5...5·5; G. = 7·1...7·5. Opaque; resinous, metallic-adamantine on the cleavage. Brownish-black; streak black (varieties with most iron) to

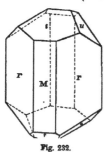

reddish-brown (most manganese). Sometimes weak magnetic. B.B. on charcoal fuses to a magnetic globule covered with small crystals ; soluble in warm h. acid, leaving a yellow residue. Chem. com. 76 tungstic acid, 9·5 to 20 protoxide of iron, and 4 to 15 protoxide of manganese, in some with a little lime or magnesia, in others 0·3 to 1·1 niobic acid. Altenberg, Geyer, Ehrenfriedersdorf, Schlaggenwald, Zinnwald, the Harz ; East Pool, Carnbroe, and mines near Redruth ; Rona in the Hebrides ; also the Ural, Ceylon, and North America. Used for preparing pigments and steel.

Fig. 232.

Blumite, Megabasite, yellowish or clove brown. H. = 3·5, with 71·5 tungstic acid, 23·1 manganese protoxide, and 5·4 iron protoxide, from Schlaggenwald and Peru, is closely related. Also *Ferberite,* from Spain.

337. COLUMBITE, Niobite.—$(\ddot{F}e, \ddot{M}n) (\ddot{N}b, \ddot{T}a)$.

Rhombic; P middle edge 83° 8', ∞P 135° 40', 2 P̄∞ 112° 26'. Tabular, or broad prismatic (Fig. 233 in other position). Macles with chief axes at 62° 40'; also foliated or granular. Cleavage, brachydiagonal very distinct, macrodiagonal less so, and basal imperfect. H. = 6 ; G. = 5·4...

Fig. 233.

6·4. Opaque ; metallic adamantine. Brownish or iron black ; streak reddish brown or black. B.B. infusible ; not affected by acids. Chem. com. 13 to 18 protoxide of iron, 3 to 7 protoxide of manganese, and 77 to 81 niobic acid (but 3 to 35 tantalic acid in some), with a little oxide of tin or copper. Middletown and Haddam in Connecticut, and Chesterfield in Massachusetts ; Rabenstein near Bodenmais, and Ilmen Mountains in granite. Evigtok, Greenland, in cryolite.

Columbite and tantalite are both isomorphous mixtures of niobic and tantalic acids with protoxide of iron (or manganese). The pure columbite would give 78·8 niobic acid, pure tantalite 86 tantalic acid. In both G. rises as the tantalic acid is more abundant; but the columbite is the best crystallised and in the finest crystals.

338. SAMARSKITE, Uranotantalite, Yttroilmenite.

Rhombic; isomorphous with columbite; mostly in flat somewhat polygonal grains. Fracture conchoidal; brittle. H. = 5·5; G. = 5·6...5·75. Opaque; strong semi-metallic. Velvet-black; streak dark reddish-brown. B.B. fuses on the edges to a black glass. In the closed tube decrepitates, yields water, incandesces, and becomes brown. Soluble in h. acid with difficulty, but wholly, to a greenish fluid. Chem. com. 50 niobic acid, 12 iron (with some manganese) protoxide, 11 uranium oxide, 6 thorium oxide, 4 zirconia, and 16 yttria with lime and magnesia. Ilmen Mountains in miascite.

339. TANTALITE.—Fe (T̈a, N̈b), *or* [Fe O . Ta³ O⁵].

Rhombic; P with polar edges 126° and 112° 30′, middle 91° 42′. Cleavages all very indistinct; fracture conchoidal or uneven. H. = 6...6·5; G. = 6·1...8. Opaque; semimetallic, adamantine, or resinous. Iron-black; streak cinnamon or coffee brown. B.B. infusible; scarcely affected by acids. Chem. com. 76 to 42 tantalic acid, 7·5 to 40 niobic acid, 9 to 16 iron protoxide, and 1 to 6 manganese protoxide. But some 1 to 10 tin oxide. (*Cassiterotantalite*) also in union with iron (manganese) protoxide. Kimito and Tammela in Finnland; Broddbo and Finbo near Fahlun, and Chanteloube near Limoges; always in granite.

Tapiolite from Tammela, black with bright lustre. G. = 7·17...7·37, has the same composition, but is tetragonal like rutile. P middle edge 84° 52′.

340. YTTROTANTALITE.—(Ẏ, Ċa, Ḟe, U̇)³ (T̈a, Ẅ, N̈b).

In two varieties—(*a*) *Black Y.*, Rhombic, in short prismatic or tabular crystals, also in grains and lamellæ. Cleavage, brachydiagonal indistinct; fracture conchoidal or uneven. Opaque, or in thin splinters translucent. Iron-black, semimetallic lustre, and greenish-gray streak. H. = 5·5; G. = 5·4...5·7. (*b*) *Yellow Y.*, Amorphous, yellowish-brown, or yellow, often striped or spotted; resinous or vitreous; streak white. G. = 5·46...5·88. Both varieties

B.B. infusible, but become brown or yellow; not affected by acids. Chem. com. 57 to 60 tantalic acid, 1 to 8 tungstic acid, 0 to 20 niobic acid, 20 to 38 yttria, 0·5 to 6 lime, 0·5 to 6 uranium peroxide, and 0·5 to 3·5 iron peroxide. Ytterby, and near Fahlun. *Hjelmite* is very like Black Y. *Azorite*, minute, greenish or yellowish white tetragonal pyramids from the Azores, seems a tantalate of lime. The *Brown Yttrotantalite* is Fergusonite.

341. EUXENITE.—$\dot{Y}$, $\dot{U}$, $\dot{C}e$, $\dot{C}a$ ($\ddot{N}b$, $\ddot{T}i$).
Monoclinic; also compact, with no trace of cleavage. Fracture imperfect conchoidal. H.= 6·5; G.= 4·6...4·9. Opaque; thin splinters reddish-brown translucent; metallic vitreous. Brownish-black; streak reddish-brown. B.B. infusible; not affected by acids. Chem. com. 18 to 38 niobic acid, 14 to 35 titanic acid, 13 to 29 yttria, 5 to 8 uranium protoxide, and 3 to 8 cerium protoxide, chiefly; the water is not essential. Hitteroe and Arendal.

342. FERGUSONITE.—$(\dot{Y}, \dot{E}r, \dot{C}e)^3 (\ddot{N}b, \ddot{T}a)$.
Tetragonal and hemihedric; P 128° 28′. Usual form $\frac{1}{3}3P\frac{4}{3}.P.\frac{1}{3}\infty P\frac{4}{3}.0P$ (z, s, r, i, Fig. 234). Cleavage,

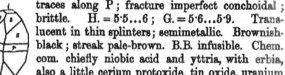

traces along P; fracture imperfect conchoidal; brittle. H.= 5·5...6; G.= 5·6...5·9. Translucent in thin splinters; semimetallic. Brownish-black; streak pale-brown. B.B. infusible. Chem. com. chiefly niobic acid and yttria, with erbia, also a little cerium protoxide, tin oxide, uranium oxide, and iron protoxide. Cape Farewell in Greenland, Ytterby, and Riesengebirge.

Fig. 234.

Tyrite, brown, resinous or semimetallic; H.= 6·5; G. = 5·13...5·36; Helle, near Arendal; is similar or identical.

343. AESCHYNITE.
Rhombic; ∞P (*m*) 128° 6′, 2$\bar{P}\infty$ (*x*) 73° 10′. Crystals long prismatic (Fig. 235). Cleavage, traces; fracture imperfect conchoidal. H.= 5...5·5; G.= 4·9...5·1. Opaque; submetallic or resinous. Iron-black or brown; streak yellowish-brown. B.B. swells and becomes yellow or brown, but is infusible; not soluble in h. acid, partially in con. s. acid. Chem. com. about 51 niobic and titanic acids with

Fig. 235.

thorium oxide (16) and cerium protoxide (18) chiefly, but also some lanthanium and didymium oxides, and other substances. Miask in the Ural.

*344. SPHENE, Titanite.—$\dot{C}a \ddot{S}i^2 + \dot{C}a \ddot{T}i^2$.

Monoclinic ; C. = 85° 22′ ; ∞P (*l*) 133° 52′, $\frac{1}{2}$P∞ (*x*) 55° 21, P°∞ (*y*) 34° 21′, 0P (*P*), ∞P°∞ (*q*), ∞P°3 (*M*), and $\frac{4}{3}$P°2 (*n*) 136° 12′. Crystals horizontal prismatic or tabular, or very often oblique prismatic (Figs. 236, 237). Macles

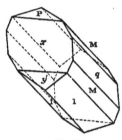   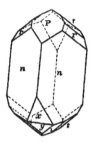

Fig. 236.   Fig. 237.

frequent ; also granular or foliated. Cleavage, in many $_{,}$∞P ; in others P°∞ (*r*) 113° 30′, imperfect. H. = 5...5·5 ; G. = 3·4...3·6. Semitransparent or opaque ; adamantine or often resinous. Brown, yellow, or green. B.B. fuses on the edges to a dark glass ; with salt of phosphorus in the red. flame reaction for titanic acid ; wholly soluble in s. acid, which forms sulphate of lime. Chem. com. 31·3 silica, 40·4 titanic acid, and 28·3 lime, with 0 to 5 iron protoxide in the brown varieties. Dauphiné near Mont Blanc, St. Gotthard, Tyrol, Arendal, Sweden, Saxony, France, America, and the Ural ; also Lake Laach and Vesuvius ; in Scotland, in Criffell, near King's House, Ben Nevis, Strontian, Loch Ness, Aberdeenshire, Fetlar and Burra in Zetland.

Greenovite, flesh-red, from St. Marcel in Piedmont, with much protoxide of manganese, is not distinct. *Schorlamite*, tesseral, black shining ; H. = 7...7·5 ; G. = 3·78...3·86 ; from Arkansas, is similar.

345. BROOKITE.—T̈i.

Rhombic; P (*e*) with polar edges 135° 37′ and 101° 3′. ∞P̄ 2 (*m*) 99° 50′, ∞P̄∞ (*h*) (Fig. 238). (Monoclinic like Wolfram, *Schrauf.*) Cleavage macrodiagonal. H. = 5·5...6; G. = 3·86...4·2. Opaque or translucent; metallic adamantine. Yellowish, reddish, or hair brown; streak yellowish-white. B.B. infusible; with salt of phosphorus forms a brownish-yellow glass. Chem. com. titanic acid, with 1·4 to 4·5 per cent peroxide of iron. Bourg d'Oisans, Chamouni, and near Amstäg in the Canton Uri, Miask, Magnet Cove in Arkansas (*Arkansite*); Snowdon and Tremaddoc, in North Wales.

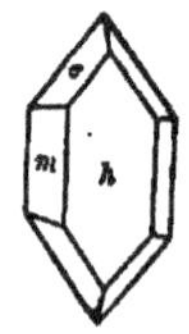

Fig. 238.

**346. RUTILE, Nigrine.—T̈i.

Tetragonal; P 84° 40′, P∞ 65° 35′. Crystals ∞P. ∞P∞. P, and ∞P 3 . P (*h, c*, Fig. 239). Macles very common (like Fig. 231) with chief axes at 114° 26′; also embedded or granular. Cleavage, ∞P and ∞P∞ perfect. H. =6...6·5; G. = 4·2...4·3. Translucent or opaque; metallic adamantine. Reddish-brown to red, also yellowish and black (*Nigrine*); streak yellowish-brown. B.B. unchanged alone; with borax in the ox. flame forms a greenish, in the red. flame a violet glass; not affected by acids. Chem. com. titanic acid, with 1·5 per cent or more peroxide of iron. Alps, Spain, St. Yrieux near Limoges, Norway, the Ural, Brazil, and North America; Craig Cailleach near Killin, Ben-y-gloe, and Crianlarich in Perthshire, Ballater in Aberdeenshire, Hillswick and Burra in Zetland. Used in painting porcelain to produce a yellow colour.

Fig. 239.

347. ANATASE, Octaëdrite.—T̈i.

Tetragonal; P 136° 36′. Crystals P . OP (*P, o*, Fig. 240), or P . ¼P. Cleavage, basal and P both perfect; brittle. H. = 5·5...6; G. =3·8...3·93. Semitransparent or opaque; metallic adamantine. Indigo-blue or almost black, red, yellow, or brown, rarely colourless; streak white.

B.B. infusible; only soluble in warm con. s. acid. Chem.
com. titanic acid with a little peroxide of iron, or
rarely tin oxide. The Alps, as Bourg d'Oisans,
Dauphiné, Valois, and Salzburg; Hof in Bavaria,
at Slidre in Norway, Ural, Minas Geraes in
Brazil; near Liskeard and Tintagel in Cornwall;
also at Tavistock and Tremaddoc.

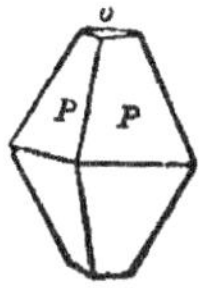

Fig. 240.

348. POLYMIGNITE.

Rhombic; P with polar edges 136° 28′ and 116° 22′,
∞P 109° 46′. Crystals long prismatic, and vertically
striated. Cleavage imperfect; fracture conchoidal. H. =
6·5; G. = 4·8. Opaque; semimetallic. Iron-black; streak
dark brown. B.B. infusible; soluble in con. h. acid. Analysis by Berzelius—46·30 titanic acid, 14·14 zirconia, 12·20
iron peroxide, 2·70 manganese peroxide, 5·00 cerium peroxide, 11·50 yttria, 4·20 lime (= 96·04). Fredriksvärn.

349. POLYCRASE.—4 Ṙ T̈i + Ṙ N̈b.

Rhombic, six-sided tables, ∞P 140°. Cleavage, not
observable; fracture conchoidal. H. = 5...6; G. = 5·0...
5·15. Opaque, or in very fine splinters translucent yellowish brown. Black; streak grayish-brown. B.B. decrepitates violently and incandesces, but is infusible; imperfectly soluble in warm h. acid, wholly in s. acid. Chem.
com. 27 to 29 titanic acid, 20 to 25 niobic (4 tantalic) acid,
23 to 24 yttria, 7 to 9 erbia, also 2·6 to 2·9 Ċe, 7·7 to 5·6
U̇, 2·7 to 0·5 Ḟe, and 4 to 3 water. Hitterö.

350. PEROWSKITE.—Ċa T̈i.

Tesseral; especially ∞O∞, also 3O3 and many other
forms. Cleavage hexahedral. H. = 5·5; G. = 4. Opaque,
or translucent on the edges; adamantine. Dark reddish-
brown, also grayish or iron-black. B.B. infusible; slightly
affected by acids. Chem. com. 58·9 titanic acid, and 41·1
lime, with 2 to 5 iron protoxide. Slatoust, Kaiserstuhl.

351. MENGITE, *G. Rose.*—F̈e, Z̈r, T̈i.

Rhombic; ∞P 136° 20′. The crystals small, prismatic;
fracture uneven. H. = 5...5·5; G. = 5·48. Opaque; semimetallic. Iron-black; streak chestnut-brown. B.B. infusible,
but becomes magnetic; almost wholly soluble in warm con.
s. acid. Ilmen mountains. *Mengite* of Brooke is monazite.

352. PECHURANE, Pitch-blende.—Ü Ü̈.

Tesseral; O; also granular, reniform, columnar, or lamellar. H. = 5...6; G. = 6·5 or 7·9...8. Opaque; imperfect metallic or resinous. Grayish, greenish, or brownish-black; streak greenish-black. B.B. infusible; not soluble in h. acid, but easily in warm n. acid. Chem. com. proto-peroxide of uranium, or 84·78 uranium, and 15·22 oxygen, but with lead, iron, arsenic, lime, magnesia, silica, and other impurities. Some contain vanadium, others also selenium (*Gummierz*, H. = 2·5...3). Johann-Georgenstadt, Marienberg, Annaberg, Przibram, Rezbanya, and near Redruth in Cornwall. Used in porcelain-painting.

Pittinerz, olive-green streak; H. = 3·0...3·5; G. = 4·8... 5·0; and *Coracite*, from Lake Superior, seem mixtures. *Liebigite*, crystalline, concretionary, apple-green, and *Voglite*, bright green pearly scales, found on pechurane at Joachimsthal, are carbonates, the first of uranium protoxide and lime, the second also of copper protoxide, both with water.

353. PLATTNERITE.—Ṗb.

Hexagonal; ∞P.0P.P. Cleavage indistinct; fracture uneven; brittle. G. = 9·39...9·44. Opaque; metallic adamantine. Iron-black; streak brown. Chem. com. 86·2 lead and 13·8 oxygen, with trace of sulphuric acid. Leadhills in Scotland.

FAMILY III.—MANGANESE ORES.

Crystallisation rhombic, tetragonal, and monoclinic. Crystals often prismatic. H. = 1...7; G. = 2·3...5. Opaque; lustre more or less perfect metallic. Colour black or brown. B.B. infusible, mostly give out much oxygen, and do *not* become magnetic; soluble in hydrochloric acid, with fumes of chlorine. The solution, saturated with carbonate of lime and filtered, gives, with chloride of lime, a copious dark-brown precipitate which acts like manganese oxide. Occur chiefly in veins in the older rocks, often along with barytes.

*354. PYROLUSITE.—M̈n.

Rhombic; ∞P (*M*) 93° 40′; P̆∞ (*d*) 140°; ∞P̄∞ (*w*) and ∞P̆∞ (*v*). Crystals short, prismatic, or pointed (Fig.

241); generally massive or reniform, and radiating, fibrous, earthy, or compact. Cleavage, ∞P, also macro- and brachy-diagonal; rather brittle or friable. H. = 2...2·5; G. = 4·7 ...5·0. Opaque; semimetallic or silky. Dark steel-gray, bluish, or iron-black; streak black and soiling. B.B. infusible, loses oxygen, and becomes brown; soluble in h. acid, with large evolution of chlo-rine. Chem. com. 63 manganese and 37 oxygen. Ilmenau, Ihlefeld, Goslar, Johann-Georgenstadt; also France, Hungary, Brazil, Cornwall, and Devon. Used for producing oxygen, chlorine, and chloride of lime, re-moving the brown and green tints in glass, in painting glass and enamel work, and for glazing and colouring pot-tery. Mostly a product of oxidation of polianite, man-ganite, and other manganese ores.

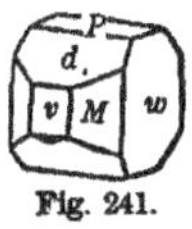

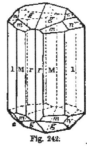

Fig. 241.

Varvicite.—With 5 water, pseudomorphs after calc-spar; also crystals with ∞P = 99° 36', or columnar, and fibrous. G. = 4·5...4·6. Semimetallic. Iron-black to steel-gray; streak black. Warwickshire.

355. POLIANITE.—M̈n.

Rhombic; ∞P 92° 52', P̆∞ 118°. Crystals like pyro-lusite, and vertically striated; also granular. Cleavage, brachydiagonal perfect. H. = 6·5...7; G. = 4·84...4·88. Weak metallic. Light steel-gray. Chem. com. identical with pyrolusite, which thus a less hard variety. Platten, Schneeberg, Johann-Georgenstadt, and Cornwall.

356. MANGANITE.—M̈n + Ḧ, *or* [Mn² O³ + H² O].

Rhombic, sometimes hemihedric; ∞P (*M*) 99° 40', ∞P̆2 (*l*) 118° 44', P̄∞ 114° 19'; also P̄3 (*g*), ∞P̆2 (*r*) 2P̄ (*m*), and 2P̆2 (*n*), (Fig. 242). Crystals pris-matic, vertically striated, and in bundles; also columnar or fibrous. Macles common. Cleavage, brachydiagonal very perfect, basal and ∞P less perfect; rather brittle. H. = 3.5...4; G. = 4·3...4·4. Opaque; imperfect metallic. Dark steel-gray to iron-black, or often brownish-black and tar-

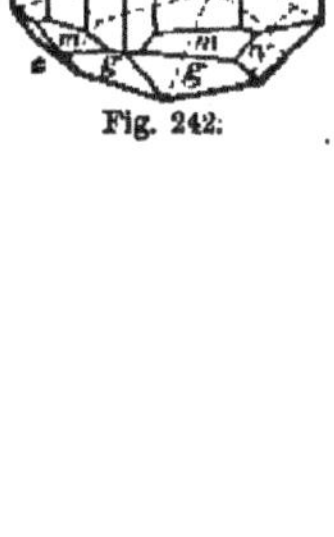

Fig. 242.

nished ; streak brown. B.B. infusible ; soluble in warm con. h. acid. Chem. com. 89·9 manganese peroxide and 10·1 water. Ihlefeld, in the Harz, Thuringia, Christiansand in Norway, Undenaes in Sweden, Nova Scotia, and Danestown near Aberdeen.

357. HAUSMANNITE.—$\dot{M}n + \overset{...}{M}n$, or $Mn^2\dot{M}n$.

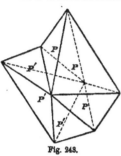

Fig. 243.

Tetragonal ; P 116° 59′, P∞ 98° 32′. Crystals P or P . ½P. Macles common (Fig. 243) ; also granular. Cleavage, basal rather perfect, less distinct P and P∞ ; fracture uneven. H. = 5·5 ; G. = 4·7...4·8. Opaque ; strong metallic ; Iron-black ; streak brown. B.B. like peroxide of manganese ; soluble in h. acid, with escape of chlorine ; powder colours con. s. acid bright red in a short time. Chem. com. 31 protoxide and 69 peroxide of manganese, or 72 manganese and 28 oxygen. Ihlefeld, Ilmenau, and in Sweden.

358. BRAUNITE.—$\overset{...}{M}n$, or [3 $Mn^2 O^2$+ MnO . SiO^2, *Rams.*] Tetragonal ; P 108° 39′; hence almost an octahedron. Crystals P and P . 0P. Cleavage, P rather perfect ; brittle. H. = 6...6·5 ; G. = 4·7.,.4·9. Imperfect metallic. Colour and streak dark brownish-black. B.B., and with acids like manganite. Chem. com. 70 manganese and 30 oxygen, but some 7 to 15 silica. Elgersburg, Oehrenstock, Ihlefeld, and St. Marcel.

359. PSILOMELANE.—$(\dot{M}n, \dot{B}a, \dot{K}, \dot{C}u) Mn^2 + \dot{H}$. Massive, botryoidal, or stalactitic. Fracture conchoidal or uneven. H. = 5·5...6 ; G. = 4·1...4·3. Dull or glimmering. Iron-black or bluish-black ; streak brownish-black and glistening. B.B. infusible. Chem. com. 4·7 to 11 protoxide of manganese, 80 hyperoxide (but 20 to 50 mixed), 6 to 16 baryta, 2 to 5 potash, 0 to 1 copper, and 0·5 cobalt protoxide ; and thus a mixture. Schneeberg, Ilmenau, France, Vermont, Cornwall, and Devon.

360. CREDNERITE.—$\dot{C}u^2 \overset{...}{Mn}{}^2$.

Granular, foliated. Cleavage, very distinct along one face of an oblique rhombic prism, less so two others. H. = 4·5...5 ; G. = 4·9...5·05. Iron-black ; streak brownish-black. B.B. very thin foliæ scarce fusible on the edges ; with salt of phosphorus in the inner flame forms a glass, first green, then copper-red ; in h. acid it forms a green solution. Chem. com. 43·3 copper protoxide and 56·7 per-oxide of manganese. Friedrichsrode in Thuringia.

361. CUPREOUS MANGANESE.—$(\overset{..}{Mn}, \dot{Cu}) \overset{..}{Mn}{}^2 + 2 \dot{H}$.

Amorphous ; botryoidal, stalactitic, or earthy. Rather brittle or friable. H. = 3·5 or less ; G. = 3·1...3·2. Vitre-ous. Black, inclining to brown or blue ; streak similar. B.B. fusible, and yields copper. Contains 16 to 17 copper protoxide and 55 oxides of manganese, 15 to 18 water, with baryta, lime, protoxide of cobalt, and other substances ; thus scarcely a true species. Silesia, Saxony, the Harz, and Cornwall.

Black copper, with 29·5 water and 30 manganese, 11·5 copper and 28 iron peroxide, is similar. Harz.

362. EARTHY COBALT.—$(\dot{C}o, \dot{C}u) \overset{..}{Mn}{}^2 + 4 \dot{H}$.

Amorphous ; reniform, sectile. H. = 1...1·5 ; G. = 2·1 2·2. Bluish or brownish black ; streak black, shining, and leaves a mark. B.B. infusible. Contains about 20 cobalt protoxide, 4·5 copper protoxide, and 21 water. Saalfeld, Glücksbrun, Riechelsdorf, and Alderley Edge in Cheshire. *Horn-cobalt*, Siegen, is a mixture with quartz.

*363. WAD.—$\overset{..}{Mn} (\dot{C}a, \dot{B}a, \dot{K}) \overset{..}{Mn}{}^2 + 3 \dot{H}$.

Massive ; reniform, stalactitic, or froth-like ; also scaly, earthy, or compact. Very soft and sectile (rarely brittle, and H. = 3) ; G. = 2·3...3·7 ; or porous, and swims on water. Semimetallic, and shining or dull. Colour and streak brown or black. B.B. like peroxide of manganese ; soluble in h. acid. Chem. com. very uncertain. Saxony, Harz, France, Devonshire, and Cornwall. *Groroilite* is a variety, and *Newkirkite* related.

Ochres.

The following substances, chiefly products of decomposition, and all compact, earthy, or disseminated, and scarcely true mineral species, may be described here :—

364. Cobalt-ochre, Earthy Cobalt.—$\ddot{\text{Fe}}$, $\ddot{\text{As}}$, $\dot{\text{Co}}$, $\dot{\text{Ca}}$, $\dot{\text{H}}$. H. = 1...2 ; G. = 2...2·65. Yellowish-gray or brown to liver-brown ; streak brown or yellowish-gray and shining. In the closed tube yields water. B.B. emits odour of arsenic, and fuses to a black magnetic slag. Saalfeld, Riechelsdorf, Dauphiné, and other localities.

365. Molybdena-ochre.—$\dddot{\text{Mo}}$.
Opaque ; dull. Straw, sulphur, or orange yellow. B.B. fuses and smokes ; soluble in h. acid. Sweden, Norway, the Tyrol, and on Corybuy near Loch Creran in Scotland.

366. Bismuth-ochre.—$\ddot{\text{Bi}}$.
Very soft and friable. G. = 4·36...4·7. Opaque ; dull, or glimmering. Straw-yellow to light-gray or green. B.B. fusible and easily reduced ; easily soluble in nitric acid. Schneeberg, Siberia, and St. Agnes in Cornwall.

367. Antimony-ochre.—$\ddot{\text{Sb}}$, $\dot{\text{H}}$.
Soft and friable. G. = 3·7...3·8. Opaque ; dull or glimmering, with glistening streak. Yellow, yellowish-gray, or white. B.B. easily reduced. Harz, Hungary, Saxony, France, Spain, and Padstow in England.

368. Stiblite.—$\ddot{\text{Sb}}$ $\ddot{\text{Sb}}$, $\dot{\text{H}}$.
Granular or compact. H. = 5·5 ; G. = 5·28. Resinous or dull. Yellowish-white or yellow. B.B. not reduced alone, but easily with soda. Chem. com. 75 antimony, 20·5 oxygen, and 5·5 water. Kremnitz, Felsöbanya, and Mexico.

369. Tungsten-ochre.—$\dddot{\text{W}}$.
Soft. Earthy ; dull. Yellow or yellowish-green. Soluble in caustic ammonia. Huntington, Connecticut.

370. Uranium-ochre.—$\ddot{\text{U}}$, $\dot{\text{H}}$.
Sectile, soft, and friable. Opaque ; dull. Straw, sulphur, or orange yellow. In the closed tube yields water,

and becomes red. B.B. in the red. flame becomes green, but does not fuse; easily soluble in acids. Joachimsthal, Johann-Georgenstadt, and St. Symphorien in France.

371. MINIUM (Native).—$\ddot{P}b + 2\,\dot{P}b$.

Massive or earthy. H. = 2...3; G. = 4·6. Dull resinous. Aurora-red; streak orange-yellow. B.B. fuses easily, and reduced; in h. acid loses its colour, and changed into chloride of lead. Chem. com. 90·7 lead and 9·3 oxygen. Schlangenberg in Siberia, Badenweiler, Anglesea, Grassington Moor and Weirdale in Yorkshire.

372. LEAD-OCHRE.—$\dot{P}b$.

G. = 8·0. Opaque; dull. Sulphur or lemon yellow. Popocatepetl in Mexico.

373. CHROME-OCHRE.—$\ddot{C}r$.

Opaque, or translucent on the edges; dull. Grass-green to siskin or yellowish green. B.B. infusible; soluble to a green fluid in solution of potash. Unst in Zetland, Creuzat in France, and Sweden. *Wolchonskoite*, emerald or blackish green, from Okhansk in Perm, is similar.

374. TELLURITE.—$\ddot{T}e$.

Spherical, and radiated fibrous. Yellowish or grayish white. Siebenbürg.

FAMILY IV.—THE RED COPPER ORES.

Tesseral and hexagonal. H. = 3·5...4·5; G. = 5·4...6. Translucent; metallic. Red or dark-gray. Soluble in acids, and B.B. fusible, except zincite. Are oxides of copper or zinc.

*375. CUPRITE, Red Copper Ore.—$\dot{C}u = [Cu^2\,O]$.

Tesseral; O, ∞O, and ∞O∞; granular or compact. Cleavage, octahedral rather perfect; brittle. H. = 3·5...4; G = 5·7...6·0. Translucent or opaque; metallic-adamantine. Cochineal to brick red, with a lead-gray tarnish; or crimson in transmitted light; streak brownish-red. B.B. on charcoal becomes black, fuses, and reduced; soluble in acids and ammonia. Chem. com. 88·9 copper and 11·1 oxygen. Siberia, the Bannat, Chessy near Lyons, Linares in Spain, Ural, South Africa; and in the Huel Gorland, Huel Muttrel, Carvath, and United Mines in Cornwall. Valuable copper ore.

376. CHALCOTRICHITE.

Rhombic or tesseral in fine capillary crystals (prisms or cubes). Cochineal and crimson red. In other characters like cuprite. Rheinbreitenbach, Moldawa, and Huel Gorland, Carharrack, and St. Day in Cornwall.

Tile-ore. — Reddish-brown, or brick-red and earthy. Chem. com. suboxide of copper, mixed with much peroxide of iron and other substances. Bannat, Thuringia, Cornwall, and Shropshire.

377. TENORITE.—Ċu.

Rhombic, in thin tables; also fine scaly or earthy. Translucent and brown; metallic. Dark steel-gray or black. On lava, Vesuvius.

378. MELACONITE.—Ċu.

Tesseral; $\infty O \infty . O$; also compact. H. = 3...4; G. = 6 ...6·3. Steel-gray or black. B.B. infusible in ox. flame; soluble in acids. Chem. com. copper protoxide, in some a little iron peroxide or silica. Near Lake Superior. Maskelyne describes melaconite from Cornwall as monoclinic with Ċ. = 80° 28′. Copper protoxide would thus seem trimorphous.

379. ZINCITE, Red Zinc.—Żn.

Hexagonal; granular or foliated. Cleavage, basal and ∞P very perfect. H. = 4...4·5; G. = 5·4...5·5. Translucent on the edges; adamantine. Blood or hyacinth red; streak orange-yellow. B.B. infusible, but phosphoresces. Chem. com. 80·26 zinc and 19·74 oxygen, but with 3 to 12 manganese peroxide. Franklin and Sterling in New Jersey. Ore of zinc.

FAMILY V.—THE WHITE ANTIMONY ORES.

380. VALENTINITE, White Antimony.—S̈b, *or* [Sb² O³].

Rhombic; ∞P 137°, P̄∞ 70½°. Crystals $\infty P̄\infty . \infty P$. P̄∞ (*M*, *h*, *p*, Fig. 244); broad prismatic, or long tabular;

also granular, columnar, or foliated. Cleavage, ∞P very
perfect, brachydiagonal imperfect. H. = 2·5...3 ; G. = 5·5
...5·6. Translucent ; adamantine or pearly.
Yellowish and grayish-white, brown, gray, and
rarely peach-blossom red ; streak white. B.B.
becomes yellow, and fuses (in the flame of a
candle) to a white mass. In the closed tube
wholly sublimes ; on charcoal forms a thick
white coating ; easily soluble in h. acid ; the
solution yields with water a white precipitate. 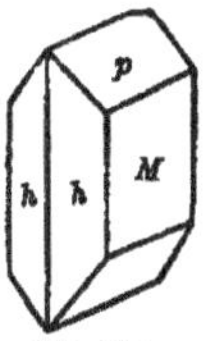
Fig. 244.
Chem. com. 83·6 antimony and 16·4 oxygen. Przibram,
Braunsdorf in Saxony, Harz, Hungary, Allemont in Dauphiné, and Siberia.

381. SENARMONTITE.—S̈b.
Tesseral ; O ; also massive. Cleavage, O imperfect.
H. = 2...2·5 ; G. = 5·2...5·3. Transparent to translucent ;
brilliant resinous or adamantine. White or gray. B.B.
and chem. com. like valentinite. Sensa, near Constantine
in Algeria, Perneck in Hungary, South Ham in Canada.

382. CERVANTITE.—S̈b S̈b.
Acicular or incrusting. G. = 4·1. Resinous. Yellow
or white. B.B. infusible, but reduced on charcoal ; soluble
in h. acid. Chem. com. 79·5 antimony, 20·5 oxygen.
Cervantes in Spain, Auvergne, Hungary, and Pereta in
Tuscany.

383. ARSENITE.—Äs.
Tesseral ; O (but also rhombic in smelting processes) ;
usually capillary, flaky, or pulverulent. Cleavage octahedral. H. = 1·5 (3, *Breit.*) ; G. = 3·69...3·72. Translucent ;
vitreous. Colourless and white. Taste sweetish astringent ;
highly poisonous. B.B. in closed tube sublimes in small
octahedrons ; on charcoal volatilises with strong smell of
garlic. Chem. com. arsenious acid, with 75·76 arsenic and
24·24 oxygen. Andreasberg, Joachimsthal, Kapnik, Alsace,
and Pyrenees. The capillary varieties are probably rhombic, like the artificial, and the substance dimorphous.

T

ORDER V.

NATIVE METALS

FORM two groups or families. The first or Electropositive group—including platina, palladium, iridium, gold, silver, mercury, lead, tin, copper, and iron—have crystallisation tesseral, mostly in regular octahedrons or cubes. Some of them—as platina, palladium, iridium, and iron—are infusible B.B., gold, silver, and others easily fusible, and mercury fluid at ordinary temperatures. The second or Electronegative group — including antimony, arsenic, osmium, tellurium, zinc, and bismuth—have crystallisation hexagonal or rhombohedral, with $R = 86°$ to $88°$ (thus almost an octahedron); they are easily fusible and burn and fume.

Metals range in H. from mercury (fluid) $= 0$ and lead $= 1\cdot5$ to iridium $6\ldots7$; in G. from arsenic $= 5\cdot7$ to iridium $= 23\cdot0$. They are all opaque, have metallic lustre and pure metallic colours (not lead-gray nor black); streak similar and shining. Are simple metals or alloys—that is, combinations of metals, as isomorphous elements in indefinite proportion.

*384. PLATINA.—Pt, Fe.

Tesseral; very rarely in small cubes, commonly in minute, flat, or obtuse grains and roundish lumps. Cleavage wanting; fracture hackly; malleable and ductile. H. $= 4\ldots5$; G. $= 17\ldots19$ (hammered $21\cdot23$). Steel-gray, inclining to silver-white. Some slightly magnetic (from iron). Very difficultly or not fusible; in nitrochloric acid forms a red coloured solution. Chem. com. platina, but always alloyed with 4 to 13 iron, 1 to 5 iridium, osmium, rhodium, palladium, or other metals. Found in diluvial deposits from serpentine in Columbia, Brazil, and St. Domingo; in the Ural; also in California, Canada, Borneo, the Harz, and France. The largest mass from South America weighs

1 lb. 9⅜ oz. ; from the Ural, 18⅓ lb. English avoirdupois. Its hardness, infusibility, power of resisting acids, and other properties, render platina a very important material for chemical, mathematical, and philosophical instruments. In Russia also used for money.

Platiniridium, Brazil, in minute silver-white grains, G. = 16·94, contains 55·44 platina, 27·79 iridium, 6·86 rhodium, 4·14 iron, 3·30 copper, and 0·49 palladium.

385. PALLADIUM.—Pd.

Tesseral ; in very minute octahedrons ; mostly small grains or scales. Malleable. H. = 4·5...5 ; G. = 11·8...12·2. Light steel-gray or silvery-white. B.B. infusible ; in nitric acid forms slowly a brownish-red solution. Chem. com. palladium, alloyed with platinum and iridium. Brazil, in gold sands ; Tilkerode in the Harz, in very small, brilliant, hexagonal tables ;—hence rhombohedric and dimorphous. Used for astronomical and other instruments.

386. OSMIUM-IRIDIUM.—Ir, Os.

(*a.*) *Light Osmium-iridium* or *Newjanskite.*—Hexagonal ; P 124° ; 0P . P . ∞P (Fig. 245), more common in small flat grains. Cleavage, basal rather perfect. Slightly malleable. Tin-white. H. = 7 ; G. = 19·38...19·47. B.B.

Fig. 245.

not altered. Not affected by acids. Analysis, 46·77 iridium, 49·34 osmium, 3·15 rhodium, 0·74 iron, and trace of palladium. Newjansk in Ural, Brazil.

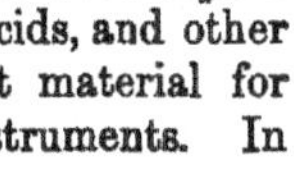

(*b.*) *Dark Osmium-iridium—Iridosmium* or *Sisserkite.*— Rhombohedral ; R = 84° 28′. Lead-gray. H. = 7 ; G. = 21·118 (*G. Rose*). B.B. on charcoal becomes black, with a very strong odour of osmium ; in the flame of a spirit-lamp shines brightly and colours it yellowish-red. In one variety Berzelius found 25 iridium and 75 osmium, or Ir Os³ ; in another, 20 iridium and 80 osmium, or Ir Os⁴. Nischne-Tagilsk in Ural, Brazil, and California. Used for pointing gold pens.

387. IRIDIUM.—Ir, Pt.

Tesseral ; ∞O∞ . O ; also small rounded grains. Cleavage, traces ; slightly malleable. H. = 6...7 ; G. = 21·57...

23·46. Silver-white, inclining to yellow on the surface. B.B. unalterable; insoluble in acids, even the nitrochloric. Chem. com., by Svanberg's analysis, 76·80 iridium, 19·64 platina, 0·89 palladium, and 1·78 copper. Nischne-Tagilsk and Newjansk. Used in porcelain-painting.

**388. GOLD.—Au.

Tesseral; O, $\infty O \infty$, ∞O, 3O3, $\infty O2$, and other forms. Crystals small, often elongated, deformed, and indistinct; also capillary, wire-like, arborescent, and in plates and grains. Remarkably ductile and malleable. H. = 2·5... 3·0; G. = 17·0...19·4. Gold-yellow to brass or bronze yellow. B.B. easily fusible; soluble in aqua regia, often with a precipitate of chloride of silver. The solution is yellow, and colours the skin deep purple-red. Chem. com. gold with silver to 38 per cent, and copper and iron under 1 per cent. In beds and veins, often with quartz, and in alluvial deposits in many parts of the world,—the Ural, Brazil, California, Australia; in the sand of many rivers, as the Rhine and Tagus; in Britain in many of the Cornish stream-works; in mineral lodes near Dolgelly, North Wales; in Scotland at Leadhills, Tyndrum, and Glen Coich, Perthshire; and in Ireland in Wicklow.

Australia yields above five millions sterling of gold annually; the United States (California, Nevada, etc.) about fifteen millions; and whole earth probably over twenty-two millions sterling.

Electrum or alloys of gold and silver occur in all proportions, with colour ranging from purest gold-yellow to brightest silver-white, and G. from 19·0 to 10·0. It has been proposed to limit the name to those with at least 15 per cent silver, and not less than 38 per cent gold.

Porpezite, from Porpez in Brazil, contains 10 palladium and 4 silver; *Rhodium-gold*, from Mexico, 34 to 43 rhodium, and G. = 15·5...16·8.

*389. SILVER.—Ag.

Tesseral; cubes and octahedrons; also ∞O, 3O3, and $\infty O2$. Crystals small and often misshapen; also capillary, filiform, arborescent, or tooth-like, and in leaves, plates, or

crusts.   Malleable and ductile.   H. = 2·5...3 ; G. = 10·1
...11·1.   Silver-white, but often tarnished yellow, red,
brown, or black.   B.B. easily fusible ; easily soluble in
nitric acid ; the solution colours the skin black.   Chem.
com. silver, often with copper, iron, gold (28 per cent),
platina, antimony, and arsenic.   Chiefly in veins, as at
Andreasberg, Freiberg, Johann-Georgenstadt, and Kongsberg in Norway (one mass 7½ cwts.); Lake Superior; Nevada,
Mexico and Peru ; St. Mewan, St. Stephens, Huel Mexico,
and Herland in Cornwall ; and at Alva in Stirlingshire.

Britain produced 761,490 ounces silver, worth £190,000,
in 1871, chiefly from lead ores.   The annual produce of
silver in the whole world, from all sources, is about eight
to ten millions sterling.

390. MERCURY, Native Quicksilver.—Hg.

Fluid ; but at − 40° congeals, and forms tesseral crys-
tals.   G. = 13·596 fluid, 15·612 solid.   Bright metallic ;
tin-white.   B.B. wholly volatile, or leaves a little silver.
Chem. com. mercury, sometimes with a little silver.   Idria,
Almaden, Wolfstein, and Mörsfeld on the Rhine, the Harz,
Peru, China, and California.

391. AMALGAM.—Ag Hg^2, and Ag Hg^3.

Tesseral ; ∞O, with 2O2, O, ∞O∞ , 3O⅔, and ∞O3 ;
also compact, or in crusts and plates.   Cleavage, traces
along ∞O ; rather brittle.   H. = 3...3·5 ; G. = 13·7...14·1.
Silver-white, and leaves the same colour on copper.   In the
closed tube yields mercury and leaves silver ; easily soluble
in nitric acid.   Chem. com. 35 and 26·5 per cent silver ;
but varieties with more silver at Kongsberg 86·3 and 95·1
occur.   Mörsfeld and Moschellandsberg, Hungary, Sala,
Allemont, and Almaden.   *Arquerite* in small octahedrons or
arborescent ; ductile and malleable.   H. = 2...2·5 ; G. =
10·8.   Chem. com. 86·5 silver.   Forms the chief ore in
the rich silver mines of Arqueros near Coquimbo.   *Gold-
Amalgam* with 39 gold, occurs in Columbia and California.

392. LEAD.—Pb.

Tesseral, but only capillary, filiform, or in thin plates.
Ductile and malleable.   H. = 1·5 ; G. = 11·36...11·40.

Bluish-gray, with a blackish tarnish. B.B. very easily fusible; on charcoal volatilises and forms a sulphur-yellow coating soluble in nitric acid. Said at Alston Moor, also near Kenmare in Ireland; in the gold sands of Olahpian, the Ural, and Altai; in dolomite at Pajsberg and Nordmark; in Mexico; and in meteoric iron from Chili.

393. TIN.—Sn.

This metal has not certainly been found native, though quoted from Cornwall and Miask. The fused metal crystallises in regular octahedrons. That formed by galvanic action is described as tetragonal, with P 57° 13′.

*394. COPPER.—Cu.

Tesseral; O, $\infty O \infty$, ∞O, $\infty O2$. Crystals small, and generally irregular and deformed. Macles united by a face of O. Often filiform and arborescent, or in plates and laminæ. Malleable and ductile. H. = 2·5...3; G. = 8·5... 8·9. Copper-red, with yellow or brown tarnish. B.B. rather easily fusible, colouring the flame green; readily soluble in nitric acid. In large masses (one measured 65 feet long, 32 broad, and 4 to 7 thick), near Lake Superior, with native silver. Cornwall, near Redruth and the Lizard; Yell in Zetland, Chessy near Lyons, the Bannat, and Hungary; Faroe Islands, Siberia, China, Canada, Mexico, Brazil, Chili, and near Ballarat, Victoria.

*395. IRON.—Fe.

Tesseral; chiefly the octahedron. Cleavage hexahedral, but often mere traces; fracture hackly; malleable and ductile. H. = 4·5; G. = 7·0...7·8. Steel-gray or iron-black, often with a blackish tarnish. Very magnetic. B.B. infusible, or only in thin plates with a strong heat; soluble in h. acid. Two varieties are distinguished :—

(*a.*) *Telluric Iron.*—In grains and plates, or disseminated. Almost pure iron, or contains carbon, graphite, lead or copper, but not nickel. Mulhausen in Thuringia, Chotzen in Bohemia; in the gold sands of Brazil, the Ural and Olahpian; in veins in Siberia, South Africa; also at Leadhills in Scotland, and in basalt in north of Ireland. Lately large masses, one of 44,000 lbs. found near Disco Bay in Greenland, it is said in basalt, but contain nickel.

(*b.*) *Meteoric Iron.*—Steel-gray and silver-white ; always contains nickel, with cobalt, copper, and other substances. Polished and etched with nitric acid, the surface is marked by lines intersecting at 60° or 120°, named Widmanstadt's figures. Has fallen from the sky in very many countries, —Siberia, Brazil, North America, South Africa, Hungary, Britain, and Ireland.

396. ANTIMONY.—Sb.

Hexagonal-rhombohedral ; R 87° 35′, but very rarely crystallised, generally massive or spherical, and botryoidal. Cleavage, basal highly perfect ; R perfect, and − 2R imperfect ; rather brittle and sectile.   H. = 3...3·5 ; G. = 6·6... 6·8. Tin-white, with a grayish or yellowish tarnish.   B.B. easily fusible ; on charcoal burns with a weak flame ; volatilises and forms a white deposit.   Chem. com. antimony, with a little silver, iron, or arsenic.   Andreasberg, Przibram, Sala, Allemont, and southern Canada.

397. ARSENIC-ANTIMONY, Allemontite.—Sb As².

Hexagonal-rhombohedral ; spherical or reniform.   H. = 3·5 ; G. = 6·1...6·2.   Tin-white to lead-gray, and tarnished with brownish-black.   B.B. gives out a strong smell of arsenic.   Chem. com. 38 antimony and 62 arsenic ; but other isomorphous compounds.   Allemont ; also Przibram, Schladming, and Andreasberg.

398. ARSENIC.—As.

Hexagonal-rhombohedral ; R 85° 36′; 0R, R, − ¼R (Fig. 246) ; usually fine granular, rarely columnar, botryoidal, or reniform.   Cleavage, basal perfect, − ¼R imperfect ; brittle.   H. = 3·5 ; G. = 5·7...5·8.   Whitish lead-gray, but in a few hours acquires a grayish-black tarnish.   When broken or heated gives out arsenical odours.   B.B. easily fusible, but on charcoal gives off dense white vapours, and may be wholly volatilised without fusing.   Chem.

Fig. 246.

com. arsenic, with some antimony, and traces of iron, silver, or gold.   Andreasberg, Annaberg, Schneeberg, Marienberg,

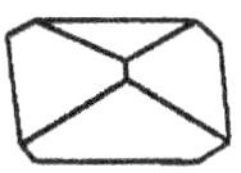

Freiberg, Joachimsthal, Kapnik, Orawitza, Allemont, St.
Marie aux Mines in Alsace, and Kongsberg; Tyndrum in
Perthshire; also the Altai, North America, and Chili.

Arsenic-silver is a compound with silver; Kongsberg.
Arsenic-glance, with 3 bismuth; $H. = 2$; $G. = 5·36...5.39$;
dark lead-gray; takes fire at the flame of a candle, and
burns; Marienberg. Arsenic is used in various pharma-
ceutical preparations and metallurgic processes.

399. TELLURIUM.—Te.
Hexagonal-rhombohedral; R 86° 50'; small prismatic
crystals; usually massive, and fine granular. Cleavage, ∞R
perfect, basal imperfect; slightly sectile. $H. = 2...2·5$;
$G. = 6·1...6·3$. Tin-white. B.B. very easily fusible; burns
with a greenish flame and much smoke, which forms a
white ring with a reddish margin on charcoal. In con. a.
acid forms a bluish-red solution. Chem. com. tellurium,
with a little gold or iron. Facebay in Siebenburg.

*400. BISMUTH.—Bi.
Hexagonal-rhombohedral; R 87° 40'. Crystals R.OR,
but often misshapen, also arborescent or reticulated; often
massive and granular. Cleavage, – 2 R 69° 28', and basal
perfect. Not malleable; very sectile. $H. = 2·5$; $G. = 9·6$
...9·8. Reddish silver-white, often with a yellow, red,
brown, or parti-colour tarnish. B.B. very easily fusible,
even in the flame of a candle. On charcoal volatilises,
leaving a citron-yellow coating. Soluble in nitric acid.
Chem. com. bismuth; often with a little arsenic or tellurium.
Schneeberg, Annaberg, Marienberg, Joachimsthal; Bieber;
Wittichen; also Modum and Fahlun; Bolivia; near Redruth; Carrick-Fell in Cumberland, and Alva in Stirlingshire. Only source of bismuth.

Maldonite or *Bismuth-gold.*—Silver-white with black tarnish; $H. = 1·5...2$; $G. = 8·2...9·7$, contains 64·5 gold and
35·5 bismuth, or $Au^2 Bi$. Granite veins Maldon, Victoria.

ZINC, said to occur native near Melbourne in Australia,
is also hexagonal or rhombohedral.

ORDER VI.

SULPHURETTED METALS.

CRYSTALLISATION often tesseral (⅔ths), rhombic (⅙d), or hexagonal and rhombohedral (⅙th), rarely other forms. H. = 1...7; G. = 3·4...9. Soluble in acids, and mostly B.B. easily fusible, many yielding fumes characteristic of sulphur, arsenic, or antimony. All (except one or two blendes) are opaque, and show metallic lustre and colour. Are all compounds of metals with sulphur, arsenic, or antimony, rarely with selenium or tellurium. Occur frequently in veins, more rarely disseminated in rocks; and many very valuable ores.

FAMILY I.—PYRITES.

Crystallisation tesseral, rhombic, or hexagonal (chalcopyrite tetragonal). Brittle, except bornite. H. = 3...6·5, the iron pyrites being the harder, the copper ores the softer; G. = 4·1...8·1, but sulphur compounds = 4·1...5·3, arsenic or antimony 6·6...8·1, sulphur with arsenic or antimony 6...6·5. Colour mostly yellow, becoming lighter or more gray in those with less sulphur. They are all soluble in nitric acid, and solutions generally coloured; B.B. all fusible, and give out fumes.

a. *Iron Pyrites.* Nos. 400 to 404.

**401. PYRITE, Iron Pyrites.—Fe″, *or* [Fe Sᶻ].

Tesseral, and dodecahedral-semitesseral. The cube $\infty O \infty$, then $O, \dfrac{\infty O2}{2}$ (Figs. 247, 248), and others (54 forms and about 90 combinations known), and macles (Fig. 249). In druses or groups, spheroidal or reniform, and massive, often in pseudomorphs. Cleavage, hexahedral or octahedral very imperfect or scarcely perceptible; brittle. H. = 6...6·5; G. = 4·9...5·2. Bronze-yellow, inclining to gold-yellow, often with a brown or rarely variegated tarnish;

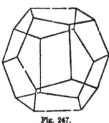

streak brownish-black. When broken emits a smell of sulphur. In the closed tube sulphur sublimes. B.B. on charcoal burns with a bluish flame, and a strong smell of sulphur. In the red. flame fuses to a blackish magnetic bead. Soluble in nitric acid with deposition of sulphur; scarcely affected by h. acid. Chem. com. 46·7 iron and 53·3 sulphur.

Fig. 247.

Very often contains gold, silver, or silicium, the gold occasionally in visible grains. Common in rocks of all ages and classes, often causing them to decompose. Fine varie-

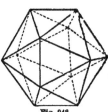

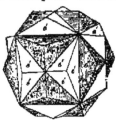

Fig. 248.   Fig. 249.

ties, Elba, Cornwall, Persberg, Traversella; also Alston Moor and Derbyshire. Auriferous pyrites, Beresof, Marmato, Mexico, Aedelfors in Sweden, and many parts of England and Scotland. Used for the manufacture of sulphur, sulphuric acid, and alum.

**402. MARCASITE, White Iron Pyrites.—$Fe'' = [Fe\,S^2]$.

Rhombic; ∞P (*M*) 106° 5′, $\frac{1}{3}\,\bar{P}\infty$ 136° 54′, $\bar{P}\infty$ (*l*) 80° 20′, $\bar{P}\infty$ (*g*) 64° 52′, also P (*c*) and 0P (*P*) (Fig. 250). Crystals tabular or thin prismatic, or pyramidal. Macles frequent (Fig. 251); also cockscomb-like groups, or spherical, reniform, and stalactitic. Cleavage, ∞P indistinct, $\bar{P}\infty$ traces; fracture uneven; brittle. H. $= 6 \ldots 6\cdot5$; G. $= 4\cdot65 \ldots 4\cdot9$. Pale, or grayish bronze-yellow, sometimes almost greenish-gray; streak dark greenish-gray or brownish-black. B.B. and with acids acts like pyrite. It is more easily decomposed by the atmosphere and changed into vitriols. Varieties are :—*Radiated pyrites*, radiated fibrous masses. *Spear pyrites*, macles (Fig. 251) very fine at Littmitz, Przibram, Schemnitz, and Freiberg. *Hepatic · pyrites*, or *Leberkies*, liver-brown, generally decomposing ;

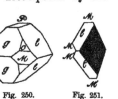

Fig. 250.   Fig. 251.

Harz, Saxony, Sweden, Derbyshire, and Cornwall. *Cockscomb pyrites*, compound comb-like crystals, often greenish, or with a brown tarnish ; Derbyshire and the Harz. *Wasserkies* or *Hydrous pyrites* contains water ; the *Kyrosite* copper and arsenic ; *Lonchidite* also arsenic.

*403. PYRRHOTINE, $\{$ $Fe' = [Fe\ S]$, *or*
      Magnetic Pyrites. $Fe'^5\ Fe''' = [5\ Fe\ S\ .\ Fe^2\ S^3]$.
Hexagonal ; P 126° 38′ to 50′. Crystals 0P. ∞P, or with P (*P*, *M*, *r*, Fig. 252) tabular or short prismatic, but rare. Commonly massive, granular, or compact. Cleavage, ∞P imperfect, laminar structure along 0P ; brittle. H. = 3·5...4·5 ; G. = 4·5...4·6. Colour between bronze-yellow and copper-red, with a pinchbeck-brown tarnish ; streak grayish-black, more or less magnetic. Unaltered in the closed tube ; in the open tube yields sulphurous fumes, but *no sublimation*.

Fig. 252.

B.B. on charcoal in the red. flame fuses to a black strongly magnetic globule ; soluble in h. acid. Chem. com. 63·65 iron and 36·35 sulphur, or 60·44 iron and 39·56 sulphur, in some with 2 to 6 nickel. Bodenmais, Fahlun, Kongsberg, Andreasberg, Moel Elion and Llanrwst in Caernarvonshire, Cornwall, Balahulish in Argyleshire, and Vesuvius ; also in some meteoric stones. Best distinguished by red colour, and solubility in h. acid.

*404. LEUCOPYRITE, Arsenical $\}$ *a.* $Fe\ As = [Fe\ As^2]$.
      Pyrites, Löllingite. $\}$ *b.* $Fe^4\ As^3 = [Fe^2\ As^3]$.
Rhombic ; ∞P 122° 26′, $\bar{P}$∞ 51° 20′, $\breve{P}$∞ 82° 21′. Crystals ∞P . $\bar{P}$∞ (*d*, *o*, Fig. 253). Generally massive,

granular, or columnar. Cleavage, basal rather perfect, $\bar{P}\infty$ imperfect; fracture uneven; brittle. H. = 5...5·5; G. = 7·0...7·4. Silver-white to steel-gray, with a darker tarnish; streak grayish-black. B.B. on charcoal emits a strong smell of arsenic, and fuses to a black magnetic globule. Chem. com. *a*, 27·2 iron and 72·8 arsenic, with G. = 7·1... 8·7; or *b*, 32·2 iron and 66·8 arsenic, and G. = 6·3...7·0; but always 1·3 to 6 sulphur, and some 13·4 nickel, and 5 cobalt. Reichenstein in Silesia; Schladming in Styria; Lölling in Carinthia; Andreasberg; and Fossum in Norway. Used for the manufacture of arsenious acid.

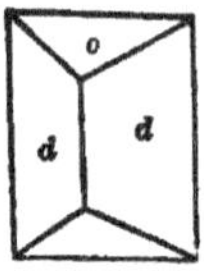

Fig. 253.

*405. MISPICKEL.—Fe S² + Fe As, *or* [Fe S² + Fe As²].
Rhombic; ∞P 111° 12', $\frac{1}{4}$ $\bar{P}\infty$ 146° 28', $\bar{P}\infty$ 79° 22', $\bar{P}\infty$ 59° 12'. Crystals ∞P. $\frac{1}{4}\bar{P}\infty$ (*M, r*, Fig. 254) (the latter with horizontal striæ) are short prismatic or tabular; macles common, also massive, granular, or columnar. Cleavage, ∞P rather distinct; fracture uneven; brittle. H. = 5·5 ...6; G. = 6·0...6·2. Silver-white to steel-gray, with a grayish or yellowish tarnish; streak black. In the closed tube yields first a red, then a brown sublimate of sulphuret of arsenic, and then metallic arsenic. B.B. on charcoal fuses to a black magnetic globule. Soluble in n. acid, with separation of arsenious acid and sulphur. Chem. com. 19·6 sulphur, 46·1 arsenic, and 34·3 iron, but some contain silver or gold, others 5 to 9 cobalt. Freiberg, Altenberg, Joachimsthal, Zinnwald, Schlaggenwald, Andreasberg, Sweden, North America, and in many Cornish tin mines. *Cobalt-mispickel*, from Skutterud in Norway. *Danaite* and *Plinian* seem the same mineral. Used as an ore of arsenic or of silver.

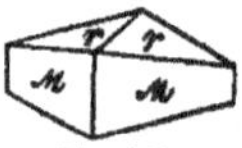

Fig. 254.

b. Cobalt-Pyrites. Nos. 405-409.

*406. COBALTINE.—Co S² + Co As.
Tesseral and semitesseral, like pyrite; also massive or granular, disseminated. Cleavage, hexahedral perfect; brittle. H. = 5·5; G. = 6·0...6·3. Brilliant, reddish silver-

white or gray, with a grayish or yellowish tarnish; streak grayish-black. B.B. on charcoal fuses with strong smell of arsenic to a gray, weak magnetic globule; after roasting forms, with borax, a beautiful blue glass. Chem. com. 35·9 cobalt (with 3·6 iron), 44·9 arsenic, and 19·2 sulphur. Skutterud in Norway, Tunaberg, Querbach in Silesia, Siegen, and St. Just in Cornwall.

Glaucodote.—Rhombic like mispickel. Dark tin-white; streak-black; with 11·9 iron, 24·8 cobalt. Huasco and Valparaiso in Chili, Orawitza.

*407. SMALTINE.—Co As, *or* [Co As²].

Tesseral; chiefly the cube and octahedron (Fig. 255), the faces of the cube convex or cracked; also reticulated, reniform, or granular compact. Cleavage, traces along $\infty O \infty$ and O; fracture uneven; brittle. H. = 5·5; G. = 6·4...7·3. Tin-white or steel-gray, with a dark-gray or iridescent tarnish; streak grayish-black. Gives out an odour of arsenic when broken. In the closed tube gives no sublimate of arsenic. B.B. fuses easily, with a strong smell of arsenic, to a white or gray magnetic globule. Chem. com. 71·4 arsenic and 28·6 cobalt, but with 3 to 19

Fig. 255.

iron and 1 to 12 nickel; others 1 to 3 bismuth. Schneeberg, Annaberg, Riechelsdorf, Allemont, Tunaberg; Chatham in Connecticut; Huel Sparnon, Doalcoath, and Redruth in Cornwall. *Gray Smaltine* has 10 to 18 iron, and G. = 6·9 to 7·3. Smaltine and cobaltine are used in preparing blue colours for painting porcelain and stoneware.

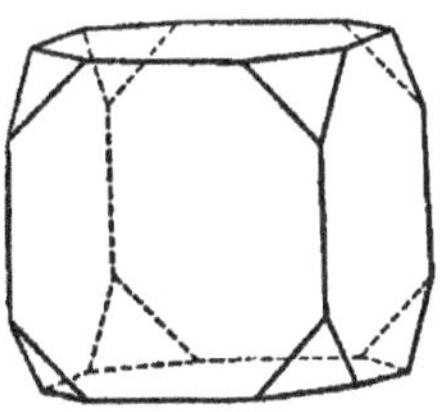

408. MODUMITE, Skutterudite.—Co² As³, *or* [Co As²].

Tesseral; O and $\infty O \infty$, or granular. Cleavage, hexahedral distinct; fracture conchoidal or uneven; brittle. H. = 6; G. = 6·74...6·84. Tin-white to pale lead-gray, some with an iridescent tarnish. Lustre rather brilliant. In the closed tube gives a sublimate of metallic arsenic; in other respects like smaltine. Chem. com. 79 arsenic, and 21 cobalt. Skutterud, near Modum in Norway.

409. LINNÉITE.—(Ni', Co', Fe') + (Ni''', Co''', Fe''').

Tesseral; in octahedrons and cubes, or macled; also massive. Cleavage, hexahedral imperfect; brittle. H. = 5·5; G. = 4·9...5·0. Silver-white inclining to red, often with a yellowish tarnish; streak blackish-gray. B.B. on charcoal fuses in the red. flame to a gray magnetic globule, bronze-yellow when broken. Chem. com. 11 to 53 cobalt, 0 to 42·6 nickel, 2 to 5 iron, and 1 to 15 copper. Bastnæs, Müsen near Siegen, also Maryland and Missouri.

410. JYEPOORITE, Syepoorite..—Co'.

Massive. Steel-gray or yellowish. G. = 5·45. Chem. com. 65·2 cobalt, and 34·8 sulphur. Jyepoor (misspelt Syepoor) near Rajpootanah in North-West India. The Indian jewellers use it to give a rose colour to gold.

c. Nickel-Pyrites. Nos. 410-418.

411. GRÜNAUITE, Saynite.

Tesseral; O and ∞O∞; also granular. Cleavage, octahedral; brittle. H. = 4·5; G. = 5·14. Light steel-gray inclining to silver-white, with a yellow or grayish tarnish. B.B. fuses to a gray, brittle, magnetic bead, yellow on the fracture, and colours the support yellow. The solution in nitric acid is green. Chem. com. nickel, bismuth, sulphur, iron, cobalt, copper, lead, in variable proportions. Grünau in Sayn-Altenkirchen.

412. GERSDORFFITE.—(Ni, Fe) As + (Ni, Fe) S².

Tesseral; O, ∞O∞; usually granular. Cleavage, hexahedral rather perfect; fracture uneven; brittle. H. = 5·5; G. = 6·0...6·7. Silver-white to steel-gray, with a grayish tarnish. In the closed tube decrepitates violently. B.B. fuses to a brittle, black, slag-like globule; partially soluble in nitric acid. Chem. com. 35·2 nickel (with 2·4 to 6 iron, 0 to 3 cobalt), 45·4 arsenic, and 19·4 sulphur; but others give different formula, with 10 to 15 iron and 14 cobalt. The Harz, Schladming, Camsdorf, Sweden; also Spain and Brazil. Craigmuir, near Loch Fyne, with 23 nickel and 6 cobalt. Used as an ore of nickel.

Korynite, in octahedrons, from Olsa, Carinthia; and *Wolfachite* from Wolfach, but rhombic, give about 13 antimony, and 38 arsenic.

413. ULLMANNITE.—Ni Sb+Ni S², *or* [Ni Sb²+Ni S²].

Tesseral; O, ∞O∞, ∞O; usually granular. Cleavage, hexahedral perfect; fracture uneven. H. = 5...5·5; G. = 6·2...6·5. Lead-gray to tin-white or steel-gray; with a grayish-black or iridescent tarnish. B.B. fuses with dense fumes, and slight odour of arsenic; soluble in con. nitric acid. Chem. com. 27·4 nickel, 57·5 antimony, and 15·1 sulphur, in some with 2 to 12 arsenic. Westerwald, Siegen, Harzgerode, Lölling, Lobenstein, and Bleiburg, Carinthia.

414. BREITHAUPTITE.—Ni² Sb, *or* [Ni Sb].

Hexagonal; P 112° 10′. Crystals, thin striated hexagonal tables of OP . ∞P. H. = 5; G. = 7·5...7·6. Brilliant. Light copper-red, with violet-blue tarnish. B.B. fumes but fuses with great difficulty. Chem. com. 32·2 nickel, and 67·8 antimony, but mixed with 6 to 12 sulphuret of lead. Andreasberg.

415. NICKELINE, Copper Nickel.—Ni² As *or* [Ni As].

Hexagonal; P 86° 50′. Crystals, ∞P, OP, very rare and indistinct; also arborescent, reniform, or generally massive. Fracture conchoidal and uneven; brittle. H. = 5·5; G. = 7·5...7·7. Light copper-red, with a tarnish first gray then blackish. It forms no sublimate in the closed tube. B.B. fuses with strong fumes to a white, brittle, metallic globule. Chem. com. 43·6 nickel and 56·4 arsenic, but with 0 to 2 cobalt, 0·2 to 9 iron, 0·1 to 4 sulphur, and 0 to 29 antimony. Freiberg, Schneeberg, Joachimsthal, Sangerhausen, Andreasberg, Chatham in Connecticut, Pengelly and Huel Chance in Cornwall, and Leadhills in Scotland. Used as an ore of nickel.

Plakodine is a furnace product, not a native mineral.

416. CHLOANTHITE, White Nickel.—Ni As, *or* [Ni As²].

Tesseral; O, ∞O∞, ∞O; also fine granular or compact. Fracture uneven; brittle. H. = 5·5; G. = 6·4... 6·6. Tin-white, but first a gray, then a blackish tarnish, and loses its lustre. Yields an odour of arsenic when broken. In the closed tube forms a sublimate of metallic arsenic, and becomes copper-red. B.B. on charcoal fuses easily with much smoke, continues long ignited, becomes invested with crystals of arsenious acid, and leaves a brittle grain of metal. Chem. com. 28 nickel and 72 arsenic, but often with cobalt; and many so-called smaltines belong to this species. Schneeberg, Riechelsdorf, Allemont, Chatham in Connecticut.

417. RAMMELSBERGITE.—Ni As.
Rhombic; ∞P 123°... 124°. G. = 7·099 ... 7·188. Colour tin-white, inclining to red on the fresh fracture. Otherwise like chloanthite, with which it occurs. The names are sometimes transposed.

418. MILLERITE.—Ni', *or* [Ni S].
Hexagonal-rhombohedral; R 144° 8', in fine acicular prisms of ∞P2. R. Brittle. H. = 3·5; G. = 4·6 (or 5·26 ...5·65). Brass or bronze yellow, with a gray or iridescent tarnish. B.B. fuses easily to a blackish metallic globule, which boils and sputters. In nitrochloric acid forms a green solution. Chem. com. 64·4 nickel and 35·6 sulphur. Johann-Georgenstadt, Joachimsthal, Przibram, Camsdorf, Riechelsdorf, Pennsylvania; near St. Austle in Cornwall, and at Merthyr-Tydvil.

419. PENTLANDITE, Inverarite.—2 Fe' + Ni'.
Tesseral; massive and granular. Fracture uneven; brittle. H. = 3·5...4; G. = 4·6. Light pinchbeck-brown, with darker streak. Not magnetic. B.B. acts in general like pyrrhotine; the roasted powder forms with borax in the red flame a black opaque glass. Chem. com. 36 sulphur, 42 iron, and 22 nickel; but mixed with pyrrhotine and chalcopyrite. Lillehammer in Southern Norway, near Inverary in Scotland, but only 11 nickel.

d. Copper Pyrites. Nos. 419 to 421.

** 420. CHALCOPYRITE, } Cu' + Fe' = [Cu S + Fe S], *or*
Yellow Copper Ore. } Cu' + Fe''' = [Cu² S . Fe² S²].
Tetragonal and sphenoidal-hemihedric; $\frac{1}{2}$ P (*P*) with polar edges 71° 20'; P∞ (*b*), 89° 10', 2P∞ (*c*) 126° 11', 0P (*a*), P and ∞P∞. Crystals generally small and deformed (Fig. 256); macles very common, like Fig. 257. Most commonly compact and disseminated; also botryoidal and reniform. Cleavage, pyramidal 2P∞ sometimes rather

distinct; fracture conchoidal or uneven.   H. = 3·5...4 ;
G. = 4·1...4·3.   Brass-yellow, often with a gold-yellow or
iridescent (*peacock copper ore*) tarnish ; streak greenish-
black.   B.B. on charcoal becomes darker or black, and on
cooling red.   Fuses easily to a steel-gray globule, which
at length becomes magnetic, brittle, and grayish-red on the
fractured surface.   With borax and soda yields a grain of
copper.   Moistened with h. acid colours the flame blue.
Chem. com. essentially 1 atom copper, 1 atom iron, and 2
atoms sulphur, with 34·5 copper, 30·5 iron, and 35 sulphur.

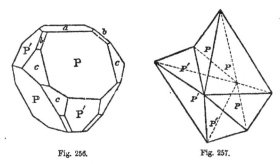

Fig. 256.   Fig. 257.

The most abundant ore of copper.   Anglesea (Parys Mine),
Derbyshire, Staffordshire, Cumberland ; Wicklow in Ireland ; also in the Cornish mines (Gunnis Lake and St.
Austle) ; in Scotland in Kirkcudbrightshire and Wigtown-
shire, Tyndrum in Perthshire, Inverness-shire, Zetland, and
other places.   Of foreign European localities, Fahlun,
Roraas, Freiberg, Mansfield, Goslar, Lauterberg, Musen,
may be mentioned ; also in Siberia, California, Canada,
the United States, and Australia.   The ores raised in
Cornwall and Devon give 8 per cent metal on the average ;
and that picked for sale at Redruth rarely yields 12, sometimes only 3 or 4 per cent.   The richness of the ore may
in general be judged of by the colour ; if of a fine yellow
hue, and yielding readily to the hammer, it may be considered a good ore ; but if hard and pale yellow, it is
assuredly a poor one, being mixed with iron pyrites.   From

U

pyrite it is distinguished by yielding readily to the knife, by its tarnish, and by soon forming a green solution in nitric acid. The produce of the United Kingdom in 1871 was 97,129 tons ore, giving 6280 tons copper, worth £475,000.

Cuban.—Cu S . Fe^2 S^3. Tesseral; or massive, with a hexahedral cleavage. G. = 4·02...4·18. B.B. very easily fusible, otherwise like chalcopyrite. Chem. com. 24 copper, 35 iron, and 41 sulphur. Bacaranao in Cuba, also Tunaberg and Kafveltorp in Sweden.

*421. BORNITE, Variegated $\}$ $\Theta u'^3 \, Fe''' = [3 \, Cu^2S . Fe^2S^3]$.
     or Purple Copper. $\}$

Tesseral. Crystals, $\infty O \infty$, and $\infty O \infty$. O, but rare, and generally rough or uneven; also macles. Mostly massive. Cleavage, octahedral very imperfect; fracture conchoidal or uneven; slightly brittle, or almost sectile. H. = 3; G. = 4·9...5·1. Colour between copper-red and pinchbeck-brown, with tarnish at first red or brown, then violet or sky-blue; streak grayish-black. B.B. acts like chalcopyrite; soluble in con. h. acid, leaving sulphur. Chem. com. 3 atoms copper, 1 atom iron, and 3 atoms sulphur, with 55·6 copper, 16·4 iron, and 28 sulphur, but often, especially when compact, mixed, and then 56 to 71 copper, and 6 to 17 iron. Crystals near Redruth and St. Day in Cornwall; massive at Killarney in Ireland; also Norway, Sweden, Mansfeld, Silesia, Tuscany, and Chili. An ore of copper.

422. DOMEYKITE.—Cu^6 As = [Cu^3 As].

Botryoidal, reniform, or massive. Fracture uneven or conchoidal; brittle. H. = 3...3·5; G. = 7·0...7·5. Tin or silver white, inclining to yellow, with an iridescent tarnish. B.B. fuses easily with strong odour of arsenic; not affected by h. acid. Chem. com. 71·63 copper and 28·37 arsenic. Calabazo in Coquimbo and Copiapo in Chili. Also near Zwickau with H. = 5; G. = 6·8...6·9.

Condurrite.—Massive, soft, and soils the fingers. Fracture flat conchoidal. Colour brownish or bluish black. G. = 4·20...4·29. B.B. on charcoal fuses, with escape of arsenic vapours, to a globule, which, on cooling, cracks, swells, and falls to pieces. With soda and borax leaves a grain of copper. Seems an impure variety. Condurrow Mine and near Redruth. *Algodonite* from Lake Superior; *Whitneyite* from Mexico; and *Darwinite* (88 copper) are also identical or similar.

423. ARSENIURET OF MANGANESE.—Mn^3 As.

Massive and botryoidal, granular or foliated. Fracture uneven; brittle. G. $= 5.55$. Grayish-white, with a black tarnish. B.B. burns with a blue flame, and emits fumes of arsenic; soluble in nitrochloric acid. Chem. com. 42.75 manganese, 57.25 arsenic, with trace of iron. Saxony?

424. LAURITE.—12 Ru''' + Os'''.

Tesseral; in very small grains or crystals of octahedrons and tetrakishexahedrons combined with cubes. Brittle. H. $= 7.5$; G. $= 6.99$. Dark iron-black, with brilliant lustre. Insoluble even in nitrochloric acid. Chem. com. 62.9 ruthenium, 5 osmium, and 32.1 sulphur. With gold, platina, and diamonds, in Borneo, and Oregon.

FAMILY II.—LEAD GLANCE.

Crystallisation, chiefly tesseral; also rhombic and hexagonal-rhombohedral. H. $= 1...2.5$, rarely more; G. $= 4.6...8.9$, and mostly 5.5, or higher. Colours generally lead-gray, and more or less dark. All soluble in acids. B.B. all fusible, and mostly very easily, and easily reduced. They are compounds with sulphur, selenium, or tellurium, known by their fumes. Chiefly occur in veins and some valuable ores.

**425. GALENA, Sulphuret of Lead.—Pb' *or* [Pb S].

Tesseral; crystals chiefly cube, octahedron, and rhombic dodecahedron; seldomer 2O and 2O2. Also massive and granular, compact, or laminar; and in pseudomorphs of pyromorphite and other minerals. Cleavage, hexahedral very perfect; fracture scarcely observable; sectile. H. $= 2.5$; G. $= 7.2...7.6$. Lead-gray, with darker, or rarely iridescent, tarnish; streak grayish-black. B.B. decrepitates, fuses, and leaves a globule of lead; soluble in nitric acid. Chem. com. 86.7 lead and 13.3 sulphur, but usually contains a little silver,—ranging from 1 to 3, or 5 parts in 10,000; rarely 1 per cent or more. Some contain copper, zinc, or antimony, others selenium, and others (the *super-sulphuret*) probably free sulphur (2 to 8 per cent). Most common ore of lead in many countries. Cornwall, Derbyshire (Castletown), Wales, Cumberland, Alston Moor, Durham (Allenhead); Isle of Man; Leadhills, Pentland Hills, Linlithgow, Inverkeithing, Monaltrie, Tyndrum, Strontian, Islay, and many other places in Scotland. In 1855 the produce was,—England, 59,592 tons; Wales, 34,373; Isle of Man, 4645; Ireland, 1105; and Scotland, 3393 tons. The total produce was about 94,000 tons ore, yielding 69,000 tons lead, worth £1,252,000; and 761,490 ounces silver, worth £190,372. The price of lead was about £19 per ton, and each ton contained 11 ounces silver.

426. CUPROPLUMBITE.

Tesseral; massive, with distinct hexahedral cleavage. H. = 2·5; G. = 6·41...6·43. Blackish lead-gray; streak black. B.B. does not decrepitate. Chem. com. 65 lead, 19·9 copper, and 15·1 sulphur (with 0·5 silver). Chili. Probably a mixture.

427. CLAUSTHALITE.—Pb Se.

Tesseral; but massive and fine granular, with hexahedral cleavage. H. = 2·5...3; G. = 8·2...8·8. Lead-gray; streak gray. B.B. on charcoal fumes, smells of selenium, colours the flame blue, stains the support red, yellow, and white; and volatilises, except a small remainder, without fusing. Chem. com. 72·7 lead (with 11·6 silver), and 27·3 selenium. Lerbach, Zorge and Tilkerode in the Harz.

Tilkerodite, with 3 cobalt; G. = 7·7; colours borax-glass smalt-blue. *Lehrbachite;* Lehrbach and Tilkerode; with 17 to 45 mercury, seems a mixture.

428. SELENCOPPERLEAD.—(Cu, Pb) Se.

Massive and fine granular. Sectile. H. = 2·5; G. = 5·6 ...7·5. Light lead-gray inclining to brass-yellow, or with a bluish tarnish; streak darker. B.B. like clausthalite, only some fuse slightly on the surface, others easily forming a gray metallic mass. Chem. com. 30 to 35 selenium, 47 to 64 lead, and 4 to 16 copper (with 0 to 1·3 silver).

Tilkerode, Zorge, and near Gabel in Thuringia. Perhaps more than one species.

429. ONOFRITE.—Hg Se + 4 Hg S.

Massive, and granular. H. = 2·5. Blackish lead-gray or steel-gray; streak shining. In the closed tube wholly volatile with a black sublimate. With soda gives metallic mercury. Chem. com. 82·8 mercury, 6·6 selenium, and 10·6 sulphur. St. Onofre in Mexico, Zorge in the Harz.

430. TIEMANNITE.—Hg Se, *or* Hg^2 Se^2.

Fine granular; brittle. H. = 2·5 ; G. = 7·1...7·4. Brilliant. Dark lead-gray. In the closed tube decrepitates, swells, fuses, and volatilises to a black and brown deposit. Only soluble in nitrochloric acid. Chem. com. 75 mercury, 25 selenium. Clausthal and Zorge.

431. NAUMANNITE.—Ag Se = [Ag^2 Se].

In thin plates and granular. Cleavage, hexahedral perfect. Malleable. H. = 2·5 ; G. = 8·0. Iron-black; splendent. B.B. on charcoal fuses; with soda a grain of silver; easily soluble in con. nitric acid. Chem. com. 73 silver and 27 selenium, with 4·91 lead. Tilkerode.

Silverphyllinglanz.—Massive, foliated; perfect cleavage; thin lamina flexible. H. = 1...2 ; G. = 5·8...5·9. Dark gray. Chem. com. antimony, lead, tellurium, gold, and sulphur (*Plattner*). Deutsch-Pilsen in Hungary.

*432. ARGENTITE, Sulphuret of Silver.—Ag' = [Ag^2 S].

Tesseral; ∞O∞ , O, ∞O, and 2O2 (Fig. 258). Crystals generally misshapen, with uneven or curved faces ; in druses, or linear groups ; also arborescent, capillary, or in crusts. Cleavage, very indistinct traces along ∞O and ∞O∞ ; fracture uneven and hackly ; malleable and flexible. H. = 2...2·5 ; G. = 7·0...7·4. Rarely brilliant; more so on the streak. Blackish lead-

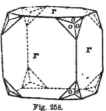

Fig. 258.

gray, often with a black, brown, or rarely iridescent tarnish. B.B. on charcoal fuses, intumesces greatly, and leaves a grain of silver; soluble in con. nitric acid. Chem.

com. 87 silver and 13 sulphur.   Freiberg, Marienberg.
Annaberg, Schneeberg, Johann-Georgenstadt ; Joachimsthal ; Schemnitz and Kremnitz ; Kongsberg ; Huel Duchy.
Dolcoath, Herland, and near Callington, in Cornwall ; Alva
in Stirlingshire.   Common ore at Guanaxuato and Zacatecas in Mexico, in Peru, and Blagodat in Siberia.   Valuable
ore of silver. *Polyargyrite*, from Wolfach, gives 7 antimony.

433. ACANTHITE.—Ag'.
Rhombic ; P middle edge 120° 36', ∞P 110° 54'.
Crystals, short pyramidal, often twisted. G. = 7·2...7·3.
Splendent.   Lead-gray, darker than argentite.   Chem.
com. like argentite, thus dimorphous.   Freiberg and Claus-
thal on argentite, also at Copiapo.

434. ANTIMONY-SILVER, DISCRASITE.—Ag² Sb, *to* Ag⁶Sb.
Rhombic ; P with polar edges 132° 42' and 92°, ∞P
120° nearly.   Crystals short prismatic or thick tabular,
and vertically striated ; macles united by a face of ∞P ;

Fig. 259.

often in stellar groups (Fig. 259) ; also massive or granular.   Cleavage, basal and P̄∞
distinct ; ∞P imperfect ; rather brittle, and
slightly malleable.   H. = 3·5 ; G. = 9·4...
9·8.   Silver-white to tin-white, with a yellow or blackish tarnish.   B.B. fuses easily ;
fumes, staining the charcoal white, and
leaves a grain of silver ; soluble in nitric acid.   Chem.
com. 64 to 84 silver, and 36 to 16 antimony.   Andreasberg, Allemont in Dauphiné, Spain, and Arqueras in Coquimbo.   A valuable ore of silver.

435. STROMEYERITE.—Cu' + Ag'.
Rhombic ; isomorphous with redruthite.   Crystals
rare ; usually massive, or in plates ; fracture flat, conchoidal, or even ; very sectile.   H. = 2·5...3 ; G. = 6·2...
6·3.   Bright.   Blackish lead-gray.   B.B. fuses easily to a
gray metallic semimalleable globule.   Chem. com. 53·1
silver, 31·2 copper, and 15·7 sulphur, but often indeterminate proportions of silver 3 to 53, and copper 30 to 75.
Schlangenberg in Siberia, Rudelstadt in Silesia, and Ca-
temo in Chili.   Ore of silver and copper.

436. REDRUTHITE, Copper Glance. — $\overset{..}{Cu}' = [Cu^2 S]$.

Rhombic; ∞P (*o*) 119° 35', P (P) middle-edge 125°
22', $\frac{1}{3}$ P (*a*) middle-edge 65° 40', 2 $\breve{P}\infty$ (*d*) middle-edge
125° 40', $\frac{2}{3}$ $\breve{P}\infty$ (*e*) middle-edge 65° 48'.   Crystals OP . (*s*)
∞P . (*o*) $\infty \breve{P}\infty$ (*p*) (Figs. 260, 261), mostly thick tabular,
with hexagonal aspect; also macles; and massive, in plates
or lumps.   Cleavage, ∞P imperfect; fracture conchoidal or
uneven; very sectile.   H. = 2·5...3 ; G. = 5·5...5·8.   Rather

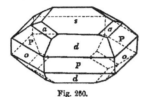

Fig. 260.   Fig. 261.

dull; brighter on the streak.   Blackish lead-gray, with a
blue or other tarnish.   B.B. colours the flame blue; on
charcoal in the ox. flame sputters and fuses easily; in the
red. flame becomes solid.   With soda gives a grain of copper.   Green solution in nitric acid leaving sulphur.   Chem.
com. 79·8 copper, and 20·2 sulphur.   Saxony, Silesia.
Norway, the Bannat, Siberia, and the United States; near
Redruth and Land's End in Cornwall; Fassnet Burn in
Haddingtonshire, in Ayrshire, and in Fair Island, Orkney.
Important copper ore.

Digenite.—Massive.   G. = 4·568...4·680 ; in other respects like redruthite.   Contains 70·20 copper, 29·56 sulphur, and 0·24 silver.   Sangerhausen, the Bannat, and
Chili.

437. KUPFERINDIG, Covelline.—$\overset{..}{Cu}'$.

Hexagonal.   Crystals ∞P . OP rare; usually reniform,
and fine granular.   Cleavage, basal often very perfect;
sectile, and thin laminæ flexible.   H. = 1·5...2 ; G. = 3·8
or 4·6.   Dull resinous, inclining to metallic.   Indigo-blue,
inclining to black; streak black.   B.B. burns with a blue
flame; on charcoal like redruthite, but remains fluid in the
inner flame; soluble in nitric acid.   Chem. com. 66·7 cop-

per, and 33·3 sulphur. Vesuvius, Sangerhausen, Baden-weiler, Leogang, Chili, Angola in Africa, New Zealand, Victoria, and Cairn Beg in Cornwall. ·

438. EUKAIRITE.—$Cu^2 Se + Ag Se$.
Massive and fine granular. Soft (cuts with the knife). Lead-gray ; streak shining. B.B. fuses to a brittle gray metallic grain. Chem. com. 43 silver, 25·2 copper, and 31·8 selenium. Skrikerum, Atacama, Chili.

439. BERZELINE.—$Cu^2 Se$.
Crystalline, in thin dendritic crusts. Soft. Silver-white ; streak shining. B.B. on charcoal fuses to a gray, slightly malleable bead. With soda a grain of copper. Chem. com. 61·5 copper and 38·5 selenium. Skrikerum in Smoland, Lerbach in the Harz.

Crookesite, from Skrikerum, contains 17 thalium, with copper, silver, and selenium. Is lead-gray, and B.B. colours the flame intense green.

440. ALTAITE.—Pb Te.
Tesseral and granular ; hexahedral cleavage. Fracture uneven ; sectile. H. = 3...3·5 ; G. = 8·1...8·2. Tin-white inclining to yellow, with yellow tarnish. B.B. on charcoal colours the flame blue ; in the red. flame fuses to a globule that almost wholly volatilises. Chem. com. 61·9 lead, with 1·28 silver, and 38·1 tellurium. Sawodinski mine in the Altai ; California.

441. NAGYAGITE, Black or Foliated Tellurium.
Tetragonal ; P 137° 52′, P∞ 122° 50′ and 0P. Crys-tals tabular, but rare ; in general thin plates or foliated. Cleavage, basal very perfect ; very sectile ; the thin laminæ flexible.   H. = 1 ... 1·5 ; G. = 6·85 ... 7·2.   Splendent. Blackish lead-gray. B.B. fuses easily, with white fumes, and forms a yellow deposit on the charcoal ; with soda leaves a grain of gold ; soluble in nitric acid, with residue of gold. Chem. com. 51 to 63 lead, 6 to 9 gold, 1 copper and silver, 13 to 32 tellurium, 3 to 12 sulphur, and 0 to 4·5 antimony. Nagyag in Siebenburg, and Offenbanya.

442. SILVANITE.—$Ag Te^4 + Au Te^3$.
Rhombic, *Schrauff*, (or Monoclinic ; C. = 55° 21′, ∞P

94° 26', –P°∞ 19° 21', P°∞ 62° 43'. *Rose* and *Von Kok-sharow.*) Crystals very small, short acicular, and often grouped in rows like letters. Cleavage in two directions, one very perfect; sectile, but friable. H. = 1·5...2; G. = 7·99...8·33. Steel-gray to tin-white, silver-white, and pale bronze-yellow. B.B. on charcoal forms a white coating, and fuses to a dark-gray globule, with soda reduced to a malleable grain of argentiferous gold; soluble in nitrochloric acid, depositing chloride of silver; and in nitric acid leaving gold. Chem. com. 59·6 tellurium, with 0·6 to 8·5 antimony, 26·5 gold (in some 30); and 13·9 silver, with 0·2 to 15 lead. Offenbanya (*Graphic Tellurium*), Nagyag (*Yellow Tellurium*), and California.

443. HESSITE.—Ag Te.
Rhombic or tesseral. Massive and granular; slightly malleable. H. = 2·5...3; G. = 8·3...8·8. Blackish lead-gray to steel-gray. B.B. on charcoal fumes, fuses to a black graiñ with white spots, and leaves a brittle grain of silver. Chem. com. 62·8 silver, and 37·2 tellurium, but some (*Petzite*) 18 to 25 gold. Sawodinski mine in the Altai, Nagyag, and Rezbanya.

444. TETRADYMITE.—2 Bi Te³ + Bi S³.
Hexagonal-rhombohedral; 3R 68° 10'. Crystals 3R. OR; almost always macles, with the faces of OR at 95°; also granular foliated. Cleavage, basal very perfect; sectile, and in thin laminæ flexible. H. = 1...2; G. = 7·2 ...7·5. Dull. Tin-white to steel-gray. B.B. on charcoal fuses easily, occasionally with odour of selenium, staining the support yellow and white; at length yields a white grain of metal, almost entirely volatile; soluble in nitric acid. Chem. com. 59·6 bismuth, 35·9 tellurium, and 4·5 sulphur, with traces of selenium. Schubkau near Schemnitz, Deutsch-Pilsen in Hungary, San Jose in Brazil, Virginia and Carolina.

*445. MOLYBDENITE.—Mo″ = [Mo S].
Hexagonal; but only tabular or short prismatic crystals of OP . ∞P or OP . P. Generally scaly or curved foliated. Cleavage, basal very perfect; very sectile, and thin laminæ

flexible. Feels greasy. H. = 1...1·5 ; G. = 4·6 = 4·9.
Reddish lead-gray ; makes a gray mark on paper, a greenish
mark on porcelain. B.B. in the forceps, colours the flame
siskin-green, but is infusible. On charcoal yields sulphurous fumes, and forms a white coating, but burns slowly
and imperfectly. In warm nitrochloric acid forms a greenish,
in boiling sulphuric acid a blue solution. Chem. com. 59
molybdena and 41 sulphur. Arendal, Altenberg, Ehrenfriedersdorf, Zinnwald, Schlaggenwald, Mont Blanc, Shutes-
bury in Massachusetts, in Maine, Haddam in Connecticut ;
Yea in Victoria ; Caldbeckfell in Cumberland, Shap in
Westmoreland, Huel Gorland, and many Cornish mines ;
Peterhead, and near Inverurie in Aberdeenshire, Corybuy
on Loch Creran, and Glenelg. Readily distinguished from
graphite by its streak, lustre, gravity, and action before the
blowpipe. Used for preparing blue carmine for colouring
porcelain.

FAMILY III.—GRAY ANTIMONY ORE.

Crystallisation rhombic, rarely tesseral or hexagonal.
H. = 3...3·5, or less ; G. = 4...6·8. Colour steel or lead
gray. All soluble in acids with precipitates ; generally
very easily fusible, even in the flame of a candle, and give
out fumes.

*446. STIBINE, Antimonite.—Sb''' = [Sb² S³].

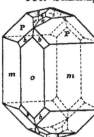

Rhombic ; P polar edges 109°
26', and 108° 21', ∞P 90° 54'. Crystals ∞P (*m*) . ∞P̆∞ (*o*) . P (*P*), or
with ½P̆∞ (*a*), 2P̆2 (*b*), ⅓P̆2 (*e*), ⅓P
(*s*), (Fig. 262). Mostly long prismatic
or acicular, with strong vertical striæ,
often in druses or stellar groups ;
also radiating, fibrous, or fine granular. Cleavage, brachydiagonal (*o*)
highly perfect, and often horizontally
striated ; also basal, ∞P, and macro-
diagonal imperfect ; sectile. H. = 2 ; G. = 4·6...4·7. Brilliant. Lead-gray, with a blackish or iridescent tarnish.

Fig. 262.

B.B. fuses easily, colouring the flame green, and volatilises, leaving a white coating on the support; soluble in warm h. acid.   Chem. com. 71·8 antimony and 28·2 sulphur.   Freiberg, Wolfsberg in the Harz, Przibram, Felsöbanya, Kremnitz, Schemnitz, Auvergne, Spain, and North and South America; also near Melbourne, Victoria; St. Stephen's, Padstow, and Endellion in Cornwall; Glendinning in Dumfriesshire, New Cumnock in Ayrshire, and in Banffshire.   Chief ore of antimony.

447. JAMESONITE.—$Pb'^3 Sb'''^2 = [3\ Pb\ S\ .\ 2\ Sb^5\ S^3]$.

Rhombic; $\infty P\ 101°\ 20'$.   Crystals $\infty P\ .\ \infty \breve{P}\infty$, long prismatic, parallel, or radiating.   Cleavage, basal very perfect, ∞P and brachydiagonal imperfect; sectile.   H. = 2... 2·5; G. = 5·5...5·7.   Steel-gray to dark lead-gray.   B.B. decrepitates, fuses easily, and wholly volatilises, except a small slag; soluble in warm h. acid.   Chem. com. 44·5 lead, with 2 to 4 iron, 34·9 antimony, and 20·6 sulphur. Cornwall, Estremadura, Hungary, Siberia, and Brazil.

448. ZINCKENITE.—$Pb'\ Sb'''$.

Rhombic; $\infty P\ (d)\ 120°\ 39'$, $\breve{P}\infty\ (o)\ 150°\ 36'$ (Fig. 263), but doubtful.   Crystals, prismatic or acicular, vertically striated, and macled in threes.   Cleavage, prismatic very imperfect; fracture uneven; rather sectile.   H. = 3...3·5; G. = 5·3...5·35.   Dark steel-gray to lead-gray, with a steel-blue or iridescent tarnish.   B.B. like jamesonite.   Chem. com. 35·9 lead, 42 antimony, 22·1 sulphur, with 0·42 copper.   Wolfsberg in the Harz.

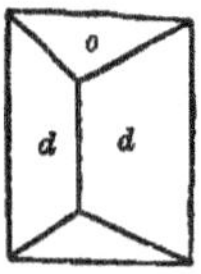

Fig. 263.

449. PLAGIONITE.—$Pb'^4\ Sb'''^3$.

Monoclinic; C. = 72° 28', P 134° 30' and 142° 3', –2P 120° 49'.   Crystals thick tabular, minute, and in druses. Cleavage, – 2P rather perfect; brittle.   H. = 2·5; G. = 5·4.   Blackish lead-gray.   B.B. decrepitates violently, fuses easily, sinking into the charcoal, and leaves metallic lead.   Chem. com. 41 lead, 38 antimony, and 21 sulphur. Wolfsberg in the Harz.

450. BOULANGERITE.—Pb⁴ Sb‴.

Fine granular, columnar, radiating, or fibrous. **Slightly sectile.** H. = 3 ; G. = 5·8...6. Silky, metallic. **Blackish** lead-gray, with darker streak. B.B. like jamesonite. **Chem.** com. 60 lead, 22·8 antimony, and 18·2 sulphur. Molières in France, Ober-Lahr, Lapland, and Siberia. *Plumbostib* or *Embrithite*, Nertschinsk, only a variety.

451. MENEGHINITE.—Pb⁴ Sb‴.

Monoclinic. C. = 72° 8′, ∞P 140° 24′, P°∞ 70° Crystals, very small, acicular, chiefly of ∞P°∞ . ∞P°∞ . ∞P, but rare ; mostly fibrous. Cleavage, orthodiagonal distinct. Splendent ; lead-gray. H. = 3 ; G. = 6·34...6·37. Chem. com. 64 lead, 19 antimony, and 17 sulphur. Bottino in Tuscany, and near Schwarzenberg in Saxony.

452. GEOKRONITE.—Pb⁴ (Sb‴, As‴).

Rhombic ; P polar edges 153° and 64° 45′, ∞P̆2 = 119° 44′, mostly massive, or lamellar. Cleavage, ∞P̆2 ; fracture conchoidal or even ; sectile. H. = 2...3 ; G. = 6·45...6·54. Pale lead-gray, with a slight tarnish. B.B. fuses easily and volatilises. Chem. com. 67 lead, with 1 to 2 copper and iron, 16 antimony, with 4·7 arsenic, and 17 sulphur. Sala in Sweden, Mérédo in Spain, and near Pietrosanto in Tuscany. *Kilbrickenite*, massive, granular, or foliated ; County Clare in Ireland.

453. STEINMANNITE.—Pb′, Sb‴.

Tesseral ; O ; also botryoidal and reniform. Cleavage, hexahedral rather imperfect ; sectile. H. = 2·5 ; G. = 6·833. Lead-gray. B.B. decrepitates violently ; on charcoal fuses readily, leaving lead and silver. Przibram.

454. PLUMOSITE, Feather Ore.—Pb⁴ Sb‴.

Rhombic ; isomorphous with stibine ; but acicular or capillary, in felt-like masses. H. = 1...3 ; G. = 5·7. Dull or glimmering. Dark lead or steel gray, sometimes iridescent. B.B. and with acids acts like jamesonite, of which Rammelsberg makes it a variety ; fuses even in the flame of a candle. Chem. com. 51 lead, 29·5 antimony, and 19·5 sulphur. Wolfsberg, Andreasberg, and Clausthal ; Neudorf in Anhalt, Freiberg, and Schemnitz.

455. ENARGITE.—$Cu^3 As''' = [3 Cu^2 S . As^2 S^3]$.

Rhombic; ∞P 97° 53', $\breve{P} \infty 100° 58'$, mostly massive and granular. Cleavage, ∞P perfect, brachy- and macro-diagonal less so; brittle. H. = 3 ; G. = 4·3...4·5. Iron-black. In the closed tube yields first sulphur, then fuses. B.B. with borax, a bead of copper. Chem. com. 48·3 copper, 19·1 arsenic, and 32·6 sulphur. Morocacha in Peru.

456. DUFRENOYSITE, *Damour.*—$Cu^3 As'''^2$.

Tesseral. Crystals ∞O . 2O2. Fracture uneven ; brittle. H. = 2...3 ; G. = 4·4...4·7. Steel-gray ; streak reddish-brown. In the closed tube gives a reddish-brown sublimate. B.B. fuses easily, leaving a grain of copper. Readily soluble in warm acids. Chem. com. 39·3 copper (with 2·8 lead, 1·3 silver), 31 arsenic, and 29·7 sulphur, but some agree with enargite, which thus dimorphous. Binnenthal, St. Gotthardt.

457. SKLEROCLASE, Binnite.—$Pb^3 As'''$.

Rhombic; P polar edges 96° 31' and 102° 41'; ∞P 93° 39'; $\breve{P} \infty$ 63°. Crystals, thick tables or broad prismatic, acicular or fibrous; very brittle and friable. Cleavage, basal perfect. H. = 3 ; G. = 5·55. Bright metallic. Dark lead-gray ; streak reddish-brown. Chem. com. 57·2 lead, 20·7 arsenic, 22·1 sulphur, with traces of silver, copper, and iron. St. Gotthardt, with dufrenoysite.

Jordanite, rhombic, with a hexagonal aspect, is very similar ; but distinguished by distinct brachydiagonal cleavage and black streak, occurs with skleroclase.

458. WOLFSBERGITE.—$Cu' Sb'''$, *or* $[Cu^2 S . Sb^2 S^3]$.

Rhombic; ∞P 135° 12', $\infty \breve{P} 2$ 111°. Crystals tabular; also fine granular. Cleavage, brachydiagonal very perfect, basal imperfect ; fracture conchoidal or uneven. H. = 3·5 ; G. = 4·748. Lead-gray to iron-black, sometimes iridescent; streak black, dull. B.B. decrepitates, fuses easily, and with soda gives a grain of copper. Chem. com. 25·4 copper, 49 antimony, and 25·6 sulphur. Wolfsberg in the Harz.

459. BERTHIERITE.—$Fe' Sb'''$.

Massive ; columnar or fibrous, with indistinct cleavage.

FAMILY IV.—GRAY COPPER ORE.

Crystallisation rhombic and tesseral. H. = 1...4, the ores of copper being above 3, the ores of silver below 3; G. = 4·2...6·3. Colour steel or lead gray, in a few inclining to black or brown. All soluble in nitric acid. B.B. fusible, often easily, with fumes of sulphur or arsenic. Mostly sulphurets of copper and silver, with sulphurets of arsenic or antimony.

**463. TETRAHEDRITE, $\{$ (Cu', Ag', Fe', Zn', Hy')' (Sb''', FAHLORE, Gray Copper. $\{$ As'''), *or* [4 Cu² S . Sb² S²].

Tesseral and tetrahedral. In crystals $\dfrac{O}{2}, -\dfrac{O}{2}, \infty O, \dfrac{2O2}{2}$

(Fig. 264, and Figs. 19, 20). Macles (Fig. 265), not uncommon; most abundant massive and disseminated.

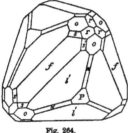

Fig. 264.

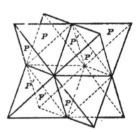

Fig. 265.

Cleavage, octahedral imperfect, with traces in other directions; fracture conchoidal, uneven, or fine granular; brittle. H. = 3...4; G. = 4·5...5·2. Steel-gray to iron-black; streak black (dark-red when containing zinc). B.B. on charcoal boils slightly, and fuses to a steel-gray slag, usually magnetic, and with soda gives copper. In nitric acid the powder forms a brownish-green solution. Chem. com. essentially Cu² S in combination with Sb² S². But part of the copper is replaced by silver, iron, zinc, or mercury; part of the antimony by arsenic. The pure antimony (25 to 28 per cent) fahlores are dark coloured, contain most silver, and fused in closed tube give a dark-red sublimate.

The pure arsenic (14 to 19 per cent) fahlores are paler coloured, contain no silver, and give in closed tube a sublimate of sulphuret of arsenic. Analyses give 30 to 40 copper, 0 to 10 silver, 1 to 6 iron, 1 to 7 zinc, 0 to 7·5 mercury, and 23 to 27 sulphur. Harz, Müsen, Freiberg, Camsdorf, Alsace, Kremnitz, Kapnik; Crinnis and other Cornish mines near St. Austle; Airthrie near Stirling, and Sandlodge in Zetland. Those with 17 to 31 silver are the *Silver Fahlore* (Freiberg). Ore of copper and silver.

464. TENNANTITE.—(Cu′, Fe′) As‴.

Tesseral; like fahlore, and scarcely distinct. Cleavage, ∞O very imperfect; brittle. H. = 4; G. = 4·3...4·5. Blackish lead-gray to iron-black; streak dark reddish-gray. B.B. decrepitates, burns with a bluish flame and odour of arsenic, and fuses to a magnetic slag. Chem. com. 49 copper, 4 iron, 19 arsenic, and 28 sulphur. Redruth and St. Day, Cornwall, and Skutterud. *Copperblende*, with brownish-red streak; G. = 4·3; contains 8·9 zinc; Freiberg.

465. BOURNONITE.—Pb‴ Sb‴ + Cu‴ Sb‴.

Rhombic; ∞P (*d*) 93° 40′, P̄∞ (*n*) 96° 13′, P̄∞ (*e*) 92° 34′, 0P (*r*), ∞P̄∞ (*s*), ∞P̄∞ (*k*) (as in Fig. 266, but in other position). Crystals generally thick tabular, very often macled by a face of ∞P, and several times repeated;

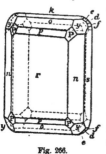

also granular or disseminated. Cleavage, brachydiagonal imperfect, traces in other directions; fracture uneven to conchoidal; rather brittle. H. = 2·5...3; G. = 5·7...5·9. Lustre brilliant metallic. Steel-gray, inclining to lead-gray and iron-black. B.B. usually decrepitates and fuses easily to a black globule, staining the charcoal first white, then yellow, and with soda leaves a grain of copper. In nitric acid a blue solution. Chem. com. 42·4 lead, 13 copper, 25 antimony, and 19·6 sulphur. Harz (Neudorf), Bräunsdorf, Kapnik, Servoz, Alais and Pontgibaud, Redruth and Beeralston.

Fig. 266.

Wölchite from Wölch in Carinthia is only a variety.

466. FREIESLEBENITE.—$Ag'^3 Sb''' + Pb'^3 Sb'''$.

Monoclinic ; C. = 87° 46' ; ∞P 119° 12', $P^\circ\infty$ 31° 41', in prisms with curved reed-like faces and strong vertical striæ. Macles intersecting; also massive. Cleavage, ∞P perfect ; fracture conchoidal or uneven ; rather brittle. H. = 2...2·5 ; G. = 6·2...6·4. Steel-gray to dark lead-gray ; streak the same. B.B. on charcoal fuses to a grain of silver. Chem. com. 22·5 silver, 32·4 lead (with copper), 26·8 antimony, and 18·3 sulphur. Rare. Freiberg in Saxony ; Hiendelaencina, Spain.

Diaphorite with the same chem. com., but in rhombic crystals, with G. = 5·90. At Przibram alone, also at Freiberg.

467. STEPHANITE.—$Ag'^3 Sb''' = [5 Ag^2 S . Sb^2 S^3]$.

Rhombic ; ∞P (*o*) 115° 39', P (*P*) middle edge 104° 20', $2\bar{P}\infty$ (*d*) middle edge 107° 48', 0P (*s*), $\infty\bar{P}\infty$ (*p*), (Figs. 267, 268), thick tabular or short prismatic. Macles frequent, repeated three or four times; also massive. Cleavage (*d* and *p*), both imperfect ; fracture conchoidal or un-

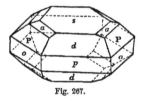

Fig. 267.   Fig. 268.

even ; sectile. H. = 2...2·5 ; G. = 6·2...6·3. Iron-black to blackish lead-gray, rarely iridescent. B.B. on charcoal (odour of arsenic) fuses to a dark-gray globule ; with soda, a grain of silver. Chem. com. 68·5 silver, 15·3 antimony, and 16·2 sulphur, but with under 5 iron, 4 copper, and 3·3 arsenic. Freiberg, Schneeberg, Johann-Georgenstadt, and Annaberg ; Joachimsthal and Przibram, Schemnitz, the Harz, Mexico, Peru, Siberia, and Cornwall. Valuable ore of silver.

468. POLYBASITE.—$(Ag', Cu')^9 (Sb''', As''')$.

Hexagonal ; P 117°. Crystals 0P . ∞ P and 0P . P

X

(Fig. 269), tabular, and often very thin ; also massive. Cleavage, basal imperfect ; sectile, and easily frangible. H. = 2...2·5 ; G. = 6·0...6·25. Iron-black; in very thin lamellæ, translucent red. B.B. decrepitates slightly, and fuses very easily. Chem. com. 64

Fig. 269.

to 72 silver, 3 to 10 copper, 16 to 17 sulphur, 0·2 to 8 antimony, and 1 to 6 arsenic. Freiberg, Joachimsthal, Schemnitz, Guanaxuato, Nevada, and Idaho. Rich ore of silver.

469. STERNBERGITE.—(Ag' + 2 Fe') Fe'''.

Rhombic ; P middle edge 118°. Crystals usually thin tabular, in macles or in fan-like and spheroidal groups. Cleavage, basal very perfect ; sectile, and flexible in thin laminæ. H. = 1...1·5 ; G. = 4·2...4·25. Dark pinchbeck-brown, often a violet-blue tarnish ; streak black. B.B. on charcoal fuses to a magnetic globule covered with silver, with borax, a grain of silver ; decomposed by nitrochloric acid. Chem. com. 34·2 silver, 35·4 iron, and 30·4 sulphur. Joachimsthal, Schneeberg, and Johann-Georgenstadt.

Flexible Sulphuret of Silver is identical ; Hungary and Freiberg.

470. STANNINE, Tin Pyrites.—Cu''³ Sn'' + (Fe', Zn')³ Sn''.

Tesseral ; in cubes very rare, generally massive and granular. Cleavage, hexahedral very imperfect ; fracture uneven or small conchoidal ; brittle. H. = 4 ; G. = 4·3... 4·5. Steel-gray (yellowish from copper pyrites) ; streak black. B.B. on charcoal fuses, forming round the assay a white coating ; with soda, a grain of copper ; easily decomposed by nitric acid, leaving tin peroxide and sulphur ; the solution is blue. Chem. com. 26 to 32 tin, 24 to 30 copper, 5 to 12 iron, 2 to 10 zinc, and 30 sulphur. Huel Rock near St. Agnes, St. Michael's Mount, and Carn Brea, Cornwall ; and Zinnwald. *Bell-metal ore.*

471. WITTICHENITE, Cupreous Bismuth.—Cu''³ Bi'''.

Rhombic ; in tabular crystals like bournonite, but chiefly massive. Fracture uneven ; sectile. H. = 2·5 ; G. = 4·3...5. Steel-gray, with lead-gray tarnish ; streak black. B.B. fuses very readily, froths, and stains the charcoal yellow ; with soda, a grain of copper. Chem.

com. 38·5 copper, 42 bismuth, and 19·5 sulphur. Wittichen in Schwarzwald.

Klaprothite, long prismatic crystals $\infty P = 107°$; with
very distinct macrodiagonal cleavage, strongly striated and
yellowish steel-gray, occurs with wittichenite, but gives
$\Theta u'{}^2 Bi'''{}^2$, or 25·2 copper, 55·6 bismuth, and 19·2 sulphur.
The *Bismuthic silver* of Klaproth is probably a mixture.

472. EMPLECTITE.—$\Theta u' Bi'''$.

Rhombic; ∞P, 102° 42', $P\infty$ 101° 38', in thin acicular prisms, strongly striated. Cleavage, macrodiagonal perfect, basal distinct; sectile. Tin-white, with yellow tarnish. H. $= 2$; G. $= 5·14...5·26$. In warm n. acid gives a
dark greenish-blue solution. Chem. com. 19 copper, 62
bismuth, and 19 sulphur. Schwarzenberg in Saxony, Freu-
denstadt in Würtemberg, and Copiapo, Chili.

FAMILY V.—BLENDES.

Crystallisation mostly tesseral; cleavage distinct. H.
$= 3·5...4·5$; G. $= 3·5...4·9$. Lustre adamantine or resinous; more or less *translucent*. Colours and streak red,
yellow, brown, or black. All soluble in acids. B.B. often
decrepitate, but fuse with difficulty.

**473. SPHALERITE, BLENDE, Zinc-blende.—$Zn' = [Zn S]$.

Tesseral and tetrahedral; $\dfrac{O}{2}, -\dfrac{O}{2}$ (sometimes as O), ∞O,
$\dfrac{3O3}{2}$ and $\infty O\infty$. Macles remarkably common, united by

a face of O (Fig. 270) and several times
repeated; frequently massive and
granular. Cleavage, ∞O very perfect; very brittle. H. $= 3·5...4$; G.
$= 3·9 ... 4·2$. Semitransparent to
opaque; adamantine and resinous.
Brown or black, also red, yellow, and
green, rarely colourless or white. B.B.
decrepitates often violently, but only

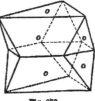

Fig. 270.

fuses on very thin edges; soluble in con. nitric acid, leaving sulphur. Chem. com. 67 zinc and 33 sulphur, but

generally in the darker varieties with 1 to 15 iron, 0 to 3 cadmium. Very abundant, the Harz, Freiberg, Przibram, Schemnitz, Kapnik, North America, Peru, Cornwall, Derbyshire, Cumberland, Leadhills, Tyndrum, and Stotfield, near Elgin. Used for producing zinc vitriol, sulphur, and recently as an ore of zinc.

474. WURZITE.—Zn'.

Hexagonal ; ∞P . P, with strong horizontal striæ. Cleavage, basal and prismatic. H. = 3·5...4 ; G. = 3.9 ...4·1. Brownish-black ; streak light brown. Chem. com. like blende, which thus dimorphous. Oruro in Bolivia, and Przibram (*Radiated blende*).

475. VOLTZINE.— 4 Zn' + Żn.

Hemispherical, curved lamellar incrustations. Fracture conchoidal. H. = 4·5 ; G. = 3·5...3·8. Brick-red to yellow or brown. Opaque or translucent ; vitreo-resinous ; pearly. B.B. like zinc-blende ; soluble in h. acid. Chem. com. 82·8 sulphuret and 17·2 oxide of zinc. Pontgibaud and Joachimsthal.

476. ALABANDINE.—Mn'.

Tesseral ; O and ∞O∞ ; usually massive and granular. Cleavage, hexahedral perfect ; fracture uneven ; rather brittle. H. = 3·5...4 ; G. = 3·9...4·0. Opaque ; semi-metallic. Iron-black to dark steel-gray, brownish-black tarnish ; streak dark green. B.B. fuses on thin edges to a brown slag ; soluble in h. acid. Chem. com. 63 manganese and 37 sulphur. Nagyag, Kapnik, Alabanda, Mexico, and Brazil.

477. HAUERITE.—Mn".

Tesseral ; O, ∞O∞, and ∞O. Crystals single or in spherical groups. Cleavage, hexahedral perfect. H. = 4 ; G. = 3·463. Semi-translucent on very thin edges ; metallic-adamantine. Reddish-brown to brownish-black ; streak brownish-red. In the closed tube yields sulphur, and leaves a green mass, which B.B. becomes brown on the surface, and is soluble in h. acid. Chem. com. 46 manganese and 54 sulphur. Kalinka, near Neusohl in Hungary.

478. GREENOCKITE.—Cd′.

Hexagonal and hemimorphic; P 86° 21′, 2P 123° 54′. Crystals 2P.0P. ∞P.P, or P.2P.∞P; attached singly. Cleavage, ∞P imperfect, basal perfect. H. = 3...3·5; G. = 4·8...4·9. Translucent; brilliant resinous, or adamantine. Honey or orange yellow, rarely brown; streak yellow. B.B. decrepitates and becomes carmine-red, but again yellow when cold; fused with soda forms a reddish-brown coating on charcoal; soluble in h. acid. Chem. com. 77·6 cadmium, and 22·4 sulphur. Bishoptown in Renfrewshire, Przibram, and Friedensville in Pennsylvania.

FAMILY VI.—RUBY-BLENDES.

Crystallisation rhombohedral, monoclinic, or rhombic. Cleavage rarely distinct. H. = 1·5...2·5; G. = 3·5...8·2. Lustre adamantine. Colour yellow, red, or gray; streak deep red, rarely brownish or yellow. Soluble in nitric acid. B.B. fusible and reduced, often with fumes, or sublime. Occur chiefly in veins in the igneous, the metamorphic, and older stratified rocks. Those with silver are valuable ores of that metal.

*479. PYRARGYRITE, $\{$ A′g³ Sb‴ = [3 Ag² S . Sb² S³], *or* Red Silver. $\{$ [Ag³ Sb S³].

Hexagonal-rhombohedral; R (P) 108° 42′, − ½R 137°

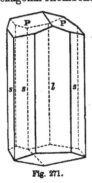

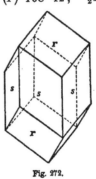

Fig. 271.   Fig. 272.

5 8′, 0R, − 2R (*r*), R3, ∞P2 (*s*), and ∞R (*l*). Crystal.

prismatic (Figs. 271, 272); macles common of various kinds; also massive, dendritic, or investing. Cleavage, R rather perfect; fracture conchoidal to uneven and splintery; slightly sectile, sometimes almost brittle. H. = 2...2·5; G. = 5·75...5·85. Translucent on the edges to opaque; crimson-red to blackish lead-gray; streak cochineal to cherry-red. B.B. on charcoal fuses easily, gives out sulphurous acid and antimony fumes, and leaves a grain of silver; soluble in nitric acid, leaving sulphur and antimony protoxide; solution of potash extracts sulphuret of antimony. Chem. com. 60 silver, 22·3 antimony, and 17·7 sulphur. Andreasberg, Freiberg, Johann-Georgenstadt, Annaberg, Schneeberg, and Marienberg; Przibram, Schemnitz and Kremnitz, Kongsberg, Mexico, Nevado, etc. ; Huel Brothers and Huel Duchy in Cornwall.

*480. PROUSTITE.—$Ag^2 As''' = [3 Ag^2 S . As^2 S^3]$.

Rhombohedral, like pyrargyrite, except R, 107° 50′. G. 5·5...5·6. Semitransparent to translucent on the edges. Cochineal to crimson red; streak aurora-red to cochineal-red. B.B. arsenical odour, and leaves a brittle metallic grain difficultly reduced to pure silver; soluble in nitric acid, with remainder of sulphur and arsenious acid; solution of potash extracts sulphuret of arsenic. Chem. com. 65·5 silver, 15·1 arsenic, and 19·4 sulphur. In the same localities with pyrargyrite, and both valuable ores of silver. (Red orpiment has a lower specific gravity and yellow streak; cinnabar volatilises before the blowpipe.)

481. MIARGYRITE.—$Ag' Sb'''$.

Monoclinic; C. = 81° 36′, P 90° 53′, −P 95° 59′. Crystals pyramidal, short prismatic, or tabular (Fig. 273); also massive. Cleavage, indistinct traces; fracture imperfect conchoidal or uneven; sectile. H. = 2...2·5; G. = 5·2 ...5·3. Opaque; thin splinters dark blood-red, translucent; metallic adamantine.

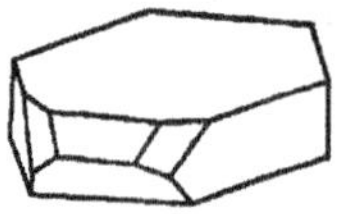

Fig. 273.

Blackish lead-gray to iron-black and steel-gray; streak cherry-red. B.B. with soda, a grain of silver; with acids, like pyrargyrite. Chem. com. 37 silver, 41 antimony, and 22 sulphur. Bräunsdorf near Freiberg, Przibram, and Potosi.

Rittingerite.—Monoclinic ; C. = 88° 26′, ∞P 126° 18′. Crystals small tabular. Cleavage basal imperfect ; brittle. H. = 2·5...3. Translucent honey-yellow to red. Colour iron-black, on 0P brown tarnished ; streak orange-yellow. B.B. melts easily, with arsenic fumes, leaving much silver. Joachimsthal.

482. XANTHOKON.—$Ag'^3 As''' + Ag'^3 As'''^{a}$

Hexagonal-rhombohedral. Crystals very thin hexagonal tables, with R : 0R 110° 30′, −2R : 0R 100° 35′. Cleavage, R and 0R more or less perfect ; rather brittle, very easily frangible. H. = 2...2·5 ; G. = 5·0...5·2. Translucent and transparent ; adamantine. Orange-yellow or brown ; streak slightly darker. In the closed tube fuses very easily, becomes lead-gray. Chem. com. 63·4 silver, 14·7 arsenic, and 21·9 sulphur. Himmelsfürst Mine at Freiberg.

Fireblende.—In thin tabular crystals (like heulandite), with one perfect cleavage ; sectile and slightly flexible. G. = 4·2 ... 4·3. Hyacinth-red. B.B. like pyrargyrite. Contains sulphur, antimony, and silver. Freiberg and Andreasberg.

483. KERMES, Antimony-blende.—Sb''^a Sb.

Monoclinic. Crystals acicular, capillary, and diverging ; also radiating fibrous. Cleavage, very perfect along the axis of the crystals, less perfect at right angles ; sectile. H. = 1...1·5 ; G. = 4·5...4·6. Semitranslucent ; adamantine. Cherry-red ; streak similar. B.B. acts like stibine ; soluble in h. acid ; in solution of potash the powder becomes yellow and dissolves. Chem. com. 75·3 antimony, 19·8 sulphur, and 4·9 oxygen ; or 70 sulphuret and 30 protoxide of antimony. Bräunsdorf near Freiberg, Przibram, Allemont, and Southam, Canada.

Zundererz, or *Tinder ore,* soft, flexible, tinder-like masses, cherry or blackish red, is a mixture. Andreasberg.

484. CINNABAR.—Hg′.

Hexagonal-rhombohedral ; R 71° 48′, R . 0R . ∞R . ⅓R (*n, o, m, i,* Fig. 274). Crystals rhombohedral or thick tabular ; also disseminated and granular, compact, or earthy.

Cleavage, ∞P rather perfect; fracture uneven and splintery; sectile. H.=2...2·5; G.=8·0...8·2. Semitransparent with circular polarisation like quartz, or opaque; adamantine. Cochineal-red, with lead-gray and scarlet-red

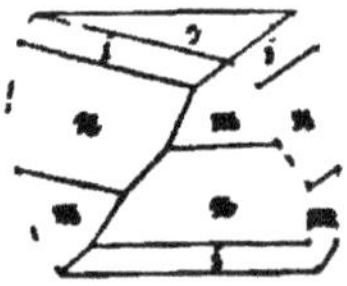

tarnish; streak scarlet-red. In the open tube sublimes, partly as cinnabar, partly as metallic mercury; perfectly soluble in nitrochloric acid, but not in hydrochloric acid, nitric acid, or solution of potash. Chem. com. 86·2 mercury and 13·8 sulphur. Idria in Carniola, Almaden and Almadenejos in Spain, Wolfstein and Moschellandsberg in Rhenish Bavaria, Hartenstein in Saxony, Szlana and Rosenau in Hungary, Ripa in Tuscany; New Almaden in California, Mexico, and Peru. Principal ore of mercury; also used as a pigment. *Fibrous and Hepatic Cinnabar* are mixtures.

Fig. 274.

*485. REALGAR, Red Orpiment.—As″, or [As S].
Monoclinic; C. =66° 5′, ∞P (*M*) 74° 26′, P∞ (*n*) 132° 2′, ∞P°2 (*l*) 113° 16′. Crystals prismatic (Fig. 275); also massive and investing. Cleavage, basal and

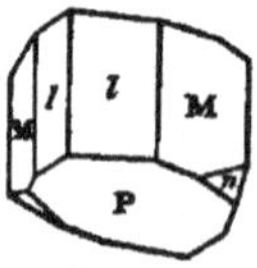

clinodiagonal rather perfect, prismatic imperfect; fracture small conchoidal to uneven or splintery; sectile. H. = 1·5...2; G. = 3·4...3·6. Semitransparent or opaque; resinous. Aurora-red; streak orange-yellow. In the closed tube sublimes as a dark-yellow or red mass; B.B. on charcoal fuses and burns with a yellowish-white flame; acids act on it with difficulty. Chem. com. 70 arsenic and 30 sulphur. Kapnik, Nagyag, Felsobanya, and Tajowa, Andreasberg, St. Gotthardt, Vesuvius, and the Solfatara.

Fig. 275.

486. DIMORPHINE.—As‴.
Rhombic, in two types; more common short prismatic, with ∞P 96° 34′ and P∞ 103° 50′; the other more pyramidal (but both derivable from form of orpiment—*Kenngott*). Very fragile. H. = 1·5; G. = 3·58. Splendent adamantine; translucent or transparent. Orange-yellow; streak

similar. Chem. com. 75·5 arsenic, and 24·5 sulphur. Solfatara, Naples.

487. ORPIMENT.—As''', *or* [As³ S³].

Rhombic ; ∞P (*h*) 117° 49', $\bar{\text{P}}$∞ (*o*) 83° 37', ∞P̆2 (*u*),
∞P̄∞ (*s*). Crystals short prismatic (Fig. 276), disseminated,
columnar or foliated. Cleavage, brachydiagonal very perfect, striated vertically; sectile, and in thin laminæ flexible. H. = 1·5...2; G. = 3·4...3·5. Semitransparent or opaque ; resinous or pearly. Citron-
yellow to orange-yellow. In the closed tube
yields a dark-yellow or red sublimate; fused with
soda it yields metallic arsenic; soluble in nitrochloric acid, in potash, and in ammonia. Chem.

Fig. 276.

com. 61 arsenic and 39 sulphur. Tajowa near Neusohl,
Servia, Wallachia, Natolia, Felsobanya, Kapnik, and Andreasberg ; the Solfatara, and Zimapan in Mexico.

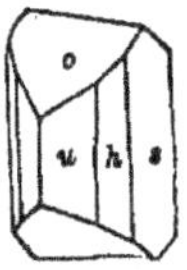

ORDER VII.

THE INFLAMMABLES.

NAMED from the substances all burning before the blow-pipe, whereas the former minerals only fused or gave out fumes, and left a residue. Few of them are crystallised, and many are rather organic remains or rocks than simple minerals. In chemical composition a few are simple elements, as sulphur and carbon, the others mostly formed on the plan not of the mineral kingdom, but of organic nature. Except the diamond, their hardness is low, or less than 2·5; and their specific gravity also 2·2, or under.

FAMILY I.—SULPHUR.

**488. SULPHUR.—S.

Rhombic; P polar edges 106° 38′, 84° 58′, middle edge 143° 17′; ∞P 101° 58′, 0P, ⅓P, P̆∞. Crystals pyramidal P.0P (*P, C*, Fig. 277), single or in druses; also reniform, spherical, stalactitic, disseminated, incrusting, or pulverulent. Cleavage, basal and ∞P imperfect; fracture conchoidal to uneven or splintery; rather brittle. H. = 1·5 ...2·5; G. = 1·9...2·1. Transparent or translucent on the edges; resinous or adamantine. Sulphur-yellow, passing into brown and red, or into yellowish-gray and white. In the closed tube it sublimes; at 227° Fahr. fuses, and at 518° takes fire and burns with a blue flame, forming sulphurous acid. Chem. com. sulphur, occasionally more or less mixed with other substances. Found chiefly in tertiary strata and near volcanoes. Sicily, at Girgenti, Cataldo, etc.; the Lipari Islands, the Solfatara near Naples, Poland, Iceland, Java, Sandwich Islands,

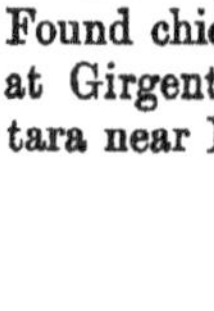

Fig. 277.

Peru, and Chili; from springs at Aix-la-Chapelle, and in Scotland. Fused sulphur crystallises in transparent mono-clinic prisms, which soon become obscure and change their form when cold. Used for making gunpowder and sul-phuric acid; in medicine, and for many other purposes.

489. SELEN-SULPHUR.

Orange-yellow or yellowish-brown. Fuses readily in the closed tube, and volatilises. B.B. on charcoal burns, and gives out fumes of selenic and sulphurous acids. Con-sists of sulphur and selenium. Vulcano, Lipari, and Kilauea in Hawai.

Native Selenium.—Brownish-black or lead-gray. Thin splinters red translucent. H. = 2 ; G. = 4·3. Culebras in Mexico.

FAMILY II.—DIAMOND.

*490. DIAMOND.—C.

Tesseral and tetrahedral - semitesseral ; $\dfrac{O}{2}$ and $-\dfrac{O}{2}$ mostly conjoined, ∞O, ∞On, mO, mOn ; or the octahe-dron, rhombic dodecahedron, and hexakisoctahedron (Figs. 2, 3, 7, and 5). The crystals have often curved faces (Fig. 278), and occur loose and embedded singly. Macles common, united by a plane of O, like Fig. 270. Cleavage, octahedral perfect ; fracture conchoidal ; brittle. H. = 10; G. = 3·5...3·6. Trans-parent or translucent when dark-coloured. Refracts light strongly; brilliant adaman-tine. Colourless, but often white, gray, or brown tints, also green, yellow, red, blue,

Fig. 278.

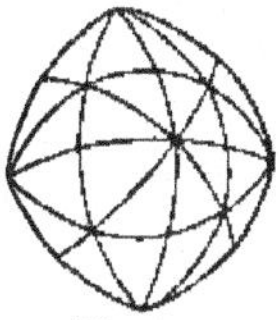

and rarely black. Becomes positive electric by friction. Insoluble in acids, and B.B. infusible; but burns in oxygen gas, and forms carbonic acid. When air is excluded remains unchanged at the temperature of melting cast-iron, but at that of melting bar-iron changes into graphite. Chem. com. pure carbon. Hindostan on the east of the Deccan, between Pennar, Sonar, and the delta of the Ganges (lat. 14° to 25°); Borneo and Malacca; Brazil in the district of Serro do Frio in Minas Geraes; also in Borneo, Malacca, the Ural, Georgia, and North Carolina, California, Arizona, and the Sierra Madre, Mexico. Also recently, very many and of large size in South Africa, north of the Cape. Used as precious stones, also for cutting glass and polishing purposes. Rough diamonds till lately were worth 35s. to 45s. the carat (= 3·7 grains). Cut as brilliants from £8 to £12 the carat, the value increasing as the square of the weight, and even more rapidly above 12 to 20 carats. In 1873 Cape diamonds were worth—yellows under 5 carats, 40s. to 50s.; above 5 carats, £3 to £4 per carat; pure white stones under 5 carats, £3 to £4; and above 5 carats, £4 to £7 or more, according to form and lustre.

*FAMILY III.—THE COALS.

**491. GRAPHITE, Plumbago.—C.
Hexagonal or monoclinic; but only thin tabular or short prismatic crystals of 0P . ∞P. Usually foliated, radiating, scaly, or compact. Cleavage, basal perfect; very sectile, flexible in thin laminæ. Feels greasy. H. = 0·5.... 1; G. = 1·9...2·2. Opaque; metallic. Iron-black. Leaves a mark on paper. Is a perfect conductor of electricity. B.B. burns with much difficulty, the foliated more so even than the diamond; and heated with nitre in a platina spoon only partially detonates. Chem. com. carbon, but mixed with iron, lime, alumina, or other matter. Pargas, Arendal, Passau, Spain, Ticonderoga in New York, Ceylon, Siberia, also Borrowdale in Cumberland, Glenstrathfarrer in Inverness-shire, Strathdon and other parts of Aberdeen-shire, Kirkcudbright, and Craigman in Ayrshire. At the latter it is evidently common coal altered by contact with trap. Is used for making pencils, and to form crucibles.

*492. ANTHRACITE.—Glance-Coal.
Massive and disseminated; rarely columnar, or fibrous and pulverulent. Fracture conchoidal; brittle. H. = 2... 2·5; G. = 1·4...1·7. Opaque; brilliant metallic. Iron-black or grayish-black; streak unaltered. Perfect conductor of electricity. Burns difficultly with a very weak

or no flame, and does not cake; in the closed tube yields a little moisture, but no empyreumatic oil; detonates with nitre. Chem. com. carbon above 90 per cent, with 1 to 3 oxygen, 1 to 4 hydrogen, and 0 to 3 nitrogen; and ashes chiefly of silica, alumina, lime, and peroxide of iron. Very common in some parts of the English, Scottish, and Irish coal-fields; in the Alps, as the Valais, Piedmont, Savoy, and Dauphiné; in the Pyrenees, and in various parts of France; in Silesia, Bohemia, Saxony, and the Harz; and in the United States, as in Rhode Island, Massachusetts, and above all in Pennsylvania. Used for manufacturing metals, and for economic and household purposes.

**493. COMMON COAL, Black, Stone, Bituminous Coal.

Compact, slaty, or confusedly fibrous; often dividing into columnar, cubical, or rhomboidal fragments. Fracture conchoidal, uneven, or fibrous; rather brittle or sectile. H. $= 2...2\cdot5$; G. $= 1\cdot2...1\cdot5$. Vitreous, resinous, or silky in the fibrous variety. Blackish-brown, pitch-black, or velvet-black. Burns easily, emitting flame and smoke, with a bituminous odour; heated in the closed tube yields much oil, and with powdered sulphur gives out sulphuretted hydrogen. Chem. com. 74 to 90 carbon, with $0\cdot6$ to 8 or 15 oxygen, 3 to 6 hydrogen, $0\cdot1$ to 2 nitrogen, $0\cdot1$ to 3 sulphur, and 1 to 11 earthy matters or ash, in 100 parts.

Slate-coal has a thick slaty structure, and an uneven fracture in the cross direction. *Cannel-coal*, a resinous, glimmering lustre, and a large or flat conchoidal fracture; breaks into irregular cubical fragments, but more solid, and takes a higher polish than other varieties. It burns with a bright flame, and yields much gas. *Torbanite*, from Torbanehill near Bathgate, dull, brown, with yellowish streak, contains 9 hydrogen, and only 4 to 6 oxygen, with 20 to 25 ashes, chiefly alumina. *Coarse* or *foliated coal*, massive or lamellar, breaks into cubical or irregular angular masses, with a more splendent lustre and less compact texture than cannel-coal, and more easily frangible. *Earthy coal*, loose powdery masses, often brown or dirty in colour, and apparently semi-decomposed. Abundant in many lands, as in England, Scotland, and Ireland ; in Belgium and France, in Germany and Southern Russia.   British America and the United States possess immense fields, specially in the valley of the Mississippi.   Also found in China, Japan, Hindostan, Australia, Borneo, and several of the Indian Islands.   Its uses are too well known to need notice.   In 1871 England produced 90,128,087 tons ; Wales, 11,620,000 ; Scotland, 15,438,291 ; and Ireland, 165,750 ; or in all 117,352,028 tons coal, worth £35,205,608.

*494. BROWN COAL.—Lignite, Jet.

Distinctly vegetable in origin, the external form, and very often the internal woody structure, being preserved. The texture is compact, woody, or earthy.   Fracture conchoidal, woody, or uneven ; soft and often friable.   G. = 0·5...1·5.   Lustre sometimes resinous, mostly glimmering or dull.   Brown, black, or rarely gray.   Burns easily with an unpleasant odour ; colours solution of potash deep brown ; heated with sulphur evolves much sulphuretted hydrogen.   Chem. com. 47 to 73 carbon, 2·5 to 7·5 hydrogen, 8 to 33 oxygen (with nitrogen), and 1 to 15 ashes. *Jet* is pitch-black, with conchoidal fracture and resinous lustre.   Brown coal occurs at Bovey Tracy in Devonshire ; also in Germany, Hungary, France, Italy, and Greece.   The *Surturbrand* of Iceland seems a variety.   Used as fuel, but much inferior to common coal.   The oolitic coals of Yorkshire, Antrim, Brora, Mull, and Skye, are intermediate varieties.

*495. PEAT.

A mass of more or less decomposed vegetable matter of a brown or black colour, closely connected with coal, and, like it, rather a rock than a simple mineral.   Contains 50 to 60 carbon, 5 to 6 hydrogen, 30 to 39 oxygen, 0 to 2 nitrogen, and 1 to 14 ashes in 100 parts.   Common everywhere in the colder parts of the earth.

FAMILY IV.—THE MINERAL RESINS.

Named from their resemblance in aspect and composition to vegetable resins, and many of them only such slightly altered. Bitumen is fluid ; the others solid with H. = 1 to 2 or 2·5. Most are amorphous, a few crystalline and monoclinic. G. = 0·6...1·6. Mostly resinous, colourless or coloured, brown, yellow, or red, with paler streak. Soluble in acids, alcohol, ether, and oils. Melt readily, and burn with flame and smoke. Compounds of carbon and hydrogen, or also oxygen, and rarely nitrogen. But many very uncertain, and hardly true minerals.

*496. BITUMEN, Naphtha.—CH^2.

Liquid. Colourless, yellow, or brown ; transparent or translucent. G. = 0·7...0·9. Volatilises in the atmosphere with an aromatic bituminous odour. Chem. com. 84 to 88 carbon, and 12 to 16 hydrogen. Varieties are :—

Naphtha.—Very fluid, transparent, and light yellow. Tegern Lake in Bavaria, Amiano near Parma, Salies in the Pyrenees, Rangun in Hindostan, Baku on the Caspian Sea, China, Persia, and North America. Used for burning and preparing varnishes. *Petroleum.*—Darker yellow or blackish-brown ; less fluid or volatile. Ormskirk in Lancashire, at Coalbrookdale, Pitchford, and Madeley in Shropshire ; St. Catherine's Well, south of Edinburgh ; Isle of Pomona ; and in many other parts of Europe. The oil-springs in the United States and Canada yield about £15,000,000 sterling worth in the year.

497. ELATERITE, Elastic Bitumen,⎫ CH^2.
        Mineral Caoutchouc. ⎭

Compact ; reniform or fungoid ; elastic and flexible like caoutchouc ; very soft. G. = 0·8...1·23. Resinous. Blackish, reddish, or yellowish brown. Strong bituminous odour. Chem. com. 84 to 86 carbon, 12 to 14 hydrogen, and a little oxygen. Derbyshire, Montrelais near Nantes, and Woodbury in Connecticut.

*498. ASPHALTUM. ·

Compact and disseminated. Fracture conchoidal, sometimes vesicular ; sectile. H. = 2 ; G. = 1·1...1·2. Opaque, resinous, and pitch-black ; strong bituminous odour, especially when rubbed. Takes fire easily, and burns with a bright flame and thick smoke ; soluble in ether, except a small remainder, which is dissolved in oil of turpentine. Chem. com. 76 to 88 carbon, 2 to 10 oxygen, 6 to 10 hydrogen, and 1 to 3 nitrogen. Limmer near Hanover, Seyssel on the Rhone ; Val Travers in Neufchatel, Lobsann in Alsace, in the Harz ; Dead Sea, Persia, and Trinidad ; Cornwall, Haughmond Hill, Shropshire ; East and West Lothian, Burntisland in Fifeshire, and near Strathpeffer in Ross-shire. The last is similar to the *Albertite* from Hillsborough, in New Brunswick.

499. PIAUZITE.

Massive ; imperfect conchoidal ; sectile. H. = 1·5 ; G. = 1·22. Dimly translucent on very thin edges ; resinous. Blackish-brown ; streak yellowish-brown. Fuses at 600° Fahr., and burns with an aromatic odour, lively flame, and dense smoke ; soluble in ether and caustic potash. Piauze in Carniola.

500. IXOLYTE.

Massive ; conchoidal fracture. H. = 1 ; G. = 1·008. Resinous. Hyacinth-red ; streak ochre-yellow. Rubbed between the fingers it emits an aromatic odour, and becomes soft at 119°, but is still viscid at 212°. Oberhart near Gloggnitz in Austria.

*501. AMBER, Succinite.—$C^{10} H^8 O$.

Round irregular lumps, grains, or drops, often enclosing insects and fragments of plants. Fracture perfect conchoidal ; slightly brittle. H. = 2...2·5 ; G. = 1·0...1·1. Transparent to translucent or almost opaque ; resinous. Honey-yellow, but from hyacinth-red or brown to yellowish-white ; also streaked or spotted. When rubbed emits an agreeable odour, and becomes negatively electric. It melts at 550°, emitting water, an empyreumatic oil, and succinic acid ; it burns with a bright flame and pleasant odour, leaving a carbonaceous remainder ; only a small part is soluble in alcohol. Chem. com. 79 carbon, 10·5 hydrogen, and 10·5 oxygen. Derived chiefly from an extinct coniferous tree (*Pinites succinifer*), and found in the tertiary and diluvial formations of many countries, especially Northern Germany and shores of the Baltic, Sicily, Spain, and

Northern Italy; rarely in England, as on the shores of Norfolk, Suffolk, and Essex, and at Kensington, near London. Often contains fragments of extinct plants, of insects, spiders, and other arthropoda (above 1000 species). Used for ornamental purposes, and for preparing succinic acid and varnishes.

·502. RETINITE, Retinasphalt.

Roundish or irregular lumps. Fracture uneven or conchoidal; very easily frangible. H. = 1·5...2; G. = 1·05... 1·15. Translucent or opaque; resinous or glistening. Yellow or brown. Melts at a low heat, and burns with an aromatic or bituminous odour. Chem. com. in general carbon, hydrogen, and oxygen, in very uncertain amount. Bovey, Halle, Cape Sable, and Osnabrück.

503. WALCHOWITE.—$C^{12} H^9 O$.

Rounded pieces, with a conchoidal fracture. H. = 1·5 ...2; G. = 1·035...1·069. Translucent, resinous. Yellow with brown stripes; and a yellowish-white streak. It fuses at 482°, and burns readily; soluble partially (7·5 per cent) in ether, and in sulphuric acid forms a dark-brown solution. Chem. com. 80·4 carbon, 10·7 hydrogen, and 8·9 oxygen. Walchow in Moravia.

504. COPALINE, Fossil Copal, Highgate Resin. } $C^{40} H^{34} O$.

Irregular fragments. H. = 1·5; G. = 1·046. Translucent, resinous, and light-yellow or yellowish-brown. Burns easily with a bright yellow flame and much smoke; alcohol dissolves very little of it, which is precipitated by water; becomes black in sulphuric acid. Chem. com. 85·54 carbon, 11·63 hydrogen, 2·76 oxygen. Highgate near London. A similar resin from Settling Stones in Northumberland, found in flat drops or crusts on calc-spar, is infusible at 500° Fahr.; G. = 1·16...1·54; and contains 85·13 carbon, 10·85 hydrogen, and 3·26 ashes; or $C^2 H^3$.

505. BERENGELITE.—$C^{40} H^{33} O^6$.

Amorphous; conchoidal fracture. Dark-brown, inclining to green; yellow streak. Resinous; unpleasant odour, and bitter taste. Fuses below 212°, and then continues soft at ordinary temperatures; easily soluble in alcohol. Chem. com. 72·40 carbon, 9·28 hydrogen, 18·31 oxygen. St. Juan de Berengela in South America.

506. GUYAQUILLITE.—$C^{20} H^{26} O^2$.

Amorphous; yielding easily to the knife, and very friable. G. = 1·092. Pale yellow. Slightly resinous. Fluid at 212°, viscid when cold; slightly soluble in water and largely in alcohol, forming a yellow fluid with a bitter taste. Chem. com. 77·01 carbon, 8·18 hydrogen, and 14·80 oxygen. Guyaquil in South America.

Bogbutter, from the Irish peat mosses, is similar; melts at 124°, easily soluble in alcohol, and contains 73·70 carbon, 12·50 hydrogen, and 13·72 oxygen.

507. HARTINE.—$C^{20} H^{14} O^2$.

Spermaceti-like masses. G. = 1·115. White; without taste or smell. Becomes soft at 392°, and at 410° melts to a clear yellow fluid; burns with a bright flame; it is not soluble in water, very little in ether, and less in alcohol. Chem. com. 78·26 carbon, 10·92 hydrogen, 10·82 oxygen. Oberhart in Austria.

508. MIDDLETONITE.—$C^{20} H^{20}$ + HO.

Round masses or thin layers. Brittle, but easily cut with a knife. G. = 1·6. Resinous. Reddish-brown by reflected, deep-red by transmitted, light; streak, light-brown. Becomes black on exposure. Chem. com. 86·43 carbon, 8·01 hydrogen, 5·56 oxygen. In the main coal seam at Middleton near Leeds, and at Newcastle.

509. OZOKERITE, Native Parafine.—CH.

Amorphous, sometimes fibrous. Very soft, pliable, and easily fashioned with the fingers. G. = 0·94...0·97. Glimmering or glistening; semitranslucent. Yellowish-brown or hyacinth-red by transmitted, dark leek-green by reflected, light. Strong parafine or aromatic odour; fuses easily (at 144°, *Schrötter*; at 183°, *Mallagutti*) to a clear oily fluid, again becoming solid when cold, and at higher temperatures burns with a clear flame, seldom leaving any ashes; readily soluble in oil of turpentine, with great difficulty in alcohol or ether. Chem. com. 85·7 carbon, and 14·3 hydrogen.

Slanik and Zietriska in Moldavia, near Garning in Austria, and Baku. Also Urpeth coal mine near Newcastle-on-Tyne.

510. HATCHETINE, Mineral Tallow.

Flaky, like spermaceti; or sub-granular, like bees' wax; soft and flexible. G. = 0·6. Translucent; weak pearly. Yellowish-white, wax-yellow, or greenish-yellow. Greasy; inodorous; readily soluble in ether. Chem. com. 85·91 carbon, and 14·62 hydrogen, or similar to ozokerite. Glamorganshire (fusible at 115°); Loch Fyne near Inverary. Also Merthyr-Tydvil (melts at 170°), and Sooldorf in Schaumburg.

511. FICHTELITE.—$C^4 H^3$.

Crystalline (monoclinic) lamellæ, which swim in water, but sink in alcohol. White and pearly. Fuse at 115°, but again become crystalline on cooling; very easily soluble in ether, and precipitated by alcohol. Chem. com. 88·9 carbon and 11·1 hydrogen. In pine-trees in a peat moss near Redwitz in Bavaria.

512. HARTITE.—$C^6 H^5$.

Triclinic, but mostly like spermaceti or white wax, and lamellar. Sectile, but not flexible. H. = 1 ; G. = 1·046. Translucent ; dull resinous. White. Melts at 165°, and burns with much smoke ; very soluble in ether, much less so in alcohol. Chem. com. 87·8 carbon, and 12·2 hydrogen. Oberhart in Austria.

513. KÖNLITE.—$C^2 H$.

Crystalline foliæ and grains. Soft. G. = 0·88. Translucent; resinous. White, without smell. Fuses at 120° to 137° Fahr. ; soluble in nitric acid, and precipitated by water in a white crystalline mass. Chem. com. 92·3 carbon and 7·7 hydrogen. Uznach near St. Gallen, Redwitz in Bavaria.

514. SCHEERERITE.—CH^2.

Monoclinic ; tabular or acicular. Soft and rather brittle. G. = 1·0...1·2. Translucent ; resinous or adamantine. White, inclining to yellow or green. Feels greasy, has no taste, and when cold no smell, but when heated a weak aromatic odour. Insoluble in water; but readily in alcohol, ether, nitric, and sulphuric acid. Chem. com. 75 carbon, and 25 hydrogen. Uznach. *Branchite*, white, translucent, feels greasy, and fuses at 167°, is similar. Monte Vaso in Tuscany.

515. IDRIALITE.—(Idrialine = C^3H).

Massive; fracture uneven or slaty. Sectile. H. = 1·0 ...1·5; G. = 1·4...1·6 (1·7...3·2). Opaque; resinous. Grayish or brownish black; streak blackish-brown, inclining to red. Feels greasy. Burns with a thick smoky flame, giving out sulphurous acid, and leaving some reddish-brown ashes. Chem. com. 77 idrialine (= 94·7 carbon, and 5·3 hydrogen) and 18 cinnabar, with a little silica, alumina, pyrite, and lime. The idrialine may be extracted by warm olive oil or oil of turpentine, as a pearly shining mass; difficultly fusible. Idria.

FAMILY V.—INFLAMMABLE SALTS.

516. MELLITE, Honey Stone.—$\ddot{A}l\ \overline{M}^3 + 18\ \dot{H}$.

Tetragonal; P 93° 5′. Crystals, P alone, or with 0P, P∞, and ∞P∞; also massive and granular. Cleavage, P very imperfect; fracture conchoidal; rather brittle. H. = 2·0...2·5; G. = 1·5...1·7. Transparent to translucent; distinct double refraction; resinous or vitreous. Honey-yellow to wax-yellow or reddish; streak whitish. In the closed tube it yields water. B.B. carbonises without any sensible odour, at length burns white, and acts like pure alumina; easily soluble in nitric acid or solution of potash. Chem. com. 40·3 mellic acid ($\overline{M} = C^4\ O^3$), 14·4 alumina, and 45·3 water. In brown coal at Artern in Thuringia, and Lauschitz in Bohemia; Walchow in Moravia, cretaceous; in true coal at Malowka in Tula.

517. OXALITE, Humboldtine.—$2\ Fe\ \ddot{C}^3 + 3\ \dot{H}$.

Capillary crystals; also botryoidal or in plates, and fine granular, fibrous, or compact. Fracture uneven or earthy; slightly sectile. H. = 2; G. = 2·15...2·25. Opaque; weak resinous or dull. Ochre or straw yellow. B.B. on charcoal becomes first black then red; easily soluble in acids with yellow colour. Chem. com. 42·1 oxalic acid, 42·1 iron protoxide, and 15·8 water. In brown coal at Kolosoruk near Bilin, Duisburg, and Gross Almerode in Hessia.

518. WHEWELLITE.—$\ddot{C}a \ddot{\ddot{e}} + \dot{H}$.

Monoclinic ; C. = 72° 41′, ∞P 100° 36′. Cleavage, basal perfect ; very brittle. H. = 2·5...2·8 ; G. = 1·833. Transparent to opaque ; vitreous. Colourless. Chem. com. 49·31 oxalic acid, 38·36 lime, 12·33 water. Locality unknown. Hungary ?

Though scarcely a simple mineral, the characters of water in its fluid and solid conditions may be noted here.

*519. WATER.—HO, *or* [H²O].

Fluid and amorphous. G. = 1·000 when pure, but seawater 1·027 and 1·0285 at 62° Fahr. When pure it is without taste or smell, and colourless in small quantities, but in larger masses green or blue. Chem. com. hydrogenoxide, with 88·9 oxygen and 11·1 hydrogen. Attains its greatest density at 39°·1, boils at 212°, and at 32° Fahr. freezes and changes to

520. ICE.

Hexagonal-rhombohedral ; R 117° 23′ (120°) ; usually six-sided tables of 0R. ∞R ; also acicular crystals, macled in delicate groups or stars with six rays. Cleavage, probably basal. H. = 1·5 ; G. = 0·918 (*Brunner* at 32° Fahr., and quite pure). *Dufaur*, as mean of 22 observations, gives 0·9175. Hence 1000 water = 1089·5 ice ; or water expands 1-11th in freezing. Transparent ; vitreous. Colourless, but in large masses greenish or bluish. Refracts double.

The water found on the earth is never pure, but contains more or less of various substances,—atmospheric air, carbonic acid, nitrogen gas ; silica, alumina, and salts (carbonates, sulphates, nitrates, phosphates) of lime, magnesia, soda, potash, protoxides of iron and manganese ; or chlorides, and fluorides of the metallic bases ; and in the sea and some saline springs also iodine, bromine, and the rare metal thallium.

521. ADDITIONS AND CORRECTIONS.

———◆———

Page 104, line 7, *for* o, p, 5, *read* r, p, s.

Page 106, line 8 from below, *for* tourmeline, *read* tourmaline.

Page 112, 3 from below, *for* ∞P∞, *read* ∞P̆∞.

Page 120, line 6 from foot, *for* Melilite, *read* Mellilite.

Page 124, No. 31. LEUCITE—

Von Rath has recently shown that this mineral belongs not to the tesseral, but to the tetragonal system : the so-called icositetrahedron, like Fig. 6, being formed in the middle by 16 faces of a ditetragonal pyramid 4P2, and on the ends by 4 + 4 faces of the primary pyramid P, both very equally formed. 2P∞ and ∞P also occur as subordinate forms. Macles, marked by striæ on the faces, and united by a face of 2P∞, are frequent. P has middle edge 73° 19¾′, polar edges 130° 3′, and the middle edge of 4P2 is 133° 58′. Leucite thus, in its primitive form, comes close to idocrase, and adds another to the remarkable series of tetragonal minerals so characteristic of Vesuvius —idocrase, zircon, humboldtilite, sarkolite, meionite, and mizzonite.

Page 152, *after* Augite *insert*

Aegirine. Monoclinic; striated or reed-like prisms of 86°:30′ to 87° 45′. Cleavage, orthodiagonal perfect, less distinct clinodiagonal, and prismatic. H. = 5·5...6 ; G. = 3·4...3·5 or 3·6. Vitreous, translucent on edges, or opaque ; greenish-black. B.B. fuses easily, colouring the flame yellow ; scarcely affected by acids. Chem. com. 3 (N̶a, C̶a, F̶e) S̈i + F̶̈e S̈i³, with 50·5 silica, 21·7 iron peroxide, 10·1 iron (and manganese) protoxide, 7·2 lime, and 10·5 soda, with a little magnesia and potash. Has the same relation to augite as arfvedsonite to hornblende. Near Brevig and Barkevig in Norway.

Page 175, line 16, *for* mantine, *read* Adamantine.

Page 245, line 27, *for* 17, *read* 71.

INDEX OF SIMPLE MINERALS.

[The Numbers refer to the Paragraphs.]

THE END.

Printed by R. & R. CLARK, *Edinburgh.*

In fcp. 8vo, cloth, price 5s.

ELEMENTS OF ZOOLOGY

FOR THE USE OF SCHOOLS AND SCIENCE CLASSES

BY ANDREW WILSON.

ILLUSTRATED WITH ONE HUNDRED AND FIFTY WOOD ENGRAVINGS.

Edinburgh Medical Journal.

THE style is clear and easily read, and while a sufficient number of examples have been given, the text is not overloaded with detail. The chief merit of the work is that any one reading it is not only put in possession of some facts in natural history, but is put in a position to carry out the study of the subject for himself in larger works.

Upon the whole, we may congratulate the author upon having supplied a want, and written a book which, if nothing very great or original, is likely to be useful.

Standard.

It is admirably adapted for the purpose for which it is intended. The author, himself a lecturer on Zoology, had long felt the want of a book which should be at once constructed on scientific principles, and giving the outlines of science required, and yet free from the great practice of that technicality which so worries and disgusts young students. The most recent and best methods of classification have been adopted, and equal attention is given to the vertebrate and invertebrate forms. The work will be hailed alike by teachers and students, and parents will find it a most welcome gift-book for studious boys and girls who are always "wanting to know."

Scotsman.

A particularly handy book, convenient in shape. Written with remarkable conciseness, and carefully calculated for the wants of students working in advanced classes. A most welcome book to a large number of students.

Glasgow Herald.

A valuable text-book for students in mastering the principles of a science which is now receiving much more attention than was bestowed upon it in the past.

Edinburgh Courant.

No better book can be placed in the hands of a young man desirous of entering upon a study which affords to the intelligent mind inexhaustible sources of delight. It is strictly what it professes to be, an elementary treatise, adapted for the use of schools and science classes, and takes in the whole field of Zoology, whilst a due proportion is assigned to each of the different parts.

[*Over.*

In fcp. 8vo, cloth, illustrated, price 4s. 6d.

JUKES'S SCHOOL MANUAL OF GEOLOGY.

NEW EDITION.

EDITED BY ALFRED J. JUKES-BROWNE,

St. John's College, Cambridge.

Quarterly Journal of Science.

WITH the exception of the classic writings of Sir Charles Lyell, there are perhaps no modern text-books better known to the student than the Manuals of the late Professor Jukes. His were no mere compilations, as elementary treatises too often are, but were the work of a field geologist, whose heart was in his hammer. The success of Jukes's larger volume, the "Students' Manual," induced the author, about ten years ago, to write an introductory work, under the title of the "School Manual of Geology." Since the lamented death of Professor Jukes, new editions of both works have been called for; the editing of the larger Manual was entrusted to the author's colleague, Professor Geikie; that of the smaller Manual to the author's nephew, Mr. A. Jukes-Browne.

Since the original appearance of the "School Manual" geology has made great advances. But whilst duty to the reader has compelled the editor to effect many alterations, he has wisely forborne, from respect to his uncle's memory, to unnecessarily interfere with the original plan of the work. Jukes's "School Manual" remains, then, what it has always been—one of our best text-books for the student of elementary geology.

Mining World.

We have been highly pleased with a new edition of an elementary work, "The School Manual of Geology," by J. Beete Jukes, Esq., M.A., F.R.S., edited by Alfred J. Jukes-Browne, Esq. Written for the express use of young persons, this work leads on gradually to the more abstruse portions of the subject, and prepares the student by easy degrees for works of more difficult comprehension; and whilst giving sufficient explanations of the different fauna which existed at each period, to make the general descriptions intelligible, must naturally awaken a desire not only to prosecute the inquiry, but also to acquire a knowledge of the kindred studies of botany, zoology, and mineralogy. In France an excellent series of elementary works on these topics by Jussieu, Milne Edwards, and Beudant, were published many years ago; but apart from the difficulty of language, they were perhaps too technical and abstruse for the use of schools. In the book before us this latter defect has been avoided; and as to the mature reader Hugh Miller's old red sandstone is a rare treat, so to the younger it must prove a charming as well as highly instructive work. There is, perhaps, no more difficult task than to write easily and with simplicity on a difficult subject, and to do so well requires the most intimate knowledge of it. This Mr. Jukes was admirably adapted to do, and he carried to his task that love which rarely fails to find a response in the breast of youth.

Well illustrated, well printed, neatly bound, and of a convenient size, the "School Manual of Geology" is a fitting specimen of what such educational works ought to be, and will no doubt be appreciated by all who have the interest of a general high-class education for the rising generation at heart.

Mining Journal.

The facility with which a sound knowledge of a science may be obtained, and the interest attaching to the study of it, is almost entirely dependent upon the character of the books whence the earlier introduction to the subject is derived, and among the most interesting and instructive volumes issued the "School Manual of Geology," by the late Prof. J. Beete Jukes is certainly entitled to the prominent place which has ever been assigned to it. To keep the work well up to the knowledge of the day a second edition has just been completed by his nephew, with the assistance of the Rev. T. G. Bonney, Fellow of St. John's, Cambridge, and the additions and emendations have even increased the value of the book. It is remarked that in preparing the new edition regard has been had to the great advance of geology and its associate sciences since the first appearance of the Manual, and that it has been found necessary to re-write some parts and to re-adjust several of the chapters. Mr. Jukes-Browne's endeavour has been to preserve as far as practicable the style and method of treatment pursued by the author, and to carry out as completely as he could his object in writing the work. The explanation of acids and bases contained in the first edition has been wisely preserved as more easily explaining facts than more recent theories, and the classification of rocks has likewise been retained, partly because it is so kept in the third edition of the larger Manual to which the school edition forms a kind of introduction, and partly because he thinks it is easier to comprehend than any more elaborate arrangement.

The general character of the "School Manual of Geology" is already well known to the readers of the "Mining Journal :" it directs the student's attention to geological operations at present going on around him, and which he can consequently examine for himself, and then explain the changes which these actions would in time bring about, accounting for the geological features elsewhere observed. With regard to the earth as a whole, it is remarked that we can hardly avoid arriving at the conclusion that the interior of the earth is intensely hot. If we were to suppose that the increase of temperature went on at the same rate indefinitely into the interior as that which regulates it in our mines and wells, or even if we allowed that it increased at a slower rate, say for instance, 1° Fahr. for every 100 feet of descent, we should arrive very shortly at an intense temperature ; at 50 miles we should have a temperature sufficient to melt steel, and at 100 miles we should get a temperature equal to more than 5000 Fahr., which is a heat greater than any we know at the surface. It is not by any means necessary, however, to suppose that the temperature does increase indefinitely into the interior, or that the rate which regulates its increase near the surface continues to be the same for such depths as those just mentioned. Neither does it follow that the materials, whatever they may be, which exist at great depths, would be melted by the same heat that would fuse them at the surface, since the enormous amount of pressure which they must experience may keep them solid in spite of the heat.

After chapters on volcanoes and earthquakes, there is an interesting one on rise and fall of ground, the conclusion arrived at concerning which is that the crust of the earth is in frequent, if not in constant, movement in some part or other ; large parts remaining stationary for long periods, while others are being elevated, and others again depressed. We know that the sea, with its present level, has once flowed over the spots now occupied by our loftiest mountains. On the other hand, there is nothing improbable in the belief that land once existed where now the deepest parts of ocean are to be found. Mr. Darwin observes of the earthquake which he felt at Valdivia in 1835 : —" It was something like the movement of a vessel in a little cross-ripple, or still more like that felt by a person skating over thin ice which bends under the weight of his body. A bad earthquake at once destroys the oldest associations ; the world, the very emblem of all that is solid, has moved beneath our feet like a crust over a fluid." The geologist, as he pursues his studies, learns to generalise this feeling and to apply it to the whole crust of the earth during all geological time. He finds that it always has been as it now is, utterly unstable, rising here and falling there, with long slow undulations ever shifting under the liquid ocean, and moving it from place to place as parts of its old bed are lifted up above its surface, and new hollows formed by the sinking of other shores. An outline of chemical nomenclature is given to prepare the way for accounts and descriptions of minerals and igneous rocks, rocks formed of animals and plants, and mechanically formed rocks. The following chapter, which is a summary of the preceding ones, concludes the first part.

The second part of the book explains the principal facts observable on the crust of the earth, the structure of rock beds, inclined beds, bent or broken beds, denudation, unconformability, metamorphic or altered rocks, concretions, and veins and fossils, and their mode of occurrence ; and the third part embraces the history of the formation of the earth's crust, deduced from the facts observable in it as interpreted by the processes now in operation. After tracing the various geological changes which have marked the several periods, it is remarked that the geological history of the earth thus closes with the appearance of man exterminating races of animals, just as preceding races have been exterminated by other animals than man. If this history were to be made complete, it should include an account of the aqueous rocks that were deposited, the igneous rocks that were intruded or ejected, the preceding aqueous rocks that were altered or destroyed, the animals and plants that made their appearance and those that disappeared during each period of the history, and for every large division of the globe. Geologists were, before the appearance of Sir C. Lyell's " Principles," mostly led away, for want of sufficient knowledge, into mere speculations as to what might have produced the earth's crust, instead of patiently studying the actions which were now operating in that production. Hence arose such notions as that granite was necessarily the most ancient of all rocks, and that after the formation of granite came that of gneiss, and so on. It is true it is remarked that the spread of a cold climate seems to have been very general over the world during part of the pleistocene period (though probably the glacial epochs in the northern and southern hemispheres may not have been synchronous) and to have formed a marked expression to the meteorological conditions that had previously prevailed. During former periods the climate of the whole earth seems to have been more genial and more equable than it is now. The change, however, seems to have been a gradual one, both in its incoming and in its outgoing, and a mere extension to lower latitude of the climate which remains now in the polar regions of the earth. However it may have been caused, we do not find here or elsewhere in the history of the earth any evidence of an abrupt termination of one order of things, and a sudden introduction of another. Few and scanty and broken as are our records of the past, they contain far more evidence of the slow and gradual and continuous action of the natural forces than of rapid or capricious or intermittent change. The present day is linked indissolubly with all past time, and that which we see around us is the result of that which has been before.

Whether considered as a separate text-book, or as an introduction to the larger Manual, this volume is worthy of high commendation. It contains an abundance of information of a thoroughly reliable character, and although the outline necessarily leaves many details to fill in, the student will have nothing to unlearn, and will learn nothing that is useless to him.

Popular Science Review.

Mr. Jukes-Browne's little book is a capital introduction to geology. It was, even when it was first brought out by the late Professor Jukes himself, an excellent work; and now the editor has taken so much trouble, and has exercised such judicious skill in the direction of his amendments, that the volume is for the present date as good a book as it unquestionably was when it first appeared about ten years since. Parts of some chapters have been quite re-written, and others have been modified in accordance with the changes that the science has undergone since. But it seems to us that the editor very wisely left the chemical part as it was. So many systems are now in vogue, and it is so impossible to say which will eventually hold its own against its compeers, that a wise discretion was shown in the maintaining of this section as in the old book. The general plan has not been altered, but many woodcuts have been introduced, and the entire work has been brought down to 1873 with skill and discretion. On the whole, we are very much pleased with this second edition, and we wish it what it deserves—a very good sale.

JUKES'S GEOLOGY—NEW EDITION BY GEIKIE.

Now ready, in crown 8vo, price 12s. 6d.

The Student's Manual of Geology.

By J. BEETE JUKES, M.A., F.R.S.,

Late Director of the Geological Survey of Ireland.

Third Edition, Recast, and in great part Rewritten.

Edited by ARCHIBALD GEIKIE, F.R.S., Director of the Geological Survey of Scotland, and Regius Professor of Geology and Mineralogy in the University of Edinburgh.

Illustrated by 166 Figures and 47 Fossil Groups.

In one vol. royal 8vo, pp. 1117, *with* 1800 *Illustrations,*
price 21s.

CLASS-BOOK OF BOTANY.

Being an Introduction to the Study of the Vegetable Kingdom.

By J. HUTTON BALFOUR, M.D., F.R.S.,

Professor of Medicine and Botany in the University of Edinburgh,
and Regius Keeper of the Royal Botanic Garden.

(*May also be had in two parts, price* 21s.)

" In Dr. Balfour's ' Class-Book of Botany,' the author seems
to have exhausted every attainable source of information. Few,
if any, works on this subject contain such a mass of carefully
collected and condensed matter, and certainly none are more
copiously or better illustrated."—*Hooker's Journal of Botany.*

" Professor Balfour's ' Class-Book of .Botany ' is too well and
favourably known to botanists, whether teachers or learners, to
require any introduction to our readers. It is, as far as we know,
the only work which a lecturer can take in his hand as a safe
text-book for the whole of such a course as is required to prepare
students for our University or medical examinations. Every
branch of botany, structural and morphological, physiological,
systematic, geographical, and palæontological, is treated in so ex-
haustive a manner as to leave little to be desired.

" The work is one indispensable to the class-room, and should
be in the hands of every teacher."—*Nature.*

" The voluminous and profusely illustrated work of Dr. Balfour is too well known to need any words of comment."—*Lancet.*

WORKS BY SIR J. F. W. HERSCHEL, BART., K.H., &c. &c.

I.

In crown 8vo, cloth, Third Edition, price 5s.

PHYSICAL GEOGRAPHY OF THE GLOBE,

CONTENTS—The Sea—The Land—Rivers—Springs—Caves—Plains—Climate—Rain—Thunderstorms—Hurricanes and Earthquakes—Terrestrial Magnetism—Mineral Products—Gems—Salt—Coal—Sulphur—Plants—Animals—Fossil Remains—Ethnology, etc.

"An admirable Manual of the whole science."—*British Quarterly Review.*

"It is utterly impossible to give an account of the immense amount of information so admirably and lucidly compressed in the volume before us."—*London Review.*

II.

In fcap. 8vo, cloth, price 3s. 6d.

METEOROLOGY.

CONTENTS—Air—Altitudes—Aurora Borealis—Balloon Ascents—Barometer—Barometric Pressures—Climate—Clouds—Cold—Currents—Cyclones—Density of Air—Dew—Dryness—Dust—Electricity—Evaporation—Fogs—Frosts—Gulf Stream—Hail—Heat—Hoar Frost—Humidity—Hurricanes—Ice—Icebergs—Kite, Electrical—Lightning—Meteorolites—Monsoons—Ocean—Rain—Rainbow—Seasons—Snow—Sun—Temperature—Thunder—Tides—Vapour—Wind, etc.

"As text-books for Colleges and School use, on the subjects on which they respectively treat, there is nothing in the whole range of our educational literature which can at all be compared with them."—*Educational Times.*

OWEN'S PALÆONTOLOGY.

In 8vo, Second Edition, with Index and Glossary, and Illustrated with nearly Two Hundred Wood Engravings, price 7s. 6d.

PALÆONTOLOGY;

Or, a Systematic Summary of EXTINCT ANIMALS and their Geological Relations.

By RICHARD OWEN, F.R.S.,

Superintendent of the Natural History Departments in the British Museum.

" *No one with any pretensions to science should be without Owen's Palæontology.*"—LANCET.

" *The Prince of Palæontologists has here presented us with a most comprehensive survey of the characters, succession, geological position, and geographical distribution of the various forms of life that have passed away.*"—MEDICAL TIMES AND GAZETTE.

UNIFORM WITH "JUKES'S SCHOOL GEOLOGY."

In fcap. 8vo, with 427 Wood Engravings, price 3s. 6d.

ELEMENTS OF BOTANY

By J. HUTTON BALFOUR, M.D.,

Professor of Medicine and Botany in the University of Edinburgh.

EDINBURGH : ADAM AND CHARLES BLACK.

CPSIA information can be obtained
at www.ICGtesting.com
Printed in the USA
BVOW06*0624201117

500893BV00012B/194/P